Vibrant with the blessings of India's Enlightened teachers, holy places and village mystics, this is a book with the power to awaken hearts and open minds. Love, travel and spiritual quest interweave, as master storyteller Alakananda Devi vividly describes her transformation from middle-class English physician and novice nun, to wild and free pilgrim, lover and wisewoman.

In her journey from patriarchy to the feet of Divine Mother, Alakananda discovers a hidden master of rare genius, encounters Shanta Durga—a goddess sensuous as a courtesan, falls in love with a Buddhist ex-hippie, and learns the secret teachings of the spiritual importance of women.

An autobiographical account of a remarkable life, in the great tradition of Irina Tweedie's *Daughter of Fire* and Reshad Feild's *The Last Barrier, Pilgrimage to the Mother* is an inspired work of great innocence and intuitive awareness.

"A very important book, destined to be a spiritual classic. Alakananda tells an impassioned tale of two mystic lovers and their incomparable guru."

~ Lex Hixon, *author of* Great Swan *and* Mother of the Universe

---

"There are many books explaining the wisdom or philosophies of East and West. However, theoretic knowledge does not erase the immediate ignorance of diversity in which we live. What is required is an equally immediate awakening to usher in the realization of unity. Alakananda Devi is in search of this awakening and tells us how she came to it. Hence, this book is an unique document useful to all seekers of Truth."

~ Pundrik C. Mehta, *Professor of Hindu Philosophy, Hindu University of America.*

Pilgrimage to the Mother

Sadananda & Alakananda

Pilgrimage to the Mother

A Woman's Journey to the Source of the Ganges

Alakananda Devi

PREMA PRESS
BOULDER, COLORADO

Published by Prema Press
1705 14th St., #392,
Boulder, Colorado 80302

Copyediting and typesetting: Susan Kay
Cover and text design: Scott Harmon
Cover illustration: Ray Geier
Cover: Nanda Devi, source of the Alakananda River

First edition, January 1999
Printed in the United States of America

ISBN 0–9657559–0–8

LCCCN 97-066228

For
Brahmachari Raghudas Maharaj

Acknowledgements

My deepest thanks to:

- Sadanandaji, for his letters, reminiscences and comments
- Celeste Rossmiller, theologian and computer expert, for her support and hours of patient work on the manuscript
- Mary Ezzell, author and editor, for her insightful comments, critique and tutoring
- Joyce and Peter Hudis, for carefully keeping my letters, and to Peter, my father, for inspiring the cover design
- Lorene Reck, for the use of Sadananda's letters
- Lex Hixon (may his soul be blessed), for reading the manuscript during the last months of his life and encouraging me to publish
- Jyoti Wind, for astrological guidance
- Swami Paramananda Sarasvati, for a writing retreat in his cabin
- Sri Anandi Ma, for her unfailing spiritual support
- Dr. Vasant Lad, for keeping me alive to write this book
- Sheikha Fariha and Sheikh Hydar, for support on many levels during the writing of this book
- Rabbi Zalman Schachter-Shalomi, for his friendship and inspiration
- Lola, for all her generous support
- Viveka, for her support of Alandi Ashram
- Devithai and the Kanyas of Sakuri, for the inspiration of their lives

~ Kabir and Habiba, Gajendra, Sagar, Manora, Netanya, Sarah, Vahid, Sumi Komo, Juan and Jennifer, Tamara Matthews, Louise Sanchez, the Neem Karoli Baba Satsang, the devotees of Denver's Radha-Govinda Temple, Kuldip and Usha Gupta, Mahalakshmi and Ravi Mahalingam, Donna de Aguera, Ramprasad Steve Winograd, Eddie and Debbie Shapiro, Muhammed Nur, Robert & Anita Meyers, Haqiqa, Jennifer Harding, Har kaur Khalsa, Mahesh Taft, Ingrid-Mangala, Brian Adler, Ron Sharp, Sita Sharan, David Ternlund, Omar, Shanti and Sunflower, Jee Yun, Jason and Bodhi, Selena,

~ and all my friends

Thank you for believing in me.

Introduction

The pages of this book unfold a tale of travel and adventure in faraway places; a spiritual autobiography; a womanstory. Yet above all, be prepared to read a love story, for here is recounted my meeting with the three great loves of my life—the hidden master who became my guru; the ex-hippie sadhu who is my soulmate; and Mother India herself—a goddess of many faces, from the most beautiful to the most dark and terrible.

In 1980, I arrived in India as a middle-class English doctor, Catholic by faith, a nun by inner dedication. Stone by stone, Mother India dismantled my fortress of orthodoxy, showing me a pathless path of inner authenticity, a way that was neither of West nor East. I left my home as a physician, a nun, a Catholic; I returned as a healer, a woman, a mystic. I left thirsting for silence, solitude and contemplation, and returned eager to serve, to sing, to celebrate, for India is the land of celebration. In five years of wandering from end to end of the subcontinent, I learnt that I could not reach the source of the River Ganges until I first encountered the Source of my own being.

A wealth of information is contained within this book—information that is of value both to the prospective traveller and to the student of Eastern religion. The maps, bibliography and resource guide have been added to satisfy the needs of those who wish to learn more about India and her many spiritual traditions. For women tired of male-oriented spiritual organizations, I have shared the little-known teachings about the greatness and glory of Woman. And for all who hunger for the feminine aspect of God, I have recounted my journey from patriarchy to the feet of Divine Mother.

The primary purpose of this book, however, is not to inform, but to inspire. My journey from outer authority to the inner guru, from limited religion to universal mysticism, is the journey of Everywoman, of every soul. The four stages of my pilgrimage—renunciation, illumination, the longed-for encounter with the "black light" of Truth and the return to the marketplace—are the classic stages of the mystic way, as described in the literature of Christianity, Hinduism, Buddhism and Sufism. It has been my fate to live a fairy tale, to experience these four steps in a very clear, intense and dramatic manner. As you read, remember that this is also your journey. Reflect upon your own seasons of renunciation and illumination, of union and mystic return; see how the gods and goddesses of Indian mythology are active in your own life. Then this book will be for you more than a travel story—it will be a guidebook for the journey of your spirit.

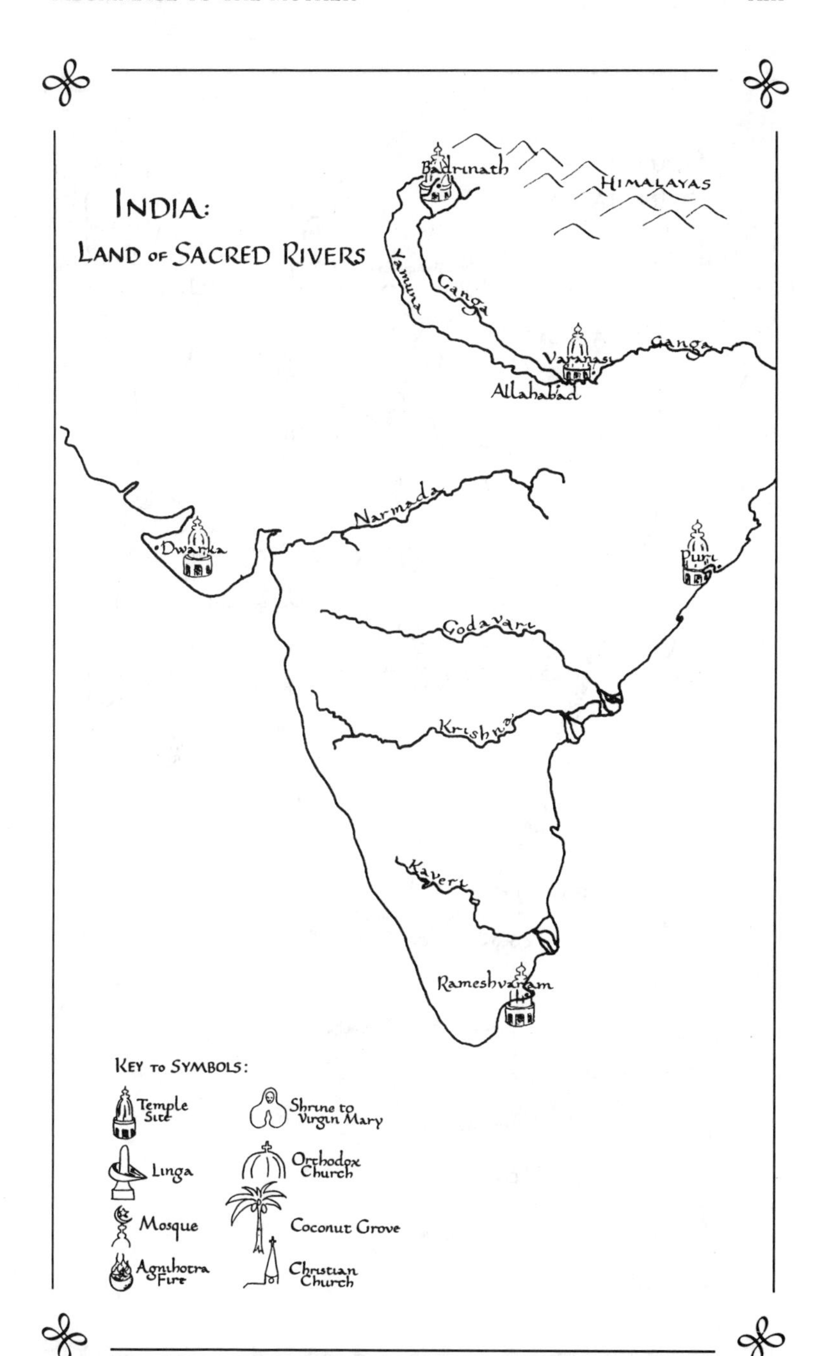
INDIA:
LAND OF SACRED RIVERS
HIMALAYAS
Badrinath
Yamuna
Ganga
Varanasi
Ganga
Allahabad
Narmada
Dwarka
Puri
Godavari
Krishna
Kaveri
Rameshwaram
KEY TO SYMBOLS:
Temple Site
Shrine to Virgin Mary
Linga
Orthodox Church
Mosque
Coconut Grove
Agnihotra Fire
Christian Church

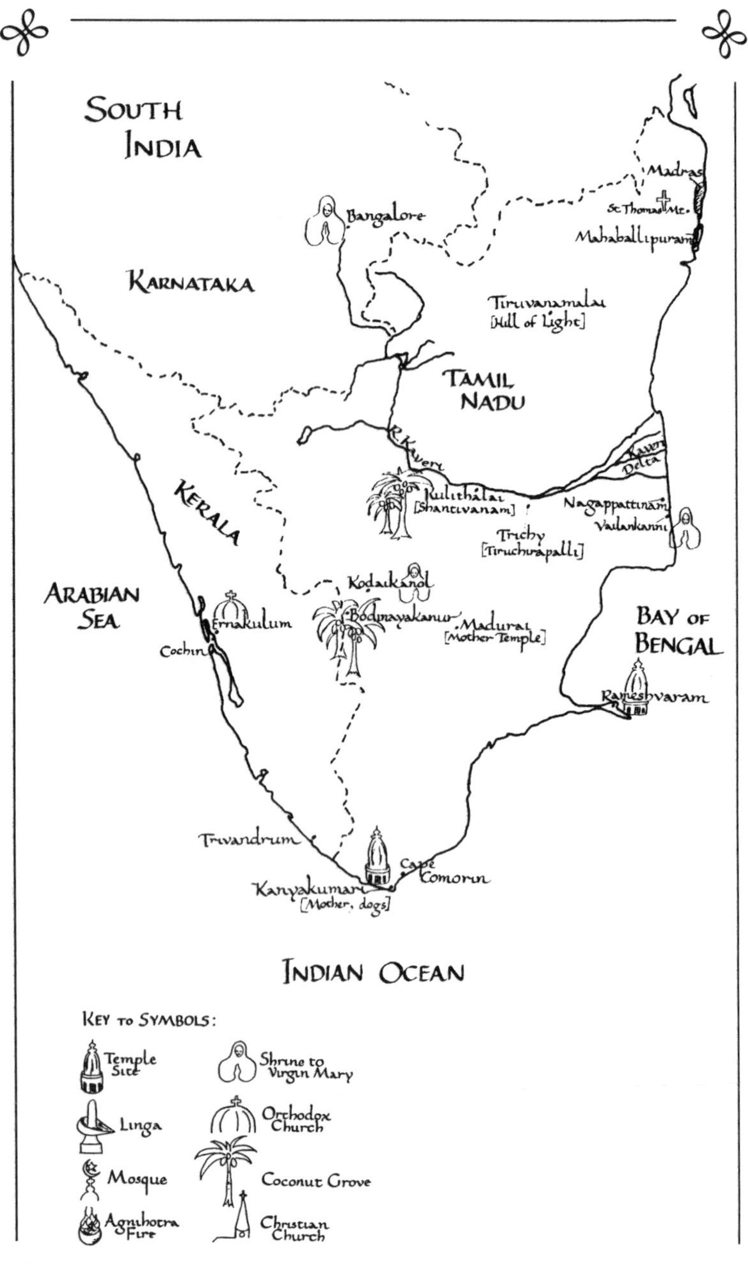
South India
Bangalore
Madras
St. Thomas Mt.
Mahaballipuram
Karnataka
Tiruvanamalai
[Hill of Light]
Tamil Nadu
R. Kaveri
Kaveri Delta
Kulithalai
[Shantivanam]
Nagappattinam
Vailankanni
Kerala
Trichy
[Tiruchirapalli]
Kodaikanal
Arabian Sea
Ernakulum
Bodinayakanur
Madurai
[Mother Temple]
Cochin
Bay of Bengal
Rameshvaram
Trivandrum
Cape Comorin
Kanyakumari
[Mother, dogs]
Indian Ocean
Key to Symbols:
Temple Site
Shrine to Virgin Mary
Linga
Orthodox Church
Mosque
Coconut Grove
Agnihotra Fire
Christian Church

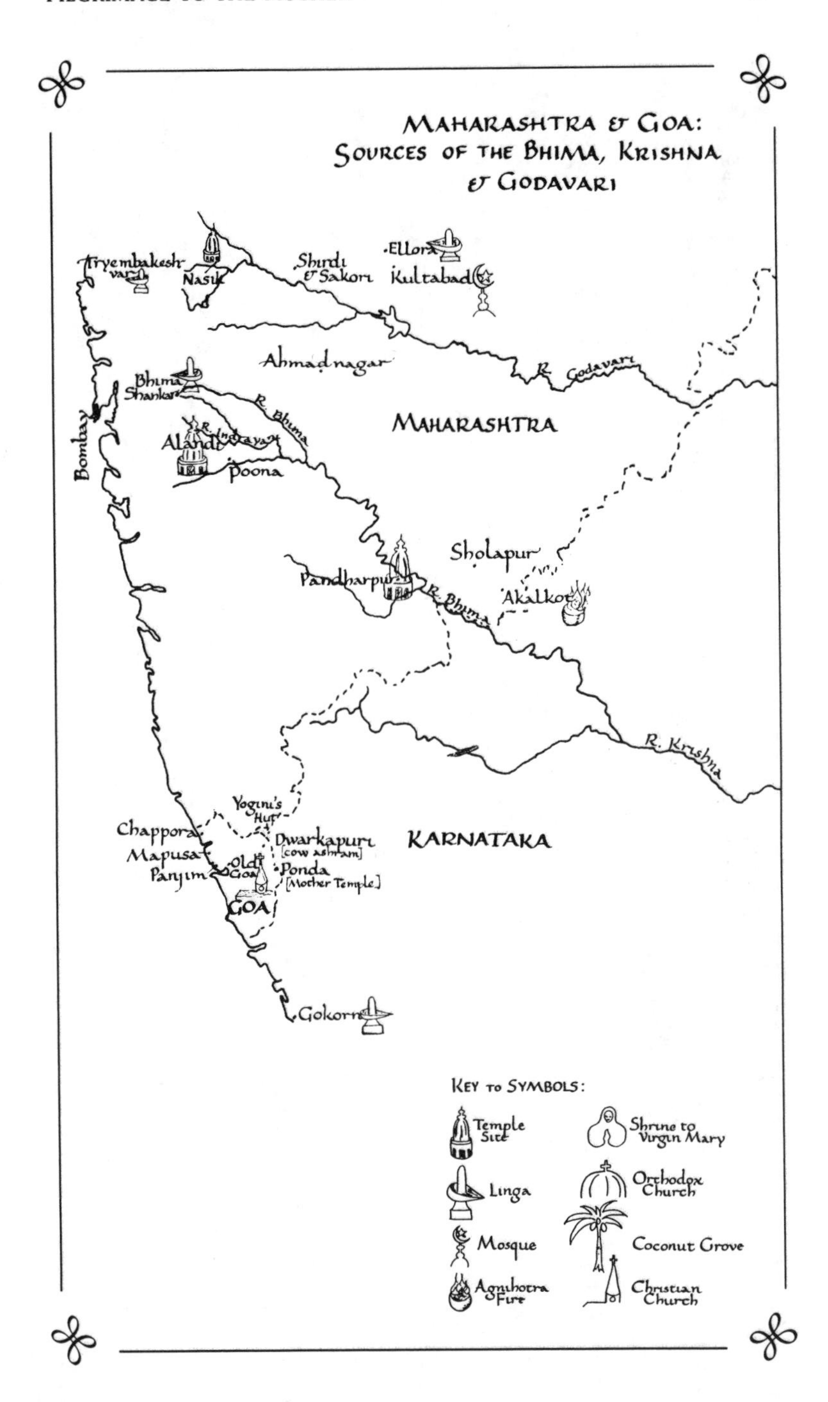
MAHARASHTRA & GOA:
SOURCES OF THE BHIMA, KRISHNA
& GODAVARI
Tryembakeshvara
Nasik
Shirdi
& Sakori
Ellora
Kultabad
Ahmadnagar
R. Godavari
Bhima Shankar
R. Bhima
MAHARASHTRA
Bombay
Alandi
R. Indrayani
Poona
Sholapur
Pandharpur
R. Bhima
Akalkot
R. Krishna
Yogini's Hut
Chappora
Mapusa
Panjim
Old Goa
Dwarkapuri
[cow ashram]
Ponda
[Mother Temple]
KARNATAKA
GOA
Gokorn
KEY TO SYMBOLS:
Temple Site
Shrine to Virgin Mary
Linga
Orthodox Church
Mosque
Coconut Grove
Agnihotra Fire
Christian Church

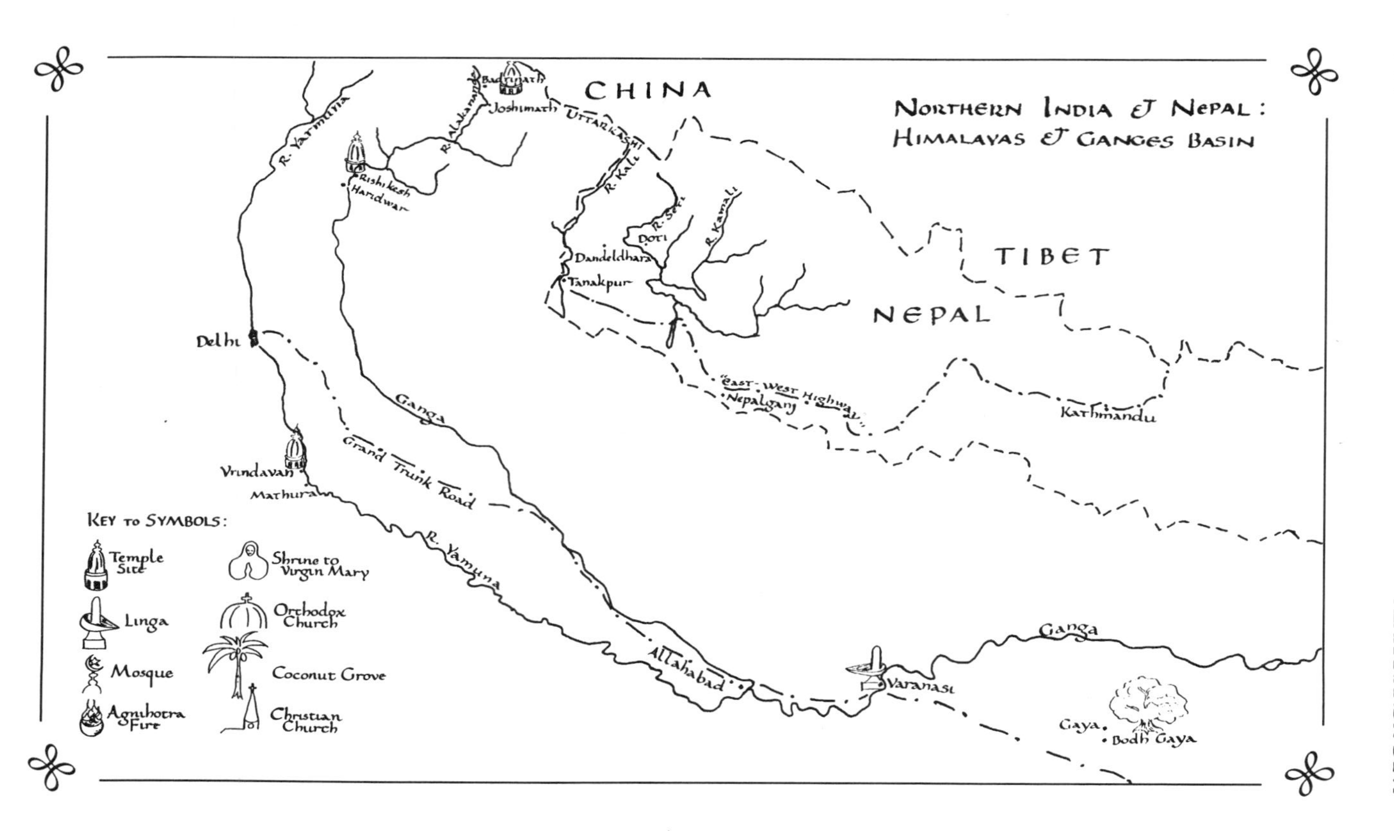
Northern India & Nepal:
Himalayas & Ganges Basin
CHINA
TIBET
NEPAL
Badrinath
R. Alakananda
Joshimath
UTTARKASHI
R. Kali
R. Seti
R. Karnali
Doti
Dandeldhara
Tanakpur
R. Yamuna
Rishikesh
Hardwar
Delhi
East-West Highway
Nepalganj
Kathmandu
Ganga
Grand Trunk Road
Vrindavan
Mathura
R. Yamuna
Allahabad
Varanasi
Ganga
Gaya
Bodh Gaya
Key to Symbols:
Temple Site
Linga
Mosque
Agnihotra Fire
Shrine to Virgin Mary
Orthodox Church
Coconut Grove
Christian Church

Prologue

"You have got to go to India! I know it!"

I stared at my youngest sister, a slender little elf barely five feet tall. Poet, musician, artist, peace activist, Oxford graduate—Ros was all these, but she was also a seer. I had never known her intuitions to be wrong. And now she had 'that look' in her huge blue eyes, the look that told me she was definitely on to something important.

"India? But, but why! I mean…they're all Hindus and polytheists and…and weird! Look, Ros, I'm working really hard at my Hebrew right now. I want to go to Israel, work on a kibbutz, get in touch with my Jewish roots."

Ros looked around the St. John's Wood room I rented at a price exorbitant even for London. Paints, brushes and canvases in various states of completion were everywhere.

"It's this art you're doing, Olivia. It all looks Indian, it really does! Yesterday I went to see an exhibition of Indian art. And I kept thinking of you the whole time. Every single thing you've painted looks like the stuff I saw there. Believe me, you're an Indian soul."

"What do you mean—an Indian soul? I'm a good Catholic. With a Jewish father. I've just tried my vocation in a convent. And it's quite enough trouble for me integrating my Jewish and Christian sides, without bringing in something totally foreign. More tea? Another scone? I baked them specially for you."

Ros's words were a shock to me. Yet I could not get them out of my head. After waving goodbye to her as she boarded the last bus back to Brixton, I stopped at the corner shop to buy a copy of *Time Out*. Immediately, I began looking through the travel section for cheap flights to India.

As my sister well knew, my life had come to a dead end. I was restless, searching, disgusted with Western materialism, hungry for meaning. I needed to travel, to go somewhere completely different, to get away from a mass culture that filled me with anger and a sense of futility. Desperate for spiritual identity, I had begun to prepare for a trip to Israel. But...suppose Ros was right? Suppose I wasn't ready for Israel yet? Did I need to make another journey first—a journey to India?

"You know," said my sculpture teacher, the next day, "you really should study Indian art. Your work looks incredibly Indian."

Yet perhaps I did not need to go to India, for India was coming to me. After weeks of searching for a room, I had ended up sharing a flat with an Indian Catholic landlady, living ten minutes' walk from the part of London popularly known as 'Little India'. The local library stocked books in Gujerati, Social Services advertised for Urdu-speaking caseworkers, notices were posted both in English and in various strange, curly scripts. A sari and cardigan were standard dress on the streets.

The local corner shop smelled of spices and incense and sold vegetables that were totally unrecognizable to me. Arriving at the cash till with my purchases for an evening of very experimental cooking, I began chatting with Mr. Patel, the proprietor.

"There is a reason, sister, why all your art looks Indian, even though you yourself are an English Christian," he said. "In Sanskrit we use the word samskara, referring to a mental impression laid down in a previous life. In another birth, indeed, I suspect, in many former births, you were Indian. At that time, you had great devotion to the various Hindu gods and goddesses. Hence, whenever you try to paint a picture or do a sculpture, the forms that are coming are those of Indian deities."

"So—do you also think I need to go to India?"

"Oh, yes, most definitely. Assuredly, that would be of the utmost benefit for your spiritual progress."

Next day, my landlady Theresa and I were walking home from Mass together. "So what do you think?" I asked her. "Should I go to India?"

"You see, the majority of people in India are Hindus," she replied. "They worship idols and believe all kinds of superstitions. Still, since you are a physician, perhaps you should go. You may be of help to the poor in the villages who have no doctor."

When Theresa retired for a Sunday afternoon nap, I sat down on my bed and began sketching pictures of the different parts of myself. There was Mummy's Perfect Daughter, the successful, organized young woman on the brink of a brilliant professional career. She, of course, wanted to stay in London and 'get on with my life'. There was the Pilgrim, barefoot, dressed in a simple robe, eager for a life of freedom and adventure. There was the Missionary Doctor, who wanted to go to a distant land and help poor, suffering people. She would willingly go to India, but she would go there with her own agenda. And there was the Nun, in her white veil and habit.

I closed my eyes. Instantly, I was back in Holy Cross Cistercian Abbey, the youngest novice in the community, almost tripping over my long robe as I ran into the chapel choir at three in the morning—late for Vigils. I saw the nuns walking in line from the choir to the chapter room, hands clasped, eyes cast down, everyone going in order of seniority, with me, the youngest, at the end of the line. I saw the wooden desk where I sat studying scripture as the rising sun touched the trees with gold, while blackbirds, wrens, robins and thrushes greeted the new day. I saw the walled garden where I dug up cabbage stumps, moved molehills and collected windfallen apples; the crowded cemetery full of the remains of sisters who had died in the full bloom of youth during an outbreak of tuberculosis. I heard the great bell that tolled thirty times a day, calling us to meals, to chapter and to prayers.

At night in the dormitory, I used to lie fully clothed in veil and habit between rough blankets, listening to the elderly sisters snoring. Just before retiring, the sweet, angelic voices of the sisters had soared in prayer as they sang, amid deepening shadows, the last hymn of the day, "Salve Regina": *To Thee do we cry, mourning and weeping in this vale of tears.* Soon I myself was crying and weeping. My soul longed for contemplation. But the life of a nun was too limited, rigid, restricted. Would I ever find my way?

Drying my tears, I picked up the copy of *Time Out.* I could not go back to the convent. I needed to go forward, to begin my life anew, in a new place—if necessary, in India. Carefully, I cut out from the magazine the address of a 'bucket shop'—a purveyor of discounted tickets—offering flights that were ten pounds cheaper than its competitors.

The bucket shop, Interworld Travel, proved to be a dingy, cluttered office in a side street of Soho. A fat, thirty-something man with long greasy hair sat behind a messy desk. My fellow clients also had long hair and were none too clean. I felt rather out of place in my tidy, conventional skirt, blouse and shoulder bag. Whilst waiting my turn to speak to the fat man, I timidly struck up a conversation with a colourfully-dressed traveller festooned with long beads who sat next to me.

"India?" he said. "No, man. I'd never go there again, man. Everybody cheats you. Bed bugs in the hotels. No decent food. And I got bad hepatitis there, man. Me, I'm off to Bali." It sounded very discouraging. Anyway, now it was my turn to sit at the messy desk.

"Three hundred and twelve pounds, return," said the fat man. "You get an open return, but you have to come back within twelve months."

"Oh, I don't think I'd be staying anything like that long. Maybe three months."

"You'd fly Aeroflot, via Moscow. It's a safe airline, never been hijacked." Three hundred pounds. Quite an affordable amount. There would still be enough in my savings to support me for more than three months in India. So it was possible, if I really was willing to exchange my room, my part time job, my little bit of security here in London, for bed bugs and parasites. But *was* I willing? True, my life was at a dead end. But, cautious as I was, I would need to think this over very carefully, discuss my decision with other important people in my life.

In the staff canteen at the prestigious hospital of St. Bartholomew, where for six years I had studied medicine, nurses in striped dresses and white caps were eating lunch. Across the table from me sat Tony, wearing the white coat, name badge, stethoscope and 'bleep' that had been my uniform, too.

"I can't understand you," Tony was saying. "You had such a good future in the medical profession. You always did well in medical school, you got good residencies at West Suffolk Hospital. Didn't your boss say you were the best junior house physician he ever had? And the patients loved you. We all thought you'd become a neurologist, rise to the top of the profession."

"But I don't know if I believe in high-tech medicine anymore."

"Oh, don't be ridiculous. You should be careful, you have this tendency to get religious. Remember what our biochem prof used to tell us: 'Man is a bag of enzymes.' There's nothing going on here except enzymic reactions. Even your religious experiences are just fluctuations of neurotransmitters in the brain. Anyway, I can't stay long. There's a coronary who needs attention. And then I have to switch off the ventilator on a motorbike accident case we're using for a kidney transplant. There goes my bleep. Have to run."

I shuddered. Tony had reminded me of everything I hated about Western medicine and its materialism and reductionism.

Leaving the canteen, I wandered outside to the hospital courtyard. Here, beside the Italian fountain, I found my old friend Sue, and we began reminiscing about our adventures in Tanzania, where the two of us did our clinical elective.

"It's super to meet you again," she said. "I'd never forget those two months we both spent on the slopes of Kilimanjaro."

"Waiting in Moshe while they bump-started the bus to Kilimanjaro Christian Medical Centre," I reminisced.

"And sewing people up with fishing line when we couldn't afford sutures. And re-using needles until they were blunt. And having to do real clinical diagnosis because x-rays and blood tests were too expensive," Sue added.

I sighed. "Did you know, every child I admitted to the children's infectious diseases ward died? Of measles, complicated by malnutrition. Perhaps you didn't have such a hard time, working on the adult ward."

"And seeing fathers of families dying of tetanus for want of an immunization that would have cost fifty pence? And case after case of TB, leprosy, amoebic liver abscess? No, I basically agree with you, Olivia. High-tech medicine just isn't the way. Two-thirds of the world's population can't afford to benefit from it anyway. What do they want with medical technology when they don't even have food? I just don't think you needed to throw the whole thing in. Me, I'm going back to Tanzania as soon as I finish with this family physician training course."

"That's wonderful, Sue. I admire you. And you have the right temperament for it. But I don't. I just can't see myself doing appendicectomies and amputations in a hut in the bush. Remember how I always used to pass out in the operating theatre?"

Sue hurried off for a ward round, leaving me to my thoughts beside the fountain. Were these the only choices for practising healing? Climbing the career ladder in a London teaching hospital or doing bush medicine in Africa? I remembered the experience that had called me into healing. I was about fourteen at the time, and had just been rowing on the River Orwell after school. As I walked by the shore with an oar on each shoulder and purple sunset colour spreading across the water, I heard a voice. Clearly and unmistakably, the voice said, *'Your mission is to heal the sick, as Christ did.'* I stopped dead in my tracks. That very night, I announced to my family that I was going to become a doctor. And no amount of persuasion ("But you're a poet, an artist! You're not a scientist. You hate hospitals. You'll never make it.")—nothing could make me change my mind. Yet neither path of Western medicine, in England or in Africa, had fulfilled that original call. Might it be fulfilled after all in India?

Back at the flat in St. John's Wood, I continued working on my art. Three times a week, I took the underground to Westminster, where I was working as play therapist for a blind girl. The job was well-paid, and I enjoyed it. My room in the flat was now full of books on Indian art, of course, and the kitchen smelled more exotic every day, as I continued my experiments in cooking the foodstuffs I bought from Mr. Patel. But I was restless, no doubt. I couldn't continue indefinitely living in a box room in St. John's Wood, doing part time work. I had to make a decision—buy the ticket for India, or go to Israel.

With these thoughts churning in my mind, I set off to visit my grandparents in Wembley, a Jewish suburb. I arrived on Saturday, when all the shops were shut for Sabbath and the car park of the Liberal Synagogue was crowded.

Granny had cooked chicken noodle soup—which I couldn't eat since I had taken to a vegetarian diet—and her famous vermicelli pudding, which I loved. My grandfather sat at the head of the table, wearing an immaculate white shirt with gold cuff links and a gold tie pin—five feet tall and dignified to the last grey hair on his bald head.

"How's the Hebrew going?" Granny asked me. "When are you leaving for Israel?" She had never given up hope that, despite the terrible disadvantage of having a gentile mother and a father who had converted to Christianity, I might still turn into a nice Jewish girl.

"You know, Granny, I don't think I'm ready for Israel yet. Ros thinks I should go to India instead."

"India! *You* should go to *India?* Well, maybe you can work in the villages, help the poor. It would be a *mitzvah.*"

At tea time, Cousin Ruth arrived. She was my second cousin, a little younger than my father and still very beautiful.

"I could have told you from the beginning, Olivia, that you were not cut out to be a doctor," she said, smiling. "And I'm a career advisor. I know what I'm talking about. You're too much of an idealist. Go to India, it will be good for you. It's time you enjoyed yourself for a change. Travel, see the world, why not?"

"A book will come out of this," added Granny firmly. "My eldest grandchild is going to go to India and write a book."

I wasn't a nice Jewish girl, of course, despite my grandmother's hopes. I was a middle-class English Christian, an ex-novice. Why was I so fascinated with my grandmother, my cousins, and everything Jewish? Would Mr. Patel say that my Jewishness was also a samskara, an inheritance from a previous life? One day, would I have to make a spiritual journey into Judaism, just as I now felt drawn to explore my spiritual roots in India?

My Jewish relatives supported my going to India. But what about my other family, my Catholic, nun family? The underground Circle Line took me to a large convent in Kensington Square. Soon I was sitting at my old place around the big oak table, sharing lunch with the community. In a niche in the corner stood the beautiful carved wooden Madonna I had brought back from Tanzania. During the last three years of medical school, this convent had been my home. Now, I was a visitor. It felt strange to be surrounded once again by sisters in purple habits and grey veils.

"So how was your experience at Holy Cross Cistercian Abbey?" asked Sister Magdalen.

"You know, in many ways, I loved it there. It really is a beautiful life. But almost all the sisters had been inside the enclosure for my whole lifetime—for the last twenty-five or thirty years. They don't seem to be able to adapt themselves to the postwar generation. It wasn't just me—none of the novices could make it. Seriously, I have my doubts about whether the abbey can even survive. Spiritually, it's fine, but culturally, it is in another world, a world that is past."

"Exactly! That's the problem. Too old-fashioned. Too nunny-bunny. Too narrow," burst out Sister Briget, a thin, energetic woman with silver hair and strong opinions. "What I don't understand is why you had to leave *us* and go *there*. The beauty of our life is, we practise contemplation in action. We live in the convent—and in the world."

I was fighting back tears. "But I couldn't get the contemplation and action together," I tried to explain. "Specially not when I was working eighty hours a week on call and living in a hospital room. I felt that I had to pick one or the other. So I chose contemplation. I *am* a contemplative. I know I am!"

"So, Olivia," asked Sister Dominic gently, noticing how emotional I was getting, "what are your plans?"

I took a deep breath. "I think I might go to India."

"To India!" a chorus of voices expressed a mixture of shock, surprise, delight and disapproval. Some of the sisters were supportive, handing me addresses of convents in India where I might find hospitality. Others were quick with warnings.

"Do please be careful," said Sister Clare nervously. "You know, you might end up joining a cult. Then what would happen to your vocation? India, remember, is a pagan country."

I had a measure of support from my Catholic family. But also a strong warning. 'Protect your vocation. Don't get involved in foreign, pagan religion.'

I was making big plans. But would my beloved parents approve them? To find out, I took the train to Ipswich, to visit the tall red brick house on Park Road where I had grown up. To my surprise, my parents expressed none of the hesitancies that had been plaguing me.

"Travel to India? Oh, how exciting!" cried my mother, who loved travelling. "And it's the perfect time for you to travel, since you need to make a career change anyway, and haven't settled down."

"You'll have a wonderful adventure, I'm sure," added my father. "And I really hope that you'll actually see the Himalayas. It's something I've always wished I could do."

"On the practical level," my mother went on, "it would save you money if you gave up that expensive room you have and stayed here for a month before leaving for India. We'll give you a good send-off."

None of my family, not even Granny, had any time for the part of me that was cautious and fearful, that dreaded giving up my security and setting off for a strange land full of wild tigers, idol worshippers, and tropical diseases. All of them saw me as a seeker, an idealist, an adventurer, someone who should travel to distant places and write books. Perhaps I would be fulfilling not just my own dreams but theirs, too.

"I have made a decision," I told my psychotherapist, a sister whose specialty was in counselling nuns and those who, like myself, had recently left Catholic religious life. "I am going to go to India. Somehow, I feel that going there is the essential next step, though I don't know where it will take me."

My wise friend's eyes sparkled. "Well, Olivia, you must go and visit Father Bede Griffiths. He has a most interesting place in South India. I have just been reading about it. They are Benedictine in spirituality, but also take inspiration from the spiritual and ascetical tradition of India. It seems to me, that if you spent your time in India there, you would discover what you were looking for, but couldn't find, in institutional monasticism."

Father Bede Griffiths! If only I could find the address of his ashram. Next day, I was queuing up by the desk in St. John's Wood Public Library, waiting to check out a copy of *Return to the Centre,* by Bede Griffiths.

"An excellent choice of book, if I may say so," said a tall, bearded gentleman who was standing behind me in the queue. "Father Bede is a wonderful being, a great spiritual guide, quite a prophet, really. And he has a beautiful place in India, you know. The Ashram of the Holy Trinity, it's called, in Shantivanam, the 'forest of peace'. In fact, I have just returned from there."

"You have! But this is amazing! That's where I want to go! Please, please, will you give me the address?"

"Most certainly. And I will lend you some other books, too, written by the original founder of Shantivanam, a French Benedictine monk named Abhishiktananda. He actually studied with a Hindu guru—quite a departure for a Catholic monk back in the 1950s. Eventually, Abhishiktananda retired to the Himalayas as a hermit. And Father Bede took over Shantivanam, where he is, one might almost say, the guru."

My mind was made up. I *had* to go to Shantivanam to meet this Father Bede.

"I envy you, Olivia," said my friend's fiancé, Khalil, an investment banker, as he gave me a ride back to the bucket shop. "You are most fortunate, to be able to drop everything and go to India. Me, I'm so locked into my life here."

"It's very easy really," I replied. "Anybody can do it. You just have to resign your job, give up your flat, spend all your savings... and set off to an unknown land. That's all it takes."

Sitting by the messy desk at Interworld Travel, I announced firmly, "I want a return ticket to New Delhi, towards the end of February."

It took a while for the fat man with the long, greasy hair to get through to his Aeroflot connection. At last, he put down the phone. "You're on. You leave London on Leap Year Day."

"My son! You think such a lot of yourself, but did you ask your teacher about that initiation, which makes a man hear what is not thought, know what is not known?... After that initiation, you know everything."

Chandogya Upanishad

One
In the Forest of Peace

At the end of a sandy lane was the gateway, crowned with a beautiful carving of a being with three heads—the three faces of the Triune God. The inscription beneath the carving read, 'Ashram of the Trinity'. On this sunny morning in the middle of Lent, as the hot season in South India was just beginning, I had arrived at Shantivanam, the forest of peace.

Taking off my heavy backpack, I straightened my dress, combed my hair, and adjusted the money belt around my waist, a girdle of security, guarding my passport, return ticket, and five hundred pounds in travellers' cheques. Hoisting my pack on again, I stood up straight, sighed deeply, and stepped through the gateway of the Triple-faced God. My new life was beginning.

On the other side of the gateway, I found myself in a beautiful, peaceful space. Everywhere I saw the slender trunks of coconut palms, their green fronds casting a dappled shade on little huts and single-storey buildings. On my right, through eucalyptus trees, I glimpsed the sparkling blue of a river. People, both Indians and Westerners, dressed in simple white clothes, were moving slowly about or sitting reading in shady corners. A white peacock stepped gracefully through the grasses.

As I stood looking about me, a tall figure appeared, like an Old Testament prophet, with white hair and white beard. From photographs I had seen, I immediately recognised Father Bede. Approaching me with a worried look, he said, "We have no room, you know. The ashram is full."

I held out the letter of invitation he had written to me. "But you're expecting me! I'm the former Cistercian novice."

"Ah, yes!" Father Bede smiled in welcome. "Our guestmaster, Brother Christodas, will show you to your room. Tomorrow at ten, come to my hut, and we will talk."

The guestmaster hurried over. He was lean and brown, not much taller than I. Like Father Bede, he wore an orange cloth around his waist; but, whereas Father Bede's cloth hung down to his ankles, Brother Christodas had his tucked up above his knees. He looked ready for anything.

Christodas set off at a rapid pace towards a U-shaped building which was evidently the guest house. He threw open the door to one of the rooms. This was to be my first Indian home. The bed, consisting of a slab of cement with a coconut mat over it, made the straw mattress at the Abbey seem comfortable. In the corner was a small table and chair. (I did not yet know it, but these latter items were non-Indian luxuries provided for the comfort of Western visitors.)

After some seeking, I found a row of dark, dank cubicles with squatting latrines, such as I had seen in rural parts of Europe. There were other dark cubicles furnished with a bucket and pitcher. These, it seemed, were the bathrooms. I filled the galvanized bucket and bathed, tipping pitcher-fulls of cold water over myself and washing with green, herbal-smelling soap.

After my bath, I began to wander around the grounds, when my attention was attracted by a large green lizard.... No, a large stone-coloured lizard.... No, a large bark-coloured lizard. I spent about half an hour chasing the poor chameleon from place to place, watching it change colour. Exploring further, I found an octagonal library with a shady verandah. Inside was an amazing collection of books on every imaginable spiritual and philosophical topic. I was sure that I would spend many happy hours browsing here. A little way past the library, I saw a white ox tethered in the shade, one of his long horns painted red, the other green. I was in a new world, taking childish delight in everything I saw. The chameleon, the library, the ox, all thrilled me.

As night began to fall, I followed the other guests past a little lotus pond to the chapel, built in the style of a South Indian village temple. It had an ornately-carved and brightly-painted dome crowned with a lotus and decorated with figures of Christ, his Mother and the apostles. Seating myself on a coconut mat on the temple floor, I tried to follow the words in a little booklet, as everyone sang a strange-sounding Sanskrit song.

When the service was over, we all walked to another building, which I gathered must be the dining hall. Lining up outside, we washed each others' hands before entering the hall, where people sat on the floor in rows. A stainless steel platter was placed before me. One server put on the platter a spoonful of pudding-like stuff, another poured on a ladle of runny sauce. During the serving, the ashramites were chanting, "*Aum shakti, Aum shakti, Aum shakti Aum,*" followed by a Sanskrit verse. It was time to start eating, but though I had food, I had no spoon. Looking about me, I saw that Father Bede, the monks and the other guests were all using their right hand to eat. Taking a deep breath, I plunged my fingers into the sticky, gooey mess on my plate and began to eat.

After dinner, I sat at the little table in my room and opened a new journal book with black binding.

8th March 1980

At last, I have arrived at Shantivanam. And after such an interesting journey. New Delhi was full of strange sights, sounds and smells. Mynah birds in the hostel garden. Women riding side-saddle on the back of motor scooters. Men urinating in the streets. Garish film posters and political slogans wherever I looked. The first time I stepped outside in my new white cotton travel clothes, I was immediately spattered with bright pink dye. People everywhere were throwing dye at each other, whilst bands of youths were riding through the streets on the backs of carts or lorries, garlanded with flowers and drumming wildly. Trust me! I had arrived in India on the day of Holi, the Spring Festival, which I gather celebrates the playful spirit of Krishna. Deep down I feel that India will destroy all my middle-class English ideas, habits and beliefs as effortlessly as she destroyed my tidy clothes with a single splash of dye.

All the shops were shut for Holi, but next day I managed to go out and buy two homespun saris, one deep green, the other turquoise.

Tomorrow, Sister Odelia, a Tamilian sister who lives in a tiny hermitage in the eucalyptus grove, is going to show me how to wear one.

Even the railway station was an experience, very different from British Rail. It was noisy and chaotic, loud with the hiss of steam locomotives and the strident cries of tea-seller "Chay; cha-a-i-i! Chay; cha-a-i-i!" *Wealthy families stood on the platform beside piles of baggage and bed rolls; a renunciant walked by in ochre robes, his hair matted, big beads around his neck, a bamboo staff in his hand. Beggars whined pathetically as they stretched out their hands for alms. Dirty urchins sneaked around looking for pockets to pick. Red-dressed, turbaned porters carried huge tin trunks on their heads. Whistles blew. And as my train rolled out at sunset, a group of white-dressed Moslems, who apparently had just returned from Mecca, began bowing and praying in the corridor.*

I was riding first class, the only reservation I could get. Next to me sat a young man, immaculately dressed in white, with a trimmed moustache.

"From where do you come?" he asked.

"From England."

"May I know your good name?" was the next question.

"Olivia." It took a while to pronounce that one. People from Southern India, it seems, tend to say it 'Woliwiya'.

Then he began to talk. I'm beginning to learn that Indians converse in speeches rather than dialogue. His speech was roughly as follows:

"I am a Brahmin. A Brahmin by caste, and a Brahmin by profession. The duty of a Brahmin is to teach, and I am a village schoolteacher. Actually, I am having Ph.D. in physics. But I am still more interested in our ancient Indian philosophy. I am a devotee of Lord Shiva. This great Lord, he lives in the Himalayas."

We were passing through the Ganges plain at the time, and this, it seems reminded my friend of a famous story about Shiva.

"Long ago," he went on, "the Ganga—Ganges, as you call her—flowed only through the heavens. In response to the prayers of one great sage, she agreed to descend, to heal and purify the earth. But the force of her flood would destroy the entire world. Now Shiva, he has matted locks, and in his locks, he caught the river as she cascaded down. Thus the world was saved. Ever since then, the Ganges has flowed down from the Himalayas, Shiva's matted locks, to this great plain which we

are now crossing. She is our mother, our greatest river. Our former Prime Minister, Nehru, called her the soul of India."

Now there are many, many Indian myths, books and books of them in the library here. So my question is, why this one? Why was this particular story the first one I heard at the start of my pilgrimage? I don't know the answer yet, but of this I am sure. The story of the descent of the Ganges must have a special relevance to my life and to my pilgrimage. And I will not forget it.

So now I'm in Tamil Nadu, the southernmost state of India, green, humid, lush, tropical; about to spend my first night in Shantivanam, the Forest of Peace. Most wonderful of all, tomorrow morning, I'll have my first meeting with Father Bede.

"So what is it that draws you here to India?" asked Father Bede, beaming at the stiff new green sari which Sister Odelia had just wrapped around me. We were seated on grass mats on the floor of his simple, bare cement hut. Gazing up at Father Bede's white-bearded face and wise, kindly blue eyes, alive with humour and compassion, I decided that I could trust him, that if nothing else of value happened on my pilgrimage to India, the journey was worth taking just to meet him.

"It's a long story," I began, "although I am only twenty-eight years old. I grew up on the edge of Melton Mowbray, a small market town in the Midlands, the eldest of four children. On the face of it, we were a typical middle class family, pillars of the Anglican parish church, my mother the local doctor.... But that was only the surface. My mother was always reminiscing about her childhood in a South London slum. And my father is actually Jewish.

"Indeed!" Father Bede nodded his understanding. "So the meeting of cultures and religions is your birthright."

"Yes, I am an interfaith dialogue in myself," I said. "In my younger years, I was always searching for roots. Gradually I've come to learn that I cannot choose one root and deny another. For as long as I can remember, oh, back in early childhood, I have had some kind of mystical inclination, but it was with the onset of puberty that I awakened spiritually. I began to feel the Divine Presence so strongly within myself, and in nature, that everything else took second place. I had no interest in boyfriends, parties, fashion, the normal teenage concerns, I just yearned restlessly for the Divine Beloved."

The words were tumbling out, for here, at last, was someone who didn't think I was crazy for being a mystic. "When I was seventeen, the inner longing drew me into the Catholic church, and since then, I have been going to Mass daily. Yet even so, I still feel unsatisfied. I went all through medical school and became a physician, because I have this deep desire to heal, to be of service, to express compassion in action. Yet the life of a doctor was too consuming. It left no space for contemplation. So I tried my vocation in a Cistercian Abbey. And I can see that it is a wonderful life. But the more I prayed and meditated, the more my heart opened, the more deeply I longed to heal people and be of service."

"So you have been experiencing a tension, a polarity, between contemplation and action," suggested Father Bede.

"I really have—to such an extent that it seems to be tearing me apart. And I have been so alone... so lonely. I know that I want to follow a celibate path, yet now that I'm not in the Abbey, I have no community, no companionship. I'm just struggling along on my own."

"So... what do you desire?"

"I want union with God. I want what all the mystics want. I want to climb to the peak of the mountain of Christ-consciousness. Even though I've left the Abbey, I can't go back to the world. In my heart, I am a monk. I have dedicated my life to God, to prayer."

I gazed at Father Bede, seated on the ground, bare-chested, in his ochre robes. He too had travelled very far from an English abbey to this hut beneath the palm trees, to a cremation ground on the shore of the River Kaveri.

"Yes," he said, "Prayer. For all of the Westerners who come here, you know, the greatest problem in meditation is simply to stop the mind. And this return from the mind to the heart, to the atman, the Self, the ground of personal being, is actually a continuation of the process of 'monastic conversion' upon which you embarked at the Abbey. Our life here, you see, centres upon

FATHER BEDE GRIFFITHS

PHOTO COURTESY OF SVEN ALGOTSSON

the hours of solitary meditation, particularly at the *sandhyas*, the times of the meeting of light and darkness at dusk and dawn. It is in these times of silent meditation that you will receive the healing you seek."

The interview was over. And I was more than pleased with my first meeting with Father Bede.

In the days that followed, I soon learnt that this remote ashram on the banks of the River Kaveri was a nerve centre of global importance. For Indian Christians, schooled in a decidedly European spirituality, Shantivanam offered the hope of reconnecting with their roots, with the soul of India, and so developing a deeper and more vital spiritual life. Indian novices and seminarians, priests and sisters came from all provinces, changing their Roman cassocks and tailored habits, at least temporarily, for a homespun sari or *lungi*. At the other extreme were the Western youths who had come to India to see Rajneesh, Muktananda or Sathya Sai Baba, to study Hatha yoga or Buddhist meditation, or simply to take the hippie trail from Goa to Kathmandu in search of peace, freedom and plentiful marijuana. These young Westerners, enamoured of the Hindu idea of simple living and high thinking, were for the most part alienated from church and synagogue, and found in Shantivanam an opportunity to reconnect with their own origins. In addition to these two main groups, I met Catholics from other Asian countries, seeking a model for a distinctively Asian Christianity; contemplatives from every continent, lured by India's ancient contemplative tradition; Hindu ascetics passing through on their wanderings; and local families, both Hindu and Christian, who came to seek Father Bede's blessings. And I encountered several people who would be important friends throughout my Indian pilgrimage.

As we stood outside the dining hall before lunch one day, I fell into conversation with a young woman from Germany. Angelika was a searching, rebellious soul, whose hatred of the West in general and Germany in particular was at such a pitch that she even refused to speak German. Although she was nearly ten years younger than myself, Angelika and I soon became firm friends. I found her a sympathetic and understanding listener, and would pour out my struggles, yearnings and ideals to her, whilst she sat and puffed *beedies*, the leaf-wrapped Indian cigarettes, in defiance of the ashram code.

Sometimes the two of us spent time with another young woman, Priya, a yoga teacher from New Zealand, who had curly blond hair and a seductive manner. Instead of the modest saris which other women at the ashram wore, Priya liked to dress in stylish Punjabis, the matching tunic and trousers favoured by Indian college girls. Angelika copied Priya's fashionable style of dress while I tried to emulate her upright Yogic posture when she sat in the chapel.

Shortly before Easter, a thin, fair young woman in a white sari appeared among the guests. Kirsti was Finnish, from a theosophical background, and had been living in India for some years, visiting saints and staying at ashrams.

"My three homes," she told me, "are Shantivanam, Tiruvanamalai, and Ananda Ashram." I looked blank, so she continued, in her soft, sweet voice, "Tiruvanamalai is an ancient temple town built at the foot of Arunachala, the Hill of Light. Many saints have lived there, but the greatest of all was Ramana Maharshi, a sage of our own century. He was just a teenage schoolboy when he realized the Self, and from that day he never departed from abiding in the Self. He ran away from home and came to Arunachala, where he spent the rest of his life. The Hill of Light was his guru. At first, few people recognized the young sage, but gradually, seekers flocked to be in his presence. He was a master who taught by silence."

I felt a thrill as I heard these words. Could I find a master like that?

"At Ramanashram, Tiruvanamalai, the emphasis is on the way of wisdom, *jnana,* through constantly enquiring, 'Who am I?' Ananda Ashram in Kerala was founded by Papa Ramdas, and is now under the care of a Holy Mother, Krishnabai. There the path of *bhakti,* devotion, is followed, in the constant chanting of the name of Ram. And here, Christ's teachings of love and service."

Kirsti fell silent and calmly watched as a mango ant, one of a species known for its vicious bite, ran over her finger.

Angelika was my confidante, Kirsti my ideal and inspiration. Meanwhile, one of my fellow countrywomen arrived at Shantivanam, a widow seventy five years old, who had lived in Poona during the British Raj and was now returning, determined to end her days in a hermit's hut far from the comforts and conveniences of her native land. Despite a severe bout of dysentery which struck her down as soon as she arrived, nothing could daunt Santoshi, as Father Bede named her. She was a woman of unfailing courage, with a kind, loving heart and a sharp tongue, and I loved to talk with her, even though I might come away smarting from her grandmotherly admonitions.

Shantivanam, 25th March 1980

Dear Mum and Dad,

In this letter I thought I would describe my daily routine here at Shantivanam so that you'd have an idea how I'm passing my time. Since I plan to stay here three months, I've moved out of the guest house to a beautiful little mud hut which faces the Kaveri. I love it! Generally I rise in the mornings at 4 a.m. and begin the day with yoga asanas. *I've been learning these postures from Brother Amuldas, one of Father Bede's disciples, who comes from Kerala and has long curly black hair and a very white smile, and is expert in hatha yoga. I do my yoga in tunic and trousers; the rest of the day I dress in a sari made of five yards of hand-woven cloth. The men, by the way, wear a lungi, a cloth that wraps around their waist and hangs down like a skirt. After Yoga, I sit for meditation on the porch of my hut until I hear the bell ring for morning prayer and mass. In the temple we all sit on the ground, and we* "Aum" *and chant Sanskrit verses as well as psalms. The celebrant at mass sits on the ground, too, in front of a low, lotus-shaped altar, and offers flowers, water, incense and a butter lamp, in Indian style, whilst celebrating mass.*

Then we all go to the refectory and eat idalis*—steamed rice-flour cakes with a spicy coconut sauce. After breakfast we help to cut green bananas or eggplants for lunch, and then I find a galvanized bucket, get water from a hand pump, and wash my clothes by thumping them on a laundry stone in the garden and scrubbing them with a bar of caustic blue soap. I spend the morning studying Bhagavad Gita, reading, writing my journal, or walking in the eucalyptus grove beside the River Kaveri. Though the Kaveri has been dammed several times upstream of here,* *and sandbanks appear in her bed, still she is a beautiful river, blue and wide, with the Hill of the Holy Bee rising on her further shore. Kaveri is known as the "Ganges of the South," one of India's seven sacred rivers.*

At noon we have a time of common prayer, then lunch, which consists of rice and sambar, *a very hot spicy vegetable soup which is poured over the rice. In Benedictine style, we listen to a reading whilst we eat—currently, Mahatma Gandhi's autobiography. By the time lunch is over, it's very hot and humid, so everyone retires for a siesta. I usually sleep until roused by the tea bell. We take tea out of doors in the shade—Indian style tea, that is, the tea, milk and sugar all boiled together in a big kettle and drunk out of hot stainless steel beakers that burn your fingers. Tea is the main time for socializing, meeting new people or chatting with Angelika or Santoshi. Then comes the best hour of the day. We all gather in a big circle beneath the palm trees whilst Father Bede lectures on Bhagavad Gita. With so many people here from all over the world—an American theologian named Adityananda, a Filipino priest, a Spanish hermit, a Dutch nun from Thailand, a serious student of Zen, to name but a few—very lively discussion takes place. The American, Adityananda, is a kind of "monk without portfolio"—I mean, he doesn't belong to an order. He always calls me a "monkess" and is encouraging me to find a monastic community where I can continue my vocation.*

After the lecture, I take a walk in the eucalyptus grove to calm the mind, then go to the river bank, for the sunset meditation. I swathe myself as well as I can, and load on mosquito repellent, but evening meditation is definitely banquet time for the mosquitos. The best solution is to wade out to a sandbank, where it's very breezy. And so to evening prayer in the temple, where we sing a Sanskrit hymn to the Trinity, praising God as Satchidananda: sat, chit, *and* ananda; *meaning Truth, Consciousness, and Bliss.*

After a light supper, I take a last walk to the cremation ground beside the river, then write my journal by the light of a kerosene lamp, and meditate until I get sleepy and crawl under my mosquito net. Sometimes there's a break in this routine when Angelika and I walk three hot, dusty miles down the river to Kulithalai, the nearest town, for essential shopping, but usually that's the pattern of the day. An English spring seems very far away indeed! The funny thing is, I don't feel like a foreigner at all. I get on really well with the Indian sisters and priests here. It feels really natural to sit on the ground and eat with my hands—the whole culture feels so familiar and nothing seems new. It's like coming home! If I believed in reincarnation, I would think I had lived here for lifetimes. For the first time ever, I don't feel like a misfit. There are others like me! I am not the only one. Deep down, I know that India is my true home, and that Indian people can understand me.

Love, Olivia

It was late afternoon, and we were gathered, hot and sticky, in a circle beneath the palm trees. Today, in honour of a group of Jesuit novices who had just arrived, Father Bede was giving his introductory talk.

"Physically, some of you have come from far away," he was saying. "From London, Amsterdam, San Francisco, Manila. For others, it has been just an hour's journey from your seminary in Trichy." Here he smiled at the Jesuit novices. "Yet spiritually, you see, you have travelled the same, vast distance, from a modern city with its airport, markets and factories to the forest. The journey you have just made has been taken by countless seekers before you, from the time of the *rishis*, the seers of ancient India, onwards; for the forest has traditionally been the place of the spiritual quest. The disciples of the *rishis* came humbly with fuel in hand as a sign of their willingness to cook and serve"—Father Bede emphasised his words with a gesture of his slender, scholar's hands—"to sit at the feet of the *rishis*, waiting patiently, for years if necessary, for the teachings to be given."

I sighed. Father Bede's words echoed deep within me. Like the seekers of old, I had come to India humbly, willing to learn, willing to wait. I longed for pure love of the Divine, for union with *brahman*, for that surely, was the goal and culmination of the spiritual journey.

By the time I had learnt to sit in half lotus in the brightly-painted little temple without fidgeting too much during the prayers, and had begun to get my tongue around the Sanskrit verses that we chanted together, the moon which lit my nightly walks to the burning *ghat* beside the river had passed through three quarters of her cycle, and the season of Lent was at an end. My first Indian Easter marked the death of an old world-view, an old paradigm, and a new birth into a wider, freer view of life, with more room for confusion and disorientation, but also for growth, change and expansion.

30th March 1980

My first Holy Week and Easter in a foreign land! And I feel that I am being resurrected into a new paradigm. So what has changed? What am I learning?

First, that a human is not a 'bag of enzymes'. That, as Father Bede says, 'the so-called laws of nature are only approximations'. That science and technology are the products of consciousness and have nothing to say about the nature or source of consciousness. In medical school, I was trained in a materialistic, reductionistic model. These last three weeks, I've spent hours in the library. I've dipped into the many books, from Victor Frankl to Shri Aurobindo to the lore of the Sioux Indians (I wonder if I'll ever meet a Sioux Indian in my life?). None of them are into the reductionistic model.

But most of all, on Father Bede's advice, I've been reading the Upanishads. And I'm finding that Indian thought is solving a very big problem for me. Due to my mechanistic medical training, I have been in a split between mind and heart, unable to hold rationally what I knew intuitively. India is providing me with concepts and vocabulary to express through reason what I feel by intuition. Here there is a science of the supra-rational, giving place for many dimensions of reality which the reductionistic thinkers dismiss as phony or pathological.

Most important of all, I have learnt that consciousness is primary to matter—that consciousness is all—that mind creates body, consciousness creates matter. That consciousness can be seen as subtle matter and matter as a gross form of consciousness. Puts Einstein's Theory of Relativity and Heisenberg's Uncertainty Principle into a new light, doesn't it! This is a very, very exciting, expansive Easter for me.

At dawn, on Easter Tuesday, I put on my green sari and took my place on the banks of the Kaveri, whilst, with Angelika as sole witness, Father Bede prepared to initiate me into *brahmacharya*. As

I watched the river change colours in the growing light, Father Bede reminded me of the significance of the step I was taking.

"*Brahmacharya* is the first of four *ashramas,* or stages of life," he said. "It is the stage of the spiritual seeker or student. Loosely translated as 'celibacy', *brahmacharya* actually means, 'chariot of brahman'. To practice *brahmacharya* is to live and move and have one's being in *brahman.* One who is thus established in *brahman* can move on to the next stage of life, that of the householder, fulfilling responsibilities to society and family. Or one can enter directly upon the final stage of life, *sannyas,* or total renunciation.

"The *sannyasi* is completely dead to the world; in fact, before taking *sannyas*, one must perform one's own funeral rites. The *sannyasi's* ochre robes, you see, symbolize flame, the flame of renunciation. Proclaiming 'Now I fear no one, and let none fear me', he dwells alone in graveyards, temple courtyards or abandoned buildings, neither wishing to live nor hoping to die, possessing nothing, claiming nothing, keeping nothing."

My heart seemed to blaze as I heard these words. At twenty-eight, I felt that I was free from attachments and that the world held no further attractions for me. Surely it would not be long before I entered into *sannyas*, into total renunciation.

"For those for whom the worldly involvement of householder life is no longer suitable," Father Bede concluded, "but who are not yet ready for the final commitment of *sannyas*, the Vedas propose an intermediate way, the third stage of life, that of the *vanprastha* or forest dweller, a husband and wife who live a retired and ascetic life together."

"For you, this initiation is not something completely new," he said. "You have already made your novitiate in a contemplative order. This is a rededication to the spiritual search, which you must now live out here in the world, not in an enclosed community. As a token of this rededication to monastic conversion, I am giving you this medallion of St. Benedict. May he guide you in becoming a chariot of *brahman.*"

That afternoon, when I was still glowing from the *brahmacharya* initiation, a group of us were sitting outside a hut, singing

Easter carols, when a thin, bronzed young man appeared, carrying a musical instrument fashioned from a gourd with a bamboo stem. His sunbleached hair was tangled, his beard was long, a rosary of prayer beads hung on his bare chest, and there was a large rat-hole in his white *lungi*. The newcomer immediately sat down, tuned his two-stringed instrument, and began to join in the singing. I stared at the wild-looking American yogi, newly-come from some jungle retreat, with a shock of recognition. In the depths of my heart, I had always known that I would find a spiritual friend, one who would walk the path of renunciation by my side. Of course, this would be an ideally pure, platonic relationship, like that of Francis of Assisi and St. Clare—or so I earnestly believed. Now, an inner voice whispered to me, *"He has come. This is the friend for whom you have always waited."*

Next day, our new guest, Francis the American yogi, found me reading on the porch of my mud hut. "I thought you might like to share this papaya," he said, rather shyly. "And I wanted to show you my Medicine Bag." Having ceremoniously cut the papaya, he carefully laid out the photographs and relics that formed the contents of his holy bag.

"I guess this is the best place to begin." Francis picked out a picture of Our Lady, standing on a crescent moon, aureoled by the sun, and wearing the starry night as her robe.

"It's very unusual," I murmured, "I have never seen this Madonna before."

"This is Guadalupe, Mother of all the Americas. In the Mexican neighbourhood where I grew up, her image is everywhere. I was raised in Denver, Colorado, at the foot of the Rocky Mountains, and there are many Mexicans there. My mother was Baptist, my father an Italian Catholic, and they left it to me, as the eldest child, to decide which church to belong to. I tried both, and chose to become Catholic, so when I was twelve years old, I was baptized. It was one of the most profound spiritual experiences of my life." As he described this, his first deep mystical experience, Francis' voice had a powerful ring.

"I felt my crown open," he went on, "and grace just flooding in. There was a tremendous sense of purity and completeness. But then I began attending parish school. The nuns there . . . perhaps they were sincere, but they were emotionally frozen, warped. They were always telling lies about me, trying to get me into disgrace. My adolescence and youth were troubled, and for a time I used drugs—that was the worst thing I ever did, to myself or to anyone."

Francis picked out an Italian holy card depicting the Sacred Heart of Jesus. "When I felt most confused and insecure, I went into a church and prayed, 'Jesus, I don't know if you exist, but if you do, help me.' And help came. Soon I was living in a milk truck with seven other young people, all non-denominational Christians. We were kind of Jesus freaks, before the Jesus freaks as such began."

The next picture he showed me was of a beaming figure with long, flowing dark hair. "Don't Worry, Be Happy," the card proclaimed. "This is Meher Baba, perhaps the greatest of the Eastern teachers who came to the West. You see, as my love for Jesus grew, I began to experience Oneness that blotted out all distinctions. Then I had an out-of-body experience, and after that, there was no more me, no more Jesus, no more God, no more Devil, just pure consciousness. I tried to communicate this experience to Christians, but none of them understood, so I turned to the masters of the East."

I stared at the picture. Beams of light seemed to be coming out of it. I could tell that the Hindu saint was full of love.

"For a long while I thought Meher Baba was my guru," Francis continued, "but he was no longer present in the body. I never met him, just attended meetings of his Lovers. Those were great days in Boulder, Colorado. We hippies were open, trusting, we cooked great communal meals, made a community garden. Everyone shared, and there were 'Holy Man Jams' where all kinds of yogis and spiritual masters imparted their teaching freely."

I sighed wistfully. Somehow I had missed being a hippie, had always been trapped within institutions, structures, orthodoxy.

"Take a look at these," Francis went on. "They are poems by Chogyam Trungpa Rinpoche, a Tibetan master of crazy wisdom who lives in Boulder. When I was in profound despair, he pulled my beard and said, 'You're okay.' And after that, I was. I had gotten into an unhappy love affair, and when that fell apart, I turned to intensive meditation under his guidance. I studied with him for three years. Then he advised me to take up *vipassana,* Insight Meditation. So I attended a three-month retreat, which helped me tremendously, and then continued studying *vipassana* for the next two years. And as I got deeper into Buddhism, I felt the need to come to India, the birthplace of the Buddha. I sold ice cream to raise the money for my trip."

I looked up from Francis' collection of serene Buddhas and Bodhisattvas. "You made that much money by selling ice cream?"

"No, I made most of it. Then winter came, and I tried selling firewood, until the truck broke down, plus I got an injured foot. I was still four hundred dollars short."

He handed me a picture of the controversial Bhagwan Shree Rajneesh, wearing a sheepskin hat.

"At the last moment, I met a Jewish woman from New York who was also on her way to India, to see Rajneesh. She gave me the four hundred dollars and told me to see Rajneesh too."

The next picture was familiar to me—a portrait of Francis of Assisi. "I flew as far as London, and then decided to travel to India overland. The first shrine I visited was Assisi, and there I dedicated myself to the pilgrimage, under the patronage of St. Francis. In Rome, I bought this *mala* from the Hare Krishnas," here he indicated the prayer beads he wore, "and I have worn it ever since. I hitchhiked to Turkey, then took a hippie bus to Kabul. It happened that I was in Kabul on the day the military coup took place."

"In the spring of '78? Now the Russians have invaded, you know. Otherwise, I would have come overland myself."

"It's just as well you didn't. Nearly everyone got sick on the journey from Istanbul to Kabul. I was the only one who stayed healthy. At Kabul we were detained in a hotel, and through the entranceway I watched the fighting, even though I heard a voice within warning me, "If you watch this, you'll get sick." There were jet bombers overhead and the sound of bombs exploding. The air was full of the crack of rifle fire, and bullets whistled past as troops battled police in the streets. Sure enough, I did get sick. I went down with terrible dysentery and couldn't travel for a week. At last I took the train to Amritsar in India. When I arrived, it was a hundred and twenty degrees in the shade, and I was shitting water."

"You could have died!"

"I just lay in a guest room at the Golden Temple, very sick. This man," here Francis indicated a photograph of a broad-shouldered, turbaned Sikh, "he befriended me and took me to his home. Then I met a Sikh ascetic named Nirgun. He had been a Rajneesh *sannyasin*, had travelled to America and lived with hoboes, spent time in a Danish prison. Me and him went travelling together, two sadhus dressed in white, two wandering ascetics, Nirgun always striding ahead and me straggling behind. He would sleep without any blanket, eat anything, drink any water. I followed his example, and of course, the dysentery just became chronic. From Punjab, we went to Himachal Pradesh."

It was oppressively hot, and the grasshoppers and cicadas droned on and on. The unfamiliar names of places and people jumbled themselves in my mind . . . Simla, Solen, Delhi, Agra, Chettapur, Khajuraho . . . the ascetics Francis had met, the yogi in Solen who had lived for years on fruit juices and who spoke for just one hour a day, the ill-tempered recluse living underground who must be propitiated with whiskey, the loving Baba Prem Ghee who nursed the sick pilgrim when he was crippled with foot abscesses and who gave up his own bed to the guest.

I came to myself, startled and wide awake, to hear Francis saying, "I met a man whose feet were lotuses."

"I beg your pardon?"

"The energy flowed from his feet like the petals of a lotus. He is a very simple old man, has no ashram, doesn't seem to want disciples. He lives at a village named Alandi, a famous pilgrim centre not far from Poona. I stayed there for some time and watched him closely—I mean, you can only be duped by so many false gurus, and then you become cautious. But I never saw a single flaw in him, never a single movement of ego. He seemed completely pure, completely humble. If anyone would be my guru, it would be him. You should meet him. There's a wonderful place in Poona where you can stay, Christa Prema Seva Ashram. It's the best ashram I've ever been to."

My spine tingled and my knees seemed to turn to jelly. The idea of actually meeting such a being was terrifying. How did one behave in his presence? Surely I would make a fool of myself. Yet I felt a keen interest in the old man whose feet were lotuses.

"How did you meet him?" I asked eagerly, but too late. The sun was sinking, the waters of the Kaveri were changing colour, and the ashram bell began to ring. It was the hour for meditation. "Please tell me the story next time we meet," I begged, as I gathered my meditation mat and mosquito repellent.

Francis' sincerity deeply impressed me. His brown eyes, with their clear, candid gaze, his high domed forehead, and the expressive mouth hiding beneath his moustache all spoke clearly of a single-hearted and sensitive nature. "I am certain," I noted in my journal that night, "that Francis will be a guru one day."

10th April 1980

Today I went to Thannirpali village, at the other end of the sandy land leading to the ashram gate. It is a very poor village, huts built of mud and straw, no running water or electricity. Everywhere you see big looms with brightly coloured weavings on them. The main source of income for these villagers is the handloom weaving of saris. I came today to visit the dispensary, run by two sisters who are connected with Shantivanam. They showed me all around and told me about their work. It's really wonderful, what these Indian sisters are doing to support the villagers.

But I realized one thing very clearly. I am not here in India to work in a village dispensary. I have come here to be healed more than to heal. I need to be here humbly, learning from India, not trying to teach her. It's not my task right now to uplift the poor villagers. First I must let them uplift me on the wings of their simple piety, their surrender to what is. In my heart is the source of war, oppression, poverty and disease. It is here, in my own heart, that I must combat the ills I see around me. First, before all else, I have to turn within and find myself—meditating in the hut beneath the palm leaves.

If only, if only, I could find a guide, a real guru like the old man Francis met whose feet were lotuses. How many hours I spent in the Abbey, lying on the cold flagstones of the chapel floor, sobbing desper-

ately because I longed to meet my guide! If only I could find the person who can teach by silence and read the inmost secrets of my heart! I love Father Bede, and I am learning very, very much from him. He will always be one of my important teachers. Yet deep inside, I know that there is someone else, someone I have yet to find, who is my true guru.

Inspired by Kirsti, I was reading Arthur Osborne's biography of Ramana Maharshi, and was profoundly affected by the book. My mind turned again and again to what Kirsti had told me, 'He was a master who taught by silence.' Shy and reticent as I was, psychologically a dweller within the high walls of a secret garden, I longed for such a sage. Until I met that being, I would always be incomplete. I knew that, although Shri Ramana had left this mortal life within a year of my birth, he would still manifest himself as guru to those who sincerely prayed to him with all their heart. So I tried. I prayed wholeheartedly and with all sincerity, and received for my answer absolutely no response, no connection. Not only was the Sage silent, he also seemed to be deaf to my appeals. He, too, was not my guru.

I had no luck so far in finding a guru. However, I did have a unique opportunity to witness at first hand the ceremony of *sannyas,* total renunciation. One cloudless morning, the entire community gathered on the grass beside the Kaveri, in the very spot where I had sat during my *brahmacharya* initiation. As the first rays of the rising sun struck the river, a lean, brown-skinned young man descended into the water. Removing his white clothes, the dress of the *brahmachari*, he let them float downriver, and stood naked in the water, free at last from all the disguises and trappings of civilization. Entering the river beside him, Father Bede whispered into his ears two things, the mantra that was hereafter to be his constant prayer, and his new name. Then he gave him an ochre loincloth. Dripping, dressed only in the loincloth, the new *sannyasi* stepped on to the shore, to receive from Father Bede's hands two pieces of ochre cloth.

"This cloth," said Father Bede, "which in India we call *kavi*, is the colour of Ganges mud. It is also the colour of the rising sun upon the waters from which you have just emerged, and the colour of fire. You are now living within the flames of your own funeral pyre. In this moment, you renounce all the three worlds, the Earth, the Air and the Heavens; the physical, the emotional, and even the merits of the spiritual world. Young though you are, this is the last initiation you can ever take. Henceforth, you must live as one already dead—and gloriously alive in *brahman*, alive in Christ, the True Person."

That night, Francis accompanied me on my regular walk to the riverside. The sound of drumming echoed through the night, and a funeral pyre was blazing a short distance away, filling the air with the scent of burning flesh. The dark river reflected flames and stars, as we took our seat on the bank.

"Please tell me the story of how you met the old man whose feet are lotuses."

"Well . . ." Francis paused and gazed out at the countless brilliant stars and the black silhouette of Holy Bee Hill. "It was like this. I had been staying in Poona, listening to Rajneesh's lectures, staying at Christa Prema Seva Ashram. There was a woman at the ashram who knew yoga and had promised to teach me, and as she was going to a village near Lonavala, I went there too, to study yoga. We both stayed at the home of a brahmin family who taught *kundalini* meditation. As soon as I arrived there, I went down with typhoid, and I couldn't leave. One thing led to another, and I wound up staying with that family for about a year.

"Anyway, in Lonavala there was a hustler Yogi, a fat man with long greasy hair and soiled white robes, who liked to hang out with Westerners. His favourite place was Alandi, shrine of the great Poet Saint Jnaneshvar, and he took me there for a visit. Every grain of dust in Alandi glistened with the power of devotion, and the place held such attraction for me that I thought of returning there for a couple of week's retreat.

"Meanwhile, I had to go to Bombay on visa business, so I visited the well-known *jnani*, or sage, Nisagadatta Maharaj, who had a *beedi* factory and lived opposite a stinking public latrine. His style of teaching was very cutting, and he came down on me heavily for moving about so much. I told him I couldn't stop wandering, that I had this intense desire to see the Ganga and the Himalayas.

"'Okay!' he said. 'Go to the Himalayas. And if there's anything left of you, come back, and I'll see you again. Where are you going now?' So I told him I planned to go to Alandi. At this he became even more intense. 'That's right!' he shouted. 'You go to Alandi! You go! Have Sant Jnaneshvar's *darshan* if you can. Get out! Get out of here! Go!' And he chased me out of the room. I tried to come back, but there he was, standing at the top of the stairs, arms akimbo, barring my way."

There was a pause, filled with the croaking of frogs and the beat of the funeral drum.

"You see," Francis went on, "when I came to India, I still had some worldly desires. I hoped to become a yoga teacher, so that when I returned to the West I would have a place in society and wouldn't have to wash dishes or sell ice cream any more. And I planned to advance my studies in *vipassana,* maybe even become a meditation teacher too. And now everything was going wrong. I was embroiled in a complex relationship with the brahmin family, who wanted me as a son, to help with their farm. Their house was crowded and noisy, and it was difficult to meditate for more than an hour or so. My visa situation was getting all tangled up, and my money was running out. I hadn't learned any more yoga than I had known when I came to India. And of the *vipassana* teachers I planned to study with, Munindra had gone to America, and Goenka to England. So I went to Alandi.

"At first the retreat seemed like a fiasco. It was marriage season, and every night there was a wedding with movie music blaring out over loudspeakers. A big pilgrimage was going on, with thousands of pilgrims crowding to the village to chant God's names with cymbals and drums. I ate some food with too much chili, and got diarrhea. Then this man, Nam Joshi, a schoolteacher who ran the brahmin pilgrim hostel, asked me to come and meet his guru. I wasn't very keen. 'Just another old Baba,' I thought, but to please him, I went along. And there, in a dark cavelike shrine, right in the central temple of Sant Jnaneshvar, was this simple old man in a loincloth and shawl. He looked like a very nice, very sincere devotee. As a matter of common courtesy, I touched his feet.

"At once, it felt as if a thousand volts of electricity were passing through my body. I was blown back, literally, from kneeling to standing. Energy shot up my back and struck my Third Eye. And I saw Mecca."

"Mecca? The holiest place of Islam? In a Hindu temple?" I was taken aback. Francis nodded.

"Yes, Mecca. I saw a bridge of light extending between Alandi and Mecca, embracing everything in the vibrational field that lay between them. Then my eyes were drawn to the old man's hand. He wore a silver ring engraved with the portrait of Sai Baba of Shirdi, a great Sufi mystic who united Hinduism and Islam. Silver beams poured out of the ring and struck me in the heart. My heart was being pierced. I felt lifetimes of poisons pouring out. I began weeping uncontrollably and praying to the old saint to help me release these poisons. At once he said through Nam Joshi's interpretation, 'I don't speak your language, but I understand all the prayers of your heart. You have done much meditation and will certainly reach the goal, but your heart has been blocked. Don't worry, I have taken care of that.'"

The funeral drum, the rhythm of the final sacrifice, still filled the air. Sparks rose from the burning corpse.

"For the next two weeks," Francis continued, "I believed that the old guru was a Moslem, even though he lived in a Hindu temple. I couldn't really see his physical form any more, he appeared to me in a body of light, emanating the silvery moon energy that I had experienced at mosques and Sufi tombs. Finally, when I sat with him one evening, I was able to see his sacred thread and the sacred tuft of hair on the crown of his head. Then I understood that he was a Hindu, a brahmin. Yet he was much more than either a Hindu holy man or a Sufi saint. He was unfathomable being."

Francis' eyes glowed in the starlight. As he talked of his guru, he seemed to grow brighter.

"And after I met him, my life took a new turn, to the way of renunciation. My visa was denied, and I was already over-stayed. The brahmin family didn't want to harbor an illegal alien, so overnight my status changed from son to unwelcome guest, even though it was they who had promised to get the visa for me—

otherwise I would have gone to Sri Lanka long before and become a Buddhist monk. They kept all my money as payment for the time I had spent there as their son, and sent me to Goa with a little pocket money. I didn't have enough to bribe the police, so even now, I'm still here illegally. For about a year I lived the life of a renunciant in the Goan jungle. Then, feeling the need to reconnect with my Christian roots, I came here."

It was late, and I had much to ponder over as I made my way back to the hut. The fortress of orthodoxy which had both imprisoned and protected me seemed to be giving way under the impact of India's *sannatan dharma,* the Eternal Way, the timeless wisdom. Francis' old man whose feet were lotuses and who was actually unfathomable being; Ramana Maharshi, the sage who taught by silence; Lord Krishna whose words formed the subject of Father Bede's daily Bhagavad Gita class—were all these great beings not the Word of God made flesh? Was Christ indeed the sole incarnation of the Word, the second person of the Trinity? Or was he one of those unique manifestations of Divine Truth who have been born in every age and every culture? Was it my destiny and the destiny of every true seeker to become ourselves embodiments of the Word?

Perplexed, I made my way next morning to the little walled garden, where Adityananda, the American sannyasi, had his hut. "I have a very big question," I said, as we sat beneath the shade of a mango tree. "Is Christ unique?"

Adityananda smiled. He would give not cut-and-dried answers; rather, food for thought.

"Only God, *brahman,* is uniquely unique," he mused. "Hence the *Upanishads* call That the One Without a Second. Yet only in the briefest flash of intuition can we contact That Transcendental Real. To be the devotee of *brahman* is impossible."

"So the Word, the Immanent aspect of That, the *atman* as it were, is made flesh as the object of our devotion? No man has ever seen God... the only son, he has made him known?" I pondered.

With an amused lift to his eyebrows, Adityananda continued. "And for you, that form is Jesus, the archetype with Whom you have lived since infancy. But now, if you were born in these parts, in the Shaiva Siddhanta sect, Shiva would be the form that the

Transcendent took for your adoration. Or, if you were one of the Shri Vaishnavas of South India, you would be singing the praises of Krishna, crowned with peacock feathers, adorned with a gold silk *lungi.*"

I wriggled uncomfortably. "So, Jesus is not unique? He is just one among many manifestations of the Divine?"

"He is not, as we have said, uniquely unique. Nevertheless, he is unique. After all, even you and I are unique. There is no other monkess Olivia quite like you." He smiled charmingly. "But now, the question you have to ponder is, what distinguishes the uniqueness of Jesus from the uniqueness of the rest of us. In particular, from those such as Father Bede, who, it cannot be denied, are vessels of Divine Grace, who radiate grace to many others."

"And," Adityananda concluded, "to give you a hint or a pointer, consider this. Divine Power, *shakti,* passes through one such as Father Bede. Yet does the fulness of Power reside in him? And in Jesus?"

Adityananda had given me much to ponder as I made my first incursion into Hindu terrain. My fellow students in Brother Amuldas' yoga class, an earnest young Dutch doctor named Aadrian and a still more earnest nurse, his wife Flore, had invited me to accompany them on a trip to one of India's ancient temple towns. We planned to travel seventy miles by train to the famous city of Madurai, stay there a couple of days during the annual marriage celebration of Meenakshi, the local Goddess, and then return to Shantivanam.

Madurai, April 1980

Dear Mum and Dad,

I am having a really thrilling time in Madurai, the ancient capital of the Pandya kingdom, today a bustling commercial centre famed for its silk saris. The city boasts a magnificent ancient temple, whose gateways are a breathtaking riot of demons and beasts, men and women, gods and heroes, all dancing. The whole city is crowded for the celebration of Meenakshi's marriage. We are enjoying the spectacle of numerous chanting Brahmins with sacred threads adorning their bare chests, loins girt with silks; hundreds of women in splendid embroidered silken saris; the idols circumambulating the temple in palanquins *to the accompaniment of pipes and drums whilst the sellers of gaudy trinkets peddle behind them on ancient bicycles; the offering of* puja *(worship), with fruits, flowers, water, incense and lights; priests breaking coconuts as a ritual gesture; sacred elephants receiving worship;* sannyasins *(renunciants) in their ochre robes; worshippers performing their ablutions; and the police station decorated with flowers and broadcasting Tamil devotional music over loudspeakers.*

There are stalls everywhere, selling bangles, hair slides, trinkets, and the ochre cords on which Tamilian women wear the golden 'mangal sutra,' *a pendant which is their equivalent of a wedding ring. Tens of thousands of women flock to Madurai on this day to renew the ochre cord and reconsecrate their marriage. Hinduism is a wonderful religion, totally confusing, neither this nor that, profound and profane, beautiful and tawdry, tolerant and bigoted, silent and cacophonous, gratuitous and commercialized, worshipping the One unknowable Absolute under three hundred million manifestations.*

Love, Olivia

In the great temple of Meenakshi, I was met with a warm welcome. The Tamilian devotees were delighted to see me there in a simple cotton sari. They daubed my forehead with vermilion powder in token of the blessing of the goddess, and much to my surprise, fastened in my hair a garland of sweet white jasmine flowers. I was too naive to realize that the flowers had been worn by the Deity, and were given to me as Her gift. Her garland was as close as I got to Meenakshi on that occasion, for, warned off by the large notices stating, 'Hindus Only Beyond This Point', I remained in the outer courts of the temple, and made no attempt to enter the inmost shrine.

A luminous Goddess, Meenakshi—'She whose eyes are like two shapely fishes', is the alluring India of beautiful women in silken saris with tinkling glass bangles and jingling silver anklets, of ancient temples, shady palm groves and sunset on the Kaveri, the entrancing land with which the newcomer falls in love. Just as, in my obedience to the 'Hindus only' rule, I was confined to the outer court of Meenakshi's temple, with its array of minor divinities, in the same way, my cautious and gradual exploration of Indian culture had brought me only to the outer court of that great temple that is India. I admired the images of the sixty-four Tamil saints, fascinated by the beauty and antiquity of it all, still innocent of the fact that the Divine Mother could be dark and terrible as well as luminous and gracious. The moon was to pass through thirty cycles of brightness and darkness before I returned to Madurai. In that time, I would learn to call the Mother 'Kali' as well as 'Meenakshi'. But for now, my Mother India seemed to me all light and beauty.

I soon found that, much as I was challenged by the faith of India, Francis was equally challenged by his renewed contact with the Christian world. A few days after my return from Madurai, he arrived at my hut looking very perplexed.

"Do you understand that talk Father Bede gave yesterday?" he asked.

"On *avatar* and Incarnation? Well, he distinguished two covenants. The Cosmic Covenant, of which Hinduism is a part, takes place in cosmic time. The *avatar* is a mythic figure. Whereas the Abrahamic or Transcendent Covenant belongs in historical time. Christ was crucified 'under Pontius Pilate'—in time and history. Christ's Incarnation is historical."

"That's exactly the part I don't understand. I can't grasp that historical time."

"Linear time? But that's the very basis of Judaeo-Christian thought. Historical time has a beginning, a middle and an end. It begins with the creation and concludes with the *eschaton,* the End Time, a great consummation when all that is now incomplete and unsatisfactory will be fulfilled. Between those two points, it is marked by God's saving acts, the passage across the Red Sea, for example, or the crucifixion. These events took place at specific points in history.

"What's the advantage of that? I thought we were trying to become free from the chains of time. Time is the product of thought. It's because our minds are thinking, thinking, only thinking of a part, never seeing the whole, that we create time. J. Krishnamurti says that time is the enemy of man."

I considered. "Yes. Thomas Aquinas wrote that everything that is, is eternally in God. So as you say, there is no time with God, Who sees the whole, not parts. But linear time is a step in that direction. It frees us from the chains of *chronos,* the slavery to time as endless meaningless repetition, and imbues time with meaning, as *kairos,* the Hour; the Hour of grace, the moment of opportunity."

Francis sighed. "I still can't grasp it. Time *has* no meaning. The notion of time creates meaninglessness, because it separates the I, who is passing through time, from the whole. I've just come from the jungle in Goa, where the leaves fall and die to create the ground for new plants to spring, where the tigress pulls down the deer to feed her cubs, and the spider spins her web, waiting for the fly. The big black ants feed upon the corpse of the spider, and the little red sugar ants carry the dead black ant to their storehouse. Everything that lives and grows feeds upon what falls and dies. The cow eats grass and gives milk, the food of life. The cobra drinks milk and gives poison, the agent of death. The cow and the cobra, both are sacred, both are faces of Divine Mother. Shiva, Lord of the Dance, bears the torch of destruction in one hand, the drum of creation in the other. This is our life, this is *samsara,* the wandering, a dragon swallowing his own tail."

"So—where is hope?"

"Hope? Hope is yet more thought and time. Hope creates a future projection. The wheel turns, but the hub, the centre, is still. In the centre, there is no I, no individual. There is wholeness. In Christian thought there is a beginning, a middle and an end, but in Indian thought this too continues for ever, the beginning and ending of Universes."

Perhaps I had as big a problem grasping cosmic time as Francis had with linear time. "I was reading something about this in Bhagavad Gita," I said, "but I didn't understand it very well. Can you explain more?"

Francis warmed to his topic. "Vishnu, the Preserver, breathes out and creates the universe, breathes in, and destroys it. His inbreath is the Night of Brahma the Creator god, his outbreath is the Day of Brahma. The whole of our so-called history is just the blinking of the eye of Brahma. And the universe continues degenerating and regenerating, passing through greater and lesser twilights, for a thousand of these Great Ages, *mahayugas*. That's just one day of Brahma."

I was awestruck. "Billions of years!"

Francis continued relentlessly, "I tell you, time had no beginning and it never will end. There's only one way out. To Awaken."

I was beginning to feel threatened. "It's very interesting," I said politely, "but these ages of which you speak, they are mythologies. And as Father Bede says, Krishna lives in mythological time, in another age than our present human condition."

"That's what I hate about Christians, their arrogance. They always claim this, that Jesus was historical, but Krishna was mythological. Krishna was a real person. He was a warrior of the Yadava clan. His father was Vasudev and his mother Devaki. And Bhagavad Gita is his teaching."

"Yes, obviously some great realized being, whom we call Krishna, must lie behind the teachings of Bhagavad Gita. But the cowherd of Vrindavan who dances with the milkmaids, what we were reading at noon prayer lately from *Bhagavata Purana*—all that is myth and legend. What Father Bede was saying is that the historicity of Krishna is irrelevant to Hindus; it is the myth that saves, whenever it is recounted. But the historicity of Christ is crucial to Christians. 'If Christ did not rise from the dead, our faith is in vain.'"

Francis sighed again, very deeply. "Christians are so gloomy, so addicted to suffering. They need some sleek cows and big-breasted milkmaids and ring dances beneath the full moon. They need to learn to listen to the enchanting flute of Krishna, to experience God as bliss. And the Hindus, they need the depth of feeling in the tears Christ shed over Jerusalem. And both need the clarity, the diamond wisdom, of the Buddha. Since I was a boy, long before I even knew what these religions were, a voice in the heart has said to me, 'I have to find the unity of these three Great Ways.'"

The following day was Priya's birthday, and she invited Francis, Angelika and myself to sing with her on the river bank. Francis led us in some *kirtan* or devotional chanting, accompanying himself on the dotar, his two-stringed gourd-and-bamboo drone, whilst Priya played finger cymbals. Francis proved to be a fine musician with a strong and melodious voice. After the *kirtan* we all walked down the lane to Thannirpalli village, where we sat on wooden benches outside the mud-walled shack that served as village tea shop, drinking chay and eating *chiki,* the Indian peanut brittle. To my eyes, Priya's manner towards Francis seemed flirtatious—after all, the man was a celibate renunciant. But perhaps I was just too prim, I reminded myself, too much the nun. As we talked, Francis realized that he had completely forgotten about his own birthday. It was now a month after the event. He confessed that he had also forgotten his age, although he thought he was 'maybe around thirty'. Evidently, linear time was really not his strong point.

Unfortunately for me, we were having an exceptionally hot Hot Season. Prickly heat broke out all over my body, and the mosquitos raised huge bumps on my sensitive skin. I slept much of the afternoon and little of the night. After a few attempts at meditating in my hut at noon, stripped to the waist with a wet towel on my head whilst sweat ran in rivulets down my back, I decided that midnight was a better hour for contemplation.

It was at the very peak of the Hot Season, a full moon in late May, that the Feast of Mariamme, the Fever Goddess, was celebrated. Despite the recent eradication of smallpox, over which she presides, Mariamme had lost none of her importance in the hearts of the folk of Kulithalai, whose town is built around her temple. One scorching forenoon, Aadrian, Flore and I made our way to the festival, with me perched rather uncertainly sidesaddle on the back of Aadrian's bicycle.

The central feature of the day's celebration was the paying of vows made to the deity for deliverance from sickness. Everywhere there were babies and small children painted with black and white spots, symbolic smallpox, and carrying crudely painted clay dolls with green branches sticking from them, an offering to the Mother.

Slightly older children promenaded, painted and dressed as various gods of the Hindu pantheon, with a metal alms box in their hands. I was both fascinated and horrified to see metal darts piercing the tongues and lips of these children. Were they sterile? I doubted it. And I was certain that there had been no anaesthesia. Who had inserted them, and how?

At the heart of all the activities were the processions of vow-payers circumambulating the temple in frenzied and ecstatic states; first drummers, playing furiously, then some wildly dancing, green branches in hand, others semi-conscious and half-carried by relatives. Some rushed around the temple holding scorching clay firepots before their faces, others bore decorated canopies attached to the flesh of their torso by forty or so steel lances, whilst smaller lances pierced their skin, lips and tongue. Did their trance state render them oblivious to the agonizing pain?

Devotees sprinted around the temple carrying on sugar-cane poles mysterious burdens tied in yellow cloth, each of which turned out to be a disgruntled and far from ecstatic baby, whilst the most enthusiastic of the worshippers soaked themselves in water and rolled in the dust outside the temple. A few of the devotees collapsed in catatonic states and were revived by showers of coconut milk. Relatives poured food and water into their mouths. The majority, however, once they entered the temple at the completion of their vowed quota of penance, immediately smoothed their hair, straightened their clothes, and assumed their usual poise. With the practised eye of a doctor, I watched as, in the shade of the temple, friends and relatives calmly pulled out the metal from the lips, tongues and torsos of votaries, wrapping the instruments of penance in cloth. Despite the utter crudeness of the operation, the pierced skin did not bleed at all.

Meanwhile, in a level, open area not far from the temple, the embers of a huge fire were smoldering. White *lungis* tucked up above their knees and sweat pouring from their bodies, four priests were raking the embers in preparation for the afternoon's firewalk, when supplicants of Mariamme would venture barefoot over the hot coals. The blazing heat was so intense and the crowds so large that I did not feel able to stay to watch the firewalk, nor did I realize how rare such events are, even in India. I would not get a second opportunity.

Venturing into the temple, I was taken to speak to the head priest, who spoke fluent English, and was a sophisticated scholar from a British university. Escorted by him, I entered the inmost shrine to receive the blessings of the Fever Goddess. I was surprised that such an educated person as the Head Priest could condone what I regarded as sheer superstition. In my ignorance, I felt myself a detached, indeed, a clinical observer of the primitive villagers' attempts to turn away the wrath of Mariamme. Full of the pride of my profession, I was face to face with the icon of Divine Mother in her aspect of Goddess of Kulithalai, She who wields the purifying power of sickness.

The India I had come to love as the realm of beautiful Meenakshi was also the land of filth and flies; the agents of disease, the servants of the wrathful goddess of plagues and epidemics. Today I turned my back on Mariamme's firewalk; exactly a year from now, I the physician was to tread the fiery path of infectious illness. Standing in the inner sanctum of the Smallpox Queen, I little guessed that within my heart she would unveil herself year by year, first as my tormentor, then as my teacher—ultimately as my healer, she who could lead me unscathed across the smoldering coals of the lower self.

The festival at Kulithalai had signalled the climax of hot season. Now, as the moon waned and May gave way to June, the weather changed. Within ten days, a sudden rainstorm flooded my palm-roofed hut, and Rohini, the windy season, began, bringing a wind at once cooling and very wearing. Meanwhile, under Father Bede's guidance, I was reflecting deeply on what it truly meant to be a monk—or to be "monk-ess Olivia".

3rd June 1980

What is a monk? Today I met with Father Bede to talk about this question and came away with some interesting articles on early Christian asceticism. Coming from my background in Western institutional monasticism, and my daily study of the Rule of St. Benedict in the Abbey, I thought of a monk as one who lives in an abbey under a written Rule and Abbot, and who has taken formal vows of Poverty, Chastity and Obedience.

Now in India, I see a monasticism that is non-institutional. The sannyasi leads a wandering life, staying three days here, three days there, begging a little food at noon, sleeping by night in a temple, burning ghat, *graveyard or abandoned building. As I've been reading lately, the early Christian aescetics were also non-institutional. They took no vows, followed no written rule, but were simply led by the Spirit into the desert. A monk is one who is* monos—*alone, that is, who is willing to confront existential loneliness. A monk is one who follows the call of the Spirit rather than the dictates of society.*

I have been all caught up in the forms of institutional monasticism. Now I must allow myself to be free to follow the call of the Spirit, wherever it leads. Then I will be a true monk, a true seeker, a true contemplative.

With these thoughts in mind, I embarked on a week of silence of both tongue and pen. Thousands of miles from every familiar scene, still grieving over the past, still confused about the future, I found silence to be a demanding discipline; yet it seemed essential for the discernment of my course in life. In the monastic tradition of India, I recognized the vision which had impelled me since I was twelve years old, and towards which a deep loneliness and sense of exile now drew me irresistibly, the vision of the one who is naked and clothed in flame, homeless and ever at home, free of all bonds, yet bound to the whole, blissfully alone beyond desire and fear, the *sannyasi.* I felt that the seeds of *sannyas* had indeed been sown in my heart, and wondered what soil would best allow those seeds to grow and mature.

While my tongue kept silence, a babble of voices lobbied me from within.

"*Look here,*" said one, "*you are nearly thirty, and it's time you made something of yourself. One must be sensible, one must be practical. Go back to England, study transpersonal psychotherapy, and support yourself in a useful way.*"

"*No, no!*" cried another, "*return to England by all means, but for contemplation, not for action. Don't be a 'do-gooder'. Where will you find a vaster desert than in the heart of the inner city? Establish your simple little ashram in that urban desert, take some part-time work, and contemplate where most it is needed.*"

"It won't work," objected the next, the voice of official monasticism. *"You're just a novice, not developed enough for such a challenge. Adityananda had the right idea, he has given you any number of addresses of monastic communities in Europe and America, which are more in line with contemporary thought than your former Abbey was. Travel to each one of them if need be, but don't give up until you find a place to live out your monastic calling."*

Listen," whispered another, the voice of the heart. *"India has much, so much, to teach you. Do not leave her now. Let her give you, if she will, some lonely corner where, like the seekers of old, you can spend twelve years in solitude. In the silence of the hermit life, you will find the one thing you desire—union with brahman. India is your teacher, surrender humbly at her feet."*

I was familiar with all these voices. Most of them were voices in the head, the urgings of different facets of the psyche, which my counsellor had referred to as sub-personalities. The Pragmatist, the Spiritual Revolutionary, the Nun—each had her own agenda, each urged me in a different direction. They rarely agreed, and it had been hard to persuade most of them to get on the plane and come to India. But the last voice was not in the head but in the heart. From early childhood, I had known this inner voice, nor had I ever disobeyed its prompting. My highest gift, my greatest blessing, the voice of the heart had never failed to guide my path, prompting me to actions that frequently seemed odd or strange to others yet which were in accord with a higher logic, an ultimate destiny.

It was this voice which had spoken to me years ago beside the River Orwell, urging me to the healer's path; this voice which guided me both into and out of the abbey, for the learning of necessary lessons. This voice had agreed with Rosalind's advice that I go to India, and this inner voice had instantly recognized Francis. Now, the same voice of intuition was calling me to stay in India.

I listened and surrendered. My surrender brought to an end the raging conflict that had been my life until now. Instead of several directions corresponding to different parts of myself, I now had only one direction, that of a plunge into India. Purchasing a stamp from Brother Christodas, the guest master, I placed my

Aeroflot return ticket in an envelope, together with a note to the travel agent requesting a refund on the unused portion of the ticket. With a trembling hand I dropped the letter in the mailbox. The girdle of security that I had been wearing when I arrived at Shantivanam was now considerably lighter. And my future was in the hands of Providence. I believed my return ticket to England was the price I must pay for my chosen hermit life in India. Not in my wildest imaginings did I think that Mother India would demand of me the sacrifice of everything—even renunciation. In fulfilment of the spiritual longing which possessed my entire being, India would lead me by a path I did not even dream of as I slept peacefully beneath the palm leaves.

"So," said Father Bede, anticipating my words as I stepped into his hut at the end of the week of silence, "you have decided to stay in India."

I gasped. "You knew! I mailed my return ticket back to the travel agent this morning, so now I'm committed. I can't leave."

Father Bede smiled. "Very nice. You can be a *sannyasi,* like Kirsti. Travel around for a time and find what place is right for you."

"When I leave here at the end of June, I plan to go to the Himalayas."

"A very good choice. But I suggest that on your way North, you visit Christa Prema Seva Ashram in Poona. It's run by women, and I think you will like the place. There's one sister there in particular that you will connect with—her name is Sister Arati."

Christa Prema Seva. I remembered that Francis had spoken of this place as 'the best ashram in India'. Perhaps I should go there for two weeks, on my way to the Himalayas. That evening, by the light of my lamp, I wrote a letter to the Acharya, Sister Sara Grant, requesting her hospitality.

I expressed my new commitment to India by taking a trip to Trichinopoly, where I invested in several metres of homespun cloth. If I was to stay in India, I must follow her customs, according to which a *brahmacharini* is not permitted brightly coloured or fashionable clothes, and is expected to wear white or yellow.

White seemed to me impractical, so I settled on yellow, and henceforth wore only that colour. After careful instruction from some Indian sisters and three months of practice, I was beginning to feel comfortable in a sari. Now I donated to Sister Marie Louise all my Western clothes, my coloured saris, even my backpack and watch. I was ruthlessly shedding all the trappings of a Western tourist.

Indeed, I no longer felt like a tourist. Despite my fair, freckled skin and reddish hair, which everywhere marked me out as a foreigner, I was feeling very much at home. And I was forming deep friendships with several Indian women who, like myself, were celibate nuns who had left institutional religious life.

One such friend, Amrita, wore the *kavi* or ochre robes of the *sannyasini*. She had very curly hair and strikingly Semitic features, and came from Kerala, on the southwest coast.

"My ancestors were Jewish Christians," she explained. "When the temple in Jerusalem was destroyed, they escaped to India. For two thousand years, we have lived here. They call us the Thomas Christians."

Of similar age, height (five feet tall), and inclinations, Amrita and I became close friends. Since both of us were interested in contemplative lifestyles for women, we went together to spend a few days at Shri Lalitambika Ashram, on the Hill of the Holy Bee, across the river from Shantivanam.

Shri Lalitambika Ashram, 20th June 1980

Staying with the yoginis*—female yogis. Disciples of the famous guru, the late Shivananda, they are a group of young and beautiful Tamilian brahmin women, who have come here to devote themselves to God-realization through yoga, meditation, rituals and service to a group of orphan children. This is a charming place. The yoginis look very picturesque in many-pleated orange robes, their hair piled in a topknot, whilst the Novices wear deep red. The atmosphere does remind both of us—Amrita and me—of an enclosed convent. There is a strict horarium, much ringing of bells, and no men, except a fat-bellied guru, allowed on the premises. But it reminds me of a mediaeval nunnery more than a modern religious institution.*

The yoginis practice a fourfold yoga: karma *yoga—action—their work with the orphan children, the cows and the garden;* hatha *yoga—similar to what I've been learning with Amuldas;* jnana *yoga—the path of wisdom and insight, which means getting up at four in the morning to meditate; finally,* bhakti*—devotion to the personal God. Their main devotional activity is the conducting of extremely long and beautiful pujas. To the accompaniment of Sanskrit chants, they decorate the image of Shri Lalitambika, the Divine Mother, with countless flowers. They make the most incredible, elaborate flower mandalas, one flower at a time with a mantra for each one. Moving gracefully with the chant, young girls in their deep red robes offer to Divine Mother the flowers that symbolize their hearts' devotion. I've never seen anything so beautiful. Even the walls of the temple are covered in deep red draperies.*

At four we rise (to a bell) for chanting, meditation and pranayama. *Then at sunrise, everyone goes outside to do Sun Salutations—a special yoga exercise to greet the sun. Then we two relax, read, meditate, whilst the yoginis do karma yoga. During the afternoon, they gather around their guru beneath a big, shady mango tree, to study Bhagavad Gita. At sunset they all do hatha yoga. I feel so proud of myself. I'm learning the headstand and the full lotus pose.*

Meals are very simple—either idalis *or rice and curds made from the milk of the sleek brown cows they tend. But for me it's an ordeal. Here I am, the only foreigner, surrounded by scrupulous brahmins. Amrita and I have to sit off to the side in an area reserved for lower-caste people. I thought I was adept at eating with my right hand—but I got really confused when I found my stainless steel* thali *(plate) filled with runny curds. I asked for a spoon—something there were only two of in the ashram, and both of them were over in the guesthouse. Of course, it didn't enter my head that you are supposed to lift the* thali *to your mouth and drink from it! And, you are absolutely not allowed to press your lips to the cup when you drink. You have to pour a stream of water into your mouth without contaminating the cup. So every time, my sari gets splashed.*

Amrita and I sleep on the guest house veranda, or at least, we attempt to sleep as much as the wind and the whine of mosquitoes will let us. We meditate together, passing most of our time in silence. When one of the yoginis *arrives at the guest house with dry biscuits and afternoon tea, we take time for talking and sharing. Amrita has been telling me both about her previous life in an enclosed convent in the Philippines and about the pilgrimage she just made in the Himalayas. I feel really inspired. I can't wait to be there myself!*

When I returned to Shantivanam, June was drawing to a close, and the time of my departure Northwards was at hand. Aadrian and Flore had returned to Holland, Kirsti had left for Ananda Ashram in Kerala, and Angelika had gone to stay with a Hindu family in Madras, from where she wrote to me from time to time. As for Francis, he was about to leave for Arunachala, a hundred miles away. Although we had shared some interesting conversations, it was obvious that the recognition I experienced when Francis and I first met had not been mutual. To him, I was just another acquaintance. *"Don't worry,"* whispered the inner voice. *"This is your destined friend. Simply follow your path, and the two of you will surely meet each other again. Go North and all will be well."* Piqued by Francis' lack of recognition of me, I decided to leave Shantivanam without exchanging an address, without even telling him where I was going next. If he really was who the inner voice said he was—he would find me.

Shantivanam was a cocoon in which I metamorphosed from an angry refugee in flight from Western materialism to a pilgrim humbly approaching Mother India, the teacher with three hundred million faces. The sojourn in the Forest of Peace had been a time of healing and hope. After the crushing defeats which I had experienced in the attempt to fulfill myself through orthodox medicine and institutional contemplative life, I began to see that there might be another way, a pathless path which, independently of any orthodoxy or institution—Western or Eastern—would lead me to the essence which I had sought in vain through traditional forms.

The rising and setting sun, the hills on the further shore, the waxing and waning moon that ushered in fasts and festivals, the brilliant tropical stars, the song of frogs and night birds, spoke words of peace and comfort to my wounded and grieving heart. The River Kaveri, the holy Mother, who year by year waters the paddy fields, had soothed my hurt as she flowed past, ever the same, ever renewed. Now the time had come to emerge from the cocoon and spread my new-found wings.

One hot, humid morning at the end of June, I took my leave of Father Bede and climbed into the ox cart which would drive me to the railway station. A rather plump pilgrim in a yellow homespun sari, with one extra sari, a Bible, Bhagavad Gita and a few belongings slung over my shoulder in a red cloth bag, I set out from beneath the gateway of the Triple-faced God, in search of my guru, *mantra* and name.

"He is the Light of Lights
shining beyond the dark,
knowledge, the knowable, goal of knowledge
Dwelling in the hearts of all."

Bhagavad Gita

Two

The Cave of the Heart

"R*am Krishna Hari; jai jai Ram Krishna Hari!"*

Cymbals clanged as ten thousand or more voices joined in devotional chanting. Spectators lining the streets were cheering, *"Jnanba Tukaram!"* and men held children up on their shoulders to watch the approaching procession. The sound of music drew closer. Wriggling through the crowd, I saw a red-clad horseman carrying a pennant, followed by a pure white horse with no saddle, the bearer of spirit. Then came the musicians, dressed in white, swaying back and forth beneath ochre banners as they sang, *"Vitthale Rukmai! Vitthale Rukmai!"*

Singing party after singing party passed, each followed by a band of *varkari* pilgrims, men and women with white markings on their foreheads and Hindu rosaries around their necks. Despite monsoon storms and rain-swollen rivers, they were passing through on their way to Pandharpur, shrine of Lord Vitthale, a hundred and fifty miles to the south. Their arrival in Poona was one of the city's greatest annual events. Suddenly the crowd became wild with excitement.

"Jnanbar Tukaram! Jnanbar Tukaram!"

At last here it was, the *palkhi*. Devotees eagerly pressed forward to offer flowers and coins as the decorated palanquin, bearing on a bed of white satin and marigolds the silver *padukas* (the sandals) of Sant Jnaneshvar, one of the greatest mystics in India's history, passed down Varkari Wadi, right in front of the gate of Christa Prema Seva Ashram.

Two days earlier, I had arrived in Poona, City of Merit, the former capital of the 'Great State,' Maharashtra. Weary and itchy after tossing and turning all night in a bug-infested sleeper car, I had reached CPS ashram just as morning Eucharist was being celebrated. Blundering in through the back entrance, I knocked on the bolted library door, tapped on the kitchen window, startling Devaki, the cook, was barked at by Anand the dog, and finally found myself welcomed by a tall, energetic sister Brigite clad in her yoga trousers. After I had bathed and taken breakfast, Brigite handed me over to a frail-looking, near-octogenarian English sister named Arati, and it was she who showed me around the ashram building, constructed cloister-style around a garden.

"The original CPS Ashram was founded in 1927 by an Anglican priest named Jack Winslow," she told me, indicating his photograph on the library wall, flanked by a beaming Ramana Maharshi. "It ran very successfully until the late fifties, when it closed. Then in 1972 we came here, seven Catholic sisters and four Anglican sisters. We re-opened the ashram as an ecumenical venture, with initial guidance from Swami Abhishiktananda, founder of Shantivanam . . . . And in this room, Mahatma Gandhi stayed." Like all the other bedrooms, it was simple and bare, with a stone floor and a low plank bed. "The original ashram was much involved in India's struggle for independence. The outlawed flag of free India was flown here, and not only Gandhi, but even Subhash Chandra Bose, leader of the Indian National Army, was entertained on the premises."

We moved on into the chapel. "The guru who guides this ashram is Jesus, so we have placed the Tabernacle on the guru's traditional deerskin seat. And this mural of St. Francis preaching to the birds was painted by the renowned Christian artist Angelo de Fonseca, one of the early ashramites. The ashram was Franciscan in inspiration from the beginning, and we still honour our Franciscan roots."

In the evening I had met the *acharya* of the ashram, Sara Grant, a woman in her fifties, slender and beautiful in a saffron homespun sari. We sat and talked in the cool of the garden. "Each ashram," Sara told me, "has its *sadhana,* the prescribed spiritual practice for members of that ashram; self-enquiry at Ramana

Ashram in Tiruvanamalai, yogic disciplines at Shivananda Ashram in Rishikesh. We are often asked what our *sadhana* is. Do we teach *mantra,* yoga, what type of practice do we recommend? Our path is a very simple one, it is contained in our name; Christa Prema Seva—Service of the Love of Christ. We are here, at the service of those who come. That is our *sadhana.* In the words of the ashram antiphon, 'That I may ever love and serve, give me, O Lord, union with Thee!'"

I stared at her. "That's amazing, I mean, it's perfect! I don't know if I could have put it so well, but you have just described my path."

Sara smiled understandingly. "In your letter, you asked to stay here two weeks. What's the rush? You can go to the Himalayas next summer, with greater benefit. Stay here as long as you wish, in the service of the love of Christ."

As the days passed, it had become increasingly obvious that Sara was right. There was no need to go anywhere. At Christa Prema Seva Ashram, I found everything I had loved about the abbey: silence, solitude, community. I also found an essential aspect which had been missing in Western monastic life.

"Our motto is freedom," Sara told me. "Each individual must be at liberty to follow his or her own *sadhana,* so long as it does not disturb the ashram in general. It is freedom of spirit which distinguishes an ashram from a monastic institution."

I soon settled into the routine of the ashram, rising at four to contemplate in the dark chapel, and sitting alone for meditation at sunset on the roof, as temple bells began to ring across the city. Three times a day, I attended the *arati,* when, to the accompaniment of songs and bells, a ghee lamp or camphor flame was waved before the tabernacle, just as it was offered in front of Shiva, Vitthale and the other deities in temples from one end of the city to the other. After morning Eucharist, I practised yoga under Brigite's supervision. Then I helped Archana, a young Indian sister, to cut vegetables and clean rice and lentils. In the evening, after the final *arati,* striped cotton mats were rolled out in the library, and we all sat in a circle to share our personal journeys in an informal *satsang,* a gathering of seekers of Truth.

CPS Ashram, Poona, 15 July 1980

Dear Ros,

Well, you were quite right! India really is the place for me at this time. So far I haven't had any dramatic adventures like meeting my guru and that kind of thing, though I have made wonderful connections with two very saintly people, Father Bede at Shantivanam and now, here at CPS Ashram, Sister Arati, who describes herself as a 'Christian Sufi'. Before she came to India, Sister Arati lived in the Middle East, and she has made a deep study of Islamic mysticism, which I'm eager to learn about.

I wanted to come to a different culture where all my conditioning would be challenged—and I got what I wanted, perhaps more than I bargained for. After more than three months meditating in a mud hut by the banks of the Kaveri, I'm here in Poona on the windswept Deccan plateau, staying at Christa Prema Seva Ashram in Shivajinagar, a marshy area on the edge of Poona. Near by is a pitiful shanty town, Shivajinagar Railway Station, and the Iyengar Yoga Institute. There are several sisters here, Sara, Brigite, Arati and Columba, all British, and a few Indian sisters, among whom I've made friends with Archana from Bombay and Elisha from Kerala. An ox cart rumbles down Varkari Wadi, the street the ashram is on; myriad insects buzz and hum in the cloister garden. The sisters are taking their siesta and soon the tea bell will ring.

From Tamil Nadu, deep in the South of India, I've come to Maharashtra, historically a very interesting area. To the North, beyond the Narmada River, lie the Hindi-speaking states which the Moslem Moghuls ruled; to the South, across the Krishna River, are the former Hindu kingdoms like Tamil Nadu, with its great temple cities. Here in Maharashtra, the famed warrior Shivaji threw off the yoke of the Moslem invaders and established an independent Hindu kingdom. This is India's hub, where elements of Northern and Southern culture, of Hinduism and Islam, mingle and merge.

It's monsoon season; rainy, cloudy, muddy, humid and very hot in the afternoons.

So how's life back in London, my dear? I don't miss St. John's Wood at all.

I cannot thank you enough for pointing me in the right direction.

Love, Olivia

A quiet, uneventful year lay ahead of me, it seemed, in the company of other celibate women; listening to Sister Arati read the poetry of Sufi mystics, accompanying the gallant Columba, who cheerfully bore the burden of age and arthritis, on her visits to the sick and elderly, and becoming acquainted with the spirituality of Maharashtra through the help of Sister Elisha, a tiny Keralite who had taught herself the local language, Marathi, and deeply appreciated the devotional spirit of the people of the land.

It was only a few days after I saw the *palkhi,* however, before an unexpected event occurred. One morning, as I was cleaning rice for lunch, a familiar thin, bearded figure suddenly appeared. To my astonishment, it was Francis, wearing a new green lungi and even a shirt—or at least the Indian equivalent, a loose tunic called a kurta—his hair carefully combed. At his side, dressed in a stunning pink and magenta punjabi suit, with red polish on her toenails and silver anklets adorning her dainty feet, was our mutual acquaintance from Shantivanam—Priya.

"What are you doing here?" asked Francis, blinking in surprise. "I thought you would maybe be in Rishikesh."

"Father Bede told me to come here, so I came. And you? What brought you here?"

"Remember that saint I told you about, at Alandi, the one whose feet are lotuses?"

"The old man who was unfathomable being? Yes."

"Well, when I was in Arunachala, he appeared in my meditation, and called me to see him again." Francis shuffled awkwardly. "Priya wanted to come to Poona, too, to see Rajneesh. So as we were travelling the same way, I escorted her."

Melodrama had suddenly entered my quiet existence, and I found myself in much turmoil. I had challenged Providence to bring Francis and myself together once again, and Providence had met the challenge with a startling rapidity. And with a strange twist. Francis was completely occupied with his relationship with

Priya, who, meanwhile, selected me as her confidante. While Francis was in Alandi, an hour's bus ride from Poona, she came to my room eager to talk.

"Frankie is a wonderful person," she told me. "He knows so much about meditation. But not so much about taking care of a girl. I think he would marry me, though, if I pushed him."

I tried to imagine Francis married to a dependent, manipulative woman. It would be a strange end to his pilgrimage.

"Then there's my old boyfriend, Patrick," Priya went on. "We came to India together, to see Rajneesh, but at Shantivanam, I left him. Which one do you think would take care of me better?"

"If it's financial security you're looking for," I said carefully, "I don't think Francis is your man. He's been a *sadhu* for years."

Priya sighed. "You're right. Patrick's family is really rich. He can buy me anything I want. I'll send a telegram to Canada and tell him to come and rescue me."

"You know, Priya, you're an adult woman. You don't have to win a man to care for you. You could take responsibility for your own life."

My words were in vain. Patrick was summoned, and arrived in Poona with all possible speed. Within two days of his arrival, the pair left for Canada. Now it was Francis' turn to seek my counsel, a hurt and angry Francis.

"I can't understand her," he groaned. "She was afraid to travel alone, so I accompanied her. But that wasn't enough. She wanted to be certain she had me. I held out for a long time, but . . . man, you don't know what an expert seductress she is. And I've been celibate for years."

"So you were vulnerable."

"And then, once I was hooked, she left me. How could she act like that?"

"She was using you. She's a desperately insecure person. And you need to acknowledge the hurt and anger. But really, aren't you glad to be out of it?"

"I guess I am. Having lost my *brahmacharya,* I was even ready to marry her. When I went to Alandi, I confessed everything to Baba—that saint I told you about."

"With the lotus feet? What did he say?"

"You know, he laughed. He just laughed, not mockingly, but in humour. Then I told him I'd bring her to see him. At once, his posture changed, as if to say, 'No you won't!' But all he said was, 'If my Guru, Sant Jnaneshvar, permits, she'll come here, not otherwise.' And she never did meet him. I tried to bring her there, but she just had no interest."

Before Priya's departure, she and Francis had been careful to introduce another challenge into my life, Bhagwan Shree Rajneesh. I could scarcely have been a more reluctant visitor to Rajneesh Ashram. Still very much the prim little nun, I was scandalized by Rajneesh's popular reputation as the 'sex guru'.

CPS Ashram, Poona, 20th July 1980

Dear Mum and Dad,

Well, finally I have encountered the most controversial figure in Poona today; hated by traditional Hindus, adored by the crowds of Westerners who flock to his ashram by the thousands, feared by fundamentalist Christians worldwide as a "cult" leader and corrupter of youth, and perhaps secretly loved by the local shopkeepers and hotel owners whose business is booming due to his ashram. Yes, Priya and Francis took me to hear a lecture by the charismatic Bhagwan Rajneesh.

*The spectacle outshone a papal audience in the precision of its stage management. Within a mile radius of the ashram, we began to encounter a stream of bicycling figures, of all ages and races, but predominately young and white, duly clad in the red or orange garb of a Rajneesh "neo-*sannyasin", *and wearing round their necks the* mala *(rosary) bearing a portrait of their guru. Inside the elegant and bewilderingly large ashram were forgathering countless red- and orange-clad devotees, with flowing robes and flowing hair; their monastic gravity and spirituality in odd combination with the prevailing amorous tone and the numerous intertwined couples and trios. Having been sniffed, frisked, exhorted not to cough, and relieved of ten rupees, we were permitted to take our seat on the bare stone floor of an enormous audience hall, where the reverent quiet gradually deepened and the mood of expectancy slowly increased until, into a pin-drop silence, came the smooth purr of a Rolls Royce and the quiet crunch of wheels on gravel. The purr faded into silence, and a small, white-clad figure noiselessly appeared on the dais above us.*

I had a vivid memory of my audience with Pope Paul VI, as all eyes focussed on the tiny figure, and the presence of a keen concentration and indomitable will made itself felt. But here the resemblance ended. Although Francis assured me that tremendous energy radiated from this 'enfant terrible' of spiritual masters, I was unable to perceive it like that myself. In his talk, Rajneesh denounced God, religion, Christianity, India, miracles, marriage, and "Polacks" (a Pole recently wrote an article unfavourable to him). He also told a number of obscene jokes. I came away with the worst headache of my life, glad to be back at CPS Ashram.

Love, Olivia

My reactions to Rajneesh said more about my own preconceptions than about the enigmatic master. Both the Priya affair and the influence of Rajneesh raised for me questions of sexuality and spirituality which in my innocence I had never considered before. Having attended a provincial girl's school and entered a convent at the age of twenty-two, I was habituated to celibacy, modesty, propriety and the society of other women, and had not even imagined that the spiritual life could be pursued under any other conditions. Apart from a brief long distance love affair with a Cambridge undergraduate when I was twenty, the sexual revolution had passed me by. And now, those of my fellow guests at CPS ashram who visited the Rajneesh ashram were telling me tales of naked encounter groups, sexual experimentation and secret tantric teachings, claiming that sex, even outside a committed relationship, could be a path to God.

Meanwhile, I met a new friend who embodied a spiritual path different both from the way of the celibate nun and from the teachings of Rajneesh. Suvasini Laddu, my Hindi teacher, was the ideal Hindu wife. A distinguished linguist and wife of a Sanskrit professor, she stayed quietly at home in her modest little house, studying the *Jnaneshvari* (the great twelfth century Marathi commentary on Bhagavad Gita) and writing articles on spiritual philosophy for various periodicals. She had no need to leave her home to attend the temple, since home was her temple, and there she meditated and worshipped the family deities. One day I asked her why she was taking so much time from her valuable research projects to teach beginners like myself.

"I have taken a vow," she replied, "to teach any pupils who ask my help, and never to mention money or fees. Also, I have promised to write one article each month. I am a linguist, therefore my duty, my service, is to teach languages. I must teach, without concern for the fruits of action. I must write articles and contribute to journals; it is my *dharma* to serve as a scholar. It is not for me to judge which is more valuable than the other. And in these actions, no reward may be sought. This is the teaching of *nishkama karmayoga,* desireless action, which we find in Bhagavad Gita. I am a married woman, I cannot go to the Himalayas and meditate in a cave; my husband, daughter and future grandchildren need my care. And the beauty of the teaching of Bhagavad Gita lies in this: the final goal, the peace that passes understanding, is not only for sages who retire to the forest. Simply by devotion to the Lord and by performing duties without concern for the fruits, one can attain God-Realization in the midst of daily responsibilities."

I stared at her. Could a woman really attain the ultimate goal whilst participating in family life? The women saints of Catholicism were mostly consecrated virgins, nuns, founders of religious orders. Getting martyred for the faith seemed to be the only way to sanctity for a married woman. Until now, everything I had read or heard about the spiritual life had suggested to me that for true contemplation, for God-realization, one must separate oneself from worldly life and embrace a celibate, renounced, path of dedication to God. And now, here was Mrs. Laddu, telling me that in her own home, amidst her roles as housewife, mother, author, teacher and linguist, she could attain the same state for which I had felt it necessary to sacrifice home, family and career. From my Christian perspective, I had to leave the world behind to seek the transcendent God. To Mrs. Laddu, the world was the body of God, spun on the warp and weft of *brahman,* who could be attained within worldly life—simply by renouncing the fruits of action. I was getting my first taste of the feminine spirituality of the land of the Mother.

Francis had many acquaintances in Poona, from the family of

shoemaker yogis who lived in a tiny shack in Shivajinagar shanty town to the head priest of the Dattatreya Temple. One evening, he introduced me to the best-loved of all his Poona friends, another householder who, like my Hindi teacher, followed the path of desireless action. Taking an auto-rickshaw to Mahatma Gandhi Road, we turned into the narrow side street where Dr. Vasant Lad, an Ayurvedic physician, had his dispensary. In the waiting room sat well-dressed brahmins, some giggling Rajneesh *sannyasins* and several poor village women in threadbare saris, who obviously could not afford to pay the doctor's fee.

At last, Dr. Lad ushered us into his room, greeted us reverently with joined palms, and spent a moment in meditative silence before asking, "What can I do for you?"

"Actually, Dr. Lad, I am not sick. I just wanted to meet you. I graduated from a London medical school, but I am so disillusioned with everything I learned."

"Healing is a spiritual discipline," Dr. Lad replied sympathetically. "It is not a question simply of taking some x-rays and blood tests. When you feel the patient's pulse, you must be so one with the patient that you do not even need to ask a single question."

I felt relief welling up and burst into tears. Never in my seven years of medical training had any of my seniors suggested that it was necessary or even desirable to feel at one with my patients. I had always regarded my natural empathy with sick people as some kind of deviation, a failure to develop proper clinical detachment.

"For years I have felt called to be a healer," I sobbed, "but I just didn't feel at home with Western medicine."

"Don't worry, don't worry. You are already a beautiful healer. Wait, and meditate much. When the fruit is ripe, it will drop. That fruit is the ego."

"But will you teach me?"

"Come back tomorrow at the end of my clinic."

"So," said Dr. Lad when I arrived the next day. "You want to know something about Ayurveda, the science of life. Then let me tell you a story."

He pressed the tips of his fingers together and leant back in his chair; eyes half-closed.

"Long, long ago, the Gods and Demons wished to churn the Ocean of Milk, to recover the lost treasures of the Golden Age. For a churning stick, they took Mount Meru, the axis of the world, and as a churning rope they used the cosmic serpent, Vasuki. But without a fulcrum, how could they churn? The Lord Vishnu himself took the form of a great turtle, and on the back of that turtle, they churned the Ocean of Milk."

Opening his eyes wide, he gazed at me as if to say, *"Listen attentively,"* and then continued, "That churning is meditation. And as they churned, deadly poison appeared. A little of that poison was enough to destroy all the worlds. Then Shiva, in his mercy, appeared and drank the poison. As a great yogi, he could transmute it and be unharmed. At last, when the churning was completed, there arose from the Ocean of Milk a Person with four arms, his complexion dark as a monsoon cloud. He wore yellow, just as you do," and here he gave me another penetrating look. "Yellow is a beautiful colour. It is the colour of Death. And in his hands, this Person carried the *amrita kumbha*, the jar of nectar of immortality. His name is Dhanvantari, the Divine Physician. It is He who has revealed Ayurveda."

I remembered my years in National Health Service hospitals; the rows of numbered beds; the smell of antiseptic. Now Dr. Lad was unfolding to me that other way of healing I had so earnestly sought, a path to wholeness that was born out of the ocean of mythic consciousness, and wore the golden robe of divine revelation, a way of service that was not separate from prayer and contemplation, but rather, was an outflowing of meditative consciousness.

Suddenly, I heard the voice in the heart that had recognized Francis, speaking to me again. *"This is your teacher, your guru on the path of the physician. Study Ayurveda. It is your way."* Though I had journeyed thousands of miles from my native place, I had come home, to the form of the healing art with which I had affinity, to the teacher who could initiate me into that art.

By late July, with Francis' departure to Alandi to sit at the lotus feet of his 'Baba', the melodrama died down, and my days resumed their monastic uneventfulness. I did a little work at the ashram and attended to my studies in Hindi and Ayurveda. The rest of the time, I followed Dr. Lad's instructions to 'meditate much'. Indeed, the sisters nicknamed me 'Nandi', after the bull vehicle of Shiva, who always sits in waiting before the Lord. I sat for hours in the ashram chapel or in a quiet corner of the garden, where Mahatma Gandhi was said to have meditated. Day by day, I churned the Ocean of Milk.

By now, I had been at CPS ashram for five weeks. My life had grown so quiet, so simplified lately, that the pages of my journal remained blank, and I found little of note to relate in letters to England except the great battle between a lizard and a hawk moth outside my room. There was nothing to suggest that I was on the brink of the most significant event of my life; nothing, that is, until Francis returned after spending a month in Alandi.

"What's been happening?" he asked me.

"Oh, nothing much. Cleaning rice, cutting vegetables. Hearing the birds sing and the squirrels chirp. Churning, churning, waiting for Dhanvantari to appear. How about you?"

Francis' eyes were brilliant and his face seemed to shine.

"It was so wonderful to spend time with Baba. The first few days, there's a kind of flushing, my mind seems to spin, and I can't really see him, just my own projections. But as the days pass, I get drawn into his silence. Then I can see that his body is made of pure light. More and more, I'm coming to accept that he's my guru. He is my closest, my most intimate friend. And Alandi itself, the shrine of Sant Jnaneshvar, is such a holy place. Some of the sisters want me to bring them there. Why don't you come too?"

It was a festival day, 23rd August, when Francis shepherded Arati, Brigite, Archana and myself on to the crowded Alandi bus.

We had arrived at Alandi, home of saints, on a sunny monsoon day. I was charmed by the little walled town, set on a small eminence where lush green banks bordered the Indrayani River. On this festival day it was bustling with pilgrims; bare-chested brahmins and toothless old women, *sannyasis* in their ochre robes and peasants in faded saris. There were beggars everywhere, offering pilgrims the chance to acquire merit by almsgiving, large halls where visitors to the shrine were accommodated, and temples and ashrams that offered free meals to all comers. The narrow streets were lined with stalls displaying prayer beads, heaps of vermilion powder, brass vessels, penny paperback books containing excerpts from devotional texts, and pictures of Sant Jnaneshvar.

"We begin here," said Francis, as he led us through the crowded entrance of the Jnaneshvar temple and around the courtyard to the feet of a pot-bellied elephant with huge goggle eyes, his body lovingly smeared with orange sindhur. "Ganesh is guardian of the threshold and Lord of Obstacles, and his grace must be sought at the outset of the sacred journey."

Next he led us to the shrine which housed the shivalinga. "Today, this is a Vaishnav Temple," he explained. "Vishnu, the Preserver, is worshipped as the Supreme. But in Jnaneshvar's day it was a Shiva Shrine, dedicated to Siddheshvar, Lord of fulfilment. And, according to Sant Jnaneshvar, non-duality or Oneness, the gift of Shiva, must be realized before true devotion can flower. So Shiva is very important here. Only he, the Destroyer, can burn our impurities to ash."

Our foreheads daubed with Shiva's ash, we continued to the knowledge-garden, where white-clad devotees sat, absorbed in reading the Jnaneshvari. Then, having circled several peepul trees, members of the sacred fig family, we entered the main building. In the hall in front of the shrine sat fifty-odd priests in red lungis, bare to the waist except for the sacred thread, performing a great puja. The sound of their Sanskrit chants rang in our ears as we entered the shrine and knelt to touch the tomb of Jnaneshvar. In that moment, I became a believer in the living presence of Sant Jnaneshvar at Alandi. Not that I cared whether the saint was in fact still sitting in samadhi beneath his monument; rather, I became acutely aware that I was experiencing a power greater even than the cumulative effect of seven centuries of devotion. Unmistakably, as I stooped to honour the marble tomb, I felt myself touched by the hand of a Master.

Now we were walking through a big hall, where about a hundred devotees sat, each with a wooden bookstand before him, as they chanted the verses of Jnaneshvari together. I felt a sense of mounting excitement. Surely we would find the guru soon!

Sant Jnaneshvar

Leading us out of the hall, Francis brought us to a handsome peepul tree. In front of me, I could see a dark, cave-like shrine.

"Here!" said Francis. "This is the place. Baba lives here, in the cave."

My heart was pounding. The hairs on my body prickled. I felt both thrilled and apprehensive. Deeper still was an encompassing sense of dread. I was about to encounter the Holy, in human form.

Hesitantly, we stood before the open doorway. Suddenly, a shape moved in the darkness. Out of the shadows he emerged—a simple old man, wearing nothing but a white loincloth. His gaze was completely inward, his face expressing a repose beyond the chattering of thoughts or turmoil of emotions. In appearance, he strikingly resembled photographs I had seen of Ramana Maharshi.

Silently he stood before us, as Francis prostrated at his feet. Still in complete silence, we all sat on the floor outside his chamber and entered a meditative state. A lightning flash of recognition lit my soul, chasing away the shadows of doubt and uncertainty. I knew this old man, as I had never known anyone before. And I had always known him. In the light of his presence, the phantom of dark, empty years spent searching, waiting and longing vanished forever, and I realized that he had always been with me, that I had never really been alone.

At this moment, as the old man in his white loincloth stepped out of his dark room to greet me, the inner Guru shone forth from the shadows of the Cave of the Heart. I had travelled from London to Poona to find the One who is closer to me than my own soul, the One who is the way back to my soul. And the journey had been entirely necessary. I needed the physical presence of this silent, simple guru to awaken the guru-nature within.

Time seemed to stand still. We sat there motionless, the ceaseless chanting of the Gita behind us, and waves of love and power flowing out from the old man who stood before us. From time to time, I felt drawn to look at his feet, from which the power seemed to flow, or to gaze up at his peaceful, recollected face. Then, just as suddenly as he had appeared, he vanished into his chamber. Encouraged by a wave of his hand, I entered, stumbling in the darkness, and knelt to touch his feet. Francis and the sisters followed me; then all five of us sat on a low plank bed as the guru, still silent, blessed us and handed each of us a *laddhu* sweet ball. Archana, the only native among us, said to him in Marathi, "Pray for the world."

Delighted to find that she spoke his language, the saint began talking to her, his face alive with quiet humour and childlike simplicity. Love flowed out from him and surrounded all of us. Very humbly, he introduced himself. When he had finished talking, Archana translated his entire speech:

"My name is Raghudas Brahmachari. I was born in the village of Duser in Satarah district, some distance south of here. At the age of fifteen I left home and set out for the Himalayas, intending to become a hermit. Travelling from one temple to another, I came to Alandi to have the *darshan* of Sant Jnaneshvar. As I knelt at his *samadhi,* I heard Jnaneshvar speaking to me. 'You stay here with me,' he said. So I stayed. There was no need to go any further. And here I began my *sadhana,* meditating on the Holy Name of Ram. I have been here for fifty six years.

"Life is like a wheel. Pleasure and pain, health and sickness, poverty and wealth, these inevitably follow one another. Dwell at the hub of the wheel, still and stable, as all these changes come and go.

"There is One who has care for all this, care for everything that lives and grows and dies. No creature, not even an ant, is too insignificant for His Love, for He has brought all to being. So then, why should we worry? He is the Turner of the wheel, all things are in His hands. Be attached to nothing, let everything come and go, the alternating spokes of the wheel that is ever in motion.

"What is the use of chasing from guru to guru, of wandering from one God to another? Are not all forms of the One? Are not all the Same? Whatever form of God you are accustomed to worship, be it Yeshu or be it Ram, abide in Him, abide in His love."

"Maharaj," I said, through Archana's interpretation, "I am feeling very strongly drawn to take *sannyas.*"

"*Sannyas* has nothing to do with forms, with externals. It is completely unnecessary to wear ochre robes, to mat one's hair or shave the head, to smear oneself with ash, or to take formal vows. This is not what it means to be a *sannyasi*. Rather, a *sannyasi* is one who is *stitha*—stable, steadfast, unshakable. And the One who is standing before you will give you this stability."

I was mystified. Who was this 'one who was standing before me'? Was it he? Had he accepted me as his disciple? I knew that the old man did not give recognizable initiations. Was this a type of initiation? Was he clothing my heart and spirit in the flame of *sannyas?*

My questions remained unasked, for I was too shy to say more. Here I sat, with Brigite, Archana and Arati, embodiments of the person I had chosen to be—pure, devout Christian nuns with special affinity for Indian spirituality. And here I sat with Francis and Raghudas, the ex-hippie *sadhu* and the Hindu saint, beings whom I had mysteriously and instantaneously recognized. I was neither a hippie nor a Hindu, yet I was drawn to both of them like iron to a magnet. And I was afraid, afraid that I could not take them with me on the path I had mapped out, afraid of the unknown to which they beckoned me.

The shock of recognition I experienced when I met Raghudas was so overwhelming that for some time I made no attempt to return to Alandi, even though the village was only fifteen miles away. As a loyal Catholic, it was hard for me to accept that in a devotee of Ram who lived in a Hindu temple, I had beheld God's love made visible, the Word made flesh. Whilst we sat together cutting pumpkins or green beans, Sister Archana and I reflected on our visit to the holy man of Alandi.

"For me it was a very profound experience," said Archana in her flawless Bombay English, "an experience of Christ. I have heard tell that the true guru will grant the vision of whatever form of God one is most devoted to. And as I meditated with Raghudas, I truly felt the presence of Christ."

"I know," I replied, "it was almost too overwhelmingly so. What has always struck me most about the Gospel was the aspect of *kenosis*, the self-emptying of Christ who humbled himself to take the form of a servant. Raghudas is *kenosis* written in flesh and blood instead of ink and paper—totally empty of self, absolutely humble and simple. The last thing I wanted when I came to India

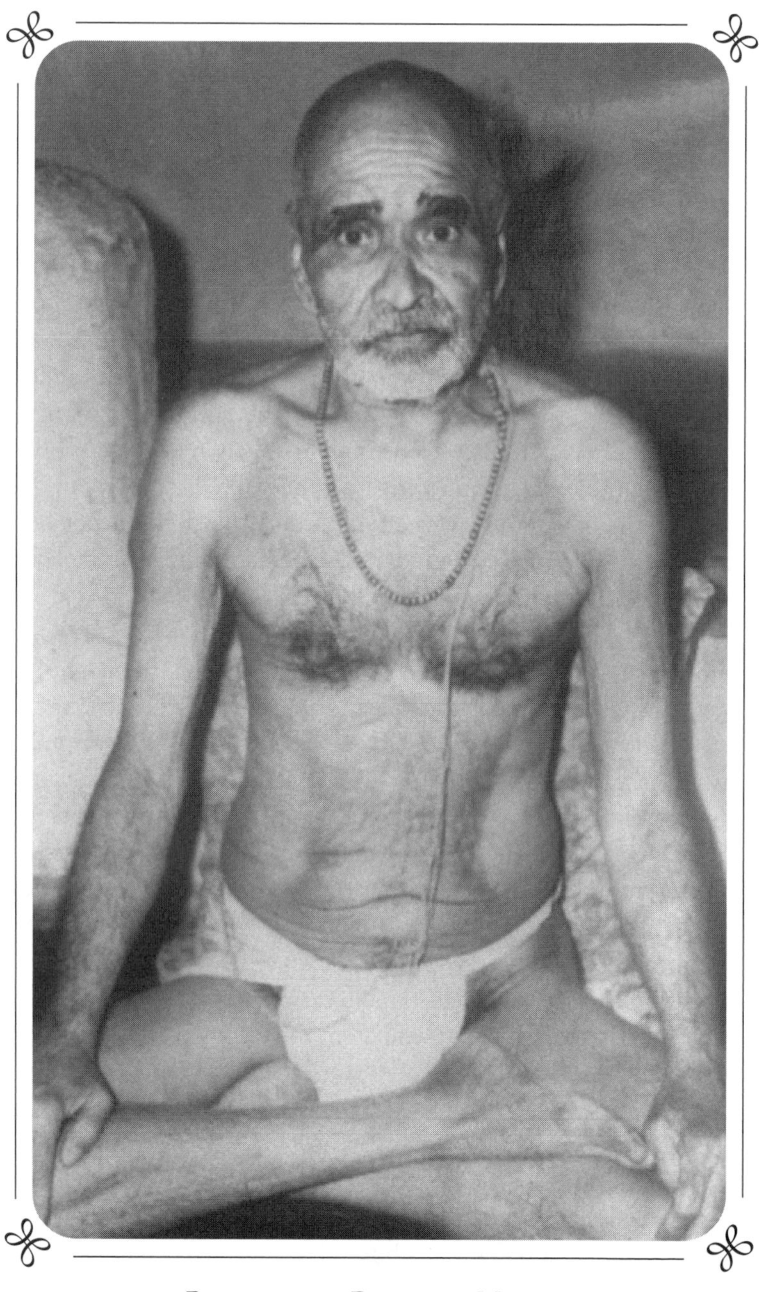

BRAHMACHARI RAGHUDAS MAHARAJ

PHOTO COURTESY OF KAMALABAI

was to get involved in a foreign religion like Hinduism, yet—and this is absolutely, strictly confidential—I have completely fallen in love with Francis' Guru. It's hard to think of anything but him. The feeling is so intense that I'm frankly scared to see him again."

"Yes!" said Archana. "Perhaps I feel the same. Meeting him—even just once—has brought me a spiritual completion I never found anywhere else. This is the mystery of *darshan,* Olivia. The word actually means sight, the incredible overwhelming sight or vision of the Holy One. The image in the temple, the Himalayas, sacred rivers like Ganga or Indrayani, the body of a God-Realized being like Raghudas—these are transparent forms, capable of bestowing the vision of God. You and I have truly had *darshan.*"

I sighed. "Meeting a Realized person changes everything. Raghudas is the true human being; the rest of us, humans in the making. He reflects so clearly, so unequivocally, our potential. What other goal in life is there except to be what he is?"

Archana smiled at me. "Didn't the Lord Jesus say, 'Every disciple, when he is fully grown, will be like his master'?"

Collecting our stainless steel bowls of cut vegetables, we brought them in to Devaki. It was time to carry on with the rest of the day's routine.

Francis, meanwhile, had been staying under a neem tree in the ashram garden, or sleeping on a sheltered veranda at another ashram when it was too rainy for the neem tree. He still had no visa, and was afraid that his illegal status could cause problems for the sisters if he were an official resident of CPS ashram. Now, hearing of a great *sadhu* fair, the *adha kumbha mela,* which was to take place in Nasik, about a hundred and twenty miles away, he set off to attend the festival in the company of a young Frenchman named Nicolas, who had recently come to CPS Ashram. I watched Francis go with some trepidation. Would I ever see him again?

"Don't worry," said Sister Sara, the *acharya*, who, intuitive as she was, had divined the connection between Francis and myself. "That young man will return."

After my visit to Alandi I knew that nothing would ever be the same, that the *darshan* of Raghudas had changed everything. It was the most important event that had ever happened in my life, and beside it, every other experience was shadowy and insubstantial. Yet outwardly I carried on as if nothing had changed; mopping floors, cataloguing books for Sister Arati, memorizing Hindi vocabulary, churning the Ocean of Milk.

Almost a month passed since the time of my visit to Alandi. One mid-September day, I arrived, mop in hand, for my morning duty of cleaning the dining area, to find an old peasant woman sitting there, clanging finger-cymbals and vigorously singing, rather off-key in a voice cracked with age.

"She is a *varkari,* a pilgrim," explained Elisha, who was also observing our new guest with interest. "The Varkari pilgrims are devoted to Lord Vittale, a special Maharashtran form of Krishna, and his consort Rukmini. His temple is in Pandharpur, in the south of Maharashtra. And they also have tremendous devotion to Sant Jnaneshvar of Alandi. Pandharpur and Alandi, these are their great places of pilgrimage. This woman, you see, is an old widow, her family is grown, and she is free to spend her whole life in pilgrimage. Always she is travelling to holy places. Some of our sisters met her in the Himalayas and told her about our ashram, so she comes here from time to time as she travels between Alandi and Pandharpur. She is named Shantabai."

I watched, fascinated, as Shantabai, having completed her *bhajans* (devotional songs), drew out from her belongings a bit of cracked mirror and a pot of sandal paste, and solemnly, indeed reverently, began adorning herself; on her forehead, the U-shaped mark of the *vaishnava,* arising from the root of the nose, and on her cheeks, ear lobes and arms, other prescribed marks.

"Why," Elisha asked her, "do you spend so much time in this adornment of yourself?"

"Because," replied the uneducated village woman, "this body is also God."

She then, with great solemnity, laid out her sacred items, the staff bearing an ochre pennant which is carried by all pilgrim *varkaris,* her pictures of Vitthale and Jnaneshvar, and some tattered, yellowed books of *bhajans,* produced in large print for the barely literate to use. Adorning each of these with sandalpaste, she offered before them one or two groundnuts and a few leaves and flowers. Then, proceeding to the garden, she began enthusiastically bowing and singing to some small shrubs that grew outside my room.

"Those are *tulasi* plants," Elisha explained, "holy basil, revered by all *vaishnavas*—all the devotees of Vishnu, the preserver God. You see those wooden prayer beads she wears? They are made from the wood of the *tulasi* plant, and are worn by those who have taken the vows of a *varkari*. You may find this hard to believe, but Shantabai is actually a respectable householder. She told me she is having a house and land near Pandharpur. And she has a bank account for the donations she receives. For her old age, she says."

This sounded strange to me, but still, I was enthralled by Shantabai. Here indeed, I thought, was the India I had come so far to find; not the land of international supergurus like Rajneesh, but that of the peasant mystics who hold in their gnarled hands the key to all we have lost in the technocracies of the West, an entirely practical spirituality that permeates every aspect of daily life.

"I am going with her," I told Sara that night. "I shall walk to Alandi with Shantabai."

And so we set off together, Grandmother Shantabai in a ragged green Maharashtran sari that tucked up between her legs like a *dhoti*, striding along briskly, with all her belongings, including pots, pans and kerosene stove, carried on her head in a white pack, and behind her me, with my fair skin, yellow sari and red cloth bag, puffing along as I struggled to keep up. Shantabai's Hindi was almost as rudimentary as mine, and we communicated mostly by signs. I tried to ignore the stares that greeted us; Grandmother liked any kind of attention, for it was an opportunity to seek donations. For a *varkari* to beg is considered a form of service, since it provides householders with an opportunity to earn merit. I soon learned that Shantabai would never pass by the chance to bestow such merit. Our progress was slow indeed, as we begged our way from shop to shop on the outskirts of Poona, receiving here a small coin from some pious old woman to whom every penny counted, and there a quick brush-off from the wealthy and sophisticated, and stopping numerous times when the owners of chay shops insisted on providing us with tea. As the strange pair, the educated English lady and her ragged and barely literate mentor, walked along, some honoured us, others mocked and jeered, and Moslem children down by the railway line pelted us with small stones. In the midst of all these alternations of praise and blame I remained calm and centred, though it is perhaps just as well that, due to my lack of Marathi, I only learned after the conclusion of my journey with Shantabai that one man had tried to offer her the sum of five rupees, or half of what a low-class prostitute earns, for my services that night.

At sundown, I found myself in a village temple, being stared at by open-mouthed children and less-than-innocent young men, whilst one woman after another placed in front of me a small offering of rice and watery *dal*, the food of the poor, taken from the family table. Just as I had finished eating this lovingly-offered meal, a clean, white-clad man appeared, held a forceful and excited conversation with Grandmother, and led us both out of the temple. What was happening? I became increasingly nervous as I followed the two of them out of our safe haven and down a dark, narrow alley. Then suddenly I found myself entering another temple, full of lights, music and devotees. It was the auspicious occasion of the birthday of Radha, Lord Krishna's consort, and the mysterious visitor had been dispatched to invite the English lady to a *kirtan,* an evening of ecstatic devotional chanting.

The scene would become, in the next few weeks, both familiar and dear to me. Women sat on one side of the temple, men and boys on the other. Around the walls were ranged musicians, wearing white *dhotis,* loose shirts and white Gandhi caps, each with a pair of finger cymbals hanging on a cord about his neck. A ceremonial carpet was placed in the middle of the temple, and here sat the chief musicians, playing tabla, vina and harmonium, whilst at the centre of attention stood the representative of Sant Tukaram, the great poet-saint and ecstatic, clad in a silk turban and multicoloured sash. His is the skill of speaking to these simple village folk of the highest spirituality, punctuating his discourse with sacred song in which all enthusiastically join, the congregation clapping their hands, the men ranged around the walls soaring with ecstasy as they sing at the top of their voices and clash their cymbals in compelling rhythm.

Before daybreak, we left the temple. The time had come for Grandmother to instruct me in the most unpleasant and unfamiliar duty of my new life, public defecation on a suitable piece of waste ground, an action surrounded by rituals and ablutions which Grandmother determinedly showed me. This was followed by the equally disconcerting procedure of bathing, fully clothed in my dirty sari, in the icy Indrayani River, as I tried to imitate the hand *mudras* and *mantras* with which Shantabai sacralized her daily bath. Shantabai and the village women bathed naked to the waist, according to local custom, but I was too shy to do anything of the kind. Retiring to some rocks, I changed, as modestly as possible, into clean clothes. As I wrung out the wet sari, I wondered when it would be dried.

Daylight found us striding along the open road, accompanied by an old varkari man, whilst both my companions sang in cracked voices, *"Jnanbar Tukaram! Jnanbar Tukaram!"* Driven off the road by a cloudburst, we took shelter in a farm building, between the tethered calves and piles of beans. Like most village structures, the shed was built of mud, with a floor made from smooth, well-dried cowdung. Shantabai and the old man continued the hoarse and tuneless repetition of sacred names above the drumming of raindrops on the tin roof.

I soon found that Shantabai had a definite "beat", with houses where she customarily received hospitality on her ceaseless journeys between Alandi and Pandharpur. Yesterday we had rested from the noonday heat and taken our meal in a middle-class house in the suburbs of Poona, where, aided by a servant girl and an enormous collection of brass pots, twenty-five people contentedly lived, ate and slept in two bare rooms with a small hallway and flat roof. Today, she brought me to a farmhouse, its cowdung floor littered with beans, strings of onions hanging from the rafters, and smoke from the cooking fire wafting through the dark room. Before eating, we hung our wet saris outside to dry; my five yards of yellow homespun tied along one side of the farmhouse, and Shantabai's ragged green Maharashtran sari, eight yards long, on the other side. Grandmother was now wearing a garment that consisted of two old saris, one purple, the other of mustard colour, crudely stitched together. She certainly did not look like a householder with a bank account. Was her style of dress a type of renunciation or an appeal to the generosity of devotees?

On the final day of our journey, we took a pleasant walk along the water meadows of the Indrayani River, from Dehu to Alandi. At a wayside booth that had been erected by some charitable organization to provide food to *varkari* pilgrims, we were provided with leaf-plates of rice, *dal*, and a potato *bhaji* that burnt my mouth with chilies. The journey with Shantabai was not having a good effect on my digestion.

As we walked, I observed Grandmother Shantabai's behaviour. True, she and the old man were always absorbed in chanting the holy names. They would even read *bhajans* from their tattered books as they walked. Yet when we neared a village, there was a subtle change. They would clang their finger cymbals just a little louder, and sing more forcefully, as if to get the villagers' attention, to remind them of their duty to make donations to the pilgrims. Perhaps my presence was a windfall for Shantabai. I attracted more curiosity, more attention, and consequently more coins clinking into her tin can.

Although the entire journey from Poona to Alandi was not much more than fifteen miles, it took us all of three days. Between bathing, drying our wet clothes, taking lunch, resting after our food, sheltering from the late monsoon rains and begging from villagers, we had only limited time for walking. It was evening, then, by the time we reached Alandi.

I followed Shantabai to a humble cottage, where she knocked on the door. A woman in a well-worn sari came out and greeted her like an old friend. Entering the little one-roomed dwelling, I saw the young men kneeling on prayer rugs. Shantabai's friends, clearly, were Moslem. Once the prayer was finished, the mother served me rice, thin *dal* and a few beans, as the whole family looked on with tremendous pride. I knew that they could ill afford to spare the food, but was also coming to understand that this temporary inconvenience was nothing to the lasting joy they would experience in having entertained in their home a devoted pilgrim who was also an English 'lady doctor'.

After I had eaten, Shantabai and I made our evening round of the temple shrines in a rainstorm. Under Grandmother's instruction, I offered flower petals, sweetmeats, and a pinch of black powder to each of the deities and trees. As we approached the place where Raghudas' chamber was, I was seized with a trembling fit. The chamber was empty, and a power cut suddenly extinguished the lights. Nearby I could see three men sitting and chatting in the shadows. Still I hesitated. The increasing downpour forced us to take shelter near the three shadowy figures, and I saw the light catch a silver ring on the finger of one of them. The ring of Raghudas, engraved with the portrait of Sai Baba—that same ring which had pierced Francis' heart—seemed to be calling me. At that moment, the youngest of the three men emerged from the shadows, and approaching me very politely, said, "Madam, do you wish to take *darshan?*" Without a word, I followed him to the feet of Raghudas. Shantabai, who sang *bhajans* and repeated the Holy Name but knew nothing of silence or meditation, quietly joined us and immediately sank into a profound meditative state.

She was still in trance when Raghudas withdrew into his chamber to take supper. Turning to me, the young man who had called me said, very diffidently, with downcast eyes, "I hope you are not offended by my bold behaviour. Actually I am not in the habit of approaching ladies, and I was most embarrassed. But Raghudas Baba told me, 'Go, call that *bai*—that woman—and bring her here.' So I had to obey."

I felt tremendously reassured. So the guru himself had called me into his presence. Now I knew that he recognized me, as I did him.

"My name is Sheikh," continued the young man. "I was placed in Baba's lap as a baby. My father, grandfather and entire family are his devotees. We are Muslims,"—this he said with pride, growing less diffident. "We venerate Baba as a *quṭub,* a perfected Master, the axis of creation. Like the great Sufi saints of old, he is one who can rightly say '*An al haq,* I am the true'."

Raghudas emerged to bid us good night.

"He wishes to invite you to *darshan* tomorrow evening," Sheikh told me. Touching the lotus-like feet of the saint, I followed

Shantabai to our sleeping place, outside the hut of the Moslem family who had fed me.

By the next morning, I was beginning to feel the need to free myself from Shantabai's ministrations, for she mothered me as if I were a child of five. But I knew that to her I was a kanya, an unmarried maiden, who should be always under the protection of a father, brother or elderly woman. She would not leave me alone; she would have to hand me into somebody's care. As I thus pondered, whom should I see walking towards me but Francis and his young French companion Nicolas. The two had just returned from the *adha kumba mela* at Nasik. After feeding all of us on a strange *khicheri* made of assorted grains and pulses which she had begged in the bazaar, Grandmother agreed to place me under the protection of these brothers. Presenting her with bananas, guavas, groundnuts and milk, I returned to more familiar companions. As for Shantabai, even though I was in some ways her 'golden goose', she seemed relieved to be free of the weight of responsibility.

"It was an amazing experience," I told Francis and Nicolas. "Grandmother showed me a way of life in which there is no separation between contemplation and action. Along the pilgrim way the daily bath, with all the embarrassment it held for me, is nonetheless an immersion in the waters of Death and Rebirth; laundry is the purification of the holy garb in which one has the *darshan* of the Lord; and cooking and eating is a partaking in God's *prasad,* His tangible grace. Even passing stool outdoors, much as I hated that experience, is a sacred act, returning to the earth an aspect of the earth element. And every step of the journey brings beneath the feet that dust which the saints have trod."

"And Shantabai?" asked Francis. "How do you experience her?"

"You know, she is very beggarly. She is addicted to begging. All the alms she begs will go into a bank account to provide for her old age. She is a rogue, no doubt about it. But she is a Holy Rogue. She has the most intense, genuine devotion that I have ever experienced. The depth of her faith is tremendous. She is truly God's lover, and His name is always on her lips. Begging and *bhakti,* that's Shantabai's life."

It was pilgrimage season, and Alandi was crowded. After three blissful days in the presence of Raghudas, Francis, Nicolas and I moved to the Janabai Dharmsala, a kind of hostel for pilgrims which also rented rooms to some long-term residents. We slept on the veranda. Near our sleeping spot, an old pundit, another friend of Francis, lived. Each morning the old man would emerge just at sunrise and seat himself by an eastern window to meditate upon the rising sun. When he had finished, his beautiful daughter would come out and coyly offer us tea, glancing sidelong at Francis and Nicolas.

"She always does that," said Francis ruefully as we left. "Her father won't arrange a marriage for her. He keeps her at home to care for him. She's bored with him and dying to escape. Last time I was here, she actually proposed to me."

After tea we always made our way to the Indrayani, where rainbows of saris lay drying on the shore and tombs of holy men stood by the riverside. Here we took our sacred bath. And at dusk each day, straw mats were laid out at Raghudas' feet outside 'Baba's cave', and Sheikh was ready to act as interpreter. On the first evening, I began explaining labouriously the complicated story of my life. I had been a doctor, but I had given it up. Now many people were criticizing me. What should I do?

Raghudas' reply was as ambiguous as my question. "What she is doing, she should continue, and I will take care of her."

This was not exactly a direct answer, and I asked Sheikh to try again.

"Baba, she is a doctor," he said, and proceeded to interpret Raghudas' answer.

"A doctor? Very good. Do your work of service. The poor people will look up to you as a god, and you will help them very much. And in serving, you will find peace."

I felt rather confused. Should I give up my pilgrimage and begin work at once?

"He thinks you're a doctor now," said Francis. "Explain more slowly; Sheikh is an erratic translator. Sheikh, tell Baba she gave it up. Now she is meditating."

"She is meditating?" Baba beamed. "Then let her meditate. And I will take care of her. My blessing is with her."

In a few words, Raghudas had told me many things at once. He had validated the choice I had made with so much agony, the decision to give up my medical career and dedicate all my energy to realizing the One without a second. He had also shown me the sheer unimportance of all decisions. I could be a hermit or a doctor or anything else I wanted to be—it was all the same to him. With a wave of his hand and a nod of his head, he had let me know that the *sadguru,* in his outer form, would not give me advice or commands; these I must seek from that same *sadguru* dwelling in the depths of my heart. And, though I did not know it at the time, he had foretold my future work of healing and service.

"Now," Baba continued, addressing all of us. "As for the Eight-Limbed yoga of Patanjali, that is not the most suitable path for you Westerners. It is too difficult. You will never arrive by that way. Simply sit and watch your breath. Be aware of the natural flow of the breath. Meditate as much as possible. That is all."

The following day, Sheikh's aunt, a plump woman who sold devotional paraphernalia at a stall in the bazaar, told us that Raghudas had invited us to the Gopal Krishna temple, upriver, at the far end of the village. The once-beautiful temple was partially ruined by a huge *peepul* tree which tugged at its remaining walls. Other great *peepul* trees flourished nearby. The deity of Gopal Krishna was housed in the front part of what was left of the temple, and in the back lived the priest and his family, longstanding devotees of Raghudas; they had given Raghudas a pair of one-roomed mud cottages which stood nearby. Here he came every noon to take his meal and rest on a wooden cot.

Today, the priest told us, Raghudas had invited us to meet a very special person, one we would never forget. Leading us to the second of the dark little cottages, the priest's daughter introduced us to an old *sannyasi,* well past eighty, who had been a disciple of Raghudas for over forty years. Totally paralysed but full of spiritual energy, he lay on the cowdung floor of the hut, exhorting us to give up everything and fix our minds upon God.

"Ramakrishna said, 'Doctors and lawyers will never see God,'" he said in a high-pitched quavering voice. "I was a lawyer. I gave it up." "Yes," I replied. "I was a doctor, and I gave it up."

The old *sannyasi* then told us the story of the pilgrimage he and Raghudas made together about ten years ago, when Raghudas was over sixty and the old man well past seventy. Apparently they had travelled together to the great shrines of North India: Varanasi, Mathura, Vrindavan, Prayag, Ayodhya, Delhi and Bhopal.

"In Mathura, the local brahmins fell in love with Raghudas Maharaj. They begged him to stay there, and offered to build him a fine ashram. But all he said was, 'I want only the company of Sant Jnaneshvar, who told me to stay at Alandi with him. And there I will return.'"

"How did you come to meet Raghudas Baba?" we asked.

"I was desperate to meet my true guru. So I went to the temple of Vitthale at Pandharpur, taking with me a sharp weapon. And standing in front of the God, I vowed to kill myself then and there unless I was shown who my guru was. Immediately, I heard a voice saying, 'Your guru is at Alandi, Raghudas Brahmachari.' So, throwing away the weapon, I went to Alandi, and surrendered my life at the feet of Raghudas. Taking the name Raghuvananda, I left my house, my profession and *lakhs* of rupees, and became a *sannyasi*. Since then I have lived as a renunciant, begging alms and sleeping in temples, cremation grounds or graveyards."

From the Gopal Krishna Temple, we were escorted to a small room in a nearby *dharmsala,* an unattractive two storey concrete building which resembled a low cost apartment complex, where devotees rented quarters. Here in a dark, cramped two-roomed apartment lived Grandmother Kamalabai, one of Raghudas' closest disciples. As I entered the room and saw the old lady in her simple cotton sari, sitting very erect upon a cot, I was moved to stoop and touch her feet. There was a kind of regal holiness about her that greatly impressed me. Her manner towards me was simple and affectionate, much as if she were my real grandmother and had known me all my life. Spontaneously, I felt myself looking upon her as a close, revered relative. Indu Thai, her middle-aged daughter, spoke to us in English, as Grandmother carefully cut an apple and shared it between us.

"My Mummy met Maharaj many years ago, and they recognized each other instantly. Since then, she has never left Alandi. My husband, son and daughter are in New York. And I myself am building a house in Poona. But my Mummy does not wish to leave here. She wants to stay near Maharaj. She and Maharaj have a very special connection. He regards her as his own mother. Those who are closest to him, he sends to meet my Mummy. You are here with her because you belong to Maharaj's intimate family; otherwise, he would not have asked that you be brought here to meet her."

That night, I tossed and turned on my sleeping mat in the heavy, mosquito-filled night. What was happening? Why did the humble, little-known saint of Alandi have such a deep effect upon me? All I had found in the pages of the Gospel—the perfect simplicity of one who has made himself as little as a little child, the purity of heart that sees God in all things, the overflowing love that knows no distinction of friend or foe—all this had sprung to life in the full moon face, silvery radiance and lotus feet of Raghudas. "All I want from you is love," he had told us, "and all I want to give is love." Never before had I met anyone who had so much right to claim, "I live now, not I, but Christ lives in me." And yet, he was to all appearances a Hindu, a brahmin, a devotee of Ram; on his shaven head grew the sacred tuft, about his chest hung the thread of the Twice-Born, and he lived in a Hindu temple.

Images raced through my mind: images of Jesus, whose devotee I had been from my mother's knee. Why did I now, in my twenty-eighth year of life, feel this extraordinary, this overwhelming compulsion to surrender myself, heart and soul, to the One I beheld in the form of this old brahmin? As I drifted into sleep, I felt Raghudas standing by my bed and repeating, "Don't worry, Yeshu and I are One."

It was the morning of the fourth day, and we were to return to Poona, where I needed to attend to my duties at CPS ashram. "You have no *mala* to wear," said Nicolas. "You should have one. Here! I got this at Haridwar, the gateway to the Himalayas. Anandamayi Ma, a great woman saint, has blessed it, and it has been immersed in the Ganges." So saying, he placed about my neck a sandalwood *mala*. Almost before I knew what was happening, I was wearing a Hindu rosary. I knew that the *mala* is a symbol of the initiated disciple. Did Nicolas' spontaneous act foretell that I was to receive initiation?

As we neared 'Baba's cave', I was overwhelmed by the need to communicate to him that the moment had come, that I was ready to surrender myself at his feet. Sheikh had gone to work, there was no interpreter, and I had no way to speak to him in words. "Then," I thought, "I shall tell him silently, and if he is indeed the one who can read the inmost secrets of my heart, he will understand."

As soon as I entered the chamber, holding this intention, Raghudas looked up, and his eyes met mine. The brilliance of a thousand autumn moons seemed to pour from his dark eyes as he spoke to me, clearly and emphatically in Marathi, in reply to my silent speech. With a wave of his hand, he beckoned me towards him. Moving carefully in the dark cave, I came forward and placed my head on his cool, smooth feet. At that moment, his feet were the centre of the universe, the heart of the blossoming lotus of creation. As I knelt, Raghudas placed his hand firmly on my head, and kept it there until my whole body burned with the love and power he imparted. This was an eternal moment. I knew that from now on, wherever I might travel, I would be here in spirit, resting my head upon his lotus feet. My long search had ended.

Boarding the bus for Poona, I returned to CPS ashram just long enough to share my experiences at *satsang* and find someone to cover my cleaning duties. Two days later, I was back in Alandi. I had come to spend two weeks at Chaitanya Ashram, a women's ashram, across the Indrayani from the Gopal Krishna Temple. Each morning, the sound of a stiff broom on beaten earth broke the silence of the pre-dawn hour, as I sat in meditation on the cowdung floor of my dark little room. The lowing of cattle, the pounding of a pestle and the slap, slap of laundry on a stone joined the growing chorus, and I usually abandoned silent sitting in favour of yoga *asanas*. By the time I emerged from the room, the sun was up.

The pattern of my days was shaped around that of Raghudas. As the new-risen sun began to warm the waters of the Indrayani, I would bathe and wash my sari in the river, before walking down the waterside footpath to the bridge. From there, I made my way through narrow streets crowded with merchants, villagers and pilgrims, to the Jnaneshvar Temple. In the main shrine, the priests were chanting as they bathed the *samadhi* of Sant Jnaneshvar with milk and coconut water. Placing my head on the wet marble, I felt myself flooded with light and blessings.

The dark chamber where Raghudas had been sitting since the small hours was filled with an almost palpable peace and stillness. Here, the two of us would sit in silence, eyes closed, while the sun climbed the sky. Without words, without gestures, the Master guided me along the path of meditation. I sat, conscious only of my breath, the flow of energy in the body, and the thoughts and feelings that came and went. Deep down, I was aware of being stripped and emptied, as layer upon layer of conditioning, lifetimes of ingrained habits of thought, were loosened. Even Raghudas' leading disciples were barred from his presence during my meditation times. If anyone tried to come in, Baba would jump up, shout at them, and furiously chase them out. Like a sculptor absorbed in his art, he would tolerate no distraction in the work of shaping the rough-hewn rock into my true likeness.

The arrival of Sahajanand Saraswati signalled the end of my meditation lesson. A thin, energetic brahmin about fifty years old with long, silver-tinged hair and ochre robes, Sahajanand had received his name, Easily-Made-Happy Swami, at a Rajneesh meditation camp. The name suited him well, for he was very happy and contented with a life that was simple in the extreme. Each day, he took *darshan* of Sant Jnaneshvar and Raghudas Maharaj, ate a small meal at the Gujarati temple, and spent the rest of the day sitting on a favourite stone outside his hut, not even meditating in any formal way, just being. His three gurus were Raghudas, Rajneesh and Mustaram Baba who lived in Rishikesh. Greatly to my surprise, he regarded Raghudas and Rajneesh as essentially the same.

"Eat little," he told me. "Eat only once a day. Now you have stone body. You must have glass body, like Raghudas, like Rajneesh."

After I emerged from the cave, blinking in the brilliant sunlight, I would explore the village, haggling over the price of bananas in the bazaar, and prostrating before the shrines on the cool marble floors of the various temples, each of which had its own flavour and added something unique to the tapestry of Alandi.

When the sun was at the zenith, I returned to Chaitanya Ashram, very hungry, for, following Sahajanand's suggestion, I had not eaten since the previous noon. Outside the ashram waited a long line of boys in threadbare white clothes, students who had come to Alandi to study devotional singing in the traditional *gurukul* system, sitting at the feet of their teacher for twelve years and living with him in forest huts. Cloths for wrapping their bakeri bread and vessels for *dal* at the ready, the boys chanted as they waited for their food. On the first day, I learned, to my distress, that I would be given the cold food that remained after all the boys were fed. This exercise in humility was too much for me, so I befriended Muktabai, the cook, sharing with her whatever little treats I bought for myself in the bazaar. In return, she would secretly call me to the kitchen, and ply me with hot bakeri, fresh from the pan.

Late afternoon found me in a favourite spot by the riverside, where I would sit in meditation for two or three hours, until the setting sun called me to cross the bridge again, for Raghudas' evening *darshan.*

"Have you had Jnaneshvar's *darshan?*" Raghudas Baba would invariably ask, as soon as I arrived. "Don't come here to see me, come for Sant Jnaneshvar. I am only his servant."

Sheikh, having lost his shyness, now regarded me as his own sister, and liked to gossip, even in front of Baba.

"Sister, how is Francis?" he grinned. "You know, he was wondering whether to remain *brahmachari* or to marry some girl from New Zealand."

"Oh, her! She left for Canada with a Rajneesh *sannyasin.*"

At this, Baba burst out laughing. He laughed totally, laughed with every pore, laughed until his whole body shook. Yet his laughter was free from either ridicule or surprise. He had known all along that Sant Jnaneshvar would not permit the young woman to join our circle. Rather, he seemed to be laughing in delight at the turning of the wheel, as if he were expressing God's laughter, the merriment of the player whose game is the universe. Eventually Akka arrived, to bring Baba his evening meal. A brahmin widow greatly respected in the village, Akka was a brisk, jolly woman, not philosophically inclined. Baba's way of teaching her was through humour. She would gossip and crack jokes, then Baba would laugh and crack more jokes, and so they would carry on, chatting and joking, for the remainder of the *darshan*, whilst I sat amazed to witness the total mindfulness with which my Baba could joke around, and wishing that I could understand what they were laughing about.

Gradually, I came to see that Raghudas could do many things at once during the evening *darshan*. He might be joking with Akka, and listening with intense seriousness as some poor villager complained about the rising price of sugar, gradually lifting the devotee's consciousness to higher and higher planes. Meanwhile two children were sitting with eyes closed, telling their beads, and I was in a state of deep meditation, hearing his voice and feeling his touch guiding me through the inner planes, as he was apparently fully engaged in laughing, chatting, patting someone's back, and having his feet massaged.

At the weekend, my friend Kathy, a Canadian yoga teacher, arrived from Christa Prema Seva Ashram. I was delighted to see her. For a couple of days, mine would not be the only white face in Alandi.

"All the sisters send their love," she beamed. "Even Anand the dog sends you a friendly bark."

Kathy had brought with her a large supply of delicacies from the Seventh Day Adventist health food store on Poona's Mahatma Gandhi Road. As I relished the nuts, cheeses and other treats, a welcome change from my daily diet of *bakeri* and pepper water, Kathy talked. She talked about the Iyengar Institute in Poona, where she was taking an intensive yoga teachers' training course. She talked about Raghudas, who had been constantly in her thoughts since I brought her with me to meet him, on the first day of my retreat.

"I was finding my yoga studies with Iyengar very difficult," she told me. "In fact, I was not making much progress and was constantly being reprimanded. But you know what? Since meeting Raghudas, everything has shifted. Suddenly I am enjoying the yoga, and progressing rapidly."

Kathy talked about Sister Columba's arthritis, about Sister

Arati's great re-organization of the library, about Devaki the cook. And she talked about Francis.

"You know," she said, in her authoritative school teacher's manner, "I've been watching Francis closely and . . . he needs a woman. But not one like Priya—not a seductress. Priya has done her work, she has opened Francis to the feminine, made him aware that he needs the company of a woman. Now he should take a *sadhu*-wife. How about you? Don't you think you'd be perfect for the job? You and he have the same interests, the same guru."

"I'm going to be a hermit," I interrupted her, as my face flushed. "I'm not going to marry—ever. And *sadhus* don't have wives anyway. You've been going to too many Rajneesh seminars."

That evening, as we sat at Raghudas' feet, Sheikh suddenly asked us, "Don't you find it a problem that you speak no Marathi and need an interpreter?"

"Not at all," we replied in unison. "Baba can hear our hearts."

Raghudas nodded his emphatic agreement without any need of translation. "Between us," he said, "there is no need of words. And in the path that you have chosen, much speaking is a hindrance."

When I returned to CPS Ashram, the glow in my face spoke volumes. Others wanted to share what I was receiving, and so my twice-weekly trips to Alandi were quite often accompanied by a friend. Raghudas loved the ashram sisters, whom he regarded as very pure and upright beings. But he was exceptionally delighted when I brought a Japanese nun to see him, for he had never met a Japanese person before. Patting her affectionately on the back, he explained, "The three of us have been drawn together from such distant lands, from India, Japan, and the Western world, because in a previous life, all three of us were close friends and companions. And so, at last, we meet again."

The little nun nodded sagely. Coming from a country with a large Buddhist population, she was more at home with the notion of reincarnation than I was. Too overwhelmed by a concept so unfamiliar to me to ask appropriate questions, I missed the opportunity to discover more about my past-life history with my guru. But one point I did not miss. If my connection with the

RAGHUDAS BABA AND WESTERNERS
(FRANCIS ON FAR RIGHT)

Japanese woman, in this life just a passing acquaintance, was so deep, then Raghudas, Francis and I musthave been intimately related in a former existence. Had the three of us sat together at the feet of Sant Jnaneshvar during his active life?

I watched Raghudas' interactions with his woman disciples closely. My mother, a feminist of the old school, and my sister Kate, a radical feminist who lived in a squat street in Brixton, South London, had done their best to share with me their values and insights. Yet as a Catholic contemplative woman, I had accepted what the church assigned to me—the cloister and veil. Now I saw that the women who surrounded my guru were anything but cloistered, indeed, many of them were very assertive and outspoken and treated the male disciples like sons.

Raghudas' ease and intimacy with his spiritual daughters was in marked contrast with the stilted and formal relationships that Indian social norms imposed between the sexes.

"Temple brahmins not liking. Women too close, saying. *Brahmacharya,* how is possible, they thinking," the wife of the priest at the Gopal Krishna Temple told me, as she and her beautiful young daughter, Surekha, explained to me the scandal that Raghudas' relationship with women caused to the hierarchy of the Jnaneshvar Temple.

Gradually, I realized that I was the only foreigner among an inner circle of female disciples which included Grandmother Kamalabai, Indu Thai, Akka, Surekha and her mother, the factory supervisor from Bombay and a Poona physician called Dr.-Mrs. Joshi. There were also two women I had yet to meet, Raghudas' niece and his sister Ganguthai, herself revered as a Realized being. The closeness and unity I felt with my godsisters, so diverse in age, social class and education, was deeper than anything I had experienced before. All of us were by nature inclined to service, and—unlike our brothers—longed not so much for *moksha,* final liberation, as for *prema,* pure love, an aspiration we shared with the sisters at CPS Ashram. Gradually I came to see that we were more than simply the equals of the male disciples. We had a special part to play in the work of the *sadguṛu,* for we were spiritual mothers, gifted with a unique ability to tend and nurture the awakening spiritual consciousness of aspirants. This new and still shadowy understanding of my ministry as a woman was later to come to full consciousness when I visited Sakuri, the home of Raghudas' sister Ganguthai and her guru, Godavari Mataji.

It was the Hindu month of Asvin, our October, and in the countryside surrounding Poona, fields of head-high *jowar* and *bazri,* the staple millets from which *bakeri* is made, were ripe for the sickle. At this harvest season, the Nine Nights autumnal festival of Divine Mother is celebrated. The Poona locals, mainly devoted to Ganesh, Vitthale and Dattatreya, paid little heed to this event, but for the city's sizeable Bengali community it was the climax of the year. One evening during the festival, Sister Brigite and I made our way to the great marquée the Bengalis had erected in Shivajinagar, not far from CPS ashram.

Inside the marquée it was hot and crowded. Drums were beating and the air was pungent with incense, acrid smoke and the sweat of the dancers. Young men and old alike were performing intricate footwork whilst holding near their faces clay vessels of smoldering coconut fibre. A couple of little girls in long embroidered satin dresses broke away from a father's handclasp and ran out to imitate the dancing.

Eventually Brigite and I pushed our way far enough through the crowd to get a sight of the elaborate image of eight-armed Durga, the Great Mother, seated upon her tiger mount, brandishing weapons and slaying the horrible buffalo demon of death, whilst black-faced Kali, the emanation of Durga's divine ferocity, stalked the battlefield, drinking the hot blood of the demons with her long red tongue. On either side of Durga were her daughters, Lakshmi the Goddess of Bounty, and Sarasvati, Goddess of Learning. The images, made of clay shaped on a straw and bamboo frame, meticulously painted, would be discarded in the Mouly River once the festival was over.

I was awestruck by what I saw. Although I had had the *darshan* of Mariamme and come to the outer court of Meenakshi's temple, this was my first encounter with India's Black Mother, destroyer of all negativity, she who is known as Durga and Kali.

A couple of days later, I was pulled back from the Great Mother and her ferocious compassion to the scholarly atmosphere of Indian Christianity. Father Francis, a local Jesuit, arrived at CPS ashram to give a seminar on Bhagavad Gita.

"We are not in the business of syncretism," said Father Francis, an English-medium educated Indian whose flawless English resembled Archana's. "We are not here to make a *khicheri,* mixing a little of this, a little of that. You cannot read Bhagavad Gita through Christian eyes, for you will read into it your pre-existing Christian concepts. No, to read Bhagavad Gita, you must develop a pair of Hindu eyes. Christians seek salvation and Hindus *moksha.* The two ideas are very different. Christianity is a religion of pure *bhakti,* supreme devotion. In Hinduism, *bhakti* is rooted in *jnana,* in wisdom. Christians see God in Christ and in the church, the body of Christ. For Hindus, the entire universe is the body of *brahman.* The Divine is seen in every aspect of nature, in rocks, in rivers, in trees, in mountains; in the cow, the snake, the monkey, the elephant."

Like Father Bede's concept of the two covenants, Father Francis' words were to influence me deeply. Thanks to him, I understood the difference between syncretism—mixing a little of one tradition and little of another; and synthesis—appreciating each tradition in its integrity, with its own special way of seeing. During the tea break, I told Father Francis about my experience as a 'nature mystic'. From the age of six, I had seen the divine in rocks, rivers and mountains.

"You are a Hindu soul," he answered, gazing deep into my eyes. "Your inclination is to see God in nature, in everything. I am trying to encourage the others to have a Hindu experience. But perhaps you should try to have a Christian experience, just for once."

I was offended. After all, I was a good Catholic—wasn't I? Even if I did have a Jewish father. And a Hindu guru.

That night, I had a dream set in a large Gothic church. Father Francis, armed with a besom broom, was busy sweeping me out of the church. Then suddenly, seated on an episcopal throne in the centre of the church, Raghudas appeared, beaming serenely. "Don't worry," he seemed to be saying, "I am here, too."

A day or so later, a catastrophic attack of dysentery struck me down, turning me overnight from a plump pilgrim into a thin one.

I lay on my wooden bed, too weak to move, whilst Sister Arati bustled in and out of my room with cups of soup and carefully chosen reading matter. As soon as I had enough strength to totter down the street, I went to see Dr. Lad, who gave me some strange-smelling little balls of herbal medicine. Now was my chance to put Ayurveda to the test.

Seating myself in a sunny corner outside the ashram chapel, I unwrapped the medicines from their paper packages and swallowed one of each kind, washing them down with warm water. They tasted bitter and slightly spicy. Immediately, I sank into such a deep meditation that I was unable to rouse myself even when Sister Sara, taking some visitors on a tour of the ashram, started an animated conversation right beside me. My breathing slowed until it almost stopped, and I became profoundly conscious of another kind of life that did not come and go with the breath, the *prana,* or vital force. I felt this force flowing through my body from the core, and knew that I was being healed. That same day, my stools became normal and the lassitude and fatigue vanished. The healing power of plants had entered my life in a way that I could never forget.

Thanks to Dr. Lad, I was now well enough to go to Alandi again. The day I returned, Sahajanand Saraswati smiled as I entered Raghudas' cave. "Just now itself," he said, "Maharaj was asking about you. He was saying that he had not seen you for some time, and that you would be coming today. He always knows who will be coming. And now he is saying that *prakruti*—your body—has been sick."

Raghudas rubbed my back and filled my hands with sweets and fruits, exhorting me to eat well and grow strong. Suddenly I realized that the dysentery had been caused not only by too much spicy food, but also by spiritual indigestion. Both Hinduism and Christianity were speaking to my soul, and I did not know which voice to listen to. "I feel confused about all these religions," I said. "Does it matter which religion a person follows?"

"Now see, if you are taking the train to Bombay, there will be Hindus, Moslems, Christians, Sikhs, Jains and Parsees, all in the same compartment. Some are eating vegetarian food, and some are eating non-vegetarian, and some are only eating bread and butter. Yet all of you will get down at Bombay.

"There are many rivers, the Ganges, the Yamuna, the Brahmaputra, the Narmada, the Godavari, the Krishna and the Kaveri. Yet in the One Ocean, all find their end. One who is established in spiritual consciousness has no concern about such small matters as this religion or that."

Francis arrived, hair still dripping from his bath in the Indrayani, and he and Sahajanand began talking about the *kumbha mela,* until Raghudas spoke.

"The *sadhus* at the *mela* are concerned about *siddhis,* the mystic powers of yoga. And *siddhis* they may have, but I tell you this. There is only one *siddhi* worth developing, the greatest *siddhi* of them all; the power to take whatever comes."

There was a moment's silence, then Baba spoke again, gazing at me. "As for you, do not worry about these complicated yoga practices. By all means, do some *asanas* for your health, but keep your path very simple. Your way is *bhakti,* the yoga of love, devotion and surrender, the Way of the Heart. Do not let yourself be distracted from this simple and easy way, the Royal Road."

The days grew shorter. It was time for our blankets to be unpacked from their tin trunks, for cold season had arrived. Kartik, the first month of cold season, brought the November feast of Divali, the festival of lights. In the days preceding Divali, Mrs. Laddu, my Hindi teacher, and all my Hindu housewife friends, both in Poona and Alandi, were caught up in a frenzy of activity—making quantities of sweet *chapatis* and other sweetmeats traditional for the festival; purchasing new garments for the entire family; cleaning and scouring their homes until not one speck of dust remained.

As Goddess of wealth and abundance, Lakshmi is of great importance to both householders and merchants. On Divali day, the streets were crowded with families dressed in their new clothes, the vermilion mark of the Mother's blessing adorning their foreheads. Wherever I went, friendly householders invited me in to admire their beautifully decorated images of Lakshmi and Sarasvati and to partake of the sweets offered to the Goddess. Even the beggars were moving about with smiling faces. They went from shop to shop, receiving sweetmeats and coins from merchants who hoped that such generosity would win them Lakshmi's favour.

At twilight, the whole of Shivajinagar became a mass of twinkling lights, as every house and shop kindled the traditional row of clay oil lamps. Firecrackers were exploding all along Varkari Wadi and the air was full of the sound of merrymaking.

December, the month of my birth, the Hindu Margarshirsha, brought me an uneasy sense of dislocation. Where was winter, the time of freezing fogs and frost on window panes? Never before had I celebrated my birthday or awaited Christmas, season of multilayered memories, in a strange culture and unfamiliar clime. My memories of December were steeped in Christian customs, the lighting of the Advent candle, the preparations for the birth of the Christ Child.

One of the great themes of the Christian Advent is the gathering of all nations. Each morning at Eucharist we read from the prophets who speak of a time when all nations, of both the Abrahamic and Cosmic Covenants, will gather together in mutual harmony and understanding. That December, at CPS ashram, the children of Abraham, Isaac and Ishmael united in prayer with the followers of Ram, Krishna and Zoroaster.

One of our visitors, a Christian lady who had come to Poona to set exam papers, brought along her two best friends, a Hindu and a Moslem. Then the Moslem lady invited another Hindu paper setter, and she in turn invited two Zoroastrians, who took up residence in my room. By now, the ashram closely resembled Raghudas' train compartment. Our Hindu and Zoroastrian friends participated enthusiastically in the *aratis;* the Moslems prayed with us. All of us were living together in peace.

"There's just one problem," I told Sara, as we sat together in the garden. "One great world religion is not represented. We have got to have a Buddhist."

Sure enough, the very next day, a tall, shaven-headed Westerner in the robes of a Zen monk appeared at the ashram gate. Born in the United States and ordained in Korea, Hey Won had come to Poona to get yoga therapy for a back injury which was impeding his meditation.

A few days later, a young man, Heinz, from Switzerland joined us, a gardener by profession and healer by inclination. Soon

Heinz, Hey Won, Francis and I were making regular visits to Alandi together. Hey Won was more attracted by Raghudas than by any of his Zen masters. At last, he felt that he had found a living Buddha. The Jnaneshvar *samadhi* deeply impressed him, too. He told us that on one occasion, when he stayed overnight at Alandi, he had a dream in which Raghudas appeared, vast in form as a mountain, thundering, "Jnaneshvar and I are one!"

Towards Christmas time, two more Westerners arrived at the ashram, both Americans. The more striking of them was very tall and looked taller because of the crown of matted locks coiled on top of his head. He had a beaming smile and wore the white robes and *tulasi* neck beads of an initiated *sadhu* in the lineage of devotees of Ram.

"Wow, it's Charandas!" cried Francis as he appeared, and he ran to hug his friend, whom he had met at the Nasik *kumba* mela. Charandas' smaller and slighter companion Richard wore a spotless white *lungi* and *kurta* and a grey silk shawl. His beard was trimmed and his hair elegantly styled. He was a well-known healer and clairvoyant, and wasted little time before telling me that in a past life I had been a medieval Catholic nun, a perception that made great sense to me—except that I was still uncertain about reincarnation.

The next day, Richard and I went to Alandi together, whilst Francis and Charandas visited the Ram *sadhus* near Poona Station. As we went around the Jnaneshvar temple, we saw Raghudas standing in prayer before the image of Ganesh. He was completely absorbed and though his eyes were wide open, he could see nothing but the elephant-headed God. Richard and I continued on to the *shivalinga*, the knowledge garden and the main Jnaneshvar shrine, then sat for a while beneath a *peepul* tree. When we reached 'Baba's cave', Raghudas, who had finished his round of the temple deities, was making the garland which he offered daily to the images in his chamber. He was still in a completely God-absorbed condition, and seemed oblivious of our presence as, with one-pointed attention, he strung marigolds. When the garland was completed, he placed it upon the statue of Vitthale and then looked up at us with a welcoming smile. After we had meditated together awhile, Sheikh arrived.

"Sister," he said to me, "Raghudas Baba is saying that you will be going away to do Buddhist meditation."

I gasped. "That's exactly right." I was still astonished to see that Raghudas knew everything about me without my telling him. "I am going to a *vipassana* retreat in a couple of days."

After *darshan* with Raghudas, Richard and I went to my favourite tea shop.

"Raghudas fills the cracks between my thought with such warmth," said Richard, as we sat on wooden benches beneath the hessian awning, sipping chay. "I have experienced emptiness before, but never this warmth, this love. Truly, he is Nobody Special, with capital letters."

CPS Ashram, Poona, 10th January 1981

Dear Mum and Dad,

I had a very quiet and austere Christmas in silence doing a Buddhist meditation course in the mountains. One reason for choosing to go away at Christmas time was that I felt that the distance would help me to find my true relation to Christ. Perhaps by stepping back from my Christian conditioning, I could experience the real Christmas. So... Christmas day came and went, the night watchman blew his whistle in the darkness, the morning star shone, the glorious sun rose from behind a dark line of hills and turned the dawn mists to golden light, the shrubs burst into bloom... pointers, pointers, but something yet lacking.

On January 1st, I returned to the ashram, prostrated myself in the chapel and suddenly had an incredibly strong experience of Christ. I was meeting Him as an exceptionally powerful guru with whom I had the strongest of connections—the unconditioned presence of a real and living person who had drawn me to himself as a disciple. No wonder the sisters say that Christ is the guru of the ashram.

Happy New Year to you all.

Love, Olivia

Raghudas was helping me to draw closer to the essence, to the reality of Christ, the Servant of Love. In the old Hindu saint, I experienced the steadfast love and unconditional acceptance which is the Christ Nature. During the meditation retreat, on full moon night, I dreamt that I was in a very strict Zen monastery, a combination of my old Abbey and Hey Won's temple in Korea. Unwittingly I committed a breach of discipline, and was brought before the abbot expecting to be judged. But as I looked up at the abbot, I saw the face and silvery beaming smile of Raghudas. All my sense of guilt, my fear of judgment or condemnation melted away in the all-accepting radiance of that smile.

It was six-thirty on a chill January morning, and already the Alandi-bound bus stand was full of pilgrims, wrapping their patterned cotton blankets more tightly about themselves and pacing up and down in the cold. At Alandi, the temple was crowded with women, each holding a big bag of white sugar candies. Today the women had come to bless the sweets they would give to all their friends and relatives, saying to each, "I give sweet things to you; please say sweet words to me." This day was Makara Sankranti, the solar transition to sideral Capricorn, the day which marks the ending of the path of smoke and darkness, and the beginning of the way of Light and Fire, the path of virtue whose cosmological symbol is the Northward journey of the sun.

It had been around the time of the summer solstice that I first arrived in Poona. During the long months of the sun's southward journey, I had travelled slowly into the darkness of the unknown, watching my body grow sick, watching concepts, mental structures and belief systems crumble to dust and old conditionings drop away. The meeting with the guru had initiated a descent into the darkness of God that was at times confusing, agonizing, even terrifying. Would I, like the sun, take a new birth? What change was in store for me at this cosmic time of change of direction?

"You should beware of staying too long in a Christian environment like CPS Ashram," Richard warned me. "Day by day I see your old self, your past life as a Catholic nun, becoming more shadowy. Every time you go to meditate with Raghudas, you return looking changed. He is taking you beyond identification with Christianity, to identity with the universal Christ."

Richard's words scared me, yet it was true that I felt an inner restlessness. CPS Ashram was the most warm, loving, home-like environment I had experienced since I left my parental home for

University ten years ago. And yet I knew I must move on. Perhaps it was time for me to go deeper into solitude, to find my own hermitage. I thought of spending my remaining money on building a hut at Alandi, so that I would be close to Raghudas for as long as he lived. But he immediately divined these thoughts and instructed Sheikh to tell me that Alandi was not the safest or healthiest place for me to live.

"He says that you should just stay here a week or so from time to time, and then return to the ashram in Poona, or to some quiet hermitage in a cleaner and less populous place." Sheikh said. Consulting with a hermit sister who was visiting CPS Ashram and staying in my room, I wrote several letters to people who might be able to help me find a hermitage, preferably not too far away from Alandi.

On Paus Purnima, the full moon following Makara Sankranti, Raghudas' disciples came together to celebrate his birthday. About fifty of us gathered in the Gopal temple to share a feast of rice, vegetables and sweets, and to offer garlands and fruits to Baba. Raghudas' niece, a serene and gentle little Madonna, came with her two-month-old son, who was so innocently attuned to his uncle's energy that whenever I took the baby in my arms, I found myself sinking into deep meditation, and had to be careful to stay awake enough to hold the baby safely.

Francis, who had slipped and twisted his ankle that morning, almost did not make it to the feast. His eventual arrival, on a pair of crutches borrowed from the hospital, was a dramatic moment. As soon as Francis appeared at Gopalpuram, Raghudas emerged from his room, where he had been resting after the meal, and embraced Francis delightedly, gazing deep into his eyes in a remarkable way. Francis' presence was the most valuable birthday gift Raghudas could have received.

The holy month of Paus had not advanced much further when one of the most revered and best-loved saints in India suddenly arrived in the City of Merit. Anandamayi Ma, the Bliss-Incarnate Mother, had come to Poona. She had come unexpectedly, for everything she did was unexpected. It was impossible for her to follow a prearranged schedule. Guided by her *kheyal*, an inexplicable inner prompting, she moved from place to place, in utter disregard of her advancing age and failing health, accompanied everywhere by a cluster of devotees who had dedicated their entire lives to serving her.

Francis, Hey Won, Heinz and I walked together down Ganeshkind Road, a broad, tree-lined street that led to the university and the Anandamayi Ma Ashram. All of us were excited by the prospect of seeing the saint who had won the hearts of the Indian people.

"When she was young, she was more beautiful than any film star," said Hey Won. "She was married as a girl, to a man named Bholanath. Whenever he tried to touch her, he would get an electric shock. She would sink into deep *samadhi* the moment he had a lustful thought and could only be revived by prolonged chanting of the holy names. So they lived as a celibate couple."

"I read about her in *Autobiography of a Yogi*," added Heinz. "Yogananda wanted to bring her to America. But her entourage of devotees refused to be parted from her, and he could not afford to bring them all. Even today, she is little known in the West."

Hey Won and Heinz had read about Ma, but Francis had actually met her. "When I stayed with that brahmin family," he explained, "she came to Bombay. Kaka Apte, the brahmin man, and I went to see her. But we couldn't get in. He kept demanding to see her, insisting on it, but her attendants refused. Then suddenly, she herself decided to come out and see him. It was unbelievable! She stood as close to us as I am to you. Then many devotees came rushing over, offering her saris, fruits, garlands, coconuts. And she gave everything to Apte. She just kept saying, 'Here Kaka, here Kaka!' So I had a wonderful *darshan* with her."

The ashram was beautiful, with large *tulasi* bushes everywhere. Today, the grounds were crowded with devotees anxious for the Mother's *darshan*. Joining a long line, we waited our turn to look through an open window at the queen of contemporary saints. As I filed past, she looked up and briefly glanced into my eyes. I remembered Meenakshi, Mariamme, Durga and Kali. Before, I had seen the Goddess in beautiful temples and images. Now, a living

Goddess of flesh and blood was meeting me eye to eye. My whole being thrilled. The Divine Mother herself had gazed upon me. I felt incredible joy.

We were all so delighted that, quite against the rules, we queued up again for a second look at the Bliss-Incarnate Mother. Next day, the four of us returned to the ashram to bid the Mother farewell, for tomorrow she was leaving for Bombay. This time, we were ushered into a large hall. Ma sat, peacefully smiling, absorbed in timeless bliss, whilst hundreds of tightly-packed devotees sang in unison, "*Hare Krishna, Hare Krishna, Krishna Krishna, Hare Hare.*" Then, one by one, we approached her seat, bowed before her, and received an apple from her hands. As we walked back home, I felt drunk with bliss. I was so full of energy that, despite being more than a foot shorter than Hey Won and Heinz, I was walking too fast for them to keep up with me. In my heart, I knew that Ma had blessed me with the strength I needed to endure whatever hardships might come my way during my Indian pilgrimage.

Only years later would I come to understand fully how profoundly Anandamayi Ma's brief *darshan* had affected me. Ma was to leave her body eighteen months later, but would never leave me. Periodically she came in my dreams, even making an unprecedented appearance in my recurrent Holocaust nightmare. The Blissful Mother in Auschwitz! Acquaintances of mine, both Hindu practitioners and Catholic nuns, fell in love with her photograph on my altar. The Saint with whom I never exchanged a word was to reveal herself as one of my most intimate friends.

Hey Won and Heinz were not satisfied with Anandamayi Ma's brief trip to Poona, and persuaded both Francis and myself to accompany them on a pilgrimage to Bombay and Shirdi, so that we could spend more time with Ma in Bombay. Accordingly, on the auspicious waning Eleventh, we took our leave at the feet of Raghudas. "Shirdi is a very good place," he said, on learning of our plans. "Sai Baba and Jnaneshvar are one. All realized beings are one and the same." Having obtained his blessings on the trip, we caught the Bombay train early next morning.

To Indian eyes, we must have seemed like a strange party. Ahead strode Heinz, over six feet tall and athletic, his blond hair cut short, his beard trimmed. He wore Western clothes and had a friendly, good-hearted smile and forceful Germanic manners, which Indians found very funny. Close behind him paced Hey Won, the American, equally tall and loud-voiced, in his grey Zen robe and felt slippers, a brown Gandhi cap on his shaven head. At a little distance behind him, limped Francis on his sprained ankle, barefoot, wearing a green *lungi* and white turban and carrying his *dotar,* the two-stringed instrument. I trailed behind, always struggling to keep up, a pale little English woman in a yellow homespun sari. Hey Won and Heinz took most of the decisions, conducting the pilgrimage at what was, to me, a breakneck pace.

Arriving at Bombay's Dardar station, we immediately noticed a large temple to which devotees were flocking, the women dressed in the distinctive Gujerati sari. We were standing in front of the Swaminarayan Ashram, and Swami himself, the current holder of a three hundred year old Vaishnava lineage, was making a rare visit to Bombay.

"Darshan," mumbled Francis, as, to my horror, all my three brothers suddenly disappeared through a doorway marked "Men Only"—leaving me standing alone on the streets of Bombay.

Now it is true, I had lived for over six years in London, a great metropolis. Yet compared to Bombay, London seemed a quiet, sedate, orderly place. All around me was whirling the most crowded, chaotic, colourful, bewildering city I had ever experienced. And suddenly, I was alone. I freaked out, tried to dive after my brothers through the "men only" door, and was firmly, if politely, stopped. Explaining that Swami had never, in his life, set eyes on a woman other than his mother, nor were his monks allowed to see the face of a woman, the man guarding the entrance called over a lady in a turquoise and crimson silk sari, who kindly led me to the ladies' gallery.

Here, across a great distance, I had the privilege of setting eyes on Swami. I could even see Francis, Hey Won and Heinz lining up to touch his feet and receive blessings. But I was filled with scorn, rebellion and confusion. What was so great about never seeing a woman? After all, wasn't Anandamayi Ma a woman? Feeling that I could have no devotion to such a saint and his ridiculous mediaeval customs, I walked—or stomped—out of the temple and sat outside by the postcard seller to wait for my brothers.

At length, the saint drove out in a shuttered limousine, and devotees began pouring from the building. The flood diminished to a trickle, then stopped. Still my brothers did not come. Had I but known it, they were receiving a courteous reception from the monks, and a special lecture on the Vaishnava philosophy of Swaminarayan. By the time they emerged, my anger was beyond control, and they were greeted by a Mother Kali breathing fire and thirsting for blood. With difficulty, I was persuaded back inside the building to partake of *prasadam,* since it was now noon. "It's the best food in Bombay," said Francis. "They make these delicious, really thin Gujerati chapatis. And you can eat as much as you like. And it's all free." It was true. This much I had to grant the despised Swaminarayans, they make wonderful food.

Much of the rest of the day was spent in an unsuccessful search for a place to stay the night. In the evening, we came to the house of a wealthy family who provided all facilities for Anandamayi Ma on her visits to Bombay. Some years previously, Anandamayi Ma had retired from public life to her hermitage beside the Narmada River. Then, inexplicably (and to our great blessing), she had returned to minister to the needs of India's rich industrialists, the class of people who had held power over the fortunes of hundreds of millions of poor and simple folk. If Ma could find the key to the conscience of only a few such capitalists, the lives of India's struggling masses would surely be eased.

Whilst waiting for the public *darshan*, we sat on a marble floor and meditated, just outside the room where Ma was giving audience. As I meditated, I could hear Anandamayi Ma and Raghudas speaking to me with one voice. "Don't worry," they were saying. "Don't worry about anything. Not even about becoming Enlightened. That is our business. We are here to guide your soul. You concern yourself with your brothers and sisters, with love, kindness and selfless service, and we will concern ourselves with you."

From Bombay, we took an incredibly crowded suburban train to the small town of Badlapur. Here, a famous householder yogi, a retired former civil servant, had an ashram dedicated to Sai Baba of Shirdi. Both he and his two sons were friendly and welcoming, offering us food, tea and sweets, and allowing us to sleep the night on the temple floor.

Badlapur Baba was famous not only as a yogi, but also as an astrologer and psychic. Heinz, who had visited him before, was much taken with his predictions, and suggested that we all ask for his guidance. Accordingly, after dinner, the yogi, clothed in spotless white, seated himself on a special chair in the temple. He was plump, with a great belly like Ganesh himself, and layers of double chin. Indeed, he so greatly resembled Ganesh that we wondered whether he was in fact an emanation of the beloved elephant God.

Francis approached the chair. Taking hold of his little finger, the yogi closed his eyes, entered into trance, and then announced, "There is only one place where you will find peace—Garudeshvar in Gujerat, on the Narmada river. Before you finish your pilgrimage, you must go there. For the previous five lifetimes, you were a yogi. Now, this is your final birth. Rest assured, in this very lifetime, you will attain *moksha.*"

It was my turn. I came up to the chair and offered Badlapur Baba my little finger. "You will stay in India and practice meditation daily," he declared. "At the age of thirty three, you will obtain the fruits of your *sadhana* and will return to the West. There, you will open a practice as a physician. But you will not be a normal physician. You will be a great healer. You will heal people by a mere touch. Many people will come and they will be healed. But always, you will spend hours in silent meditation. Your life will be a harmonious balance of contemplation and service."

What was the meaning of the yogi's words? Would they prove to be true? Hey Won and Heinz were not about to give me much time to think about it. We were off again—this time to Shirdi via a long and bumpy bus journey through very beautiful mountains.

Sai Baba, who left his body in the early years of this century, is one of the most famous saints of modern India. I was familiar with his image, for I saw his picture everywhere in Poona's temples, chay shops and homes—and, of course, on the silver ring of Raghudas. From my studies of Sufism, under Sister Arati's direction, I understood that Sai Baba of Shirdi was a great Sufi mystic, part of a tradition of Indian Sufism, who baffled brahmins and Moslems alike by plumbing the depths of both Hindu and Islamic mysticism.

We spent the night in a large hall, where numerous pilgrims from all parts of India spread out their blankets. Early next morning, we got into a horse-drawn *tonga* to travel three miles to the ashram of Godavari Mataji. Here Upasani Maharaj, Mataji's Guru, the Hindu saint who was the spiritual heir and "chargeman" of Sai Baba, had transformed a desolate graveyard into a little paradise.

Dedicated to Kanya Kumari, Divine Mother as a Little Maid-Child, the Upasani Maharaj ashram at Sakuri village is a place of purity and sweetness. In the beauty and cleanliness of its buildings and gardens, in its harmony and tranquillity and its abundance of trees and flowers, it seemed to me like a reflection of Krishna's celestial Vrindavan. And like the milkmaids of Vrindavan, the *kanyas,* or consecrated maidens, wearing colourful cotton saris, with bangles at their wrists and the red dot painted on their foreheads to symbolize their spiritual marriage to the *sadguru,* perform traditional ring dances around a charming image of Gopal Krishna.

Francis, who had been to Sakuri before, showed us the tomb of Upasani Maharaj, the cage where he had incarcerated himself for fourteen months (consuming nothing but a cup of coffee daily), the beautiful marble image of Kanya Kumari, and the temple of Dattatreya, the Triple-faced God.

"Dattatreya's face looks like a young woman," I remarked.

"It does indeed. The image has the face of Godavari Mataji, Upasani Majaraj's successor, who is believed to be the reincarnation of a wild, naked, *ganja*-smoking saint of tremendous spiritual stature. Before he left the body, the saint told two of his disciples that he would be reborn as their daughter, and should be named Godavari. And you know what, that couple, who always travelled around because the husband worked on the railway, just happened to be stationed at the saint's shrine on the day Godavari was born. When she was nine, her parents brought her to Upasani Maharaj, who immediately hailed her as his successor. A few years later, when she was hardly a teenager, he announced publicly that she was completely one with the *adi shakti,* the primal power, and put her in charge of the ashram."

IMAGE OF DATTATREYA AT SAKURI

PHOTO COURTESY OF SRI UPASANI KANYAKUMARI STHAN

It was a wonderful story, and I was excited to meet Godavari Mataji. Leaving the Dattatreya temple, we hurried over to the *bhajan* hall, where morning *arati* was just beginning, in the presence of Mataji. She was now about fifty years older than the beautiful girl depicted on the statue. Her face was heavier, her body plumper, and she wore glasses. At first glance, she did not look so extraordinary.

But when I prostrated myself before her, I felt as if her glance penetrated to my inmost being. She sat on the ground, one knee drawn up, in her characteristic pose. Her body was motionless, her face expressionless, and she seemed utterly self-sufficient, absorbed in a reality beyond my ken. Yet as she raised her hand in blessing, I felt that she radiated infinite love and benevolence. Indeed, I could scarcely look at her, for she appeared to me with the brilliance of a thousand suns.

After Mataji had read the notes we all handed her, the ashram manager, who spoke fluent English, delivered her messages to us.

"Mother gives you her *ashirvad,* her blessings. And she is delighted that you are disciples of Raghudas Maharaj. Mother is quite familiar with him, for his sister, Ganguthai, is her right-hand woman. In fact, Raghudas came here once and met Upasani Maharaj, and the two liked each other greatly. Mother says that your guru is certainly a God-realized being, and has been so these many years. Indeed, we regard him as a Governor in the spiritual world. Truly, he is a *sadguru*, a perfect master.

"You have all asked many questions, and Mother has replied simply with her *ashirvad*. However, Francis, she has made some answer to your very long letter. As to your problem with meeting that woman from New Zealand and losing your *brahmacharya*, Mother is saying, no need of worrying about this. She will give her *ashirvad*, and you will regain your *brahmacharya*. Simply she is instructing you to look upon all women, young or old, ugly or beautiful, as forms of the Divine Mother. Secondly, you were telling of your strong desire to see the Ganga and the Himalayas before you leave India. Mother says, don't worry, these are good desires, and you will fulfill them. Mother understands that you have some problem with your visa, and that you have been long gone from your family, and she is blessing you like this; first, see

GODAVARI MATAJI

PHOTO COURTESY OF SRI UPASANI KANYAKUMARI STHAN

the Ganga and the Himalayas, and then only leave India. She has given her *ashirvad* for this. So have no more concern, Mother will take care."

"What was it like for Mataji," I asked the manager, "being given so much spiritual responsibility at a very young age?"

"Mother has told us that she had a very difficult time," he replied, obviously happy to talk about his beloved guru. And as is the custom of high class Indians, he proceeded to deliver a speech inspired by my question, rather than a direct answer. "At first Upasani Maharaj's disciples refused to accept that a teenage girl could be his spiritual heir, equal to him in realization. For many years, she was tormented and criticized. Now the whole country respects her. When she visits a big city like Bombay, tens of thousands flock for her *darshan*. Many people believe that it was her prayers that saved India from invasion by the Chinese in 1962. At that time women were donating their gold on behalf of the nation. Mother sent a gold ring to Pandit Nehru with her blessing, and the promise that there would be a ceasefire within a few days. And indeed there was."

"And she was really a naked yogi in her previous birth? What a different life she has chosen this time!"

"Yes, Madam. In front of many disciples, myself included, Mother once revealed her true form as Dattatreya. She is *datta-vatar*, the incarnation of the Triple-faced God. As Gajanan Maharaj, the naked yogi, Dattatreya manifested as *avadhuta*, the one who has passed beyond all social and religious norms. Now, in the form of Godavari Ma, he has come to reveal the greatness and glory of woman. In order to liberate thousands of souls, that great yogi promised to take rebirth in a female body. For as Upasani Maharaj has taught, the woman who has realized her true nature has an unrivalled power to benefit humanity and lead others to Absolute Bliss. The mere sight of such a one can wipe away lifetimes of sins."

This was truly astonishing. After ten years in the Catholic Church, I was embittered about the spiritual disenfranchisement of women.

"You mean, I'm not spiritually second class, doomed to an unfortunate birth?"

The manager shook his hand, the Indian gesture of negation. "Not at all. According to Upasani Maharaj, your birth is the more fortunate. On account of our obstinate egos, we men must perform much *tapas*, much austerity, to attain the goal. But a woman innately knows that Absolute Bliss is her true nature. She has not to do severe penances; some *bhajan* and *puja*, some devotional singing and deity worship, and remembrance of the Holy Name whilst she performs her daily duties, this is enough to give her what a man can obtain only by great effort."

Now I understood why Raghudas had surrounded himself with an inner circle of women. Through our feminine nature, our inborn qualities of service and devotion, we furthered the work of the *sadguru*. As we went about our daily duties on the factory floor, hospital ward, ashram, home or village temple, Raghudas extended his blessings to everyone we met. We, the womenfolk, were chosen vessels of his grace. What a reversal! I, a liberated woman from the West, daughter of a feminist, had found in India—where the plight of women appeared to me pitiable indeed—the one key I needed. I had come from a world where women had won some social, but little spiritual, equality, to discover, in this remote Maharashtran village, a true feminine spirituality that restored to me the dignity I felt the Catholic Church had stolen from me. Hurrying over to the ashram bookstore, I purchased a volume of Upasani Maharaj's talks on the "glory of a woman's life".

Profoundly though Anandamayi Ma and Godavari Mataji had affected me, the interaction with my fellow pilgrims had been the most significant aspect of the journey. Hey Won, the monk, respected me as a nun, and encouraged me to remain as quiet, modest, and suppressed as ever. Heinz, the healer, saw in me a great healer, and insisted that I be more forthcoming and assertive in expressing this potential.

As for Francis, unfailingly frank and spontaneous, he, the barefoot little brother, as welcome in the shanties of the poor as in the homes of wealthy Poona brahmins, was all that I longed to be and feared to become—the free, untrammelled pilgrim who had passed beyond the bounds of limited religion and conventional culture. I was still far too modest to tell him about the voice in my heart and my immediate recognition of him. But now Francis was getting intuitions about me.

"I dreamt last night of you and Raghudas," he told me one morning. "The three of us were sitting together, you and I opposite one another at the base of a triangle, and Raghudas at the apex. A field of blue *shakti* enveloped us and circulated between us. The sexual energy was flowing, uniting us." I tried hard not to blush. "It didn't feel like a dream. It felt real. Perhaps," he added thoughtfully, "I shouldn't have told you about it. I was afraid you would get angry with me. I mean, you're a nun, and here I am talking about *shakti* and sexual energy." Though I was English enough to conceal my emotions, inwardly I was trembling with shock at his words.

When I returned to CPS ashram from the pilgrimage, two letters awaited me. One, from a Christian Swami, instructed me to proceed immediately to an ashram in Gujerat, "where you will have a hut and all you need for the hermit life. The Bishop will take care of you financially." The other letter was from a French lady, a former enclosed nun with whom I was acquainted, who wanted me to help her start an ashram beside the Indrayani, conveniently close to Raghudas.

Meanwhile, Francis approached me politely. "I am planning to make a pilgrimage to the sources of the Ganges, in the Himalayas. If you like, you can accompany me. I know you want to see the Himalayas, and it would be better for you to travel with an escort."

I gasped. Only a short while before, Raghudas had said to me, "Don't travel around alone. Stay with Francis. He will take care of you." I was a very independent young woman and had travelled alone to Stalinist Rumania at the age of twenty. Why did I now need a male escort? However, protection apart, there was no doubt that Francis would be a wonderful travelling companion. Should I take up one of the hermitages offered to me, or set off for the North with Francis?

"You will not have many opportunities to travel to the Himalayas with someone as spiritual as Francis," said Sister Brigite, as I discussed my situation with her over a cup of tea. Her words

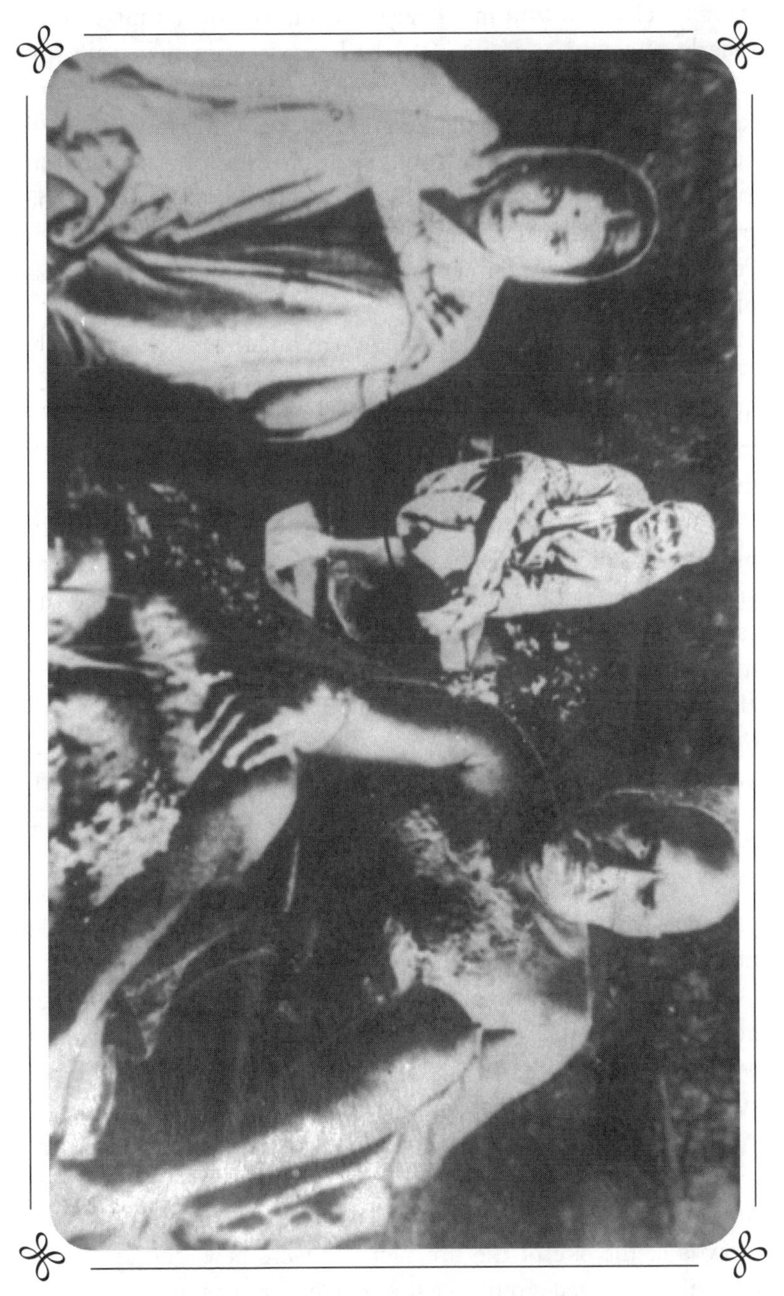

GODAVARI MATAJI, SAI BABA (CENTRE) AND UPASANI MAHARAJ

PHOTO COMPOSITE COURTESY OF SRI UPASANI KANYAKUMARI STHAN

struck a chord within me. I regarded Francis with a mixture of sisterly affection and awe. (If I had any feelings that were not purely sisterly, I hid them—even from myself.) Apart from Raghudas and Father Bede, he seemed one of the most evolved beings I had ever met. He could sit in meditation for hours on end. Everyone—the sisters at CPS ashram, Raghudas' disciples, the priests at the Dattatreya temple, Dr. Lad—respected Francis as a yogi and renunciant, for beneath his humility lay a true greatness of soul.

In practical affairs, Francis had the reputation of being unduly innocent; where spiritual life was concerned I obeyed his guidance implicitly. Why did such a lofty being want a simple novice like myself as a travelling companion? I sought Richard's counsel with this question.

"You too have something to offer Francis," said Richard. "In his previous life, Francis was a yogi living in a cave in the Himalayas. He practised tremendous austerity and fiercely avoided the society of women. Thus Francis is very developed spiritually, yet needs to become a little more rounded. By travelling to the Himalayas with a woman—particularly with you—he will learn the feminine softness and gentleness which you have so abundantly. And his influence will free you from your obsession with structure and orthodoxy. If you go with Francis, my prediction is this. The journey to the Himalayas will be of far more value than the arriving. And," he continued, giving me a penetrating look, "on your way to the Himalayas, you will find something which you do not yet know you need."

Richard's words gave me a shift of perspective. It had never occurred to me that *I* could be of help to Francis. But if Richard was right, what better service could I render to Raghudas than to support and assist his beloved disciple?

Whilst pondering on this matter, I went to spend a week at Alandi. It was late January, the sacred month of Magh, and a great fire sacrifice, the *mahavishnu yagna,* was in progress. The noise and crowds at the site of the fire sacrifice were bewildering. In the centre of the *yagna* grounds, a group of brahmins squatted around the sacred fire, chanting the Vedic mantras and throwing rice, sticks, sacred grass and ghee into the fire with cries of "*Svahah!*" It was almost impossible to hear the mantras, however, since on one side a hundred and eight brahmins were chanting Bhagavad Gita over a loudspeaker, and on the other side, a discourse on *Jnaneshvari* was being delivered over a loudspeaker at yet higher volume. Just as I felt that I could bear the noise no longer, in walked the local brass band. By the time they had finished their piece and marched out, I had to accept that the remaining sound level was, relatively speaking, quiet.

Every time I went to see Raghudas, he would ask, "Have you taken *prasad?*" If my answer was in the negative, he would send Akka and myself off to the *yagna* site to share some of the consecrated food. Thus, I lived for a week almost entirely on the *prasad* from the fire sacrifice. On one occasion, however, I was carried by the press of the crowd out of the *yagna* site to an adjacent meadow.

There must have been about five thousand villagers gathered there, the men dressed in baggy white pants, long shirt-tails and white caps or turbans; the women in deep-coloured saris—purple, indigo, royal blue, sea green. We sat in long rows on the ground, a leaf plate and little boat-shaped leaf bowl placed before each person. These utensils, made of freshly-dried leaves stitched together with grass, caught my fancy. What wonderful pieces of disposable, renewable, environmentally safe technology! About a hundred servers, tall, strong men wearing *dhotis*, filled the plates with *khicheri* (a rice and *dal* mix), *halvah* (a sweet dish made of farina), and fried sweets. In the bowls, they poured buttermilk. Meanwhile, five thousand voices joined in singing the name of Gopal, the cowherd God. It was a luxurious meal for peasants who lived on *bakeri* and pepper water, and the servers moved down the rows constantly, refilling plates. I had always wondered what it would have been like to be present at the feeding of the five thousand described in the gospel. Today, I felt that I was truly experiencing it. For me, this was more than a meal; it was a heavenly banquet.

On the last night of the *yagna*, as I lay on the floor in my room at Janabai Dharmsala, I had a kind of waking dream in which I saw Lord Vishnu in a form of golden light. I realized that the blessing of this vision was the result of my eating the *prasad* from the *mahavishnu yagna*. Appreciating the holiness of food offered in this context, I now understood why Raghudas had been so insistent on my taking the *prasad*.

Next morning, at the usual hour for my meditation with Raghudas, I was waiting outside 'Baba's cave'. Gondaliker, a brahmin sweet-seller from Poona who occupied a position of eminence among the disciples, was inside. Afraid to disturb him, I moved around the corner, well out of sight. However, I could not hide from Baba, who immediately sent for me. Raghudas had something important to say to me, and Gondaliker was to act as interpreter.

Waving his head reassuringly from side to side, he began, as Gondaliker interpreted, "Don't worry. We are not two. Yeshu and I are the same."

I was amazed. "You told me that in a dream, months ago."

"And now I am telling you in words."

I listened carefully.

"Today," Raghudas went on, "you must choose a *mantra*. Choose any one you wish. That is up to you. But once you take the Name, abide steadfastly in it. Your path is to keep the constant remembrance of God, to have the Holy Name always in your heart. What *mantra* do you choose?"

When I had come to see Baba on the festival of Makara Sankranti, the crowd of women with their bags of sweets to offer had made the whole temple noisy. Even inside the cave, I had not been able to meditate quietly. Suddenly, I had found myself repeating a *mantra* which combined one key word from the Hindu and one from the Christian tradition. Somehow, it had felt right.

"This will be my *mantra*," I told Baba, repeating the "Vedic-Christian" prayer.

Raghudas' hands became electric. Beams of silver light flashed toward me from his fingertips as he made a gesture of assent.

"That is it! That is right! This will bring her to understand that the two are both the same, that they are essentially one." I felt a sense of awe. Baba had never been to church or read the Bible. How could he possibly understand the significance of the semitic word which I had incorporated into the *mantra*? Yet undoubtedly he did understand, and far more deeply than I myself did.

"Repeat the *mantra* again." I repeated it.

"I have empowered this *mantra* for you to recite. Whenever you repeat it, I am with you. Never reveal this *mantra* to anyone. Not to your own mother, not even to Francis. Never change your practice, nor accept a *guru-mantra* from any other person. Henceforward, this is your path; do not waver in it. When you came to me, I did not speak to you of divorce, and today I tell you solemnly, I will never divorce you. I am the guru, you are the disciple, forever." I felt indescribably privileged. Raghudas very rarely claimed to be a guru.

"The covenant between us can never be broken; it will always endure. Abide steadfastly in it. I am your gardener, your guide, your guardian and protector, your teacher, your mother and your father. Everything that happens to you is known to me. So now, you must surrender completely. Don't keep any power for yourself. So long as you imagine that you are the Controller, the Doer, you will continue to be bound by the fruits of your actions. Instead, surrender to me, and actions can no longer bind you, for they are not the result of your own wishes and desires. You are the train, I am the signal master. And today, I say to you, 'Full Speed Ahead!'"

Only years later did I realize the significance of this statement. Adopting the cryptic metaphorical speech typical of Sai Baba of Shirdi and other Sufi masters, Raghudas was promising that I would not have to stop at any of the various planes of consciousness, that his grace alone would bring me to the journey's end.

"Our bond is now cemented, and you no longer need to remain here. Go wherever you wish. Go to the Himalayas, go to New York, anywhere. I will always be with you, wherever you go. My care and guidance will never fail you."

Tears were in my eyes as I left the dark chamber and blinked in the sunlight. It seemed unbelievable that such a graceful experience could have happened to me, barely a year after I had stepped off the plane at New Delhi Airport. On this day, I was truly a new person, for the guru had become both my mother and my father.

That evening, Francis joined me for Raghudas' *darshan* hour. Baba was sitting on the step outside his chamber, whilst Francis and I took our places on the mats below, facing one another, exactly as in the dream Francis had shared with me.

"Baba," Francis said, pointing towards me, "we were thinking of going to the Himalayas together."

Baba beamed. "Very good!" he replied. My doubts about the pilgrimage were finally settled. Difficult though it was to leave my friends at CPS Ashram, Dr. Lad, and above all my regular visits to Raghudas, the inner voice was clearly telling me that it was time to move, that the pilgrim way had lessons to teach me that I could not learn in the city.

The night before the pilgrimage was due to start, I had a dream in which I was setting off from the Alandi bus stand, in the company of Gondaliker. The full moon was shining, shedding a soft golden light all around. When I awoke, the sweet taste of the dream was still with me. I was journeying towards illumination, and fullness of being.

"O fragrant Lord of Sacrifice, you of the Three Eyes, free us from evil and the bonds of death, as the ripe fruit drops from the vine; free us, for immortality."

Mahamrtanjaya Mantra, from the *Vedas*

Three
The Triple-faced God

"I like Dattatreya very much," Francis told me, as we sat outside Poona's Datta Temple in the shade of the wild fig, the god's sacred tree. A beautiful, beardless youth of androgynous appearance, dressed in a gold silk *lungi*, Dattatreya has three heads and six arms. In his hands he carries the lotus of blooming creativity, the conch that holds and maintains all beings and the discus that protects them, the trident that destroys evil and the water pot containing the flood of final dissolution. He turns towards his devotees the face of Vishnu, the aspect of love and nurturance. Four dogs, representing the four *vedas,* sit at his feet, gazing up at him adoringly, whilst behind him stands a beautiful white cow, embodiment of the nurturing feminine principle.

"When I went to Goa with no visa and no money," Francis continued, "it was at the Datta Temple that I found refuge. Ever since then, he has been my patron. His three faces are the faces of Brahma, Vishnu and Shiva; Creator, Preserver and Destroyer, for he is the simultaneous *avatar* of all three. Isn't that the same as the Trinity?"

"There are many Christian theologians who would strongly disagree with that," I replied. "But for myself, I find it impossible to separate them. Dattatreya is so graceful, he seems to express the Dance, the mutual interpenetration of the Persons of the Trinity. When I was at the Abbey, I took the name, Olivia of the Trinity.

So we can both take Dattatreya for our patron on this pilgrimage, since he embodies the Trinity of India."

That evening in the ashram library, I read the story of the birth of Dattatreya. The story was a fascinating one, for it showed the tremendous spiritual power of the women sages of ancient times. Dattatreya's father, Sage Atri, was blessed to have as his wife the most beautiful woman in the world, Anasuya. More inclined by nature to prayer than to sexual adventures, Anasuya lived contentedly in their simple little hut, whilst kings on their beds at night dreamt of possessing her. Eventually, news of her beauty and chastity reached even the halls of heaven. Smitten with jealousy, Sarasvati, Lakshmi and Parvati incited their consorts, Brahma, Vishnu and Shiva, to destroy Anasuya's reputation. Descending to earth in the guise of aescetics, the three gods knocked on the door of Atri's hut, begging Anasuya for hospitality. The sage and his wife lived such a poor and austere life that there was no food in the house. Nonetheless, it was Anasuya's duty to feed wandering aescetics. The disguised gods, in order to break her chastity, demanded that she suckle them at her breast. "Certainly," she replied. "But first, all three of you must become babies." Since Anasuya always spoke truth, her words inevitably came true. Instantly, those great gods, Brahma, Vishnu and Shiva, were transformed by a human woman into helpless babies. Time passed, and the goddesses' consorts failed to return. Hurrying to Atri's house, the three Queens of Heaven found their beloveds happily gurgling and cooing on Anasuya's lap. She would allow them to assume their usual forms only when all three of them promised to take birth simultaneously as her son. From this boon, Dattatreya was born.

A few days later, I was sitting in meditation in the chapel at CPS, seeking some guidance for the way ahead, when three images emerged to consciousness: a round cave, rocks overhanging the entrance; a mosque with shining minaret; a carved stone fish, pointing west.

That night, taking out a clean notebook decorated with a picture of Sarasvati, Goddess of speech and poetry, I wrote the first words of a new journal, which I intended to keep as a record of my journey to the Himalayas. Though I did not know it at the time, it was to be the last journal I ever wrote as Olivia of the Trinity, the English Catholic nun.

21st February 1981

The Round Cave—the Orient, Hinduism and Buddhism, intuition, the Way of Wisdom; Aum, the Word, in the silent darkness of the Cave of the Heart. The Stone Fish—carefully chiselled form; Christendom, Roman culture, the West; mind and hands, doctrine and codification, the Way of Work. And between them, the Middle East, Islam. Uniting the hands and the Eye, the Heart, compassionate, passionate, open to joy and to pain; joining Wisdom and Work, the Way of Love. Formless, unmanifest, beyond all, within all, drawing all to Himself in the Cave, the Father. Taking form, swimming out from the primal sea, deliverer, saviour, Word. Falling on the Prophets, fanning flame in the Heart, sweeping all things together, Spirit. The Cave, the Fish, the Minaret, three roads that meet on the way to the Triple-faced God.

Shiva enters our consciousness. He comes in our sleep, our dreams, broods over the image of Dattatreya. The streams flow into the Ocean; in the Tomb, the Cave, the Darkness, all roads end, all paths begin. For He whose hands heal and restore, She of the passionate heart, is ultimately That which draws all to Itself in the Cave. Our pilgrimage, a journey from Vishnu to Shiva, for Alandi is the heart of Vishnu's land, the Himalayas the abode of Shiva. A journey and a return of the changed, nail in the hands, sword in the heart, who seek the new perceiving, the Single Eye. A search for the poise, the Dance, the way to the Triple-faced God—and Beyond.

It was late February, and the Himalayan passes would be snowbound until May. Francis, however, was eager to be moving. Because of his visa problems, he did not like to stay too long in one place lest the local police hear about him. Our plan, therefore, was to spend about a month visiting some of the chief holy places in Maharashtra, and then to go North to Varanasi and Calcutta, reaching Rishikesh, at the base of the Himalayas, just as the passes opened. Meanwhile, we would be looking for a suitable spot for my hermitage. By the time the monsoon broke, in July, our pilgrimage would be completed—or so we thought. Francis would then see me safely settled in my solitary hut before he departed to America to visit his parents.

The connection between us seemed to be deepening day by day; yet each of us had our own agendas. I was bent upon the celibate hermit way; Francis was a *sadhu,* a yogi, and felt that too much involvement with women would drag him into worldly life. The idea that our intimate connection would last for only six months or so, after which we would go our separate ways, was a safety net for both of us. Yet all the while, the voice in my heart was whispering, *"Remember! This man is your lifelong companion."*

Our first destination was the site of Bhaja caves, the oldest Buddhist cave temples and meditation cells in the Deccan. Taking the Poona-Bombay passenger train to a small station set amid rice fields in the Western Ghats, a rugged mountain range, we climbed up a steep and rocky path just before sunset, carrying our bed rolls. It was twilight by the time we began exploring the caves. At first, I was disappointed. All the caves were rectangular, with a square-cut door and lintel. Then suddenly, right at the end of the group of caves, there it was, the cave I had seen in my meditation.

26th February 1981

It is a round cave. The cliff face overhangs the entrance arch. I have never walked down this path before, yet I recognize it instantly. The hills, the rocky ground, the scrubby bushes near the entrance, the Round Cave; for years this landscape and this cave have formed from my paintbrush or pencil, have beckoned to me from the land of the heart. Awed and trembling, I enter. We enter together. From here, our pilgrimage begins, a journey to new life.

Innumerable stars. We stand outside the main hall of the monastery. The arch gleams in the starlight. Within it, the Void, Nirvana. Dreadful, dreadful yet compelling, the movement through the glittering arch, into the formless dark. And the return. The arch an edge of darkness, and through it, the starlit world appearing: shapes of hills, patchwork of fields, a gleam of wings. Innumerable stars, infinite forms. From the shining arch to the dark, from definition to the void, utter emptiness, limitless possibility, Shiva. From the edge of darkness to the starlit forms, from the unmanifest to the manifest, countless loves, countless limitations, Vishnu. To find the poise between the edge of darkness and the gleaming arch, the formless and infinity of forms, freedom and commitment, distance and involvement, this is our pilgrimage.

The moon rises over the cliff as we return to the Round Cave. It is the Silent Tomb, the journey from Being to Non-Being. It is prakriti *unmanifest, empty, full of the seeds of life. It is the Womb, the journey from Non-Being to Being. It is the Sepulchre, the place of passage, the journey from darkness to Light, from death to Immortality. The Round Cave, silent nurturer, receptive emptiness, fruitful darkness, womb of earth, the Mother. I am that. Above the cliff, the moon rises, lighting our journey to new life.*

Next morning, as I was rolling up the blue cotton mat and colourful quilt made from patches of old saris that served as my bed, I noticed something tied in an orange cloth, hanging from a nearby tree.

"What's that?" I asked Francis.

"Oh, it's my passport," he replied, with some disgust. "I was kind of hoping I would forget it, get rid of it somehow. I'm fed up with being illegal and worrying about the police putting me in jail. And I've been sick so much, and you can't get clean drinking water in jail, which means I could easily die there."

"Losing your passport won't help. It's illegal to travel without one."

Francis thought for a moment.

"You know," he said, "I have such intense aversion to all that my passport symbolizes, it's almost like I *want* to lose it. Could you carry it for me?"

I carefully wrapped both passports, the cheque for a hundred dollars that Francis' parents had sent him for Christmas, and the remainder of my money and traveller's cheques—about a hundred and fifty pounds—in the orange cloth and tied them round my waist. Even the traveller's cheque records were wrapped in the same cloth. I was breaking the most elementary rule of safe travel: 'Divide your money.' And I was not to be let off lightly.

The brahmin family with whom Francis had spent a year lived near Bhaja caves in a remote village at the base of the Western

Ghats. We stayed on the porch of their ramshackle brick farmhouse for a couple of days, in the world of householders: the shy young bride, who seemed little more than an unpaid servant, the arrogant teenage sons, the two dogs, 'Jackie' and 'Bruce Lee', the water buffalo that provided the family with milk, the servants slapping laundry upon a stone, the womenfolk endlessly cooking, preparing a bewildering variety of dishes for meals and snacks.

1st March 1981

The householder state is a life of much love and many bondages, a life enclosed in the structure, the house, caught in the limitations of form, Vishnu. And the traditional sannyasi *life: ultimate freedom, yet coldness of heart, the life of a bird with no branch to rest on, a quest of That which has no form to love, Shiva. To seek the poise between these two* ashramas, *two ways of life, the reconciliation of opposites in a life of love and liberty; to find the gleaming arch that spans the formless dark, to know the edge of darkness, wrapping in mystery the world of forms, such is our journey.*

The mother of the family was one of Francis' few friends who actually had a bank account. She cashed the cheque from his parents for him, giving him eight hundred rupees in cash, and a cheque for eight hundred rupees drawn on her account, which he would be able to encash in three months, after the deposit cleared.

The dark of the moon was approaching, and with it the Great Night of Shiva, Mahashivaratri, when a *mela,* or religious fair, would be held at the remote mountain shrine of Bhima Shankar, sacred to Lord Shiva. After asking directions from numerous people, we set off by way of Kurjat to Kamdao village. "Half an hour's walking," we were told, would bring us from Kamdao to Bhima Shankar. As we began the climb, my *chappals* suddenly broke, so that I, like Francis, had to walk barefoot. We climbed half an hour, an hour, uphill in the noonday heat, over burning rocks and scorching sand, whilst party upon party of hardy peasants overtook us. At length we met a group of pilgrims who spoke English, and politely informed us that Bhima Shankar lay fifteen miles ahead, at an altitude of eleven thousand feet. We had fasted on watermelon the previous day, indeed, Francis had fasted the previous two days, and we had no provisions, about a cupful of water, and our cloth bags and bedrolls.

Reflecting grimly that it was, after all, Shrove Tuesday, and a good day to begin our Lenten penance, we toiled on, dizzy with thirst, begging occasional sips of water from fellow pilgrims. Gasping my *mantra* at each step, I tried to raise my mind from my blistered feet to the incredible beauty of Shiva's mountains. Hours passed; still we walked. Darkness fell; still we were stumbling along. I thought I heard the swish of some large beast of prey, a mountain lion or tiger, stalking through the undergrowth. At last, at a turn of the road, we heard voices and saw lamplight and two huts. Here we were supplied with drinking water, tea and bananas.

As we laid out our beds and sat gazing at the brilliant stars, Francis said to me, "I think I can hear angels. There's a faint sound of music."

I listened. "It can't be angels, because I can hear it, too, quite distinctly. There are people singing. They must have a loud-speaker."

We listened more carefully. High pitched women's voices were singing in harmony, a choral sound completely foreign to India, to the accompaniment of sitars and harps. The music, a unique blend of Eastern and Western elements, was sometimes almost deafeningly loud, at other times barely audible, and behind it was a ringing and humming, like the music of the spheres. Eventually, even I agreed that the sound must really be an angelic choir. When we finally reached Bhima Shankar the next day, we found that the little pilgrimage centre had no electricity, no generators and no loudspeakers. We asked everyone we met about last night's music, and were answered with blank stares. No one had heard any music faintly resembling the choir we listened to that night. All around us was wilderness, the abode of wild boar and panthers. No women's choirs had been singing with sitars and harps anywhere in the area. With senses sharpened by fasting, Francis and I truly must have heard the music of angels.

Ash Wednesday dawned, and we climbed to the crest of the mountain before the heat of the day, and then walked along a stony forest path. After the rugged beauty of the wilderness, we arrived at last at Bhima Shankar, crowded with ash-smeared *sadhus*, pilgrims and layfolk. We had reached our goal, purified more by the journeying than the arriving. Draped in a *lungi*, I plunged, in company with jostling Indian women, into the 'sacred tank', a rectangular stone bathing pool, whose waters are drawn from the very source of the Bhima River. Now I was ready to enter the temple and bow before the *linga*.

"This is a *jyotirlinga*, a pillar of light," Francis explained to me. "It is told that here, at the site of the light *linga*, the earth split open and an infinite column of light appeared, having neither top nor bottom. This column of light is actually the full manifestation of Shiva, whilst the Shiva-Shankar whose picture you see on the walls of temples and teashops, the ash-smeared yogi clad in tiger skin, with cobras coiled about his arms and throat and a trident in his hand—that form is the partial or qualified manifestation of Shiva. I have heard that there are twelve such *jyotirlingas* throughout the length and breadth of India."

4th March 1981

As I touch the linga, *I receive a burst of energy; peace, light, warmth, a glimmer through the Eye. Shiva is fire, light, brilliance, both tapas, the heat of aesceticism, and* tejas, *the radiance of the Adept. He is the scorching noonday sun, the black rocks that burn the feet, light from the* linga, *the piercing light of the Eye. He is the sacred fire the sadhus tend, and the relentless fire in the heart, burning all secondary things, consuming all that is not That. Our God, a consuming fire. Ash Wednesday.*

Hearing that we had fasted the previous two days, a kindly passerby led us a little way down the mountain, to one of Bhima Shankar's few permanent structures, the home of the temple priest. The father of the house was extremely kind. Apologetically, he explained that, since this was a fast day, no rice, *dal* or *chapatis* had been prepared. Could we content ourselves with the little they had, merely some fried tapioca pearls and potato *bhaji?* It was a wonderful meal, and served with great love.

Clustered near the Shiva temple were homes of the priests, temporary booths erected for the *mela,* and some aescetics' huts. Further uphill, we found a small, dark Dattatreya temple, to which was attached a mud-walled shelter for the half dozen sadhus who were caretakers of the image of the Triple-faced God. Entering the building, we saw a number of ochre-robed ascetics seated around their *dhuni,* the sacred fire. By the large bone rings in their slit ears and the bone whistles hanging from black cords on their chests, we recognized them as members of the *kaphata* or 'slit-eared' sect, popularly known as Nath Babas, because their names all end in Nath, 'Lord'. They are practitioners of the esoteric tantric yoga of Gorakhnath, and devotees of Dattatreya.

One of the *sadhus* immediately recognized Francis from the Adha Kumbha Mela at Nasik, and invited him to join the circle around the fire. I stood on the fringe, hesitating. This was a test case. Would the *sadhus* accept me? And would they accept Francis, once they realized that he was travelling with a woman?

"Oh, by the way, this is my sister, my godsister," said Francis, barely glancing at me as he waved a hand in my direction. Although he had invited me to join his pilgrimage and was happy to offer me protection, he did not want to lose the respect of his *sadhu* brothers, who are supposed to shun women. In their presence, he was distancing himself from me.

At his words, a heated debate broke out among the aescetics. Should the woman be allowed to join the circle or not? The case was settled in my favour, and I took my place beside the *dhuni.* Indeed, I was eventually given the honour of unrolling my bedding beside the sacred fire, at a suitable distance from Francis and the *sadhus*. It was a cold night at eleven thousand feet, and I was glad of the warmth from the embers.

Instead of leaving Bhima Shankar on foot by the back-country route, we planned to travel by bus and train, a roundabout trip. A huge crowd was assembled at the bus stop, and, hampered by our lack of language, we continually missed our turn, and did not get a bus until after dark. Our companion in misfortune was one of the Nath Babas, and as we could not possibly reach our destination that night, we got down at his village and passed the night in his little hut beside a river.

At the railway station, we learned of a terrible train crash the previous day, on the very line on which we would have been travelling, had we been able to get an earlier bus. I was beginning to learn that what seemed to be misfortune might actually be divine protection.

Returning to Poona, we took "permission to go" from Raghudas, who gave his blessings for the journey to the Himalayas. We also said our farewells to Sisters Sara, Arati, Brigite, Columba, Elisha and Archana. For me, it was a significant moment. Up to now, I had passed my entire time in India, exactly one year, in the Christian environment of Shantivanam and CPS ashram. Now, for the first time in my life, I was stepping beyond the confines of the Christian world, out on to the roads of India, for a strange new encounter with Christ, who seemed so palpably present in this land of the cosmic religion. Here were the fingerless lepers living in their hovels "outside the camp", the good-hearted harlots, the blind beggars, the pious old widows, the erudite and spotlessly clean members of the priestly caste, great temples and fire sacrifices, crowds assembling for some annual festival. And here were those whom Jesus loved, the children, everywhere on the village streets; plump, naked toddlers and beautiful children with *khajal* around their bright inquisitive eyes, never too small to be carrying in the crook of an arm a smaller child, or a curly-haired baby with sunbonnet and tiny anklets.

After travelling by bus about a hundred miles north of Poona, we came to Nasik on the Godavari River—situated, it is said, at the spot where Ram, Sita and Lakshman, wandering in the Dandarka forest, met a hideous demoness. When she insisted on having one of the brothers for her husband, Lakshman sliced off her nose. The furious demoness, returning home to her brother Ravana, incited him to abduct Sita to Lanka, thus setting in motion the great drama of the *Ramayana*.

On our arrival, we bought some bananas and ground nuts in the bazaar and found a chay shop, where we could drink warm milk with our simple lunch. Inside the chay shop, which called itself 'Imperial Grand Hotel', it was dark, hot and humid. Flies buzzed around the heaps of sweets, dirt was caked on the refrigerator; pictures of Krishna among the milkmaids adorned the walls. Workmen slurped tea, drinking out of saucers; a mangy stray dog wandered in, looking for scraps.

"*Apka desh kaun hai?* (What's your country?)" asked the proprietor in Hindi as we placed our order.

"*Kaun desh?* (Which country?)" asked the ragged boy who brought us sweet, watery buffalo milk.

A man of about fifty entered and seated himself on the bench opposite us.

"Where do you come from?" he asked.

"America," answered Francis.

"England," I said.

"Ah, yes." He gave me a polite but cold smile. "The English. Our former rulers." I could sense the hatred beneath his polished manners.

"I wish they had never left," muttered an old man at the next table. "When the British were here, the trains ran on time. Now, the whole country has gone to the dogs."

Irritated, the man sitting opposite us quickly finished his tea and left.

"I'm tired of this," I said to Francis. "I'm tired of being blamed for the British Raj. I'm tired of saying, 'I come from England,' twenty times an hour."

"I know," Francis sighed. "It gets to be like a *mantra*. 'I come from England,' 'I come from America.' And it isn't even true. That's all *maya*, all illusion. You don't come from England. You come from *brahman*."

I thought for a moment.

"Well, in that case, I want to speak the truth. I'm not going to talk about my country of origin any more, since it's all *maya* anyway."

Francis smiled. "Okay, that's a great idea. I'm with you. We won't speak of our past countries again."

A high class gentleman dressed in spotless white came in. Stopping by our table he asked, "From what country do you come?"

I took a deep breath.

"The universe is my home," I said firmly.

The brahmin gentleman smiled.

"Very good, very good. In Marathi we have a saying, *'Vishvaje muje ghar.'* It means exactly that, 'The universe is my home.' You have definitely taken to a spiritual way of life."

From that moment on, *'Vishvaje muje ghar'* was our answer to the inevitable questions about nationality.

It was a warm spring day, and the riverfront at Nasik was a lively and colourful place. Temple bells were clanging, worshippers chanting, dogs barking, children playing, bathers performing their ablutions, women slapping laundry, whilst saris, green, blue, purple and gold, lay drying in the sun. Men scrubbed the sleek, dark coats of water buffaloes, ascetics squatted by the river's edge to scour their brass vessels with mud, vendors rang handbells to advertise their wares, and beggars pathetically displayed a picture of Ram or Hanuman. We in our turn descended the slippery steps to bathe in the Godavari, and then visited various of the riverside temples. As we wandered past them, the *sadhus* sitting over their *dhunis* would wave a hand and cry, *"Bas, bas!* (Sit down!)" Immediately, a blackened pot would be placed over the fire, and tea prepared and solemnly offered to us.

Toward sunset, Francis, who was familiar with Nasik, led us outside the city to Panchvati, where several tributaries of the Godavari meet. The confluence is a privileged spot for aescetic practices, and here we spent the night at an ashram of white-robed *vairagis,* renunciate devotees of Ram. The *vairagis* welcomed us hospitably, and fed us on *kheer,* or sweet milk rice.

Very shy of staying with *sadhus,* I rolled out my bed by the *tulasi* plant which grew on a stone stand in the temple courtyard.

"Tandi, tandi! (Cold, cold!)" cried one of the *sadhus,* rushing over to me. The March nights were still chilly, so he wanted me to sleep inside the temple where Francis and the *sadhus* were spending the night. So as usual, I spread my patchwork quilt out a few yards from Francis' goat hair blanket. He and I were together twenty four hours a day, almost always sleeping in the same quarters, yet steadfastly observing the utmost decorum; I the modest nun, he the yogi aloof from woman and her snares.

At four in the morning, we all woke to the sound of a conch shell blown by one of the *sadhus*. We rolled up our beds and took an icy dip in the Godavari, before celebrating *arati*, which was accompanied by a long hymn in praise of Ram, with much ringing of bells and beating of drums and gongs. The ceremony was followed by the inevitable milky chay, the customary breakfast of most Indians, *sadhus* and layfolk alike.

Francis was eager to show me a holy place he loved better than any other, Tryambakeshvar, where he had attended the *adha kumbha mela*. Squeezing ourselves, along with perhaps a dozen others, into a public taxi, we made our way up the winding road into the hills above Nasik. Just as I felt about to suffocate, we reached Tryambakeshvar, one of the twelve *jyotirlinga*. In place of the usual single black column, the light *linga* of Tryambakeshvar, echoing the sacred geography of the place, is a hollow containing three small mounds, representative of the triple peaks which tower above.

14th March 1981

Tryambakeshvar, at the source of the Godavari. A morning bath at the sacred tank, for hundreds of years a bathing place of the utmost holiness. Godavari, mother, nurturer, bountiful one, giver of food and life, the feminine power of this holy place, the river within the Bowl. And the triple crags, the triple lingas; *Brahma, Vishnu, Shiva. The landscape of Shiva, the wilderness, burning rocks, yet always seeking the balance, the poise, the dance; the* linga, *formless forms of the Triple-faced God.*

In the temple, the priests chanted "*Aum Tryambakam Yejamahai*... O fragrant three-eyed Lord of sacrifice, free us from evil and the bonds of death; as the ripe fruit drops from the vine." Tryambakeshvar is the Lord of the Three Eyes, the three ways of seeing. His *mantra*, which I already knew by heart, since we had chanted it each morning at Shantivanam, entered my being in a new way at Tryambakeshvar.

By the time we had circumambulated the temple, had *darshan* of the *linga*, and sat for some time in the outer court chanting,

"Aum Bhagavan," the sun was high in the sky, and we were hungry. A passing *sadhu* directed us to the house of a learned brahmin, who, he said, was dedicated to the fivefold sacrifice of the Vedas. This brahmin, the *sadhu* explained, was renowned throughout Maharashtra for his skill in conducting the Vedic fire sacrifice, and was equally careful to fulfill the sacrifice of hospitality. Each day his wife prepared a big pot of *khicheri,* which he himself served to pilgrims, ascetics and beggars. Accordingly, we climbed uphill to his house. In the courtyard we found the brahmin, a slight, quiet, humble man, who served us very courteously. We were lucky, for *khicheri,* an Ayurvedic preparation made from rice and *dal,* is a very easily digestible food. Francis was still suffering from the poor health that had troubled him ever since he watched the fighting in Kabul, and since neither of us could tolerate chilies, ubiquitous in Indian food, we often went hungry. After eating our fill, we continued up the hill in search of accommodation.

Eventually we came to Nirmal Akara, the ashram of a Sikh *sannyasi,* who offered us hospitality for a few days. Nirmal Swami was a young man who spoke fluent English and had formerly, he said, been a wealthy doctor. He still had many of the habits of his previous life, as I was soon able to observe. Francis and I slept on the veranda, and each morning I woke at dawn, sat for meditation, and practiced yoga *asanas.* Eventually, a little before nine, our host emerged from his bedroom, and from my corner, I would watch his morning *'sadhana'* with fascination.

When he appeared, his jaw would be tied up in a strange-looking cloth, which, I soon discovered, was a beard press. Removing it, he would comb and preen his beard in front of a mirror until it followed the classic curve. The twirling and waxing of the moustache next received his attention, then the solemn winding of a big orange turban. Adjusting his dress, an orange polyester *kurta* and *lungi,* with not one wrinkle, Nirmal Swami then donned his embroidered slippers and took up his ebony and silver cane. Thus attired, he was ready to conduct us a few hundred yards up the dirt track to visit the *vairagi sadhus,* with whom Swamiji liked to smoke *ganja.*

So there we would sit, on the beaten earth floor of the *vairagi math* or monastery, accommodated on hessian sacks. The *vairagis*, wheezy old men with yellowish-white matted locks, wearing threadbare yellowish-white cloth, noisily slurped their tea from saucers, while Nirmal Swami, seated in a perfect posture upon his sack, his expression calmly aloof, elegantly sipped from a cracked cup.

"Since your digestion is bad, please go to the bazaar and bring some milk for yourself," said Nirmal Swami to Francis, one evening a little past sunset. Innocently, Francis set off for the bazaar. "But our Olivia is hungry," said Swamiji, as soon as Francis was gone, turning to me with a suggestive lift to his eyebrows. "She will dine with me." So saying, he threw open the door to his inner rooms, where dinner for two was carefully laid out. What a breach of Indian etiquette! How could I possibly dine alone with a Swami, in a closed room? But I was too shy to demur, so in a few moments, there I was, much embarrassed, sitting at table—a strange Western affectation here—eating *nan* bread and mung *dal*, and trying to fend off Swamiji's charming and amorous remarks. Saying that I was tired and had little appetite, I rose from the table.

Nirmal Swami followed me, pouting his lips and begging, "One kiss!" I was shocked. This was too much from one who wore the ochre. Pointing to my yellow cloth, I declared hotly, "*I am brahmacharini!*" and fled to the veranda. My host followed and sat on the bench beside me, entertaining me with the story of Krishna and his sixteen thousand wives.

"Yet Krishna was a great *brahmachari*. You see, *brahmacharya* is something internal, not physical," he continued persuasively.

Moving further down the bench out of Swamiji's reach, I sat up in the half lotus. It was my turn to maintain a perfect posture and calmly aloof gaze, now markedly lacking in my host, as I tried to prevent myself giggling at the incongruousness of it all. When would Francis be back? But my trials did not end with his return. Swamiji promptly brought both of us into his room, put a jazz record at full volume on his gramophone, and invited both of us to dance. Francis, who was still innocent, happily danced, and tried to persuade me to do the same. I sat in a corner, trying to keep well out of the way.

"Why do you have to keep telling these lecherous *sadhus* that I'm your sister?" I practically yelled at poor Francis, when we were finally alone. Pouring out the whole story, I demanded, "Why can't you just leave our relationship vague and ambiguous, so that people can draw their own conclusions? Those with lustful minds will conclude I'm your woman. They won't risk your anger by making a pass at me. When you spell it out that I'm your sister, they think I'm up for grabs! They probably think I'm *wanting* some kind of sexual attention from them."

Francis could not help laughing at the absurdity of Swamiji's behaviour. After all, I had come to no harm, nor been in serious danger.

"But we can't leave ambiguity in the minds of our Indian friends," he said, wiping his eyes and becoming serious again. "There are only two categories here, culturally speaking, married householders and celibate renunciants. If we leave things hazy, the people we are here to learn from will call us 'Rajneeshis' and shut the door in our faces."

It was true. As foreigners, we were always suspect. And the irony of it all was that the *sadhus*, who scorned the society of women, could often not restrain themselves in the presence of even the most chaste female, whilst Francis, who was breaking the rules by travelling with a woman, was a genuine yogi and sincere *brahmachari* who respected me for the nun that I was.

As the full moon approached, a family of poor and intensely devout villagers who ran a makeshift tea stall opposite Nirmal Akara advised us to climb the mountain to the hilltop shrine, Brahma Giri. A stout young man with a soft, beardless face sat by his begging bowl at the edge of the dirt track, dressed only in an ochre loincloth. He looked so unmanly that at first I thought he was a very immodestly dressed woman, until Francis explained to me that he was a eunuch. With a shy charm, the eunuch smiled and waved as we walked past him to begin our climb.

19th March 1981

Ascent of the mountain to the headwaters of the Godavari. Towards sunset, we reach the first of the rock shrines, where water sweet as nectar trickles from the bull's mouth. In the subterranean cave below, the infant river. The mountain, the crags, not solid, but full of hidden water: in the womb of earth, the unborn river sleeps. We gaze down at Tryambakeshvar village. Bowl and crags, passive and active, emptiness and form, the bowl patterned with forms—temple, cottage, tree—the crags porous, containing emptiness.

We sat at the rock shrine, watching the light of the setting sun glint on lakes, streams and irrigation ditches. "Those are the sparkles on Parvati's sari," murmured Francis, as we gazed down upon the valley. Climbing on, we reached the monkey shrine, a little way above the cave where the underground river flowed. Here, the sacred monkeys of Tryambakeshvar scampered over a great statue of Hanuman, the monkey god, while sweet, cool water flowed from another spring. We lingered, watching the monkeys play and feeling a great energy of love, like the beating of the strong heart of Hanuman, until the moon had climbed some distance up the sky, shedding enough light for us to continue our ascent.

I puffed and struggled to keep up as the path climbed steeply to a great cleft rock. Once we had passed through this rock, the way was less steep, and the path, glittering in the moonlight as if made from tiny diamonds, swept on for a couple more miles, past shimmering stones and great white boulders breathing moonlight, to Brahma Giri, the summit of the light *linga.*

Here, it is told, Gautama Rishi, one of India's legendary Seven Sages, together with his wife Ahilya, performed penance for ten thousand years. In time of terrible drought, they won from Varuna, the Lord of Waters, the perennial spring that flows on the hilltop. Gautama Rishi immersed himself in spiritual practices, meditating, fasting and performing all kinds of austerities. Meanwhile, Ahilya, an eminently practical woman, took care of the hermitage, gathered fruits and roots, fed and milked the cow, wove flower garlands, prepared medicines, made garments, gave hospitality to nearby aescetics and tended to her husband's needs. At length, Shiva himself, accompanied by his beloved Ganga, appeared to Gautama and Ahilya.

"Great is the penance of Gautama Rishi," they said, "but

greater still is the service of Ahilya. Oh noblest of women, ask for any boon you desire."

"Dwell here for ever, O Shiva, O Ganga," replied Ahilya, "that we and all who come after us may serve you and receive your *darshan.*"

"As you ask, so shall it be," the divine pair replied. "Here we will dwell forever, to bless all who pass this way."

We had arrived at Brahma Giri just in time for Holi, the spring Festival, and the mountain top was crowded with pilgrims: young factory workers from Nasik; older men with *dhotis* tucked up above their knees for the climb; farmers in shirt-tails and Gandhi caps; little girls in frilly dresses; women carrying steel tiffin boxes full of rice and *dal;* grandmothers toiling up the steep track. Meanwhile, in the village below, youths were assembling wood for the great bonfires which would be kindled at nightfall, to burn up the sorceress Holika whose destruction is celebrated during the festival. In search of a quiet spot for meditation, Francis and I descended as far as Gorakhnath's cave, midway down the mountain, where seven centuries previously the young Nivrittinath, the elder brother and guru of Sant Jnaneshvar, had met his guru, the great Gahininath. At this cave, I meditated on the three *gunas* or modes of nature—*sattva,* the mode of Goodness; *rajas,* the mode of passion; and *tamas,* the mode of ignorance. To me, the cave embodied the state of transcendence, beyond the three *gunas,* beyond the white, the red, the black.

21st/22nd March 1981

Moonlight and firelight, Holi. The moonlight—clarity, purity, sattva, *filling the empty bowl, highlighting forms distinctly, sharply, yet with calm detachment. Below, in the valley, the red fires leaping, dancing, voices shouting, passion, excitement—*rajas. *And we midway up the mountain, beneath the moon, above the fires, outside the darkness of the Cave. Midway up the mountain, within and beyond the* gunas, *in sight and hearing of the valley, yet distanced, gaining perspective. Midway up the mountain, aware of both peaks and plain, not immersed in the world nor in flight from it, but in search of the poise, the Dance; love and liberty united in the Cave, the open heart.*

Sunrise, and a bath at the source of the Godavari. Living water, water from rock, the cleft rock, the wounded heart. 'From his side shall flow streams of living water,' the inexhaustible fountain at the Heart of the Universe, stream that pours through the wound of compassion, where the rock of our being is willingly cleft.

It was the Third Sunday of Lent. The people in the mission stations of the plains and the sisters at CPS Ashram must have been listening to the words of the 'Great Gospel', "The water that I shall give him will become in him a spring of water, welling up to eternal life."

22nd March 1981

A morning scrambling above the cliffs; on the ridge between two valleys, the one patterned with villages, temples and farms, the other wild, remote, inhabited only by tribals. A lake shines blue in the distance; the sun climbs. We explore the ridge of triple peaks, the lingas, in a landscape of triple hills, triple crags, triple faces of the rock spirits. There is not just a twin-ness but a tripleness in things. The world of the multiple hides and reveals the rhythm, the dance, of the three that is only One; for there are, in the end, no opposites, no partners in the Dance of Love.

Night vigil at the Cave, midway up the mountain, at the point of struggle, tension, between peak and plain. Beneath the stars, above the village, where hawk and swallow nest, on the cross of the human condition, centre of struggle and reconciliation.

We had fasted on Sunday out of sheer expediency. Tourists from Bombay were everywhere, and the deserted knife-edge ridge was the only quiet place. Now, as we had vowed to fast in honour of Shiva on all the Mondays of Lent, we remained at the cave, watching the thin, bluish veil of smoke from cowdung cooking fires waft over the valley, the hawks wheel, and the gilded pinnacle of the temple glitter in the sun. Towards sunset, we descended to the teashop at the bottom of the track and sipped lemon tea. Inviting us to spend the night with them at the tea stall, which doubled as their home, the family explained that the following day was very auspicious for the worship of Ganesha.

Everyone in Tryambakeshvar would be fasting, and we should definitely continue to fast. Although I was very attached to food, I was coming to accept that fasting was an integral part of the *jyotirlinga* experience.

Next morning, as we took the dirt road back to the village, we saw a short, thin old woman with matted hair walking in the other direction. She had the sunken nose of a leper. "*Ananda, ananda!* (Bliss, bliss!)" she cried, her beaming smile revealing broken and blackened teeth. And she immediately turned around and accompanied us back to the village, chatting in unintelligible broken Hindi. Because of her joyous nature, we named her the "Blissful Leper".

As we arrived in the bazaar, looking for a public taxi to take us to Nasik, we saw a young blond woman wearing an elegant black punjabi suit and silver jewellery. Our eyes met, and we recognized each other as kindred spirits. Rushing over, she greeted us.

"My name's Lakshmi. I'm from America, and I'm here guiding a tour of psychics to sacred sites in India. They have three shopping days, so I came here. I used to be a *sadhu* like you guys. I lived here in Tryambakeshvar and in Gujerat. Have you met the Naga Babas yet?"

Within minutes, Francis and I decided to stay two extra days in Tryambakeshvar, to enjoy Lakshmi's company. Buying some vegetables in the bazaar to offer to the *sadhus,* we followed our new friend to the Naga Babas' ashram. I tried not to stare or look shocked on finding myself surrounded by eight completely naked men, smeared with ash, long matted locks coiled on their heads. The Nagas recognized Lakshmi, and were totally unembarrassed by the presence of two women. They just continued sitting by their sacred fire, drinking chay, smoking chillum and coughing as they smoked. We cut the vegetables we had brought them, and one of the *sadhus* cooked lunch, whilst another shaped *chapatis,* patting them in his hands.

Soon Lakshmi and I were chatting together. I told her about my strange experience with Nirmal Swami. At once she burst out laughing.

"Oh no! He tried it on you, too! I met him when first I came to Tryambakeshvar, the day before I met you. And he did exactly the same line, about Krishna and the sixteen thousand wives! But you're so modest, so much the *brahmacharini!* I can't believe he dared to do a number like that on you!"

That evening, Lakshmi led us over to the hilltop temple of Dattatreya. While Francis sat immersed in meditation before the image of the Triple-faced God, she and I stood on the balcony of the temple, watching the sunset. As the first star appeared, she began softly chanting the mantra of Tryambakeshvar.

"Aum Tryambakam yejamahai..."

I joined in. *"Mrityor mukshiya mamritat."*

Lakshmi stared at me. "Where did you learn that *mantra?*"

"At a Christian ashram in South India."

She giggled. "Sounds like a funny place to learn one of the greatest *mantras* in the *vedas.*"

"Not so funny," I shrugged. "Where did you learn it?"

"From the most radiant, loving being I've ever met. His name is Shree, and he teaches the Vedic fire sacrifice to everyone—foreigners, untouchables, everyone."

My heart gave a leap. That same inner voice which had recognized Francis, Raghudas and Dr. Lad was speaking.

"Listen. This is very important. You must meet Shree. You must learn the fire sacrifice."

Yet somehow in the excitement of two days spent cooking with the *sadhus,* meditating in the Datta temple, and walking, talking and sharing with my beloved new friend, another woman who was truly interested in *sadhus,* pilgrimage and aescetic practices, I forgot about getting Shree's address until it was too late, and we had waved goodbye to Lakshmi's taxi. How would I ever find the remote place where her guru lived?

Soon, it was time for us too to leave Tryambakeshvar and return to Nasik. This time, we were not staying at the Panchvati, reserved for *sadhus* and aescetics, but in Nasik itself. On my last visit, I had seen the dwelling of Ram; now I saw a modern industrial city, where two Westerners in pilgrim dress were definitely an oddity.

29th March 1981

Today we experience strongly the persecution which the foreigner, the stranger, meets: mockery, trickery, jeering, cheating, staring. We are foreigners, worse still, we are unconventional foreigners. To act not as pulled by the puppeteer of conditioning, but from an inner dynamism, a personal necessity, is to become the stranger, challenger of society. It is to taste the loneliness of the Son of Man, the wholly authentic person, expression of the inexpressible, the Living One who is sought in vain among the dry bones of traditionalism, the Eternal Stranger.

A day of dark mood and drooping spirits, and behind it a tremendous loneliness, the pain of going beyond, always beyond; the relentless fire of Shiva. To follow the Son of Man, the fully authentic person, is to leave all behind, the good as well as the harmful. To be free is to become naked, without culture and without cult, it is to be stripped and nailed to the crux of the present moment. In this loneliness even He is lost, the Son of Man, leaving only the sword in the heart, the nail in the hand. Now nothing remains, but the boundless abyss of compassion. That I am.

Evening Mass at the shrine of the Infant Jesus, impeccably Roman, undeniably powerful. The last of the great Lenten gospels, 'Lazarus, come out!' From the closed tomb, winding cloths, the living death, the land of shuffling shadows that can never meet or share, from the dry bones sighing their familiar prohibitions, the worm-eaten lawbooks and the withered ritual offerings, come out, O humankind, into the light, naked and free, as the ripe fruit drops from the vine.

Next day, we were on the bus, riding across the city. A young girl who sat nearby smiled at us. "Come to my house!" she begged. Her mother, a fat jolly woman, nodded her agreement. Getting off the bus with them, we followed our new friends to a little settlement on the edge of the city: a group of rundown cottages at the end of a dirt lane. Chickens scratched in the dust and dogs barked at us. The girl, her mother, and everyone else in the settlement had a mark tattooed on the forehead—poignant reminder of centuries of untouchability. Soon, we were enjoying a meal in a chaotic, happy-go-lucky household, as skimpily-clad children from neighbouring houses peered through the doorway at the strange white visitors.

"Christian," said the girl, Sujata, pointing at her mother. "Hindu"—as she waved a hand towards her father. "Church going, temple going. Same, same." And she began showing us the cheap, highly coloured pictures that decorated their walls: portraits of Christ, Buddha, Sai Baba, Mahatma Gandhi, and Dr. Ambedkar, the social reformer who brought Buddhism to the untouchable castes. Evidently, our hosts went to church on Sunday, and poured water over the *shivalingam* on Monday, while on Thursday, the day of the guru, they joined the local procession in honour of Sai Baba.

Sujata and her family were ignorant, unlettered people. They had never read either Gospel or Gita, most certainly they had never heard the concept of the Cosmic and Abrahamic covenants. Yet they had grasped the essence of the teaching that Raghudas gave in the parable of the train compartment, that all rivers end in the one Ocean. The issue that caused me so many sleepless nights, so much spiritual and physical indigestion—the tension between Jesus and Krishna, between Mary and Kali, between the Vine of Christ and the Cosmic Banyan Tree—was for them, quite simply, not a problem.

Later in the evening, Sujata's elder brother arrived from the factory. The best English speaker of the family, he explained to us that Sujata suffered from epileptic fits. From the look of me, I was obviously a great healer, able to bestow blessings. Would I help Sujata?

It never failed to astonish me that the simple folk of India instantly grasped those hidden truths about us that the fat yogi in Badlapur had learnt by holding our little fingers. It seemed as if they could read our souls, our highest potential, at a glance, and felt no embarrassment in asking us to be who we truly were. Invariably, they perceived Francis as a yogi, an evolved being on the way to liberation in this life, whilst they saw me as a great healer, able to bless them by a single touch.

No one had ever called upon my abilities in quite this way. Requesting some oil, I performed an impromptu anointing upon Sujata. After this I was asked to bless the baby . . . then the rest of the family, one by one . . . then the house. At length, all of us fell asleep, the men in one room, the women on the kitchen floor.

Francis, who loved Sai Baba, did not want to leave Maharashtra for the North until we had revisited his shrine, which we had last seen with Hey Won and Heinz. Thus, although we were already behind schedule for our journey to the Himalayas, we set off for Shirdi in a bumpy local bus, crossing arid hills sparsely wooded with thorn bushes and neem trees. It was the eve of Palm Sunday when we arrived, and we discovered that the greatest of Shirdi's annual festivals was to be celebrated the next day, which also happened to be Francis' birthday. When the village elders approached Sai Baba and asked him to choose a day for an annual festival which would draw together his Hindu and Moslem devotees, Baba had replied, "Arrange it on Ram *navami*, the birthday of Shri Ram."

12th April 1981

The whole scenario of Holy Week is here, the vast crowds just arrived for the feast of Ram navami, *filling the hospice to overflowing, pushing through the streets, queuing to enter the temple; the worshippers pressing forward to make their offerings, the sale of sacred cloth in the temple precincts; corrupt priests, callous policemen, blind beggars and ragged children, heat, dust, flies. Palm Sunday, and the crowds are celebrating, waving flags of ochre and green, the holy colours of Hindu and Moslem, dancing and processing through the streets, with cries of* 'Shri Sai Baba sadguru ki jai!'

I was amazed that, with no planning on our part, we had arrived in Shirdi on the greatest day of its pilgrimage year; a time specially dedicated to celebrating the union of Hinduism and Islam. I was also overwhelmed by the crowds of devotees who had gathered for the festival. Here were simple folk from the villages, wealthy Bombayites in silken saris, old widows, teenagers in jeans, children and babies in arms. In the bazaars and streets of Shirdi, layfolk, both Hindu and Moslem, from every part of India mingled with *sadhus* in white or ochre robes, green-clad *fakirs*, beggars, and boy *fakirs*, part beggar, part spiritual seeker, carrying an alms bowl and a peacock feather fan.

SAI BABA OF SHIRDI

"My tomb shall bless and look to the needs of my devotees," Sai Baba had declared. "My mortal remains will speak from the tomb."

And so they came: the sick in search of health, the childless, desiring sons; the rich, anxious to be richer; the poor, requesting protection; the young girls wishing a good husband; the students, for success in exams. "Before I heard of Sai Baba, I was embarrassed about our religion," said a young man in blue jeans, a student at a Catholic college in Bombay. "What does a God with an elephant's head mean to me? But Sai Baba—he has a human face. Due to him, I have faith again. And definitely, he will help me to pass my B.A."

"I give people what they want," said Baba, "that they will come to want what I have to give them."

When the young Sai Baba arrived in Shirdi, he came first to the temple. "Get out!" said the priest, noticing the youth, who was dressed in a simple white tunic, the garb of Moslems, a white cloth tied about his head, after the style of the Fakirs. "You cannot stay here. This is a Hindu temple. Go to the Mosque."

So the saint took up his abode in the little mosque, the Dwarka Mayi. It was a humble building, and much less crowded than the great marble temple built around his tomb. The air was smoky, for the sacred fire that Sai Baba had lit more than a century before was still burning, its ash—which Baba had used as a vehicle of healing—still reverently collected by pilgrims. Near the fire was the saint's grindstone, with which he had ground wheat to flour whilst grinding the sins of his devotees.

The walls of the Dwarka Mayi were decorated with pictures of all the saints who, like Sai Baba, were revered as incarnations of Dattatreya, the Triple-faced God. At the rear of the building was the rock on which Baba loved to sit. Kneeling, I placed my forehead on the rock. At once, I felt exactly as if I had my head on the lotus feet of Raghudas. The same vibration of incredible, overwhelming love and compassion was washing through me. Now, I knew that Sai Baba and Raghudas were one, and that Sai Baba loved me with just the same intimacy and tenderness that Raghudas showered upon me. The saint of Shirdi was my spiritual grandfather.

At the start of our pilgrimage, I had seen three images, the cave, the carved stone fish and the minaret. The cave had prefigured our experiences at Bhaja caves and at the cave of Gorakhnath, midway up Tryambakeshvar. The carved stone fish symbolized the churches where we had attended Mass and listened to the Lenten gospels. The minaret represented the Dwarka Mayi, mosque of Sai Baba, the true *fakir,* who could teach me to unite the ways of the cave and the fish. And the minaret reminded me that I was more than just a "Hindu Christian"; I was also a Sufi, a spiritual grandchild of one of the greatest Sufis in modern history. Islam too had a part to play in my spiritual journey.

Near the Dwarka Mayi, we visited the home of Abdullbaba, Sai Baba's chief Moslem disciple. His son, who now lived there, was Sai Baba's Islamic lineage holder, leader of Shirdi's fakirs, the "poor ones" who are the holy men of the Moslem tradition. He was, for the most part, ignored by the crowds of Hindu pilgrims. *"Salaam aleikum!"* Abdullbaba's son came out to receive us when we entered the little cottage. A silver-haired old man wearing a white tunic in the Moslem style, he was completely blind, and was guided by his plump, homely wife and a daughter in a worn green sari. As he sat on the bare floor and handed us little packets of ash from Sai Baba's *dhuni,* I sensed his simplicity and quiet radiance. By signs, he asked me if Francis was my husband.

"Nahin," I replied in Hindi. "Allah is my husband."

The *fakir* smiled at me, wagging his head from side to side, the gesture of assent or reassurance. *"Achchaa, achchaa,* (Good, Good)," he said.

Hearing of Francis' digestive troubles, the old man advised him to repeat the *mantra "Sai Aum".* Then he gave me a bottle of coconut oil, instructing me to anoint Francis' head, hands and feet. I knew little about fakirs, yet I realized that, with Abdullbaba's son, the smallest action had many levels of significance. I was receiving a healing transmission from the heir of Sai Baba, a gift that would mature and ripen over the years. Tapping each of us with peacock feathers in a gesture of blessing typical of the *fakirs,* the old man sent us on our way.

After swallowing the ash from Abdullbaba's son, I began to feel increasingly blissful and intoxicated, despite the heat, the flies and the crowds. Each detail of the little sacred universe that was Shirdi village held a special meaning for me; it was quite unlike any other place on earth. Opposite Abdullbaba's house we visited the room where Sai Baba himself used to sleep, containing the sedan chair in which devotees formerly carried the aging saint in procession, and the strange bed, a plank suspended from the ceiling by ropes, on which he used to spend his nights. In and around Sai Baba's bedroom lounged the dogs of Shirdi. Since Dattatreya is accompanied by four dogs, saints in the Dattatreya lineage such as Sai Baba, whom Hindus revere as an incarnation of the Triple-faced God, always show an unusual fondness for dogs. Indeed, the dog is believed to possess special properties of removing sins, and is used by advanced beings to help them in their work of uplifting souls. Tradition recommends that by feeding dogs, devotees will have their sins eaten away. Accordingly, these mangy strays were reverently fed with milk by numerous pilgrims each day.

Next we came to the *neem* tree that grew by the tomb of Sai Baba's guru. *Neem* is one of the most bitter trees, but devotees claimed that Sai Baba's grace had turned the leaves of this particular tree sweet. I ate a few leaves, according to custom, and found that, though not exactly sweet, they tasted more like lettuce than like the bitter *neem* outside CPS ashram.

Sai Baba was for me one of the most significant of India's saints, and it was important to get to know him in ever-greater depth. Firstly, he was truly my spiritual grandfather, the head of our lineage. Raghudas wore a ring engraved with Sai Baba's face, and was felt by many devotees to embody his spirit. Godavari Mataji and Raghudas' sister Ganguthai were Sai Baba's heirs, via his chief disciple and chargeman, the great Upasani Majaraj. As these God-realized elders passed on, I myself would become one of the bearers of the mantle of Sai Baba, helping to bring the light of his lineage to the world.

Secondly, Sai Baba, the Sufi who had plumbed the depths of both Islam and Hinduism, embodied, in a remarkable way, the union of the Cosmic and Abrahamic covenants. The task which Raghudas had laid upon me when he gave me my *mantra*—to "see that the two are the same", that the religion of Moses and that of the *Vedas* are essentially, eternally one, had been fulfilled, to an extraordinary degree, by the *fakir* of Shirdi. He was my greatest inspiration, the highest exemplar, the most skilful guide in the life work which I had been given—the work of uniting and synthesising the world's great spiritual traditions.

My journey to Shirdi was a quest for the true *fakir,* the Poor One of Allah. I had come to Shirdi, where Baba had promised to dwell at his tomb for a thousand years. Yet even as I visited his shrines, I knew that the true Sai Baba lived not in marble temples, but in the minds and hearts of his devotees. To find the real Saint of Shirdi, I must come to know myself as eternally naked and free. Could I reach the true *fakir* in my own heart?

Four-thirty in the morning, and the voice of a woman, high and shrill over the loudspeaker, chanting a morning *raga* to the Sanskrit words, "Arise, awake," signals the moment to leap from my sleeping mat and make a dash for the bathrooms, which are much in demand. Soon pilgrims are hastening to the temple with offerings of roses, rosewater and milk. This is my favourite moment of the day at Shirdi, when the image of Sai Baba is bathed with a mixture of milk and rosewater. Jostled by the other women, I crowd as close to the image as I can get. I feel the grace of Sai Baba, flowing forth as the milk pours over him. And in the fragrance of roses, I catch the scent of ecstatic divine love, the oneness of lover and beloved. In the grey dawn, the priests wave brilliant ghee lamps, bringing to light the image of Sai Baba, the true guru, the *qutub,* axis of creation. After the *arati,* all of us file past to venerate Baba's tomb and to catch a little of the milk from the bathing ritual, flowing out of a marble bull's mouth at the rear of the shrine.

Our days at Shirdi followed a regular pattern. After drinking a beaker of milky tea, offered by the temple organization at a third of the usual price, Francis and I would go to visit an old lady, the daughter-in-law of Lakshmi Bai, who used to feed Sai Baba daily. The dark little room where the Saint formerly ate was our favourite meditation spot, and here we would sit until pilgrims began arriving to venerate the coins given by Sai Baba to Lakshmi Bai. When I roused from meditation, I was invariably obliged to listen as the old lady gave a long account of her troubles. Piecing together the few words I understood from her rambling Marathi, I gathered that her husband had taken *sannyas,* her children were neglecting her, and she felt quite abandoned.

At noon, we usually went to the *bhojanalay* or community dining hall for a two rupee meal of chapati and buttermilk. *Sabji* or curried vegetables and *dal* was also served, but was usually too spicy for us to eat. One day, however, we decided to take our place with the beggars of Shirdi, and see how they fared, for the temple authorities proudly proclaimed that all beggars would be fed. So there we all sat, Francis, myself and the beggars, squatting on the ground, growing hungrier, whilst the blind beggar woman's little daughter entertained us, dancing gracefully and twirling her beggar's scarf. Eventually a window was opened, and a few of the taller orphan children rushed up and grabbed some *chapatis,* the remnants of the mass feeding. The rest, some blind, some lame, some fingerless lepers, wandered sadly away.

The latter part of the afternoon was usually spent in the Temple, which was less crowded than usual at this time. Here we sat in meditation before the image of Sai Baba, whose eyes glittered like wish-fulfilling gems, whose bones were the roots of the wish-fulfilling tree. On our first day, both of us made our petitions to the Saint.

"I asked for only two things," Francis told me afterwards, "to be able to love people and to digest food."

As for me, I prayed with great intensity, "Make me like you, a true *fakir,* a true Poor One, claiming nothing for my own. Set me free from bondage to security and to human respect." The magical eyes glittered, our prayers arose, prayers sincere and heartfelt, boldly, rashly uttered before the one who hears and grants every request.

"Arati Sai Baba!" A ringing of bells and droning of the priests' voices over the loudspeaker drew pilgrim crowds to the evening *arati.* Usually we were already sitting in the temple; if not, we, like everyone else, came running to attend the ceremony. After *arati,* at dusk, we walked in the little park, where a lamp burnt before Dattatreya's image, and then returned to the temple, where devotees were gathering to sing Sai Baba *bhajans.*

"Not rituals, nor tulasi leaves
nor dips in the holy Ganges—
Nothing but true and loving devotion
Can please thee, O Lord Sai!"

We passed four days at Shirdi in this way. By now, I had stayed long in the Hindu world, and my Christian roots were pulling on me. So we went to nearby Rahata, close to Sakuri, Godavari Mataji's seat, to spend the Easter Triduum at the Catholic Church, in a mission compound much like those I had stayed in—and hated as paternalistic institutions—when I was in Tanzania.

Rahata Catholic Church, Easter Sunday 1981

Dearest Mum and Dad,

Christ is risen, Alleluia, Alleluia! And sitting here under the neem trees, in the brilliant sunlight, I am thinking of you all and wishing you all the peace and joy and newness of life which is the grace of this season. Since Wednesday night we have been given hospitality at this Christian compound in a village a couple of miles from Shirdi. Normally a mission compound such as this would give me the willies, but coming in from the chaos of a Hindu environment, I appreciate the blessings of a quiet, orderly place (institution!), own room, peace for meditation, and chance to share the Easter liturgy—in Marathi.

I was able to make the full three days Easter fast, which was a great help towards quiet, clarity of thought, and meditation. Being in a Christian environment, however, also causes me much confusion, after such an intensely Hindu trip, for it seems to be my fate to be at once at the heart of the Christian thing, and also outside the door. Outside in the sense that I cannot fit the structures, and that enlightenment which I could not get from the church has come to me from the sages of the East; at the heart in the sense of being imbued with the traditions of the Church, and having such a strong connection with Christ, such a burning desire to live, fully live, the Gospel. This is to be the true fakir.

So may the risen Christ who has passed beyond form bless you all with joy and freedom.

Love, Olivia

Our whole Lenten pilgrimage, the fiery climb up Bhima Shankar, fasting in the wilderness above Tryambakeshvar, the harshness of Nasik, the hours spent sitting with the beggars of Shirdi, the search for the true *fakir,* all had been a journey to the Passover, a preparation for the death to an orthodoxy that had served its purpose, the arising of one open to the unknown.

Falling asleep after the Easter vigil, I dreamt a dream. In this dream, just as in daily life, I was carrying round my waist all the money belonging to both Francis and me, and both our passports. It was Easter night, and I had to cross the Red Sea, to ford the river of death and rebirth. Francis, setting off ahead of me, strode boldly towards the further shore, but I found myself handicapped by the money and passports I was wearing. If I entered the waters, they would be ruined! Miserably, I stood on the shore, unable to enter the waters, left behind by my friend. How could I be aloof from such encumbrances? When would I be free to plunge naked into the waters of new life?

19th April 1981

Easter morning, a time for tears. They have taken away my Lord. A time of tears, for nothing can be recaptured, and the place of grace is a place of no returning. A time to mourn the warm womb life, to lament the shattered fragments of the shell, to regret what was valid two days past, and yesterday a corpse, so carefully embalmed. Today, where have they laid him? Easter, a day to enter the tomb, to stare into the formless dark, and coming out, to see afresh the One Who Is Not Here. He is the sunlight that shines on the dust grains, now, only now; the water that freshly drips from the rock, the bakeri *broken, eaten, consumed. He has risen and left you only his sword; wear it in memory of Him, bear it within your heart. You too shall be broken, you the* bakeri, *you the sunlight that sparkles and slips beyond, for the One Who Is Not Here is beckoning, now, only now, past the formless dark. There is One who shines beyond the darkness; only by knowing Him, one passes beyond death. Now, only now, you are That.*

A whole year had passed since my Easter initiation into *brahmacharya,* on the banks of the River Kaveri. Last Easter, at

Shantivanam, I had been letting go of the Western rationalistic paradigm, as I was born into the ancient Indian world view. This year, I experienced the Paschal Mystery on a deeper level. It was time, as Richard had prophesied, for me to die to Christianity, to the form of religion that had nurtured me from my birth, and to rise to a more cosmic, more universal understanding of Christ, whose picture hung in many Hindu homes, alongside highly-coloured representations of Krishna, Lakshmi, Ganesh and Indira Gandhi. My quest to live the evangelical life had brought me to the 'One Who Is Not Here', the Christ that I could not embalm in my limited understanding, who did not rest in the tomb of limited religion. Henceforth, the risen Lord was always ahead on the road, leading me beyond the known.

It was the last day of our stay at Rahata. The priest, who had to go to Aurangabad, offered us a ride. Just a short distance from Aurangabad lay Ellora, famous for its rock-cut cave temples. It was an excellent opportunity to visit one of the greatest shrines in Maharashtra.

By now it was early May, Vaisakh, the hottest month of the year, and the plains of Maharashtra were hard and cracked. Women crowded around stagnant pools in the dry river beds, beating their laundry. Dust rose beneath the hooves of skinny goats and water buffalo as flocks and herds trotted home at sunset after another day of sparse grazing. In the villages of mudwalled huts, landless labourers shrugged their shoulders in resigned misery, for the sugar cane factory is laid off at this season, and work is hard to come by. Speeding across the arid landscape, we watched the heat-haze through the windows of the priest's car, arriving at Ellora village in unprecedented style.

"This is your own place," declared the Principal of the Jain school, a middle-aged, white-robed *brahmachari* who had left home and family to serve the cause of religion. "We are here for spiritual seekers. I too am a seeker. Please be at home here." And so saying, he accommodated us, since it was the summer vacation, in an empty classroom. At the Jain school, the diet was strictly vegan, with no dairy, honey or even root vegetables, since taking milk or honey meant robbing cows and bees, whilst eating root vegetables involved taking the life of a plant. Muslin filters covered the taps, so that no tiny creatures could be ingested in the water, for the Jains are a strict sect who strive for total non-violence.

The area around Ellora is sacred to four of India's great religions. Above Ellora is the hilltop city of Kultabad, once a royal seat of the Emperor Aurangzegeb, which houses the tomb of one of India's greatest Sufi saints. Below the hill are thousand-year-old rock-cut shrines, Hindu, Buddhist and Jain, whilst in Ellora village, one of the twelve *jyotirlinga*, the pillars of light, is venerated.

In the cool of the evening, we walked from the village up to the Buddhist caves. In these shrines, I had expected to see the familiar form of the Buddha, seated in the full lotus position. But as I followed the beam of the flashlight Francis held, I experienced a shock of surprise. There was a stately figure seated on a chair, his feet on the ground. "Who is it?" I asked. "He's seated on a chair like a Westerner!"

"That's Maitreya," answered Francis, well-versed after his years of Buddhist studies in Boulder. "He's the Buddha of the future; the embodiment of friendliness and loving-kindness."

"He reminds me of Shirdi Sai Baba on his rock, with one foot touching the ground," I reflected.

"Yes," Francis said. "And when I saw Krishnamurti in America, he was sitting on a chair, teaching. This is the age of Maitreya Buddha—an age when all paths converge."

I was deeply struck by this image. The Buddha of the future! In my mind, he was the symbol of the meeting of East and West, uniting the love of Christ and the Wisdom of Buddha. Surely the work we were doing, in finding the union of the two covenants, was helping to bring Maitreya to the earth.

5th May 1981

Buddhist caves by night. Into the formless dark, until the beam of the torch reveals Maitreya, the Buddha to come, seated not with feet upturned, but rooted in the dust of earth. There is no God, no God but the sea of Light that beams from the single Eye, that streams from the opened Heart. And there is nothing but this: the endless flux of particulate light; meeting, merging, mingling, breaking, living, and dying and living again, Nataraj with drum and flame, the dance of the cosmic Christ who is Lord of the living and dead, fullness and emptiness, nothing and all, beyond the dual and the non-dual too, where wisdom and love are one.

"Look," said Francis, as we sat one sunset at our favourite vantage point outside the Buddhist caves, above Ellora village. "The colours of the sky—they're all spread out like a fan, like a peacock's tail."

I looked carefully, "And see where they're pointing—the focus of all the colours radiating into the sky? Isn't that the ashram where they're going to do the ceremony?"

Francis nodded. "You're right. It must be connected to the fire sacrifice."

All the villagers had told us of Janardan Swami, a great yogi who had sat in *samadhi* for twenty full years. And for this past week, Ellora had been buzzing with talk of the preparations the yogi and a group of brahmins were making for the performance of a great fire sacrifice. Today, as the heavens bore witness, the preparations were complete.

Next morning, the three fires were blazing in rectangular fire pits adorned with the *yoni*, the symbol of Divine Mother. Around each fire sat a group of brahmins, bare-chested, wearing scarlet dhotis. Beads of perspiration stood out on their brows as they chanted Sanskrit *mantras* at the top of their voices, throwing ghee, rice, sticks and *kusha* grass into the flames with resounding cries of *"Svahah!"* Under a great awning, numerous smaller fires were burning, a married couple seated before each fire, the husband spooning in the *ghee*, the wife holding his arm to empower the ritual act.

The most dramatic time of each day was the early morning, when the first flame was kindled by twisting an upright stick back and forth in a hollowed plank. The task was a difficult one, and brahmin after brahmin would retire defeated, until at last the yogi himself came forward to kindle the flame. Immediately, fire sprang forth. As I sat watching at the edge of the awning, outside the sanctified area, thoughts flickered through my mind like the flickering flames.

The twisting of the stick, the churning of the Ocean of Milk. Grind, grind, grind, the dualities, the polarities, good and bad, pleasure and pain, praise and blame, I and It... grind, grind, on the pilgrim way, on the yogi's path. Then flash . . . the first spark of inner fire, the first kindling of the flame of tapas, flame of the spirit. And up it goes, dung and ghee alike, all but smoke, all but ashes. The firestick, the Paschal candle, the One who comes to cast fire on the earth. 'Christ our Light', Christ the flame of the Heart, linga of Light in the innermost shrine, the kindler, fuser of polarities, destroyer of good and bad, of I and It. The yogi, upright on his litter, he who is more a yagna than any visible fire, kindler of fervour in the hearts of his devotees. The rising flame, the rising kundalini, ascending consciousness, 'I am Who I AM.' The descending rains, nectar entering through the yogi's crown, waters of the Ganges, dissolving, dissolving, nectar of immortality.

Yagna flames were not the only fires at Janardan Swami's ashram. Along the side of the ashram building, a row of huge cooking fires was burning. Women, flushed and sweating, stirred huge blackened woks of vegetables and halvah; others stood beside enormous pots of steaming rice. In the early afternoon, at the conclusion of the day's ceremonies, hundreds of people received a leaf plate of *prasadam*. The yagna was the bringer of abundance, both in the form of food and in the form of rain.

The plains around Ellora were scorched and arid. Village women coming to market in Kultabad had little to buy or sell but wormy eggplants, a few small tomatoes and some melons. It would be at least a month before the first rains of the monsoon. Yet as the cries of "*Svahah!*" echoed about the village, clouds gathered overhead, and soft showers refreshed the weary land.

On the final day of the *yagna*, coconuts were broken, and new silk saris and *dhotis* thrown into the fire. At last the sanctified area was opened to the public, and we, together with hundreds of villagers, rushed in to offer a handful of rice to the final flames, and smear ourselves with the sacred ash. The brahmin who had fed us *khicheri* weeks ago when we arrived in Tryambakeshvar, the renowned fire sacrifice expert, came over to greet us, glowing with inner light. He had been overseeing the entire *yagna*. Now that the ritual was over, and he was out of seclusion, would we oblige him by taking lunch with his family? In a complete abrogation of brahmanic rules and regulations, which forbid brahmins to take food with other castes, we all gathered like one family in a bare cement room and happily ate together.

The sacrifice was over. Bidding farewell to the Jain schoolmaster, our kind host, we boarded a bus in the direction of Shirdi. It was time to return to the feet of Sai Baba. As we travelled, my head began to ache more and more intensely, and my body to feel hotter.

Must have sat in the sun too long. Shouldn't have travelled in the heat of afternoon. Flames, my head is full of flames, fires leaping and flickering behind my eyelids. Why did I watch the yagna? *I too have caught fire, like the handful of rice I dropped into the flame. Is the sacrifice over, or has it just begun?*

For the next few days, the fever raged. I lay on a wooden bed in the pilgrim hostel at Shirdi, semi-delirious, a wet towel over my head, as flies buzzed about the room. Images of Christ and Buddha, of Maitreya and the Jain Passage Maker, of Raghudas and Janardan Swami, danced in my head.

The fever passed, leaving me icy cold, with a head like cotton wool. Wrapped in my shawl, and shivering violently despite the noonday heat, I visited the outpatient department at Sainath Hospital.

"It is a head cold," declared the young doctor.

I stared at him. "But I had a terribly high fever!"

"Yes, yes. It happens like that sometimes. You are unaccustomed to the heat."

Still shivering and in a cold sweat, I stumbled out. Since all I had was a head cold, I must definitely pull myself together. Get moving. Furthermore, we had already overstayed the three days allotted to pilgrims at the hospice.

"Come," said Francis, as I dragged myself out of bed at nine the following morning. "Today we have to go to Sakuri. I found you a room there. And see what I have for you."

Francis had attended the morning *arati* and was proudly carrying a lota full of the milk and rosewater that had bathed Sai Baba's image. Obediently, I drank the entire lota. At once, my body began buzzing with energy, so much so that I boldly walked the entire three miles to Sakuri, through sugar cane fields and pomegranate orchards.

We could not have chosen a better day to visit Kanya Kumari Sthan. Once again, quite unplanned, we had been brought to the right place on the most auspicious day of the year. It was Upasani Majaraj's birthday celebration, and devotees had gathered from far and wide. The *kanyas,* wearing ceremonial saris of golden silk, were gathered around a huge firepit, chanting Sanskrit mantras as they offered rice and ghee into the flames. According to Upasani Maharaj's instructions, and in total defiance of orthodox Hindu tradition, which considered women to be incapable of learning Sanskrit, they performed the Vedic rituals themselves, without the assistance of a male priest.

Despite the huge crowd, our presence was immediately noticed by Godavari Mataji, as we realised when a girl in a pink and white sari ran up to us. "Mataji wishes you to come and meet her mother," she said breathlessly, and led us across the garden. The frail old lady, who passed her days at the ashram, devoted to spiritual practice, nodded and beamed at us as we reverently touched her feet. I felt deeply privileged, for in introducing us to her mother, Godavari Mataji was letting us know that we were members of her intimate family.

The manager bustled over with fresh directions. "Mother insists that you take *prasad.* She said, 'Since all are celebrating, see to it that they are not left out.' Please come to the dining room."

After eating, I leaned against a pillar in a shady corner of the crowded temple, listening to the sound of Sanskrit chanting. *Kanyas* in gold silk tending the flame. Dattatreya, the Triple-faced god, in his golden *lungi,* the perfect *brahmachari*. Pure, no dross, no traces left of bitterness or resentment, no greed or attachment, nothing but golden sunlight, golden *ghee*, poured forth upon the flames. Shivering, I wrapped my yellow sari, colour of death, more closely about me. For he is like a refiner's fire. These words of the Bible began to dance in my head above the Sanskrit mantras. *Svahah!* The offering! Unto the Beyond!

The room that Francis had found for me was located in the Parsee Rest House. Upstairs lived an old Parsee widower, who welcomed us into his room, adorned with pictures of Godavari Mataji, Meher Baba, Jesus and Zoroaster.

"When I saw you coming," said the old man, "I thought you were a Parsee lady, since you have fair skin and wear a sari."

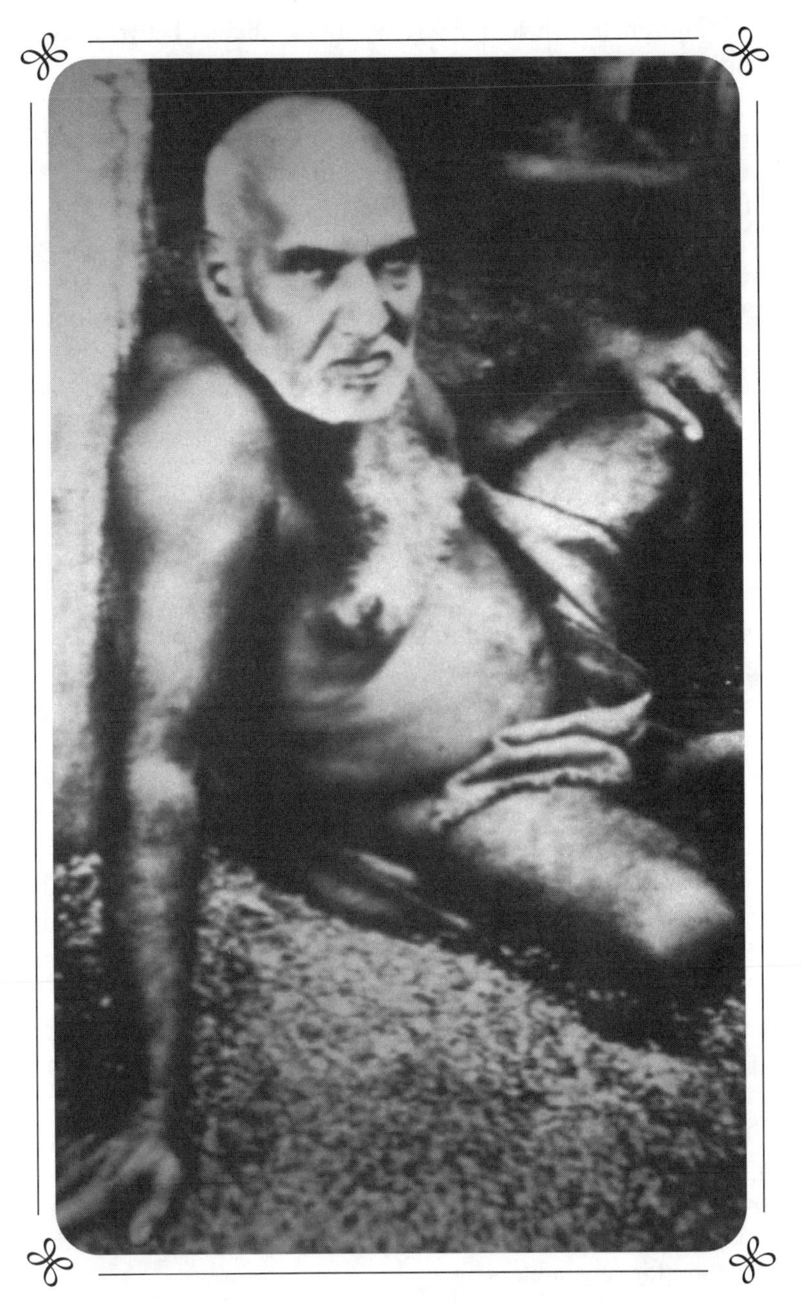

UPASANI MAHARAJ WITH KRISHA MANIFESTING FROM HIS HEART

PHOTO COURTESY OF SRI UPASANI KANYAKUMARI STHAN

"But I am Jewish, and there is some resemblance between Jews and Parsees."

"Certainly. I am delighted to meet you. Jews and Parsees have been the best of friends since ancient times. It was our Cyrus the Great of Persia who allowed the Jews to return to their own land and rebuild the Temple."

Parsees follow an ancient religion, and have, it seemed, very long memories, stretching back to the days of Cyrus.

Upasani Baba's birthday *yagna* continued for several days, and I attended as much of the ritual as I could, amazed that a mere head cold could have left me so weak, so nauseated, and so lacking in appetite. As the celebrations drew to a close, one of the senior *kanyas* called me.

"Mataji is worried about you. You are losing weight. Please see a doctor. There is one in the village."

The doctor's room was a dark little cottage with a low ceiling. There was no diploma on the wall, and the physician's behaviour was casual and hasty. "You are anaemic," he pronounced, after looking at my eyelids. "Take these."

I left, clutching a few pills wrapped in paper. It was Francis who finally made the diagnosis. "Anaemic? Let me see your eyes. My God, they're yellow! You've got hepatitis!"

The *kanya* who had spoken to us returned. "Come to see Mataji at once. She is very concerned about you."

I prostrated before Godavari Mataji, who smiled and said, through the *kanya's* interpretation, "You must go to hospital. Hepatitis is a serious illness. Leave at once, go to the hospital in Shirdi. You will surely recover. I give you my *ashirvad.*"

As Mataji spoke, I felt a golden energy, like the light of the rising sun, like the robe of Dattatreya, streaming into my solar plexus. My heart merged with the radiance of her being, brighter than a thousand suns. I stepped back, awed at the power and spiritual light hidden within the form of the aging woman, a purple and gold sari draped modestly over her head. Within me was a strange gratitude for the sickness which had been the occasion for such a blessing.

"And our pilgrimage to the Himalayas?" asked Francis. "We are meeting with so many obstacles. First I got sick, and we had to stay in Nasik. As soon as I feel better, she becomes sick."

"I already gave my *ashirvad* for your pilgrimage. At the proper time, you will reach your goal, the source of the Ganga. Now it is her health that is my concern. Today, my *ashirvad* is for her."

Lacking the funds to pay hospital bills, we ignored Mataji's instructions and checked in at the pilgrim hostel. Next day, we visited the outpatient department at the hospital in the hope of getting an Ayurvedic remedy. Dr. Despande, the head physician, had an aura of learning and clinical acumen that inspired immediate confidence.

"It is by no means a light case," he said. "The liver is considerably enlarged. I am going to admit you immediately. If you cannot pay the bill, don't worry."

To be sick at Shirdi seemed to me a great blessing. I was profoundly aware of Sai Baba, Godavari Mataji, and even the Catholic Church at Rahata. Weak and befogged as I was, my mind had lost its usual power to defend me from what I truly desired, and there was nothing to do but lie back and surrender to the *sadguru*, the *qutub*, the Christ. And to the Divine Mother, the dark-faced one. A year ago, I had been witnessing the festival of the Fever Goddess in Kulithalai—and how immune I had then felt myself to her destructive power. Now it seemed as if the darts and lances of her votaries were piercing my liver as I trod the firewalk of raging fever. For the first time in my life, I was in hospital as a patient, not as a physician. And for the first time, also, I was learning to honour the dark and wrathful aspect of the Mother. Terrible as Mariamme now seemed to me, even she was but an aspect of the ferocious compassion of Kali, the Black Mother.

Perhaps my illness provided an opportunity for Francis, also, to come closer to Sai Baba during our enforced stay in Shirdi. The hepatitis was delaying our journey to the Himalayas and already the pre-monsoon clouds were rolling in. Why did Francis not bid me farewell and set off for the North alone? He was tired of being sick and illegal in India, and wanted to complete his pilgrimage and 'resolve his *karma*' with his parents in America. Was he staying because of commitment to me, because of dedication to the pilgrimage we had vowed together, or just because of the kindness and compassion that would often take him out of his way for a complete stranger?

"I couldn't just leave you here," he said, when I questioned him about this. "You need someone to take care of you while you're sick."

So it was just kindness, then? I still was not sure. Beneath the camaraderie of fellow pilgrims and the brotherly and sisterly affection we felt for each other as disciples of the same guru, I sensed a tension, an increasing magnetism. My illness made me feel more emotionally vulnerable, less guarded. Yet both of us were clinging tightly to our roles as yogi and nun, for if we let them slip for a moment, we might encounter each other as man and woman.

On Upasani Maharaj's birthday, Francis had asked Godavari Mataji to give him a Sanskrit name. Accordingly, he returned to Sakuri on the day appointed by her as auspicious for *nam diksha*, the bestowal of a spiritual name.

"Well, what did she call you?" I asked, as he walked into the hospital room, looking radiant.

"Sadananda. It means ever blissful, or eternal bliss."

"Wonderful! That's really your true name."

"It was a very simple ceremony. She just told me the name, and a *kanya* wrote it down in Sanskrit and English. But I felt such an energy. Very powerful. And they told me I am the first Westerner to receive a name from Mataji."

"What an honour, Sadananda. And I am the first person to call you by your new name."

After eight days in bed, when I was out of immediate danger, though still very weak, I was discharged from hospital.

"You are not out of the woods yet," Doctor Despande told me. "For three months, you must take a diet absolutely without oil or chilies."

This sounded difficult. It would mean buying my own food and cooking for myself. 'Thank God,' I thought to myself, 'I still have some money left. Now I'm really going to need it for food and Ayurvedic medicines.'

When I left the hospital compound, Sadananda introduced me to his new acquaintance, Enrico, an Italian with missing teeth and a spotless white *dhoti*, who was the only other Westerner in Shirdi. Enrico complained that he felt unwell, so we took him with us to a well some distance out of town. The well was a deep one, in the centre of a mango orchard which had come to a poor devotee as a result of Sai Baba's blessing. For us, it was a holy place of healing, where we liked to come each day, to drink sweet water and rest in the shade of the mango trees.

Drawing a bucket of water, I bathed, then slowly and labouriously washed my clothes, keeping a watchful eye out for any passing farm workers or boys who might take a fancy to my valuables. Sadananda slept beneath a tree, and Enrico lounged in the shade, watching, as, nearly exhausted by the effort, I spread my sari out to dry in the sun.

"Ciao . . . . See you later. I go to town." Enrico went. The afternoon sun soon dried my clothes, and as I folded the sari, Sadananda emerged from his nap.

"I saw the strangest omen here in the woods before I fell asleep. An owl flew out, in broad daylight, chased by some crows. It flew up to me, until it stared me right in the face. The crows mobbed it, but eventually it escaped."

I shivered. "Well, let's get going. I have this huge appetite. Let's go and buy buttermilk and *roti.*"

I picked up my red cloth bag. "Sadananda! The money and passports! They're gone!"

Frantically, I searched through the bag. I was panic-stricken and also guilty. At Easter, I had dreamt that the money and passports were an encumbrance to me. And now I had lost them. I had lost everything, even the travellers cheque record.

"They're really gone! I watched all the local people like a hawk. It must have been Enrico. I didn't keep an eye on him because I trusted him. I thought he was a friend."

Sadananda's face grew red and his brown eyes became piercingly bright.

"Don't you understand?" he shouted, gesticulating wildly. "Don't you realize that there are people who survive by stealing passports and selling them? How could you be so careless? What are you going to do now? You're sick, you need this special diet! What are you going to do?" Sadananda ranted on, boiling with anger.

I was trembling, immobilized like a frightened rabbit. Nothing in my genteel, understated English background had prepared me for this kind of flamboyant rage.

"Do you know where we're going now?" Sadananda was yelling. "We're not going to the Himalayas. No, we're going to Bombay. Bombay! Do you understand? With no money, and no papers. I hope you're ready to struggle. We're going to Bombay to get new passports, because *you spaced out.*"

He paced up and down, glaring at me. Then, regaining his usual emotional detachment, he shrugged his shoulders, saying to me coolly, "Well, no *roti* and buttermilk tonight."

Stunned, we set off toward the village. As we came to the outskirts of Shirdi, a man passed us, dragging three performing bears, muzzled and chained. Another omen. Before we reached the temple, the day's third omen appeared, a naked madwoman wandering the streets. I began laughing and crying hysterically.

"It's me! It's me! I *am* the naked madwoman. I prayed to Sai Baba for renunciation, for the state of the true *fakir.* I lost the money and passports because I needed to know what it was like to live without them, because I secretly desired to be free from material encumbrances."

"Didn't I tell you," said Sadananda, "that the trees beside the well are wish-fulfilling trees? Whatever your heart desires, they will grant. You chose poverty and the fires of Shiva, and the wish-fulfilling bones of Sai Baba have given you what you desired. You died in the flames of hepatitis, and have been reborn as the Poor One, the *fakir.* So . . . welcome to God's palace!"

"The Self is dearer than all else, dearer than son, dearer than wealth, dearer than anything. If persons call anything dearer than Self, say that they will lose what is dear, of a certainty they will lose it; for Self is God."

Brihadaranyaka Upanishad

Four
In God's Palace

I sat crushed into the corner of a wooden seat, with Sadananda squatting on the floor beside me, amid babies, chickens and baskets of guavas. Here we were, two ticketless travellers in the third class compartment, as the night passenger train inched its way across Maharashtra towards the Western Ghats. The train heaved in and out of stations, to cries of "Chay! Chay!" Between halts, I slept fitfully, the fat man beside me continually threatening to dislodge me from my seat as he snored. Events at the wish-fulfilling well flashed through my mind like the passing silhouettes of *neem* trees. When I became sick, I had worried about my dwindling savings, concerned that I might not be able to buy all the special foods and medicines I needed to get well. Now that all was gone, nothing remained to bother about, and I felt a strange lightness, an anticipation of adventure. I glanced across at Sadananda, who lay peacefully asleep on the Poona Herald, curled into a three foot area, his head pillowed on an old woman's bundle. Welcome to God's Palace!

I had been on the pilgrim way for some months now, and it had brought me a very different experience from that which I had received at Shantivanam and CPS Ashram. The ashram experience had been, as Father Bede hinted, not so different from my life at the Abbey. True, in the Abbey, my days were regulated by a bell. I had been following a cenobitic or communal life, all of us working, resting and praying in synchrony. At the ashrams, the life was semi-eremitical; I was more of a hermit, with more solitude, more freedom was semi-eremitical; I was more of a hermit, with more solitude, more freedom to follow my own path and to meditate and retreat as much as I chose. Yet in both cases, I had separated myself from the world, and from the ordinary lives of common folk. And in both cases, it was the hours when I sat in silence that constituted my *sadhana*, my spiritual path.

Now I was out in the world, on the dusty roads. Sometimes I meditated and fasted in remote caves, sometimes I jostled other pilgrims for a glimpse of the sacred image, sometimes I sat by the *dhuni* of *sadhus* and sometimes at the table of the poor and lowly. True, each day we sought out some quiet space to spend a few hours in meditation. We also spent a lot of time trying to get one simple meal. Now it was not just meditation that was the *sadhana*. Hunger was the *sadhana*, uncertainty was the *sadhana*, and thirst and heat and cold. Tired limbs and sore, cracked feet—these austerities replaced the austerities of silence and prolonged contemplation. Bathing at some sacred river or temple tank, washing clothes, sleeping at hallowed spots, walking the dust the saints had trod; all this was the spiritual path. My teachers now were not only whitebearded sages, holy nuns and revered gurus; they were also ordinary people of all walks of life. Now the whole of India was my ashram and each one of her teeming masses the face of Raghudas. The pilgrim path had broken down the division between *sadhana* and life. And now that I had, for the time, no money and no papers, I would no doubt have a fuller and more complete experience of the pilgrim path, without any buffers. This was my opportunity to walk the way of the *fakir*.

It was dawn when we reached our destination, the village in the Western Ghats where the Aptes, Sadananda's old friends, lived. Since a cheque on Mrs. Apte's bank account had been among the items stolen from us, we were hoping to get to her bank at Lonavala in time to stop its encashment.

The Apte's farmhouse was full of the squalling of babies. The eldest daughter had, according to custom, returned to her parental home for the birth of her first child, and was now proudly nursing her newborn son, as family members cooed and clucked approvingly at the man-child. Meanwhile, the young daughter-in-law sat neglected in a corner, playing with her baby. To the indignity of being the unpaid servant was now added her manifest failure in having produced "only" a daughter.

We arrived at the bank next day to learn that two Westerners had come the day before and attempted to cash Sadananda's cheque. An astute bank clerk, noticing that the face on Francis' stolen passport was definitely not that of the man standing at the counter, had refused payment and notified the police. With a few hundred rupees in Sadananda's hands, we left the bank.

It was three weeks before I was strong enough to make the journey to Bombay to get replacement passports. In the meantime, the money Sadananda had was quickly spent, mostly on Ayurvedic medicines for me. I felt embarrassed about this, yet Sadananda did not seem to feel that I was in any way indebted to him.

By the time we finally reached Bombay, penniless once again, it was July, and the city was in the grip of the monsoon; the streets around Victoria Terminus were awash with a mixture of rainwater and drain overflow. The entire waterfront was flooded, disrupting the train service, and old and overcrowded buildings had collapsed. Homeless families huddled under bridges and along the pavement in makeshift polyethylene shelters, while outside the gates of the rich, watchmen shivered in their guardhouses.

These seasonal hazards were added to the routine exasperations of life in Bombay; the undrinkable water and the overburdened transport system, under the press of which, thousands of people travelled to and from work hanging out of the doors of buses or clinging to the outside of suburban trains.

Bombay was a bewildering whirl of contrasts, a busy and chaotic metropolis touched by unpredictable moments of grace. It was the overwhelming opulence and glittering chandeliers of Taj Mahal Hotel or Oberoi Towers, and the ruined shacks of the homeless poor, demolished without warning by the police on the worst day of the monsoon. It was women in silk saris embroidered with gold and tinkling with jewels, and a *harijan* family, dirty and louse-ridden, the children rickety and malnourished, yet with light in their eyes and laughter in their faces. It was pilgrims walking out on a causeway in the ocean to visit the tomb of a great Sufi mystic, on a day so stormy that umbrellas blew inside out and wind drove the rain horizontally, and it was the anonymous *sadhu* immersed in contemplation in the midst of the crowded bazaar. Bombay was a beggar lad cheerfully taking off his hat as a container for a spoonful of free *khicheri*, and it was a blind street musician playing on an instrument fashioned from pieces of trash.

On arrival in Bombay, we went first to Juhu Beach. After wandering for some time along the beach and around streets of fabulously wealthy houses, protected by high walls topped with sharp pieces of broken glass, we finally found Hare Krishna Land, where western followers of Bhaktivedanta Swami readily offered us hospitality.

Sadananda was accommodated in the *brahmachari* ashram and I on the roof of the women's ashram. Kirtana Rasa, the devotee in charge of the women's ashram, eyeing my stained and threadbare clothing with some disgust, presented me with a beautiful white sari with a lotus-pink border. I was relieved. After my bout of jaundice, the colour yellow repelled me; yet I had only yellow clothes. I was only too glad to move from the colour of death to that of purity; from the flames of Shiva to the nurturance of Vishnu. From then onwards, I wore only what was given to me, and invariably received a new white sari before the previous one fell to pieces.

Whilst in Bombay, we received two unusual interventions of Providence, each one coming as a result of a vow made by a devout Hindu, of which we were the beneficiaries. Both had a playful twist that seemed to come straight from Krishna.

One afternoon, we were on our way to visit the British High Commission about my passport. Rain was pouring down, and we took shelter beneath a shop awning near Victoria Terminus. On our backs we carried everything we owned, including our bed rolls, which grew steadily wetter. Suddenly a well-dressed Indian businessman rushed up to me. Noting our simple clothes and the *malas* we wore around our necks, the mark of pilgrims and spiritual aspirants, he said, "You have no umbrella? He also has no umbrella? Come, come!" We followed him through the downpour to his car, where he opened the trunk and proudly produced two brand new umbrellas.

"I have made a vow to give one gent's and one lady's umbrella each monsoon, in memory of my parents, to persons who have no umbrellas. I have been standing here all day in the rain, trying to find someone who is not having an umbrella."

It was true. Even the beggars had some kind of patched umbrella.

"I am delighted to be able to give these umbrellas to pilgrims such as yourselves. Please remember to pray for my parents."

And stooping to the ground, awash with dirty water, he reverently touched our sodden feet, and, jumping into his car, departed.

A few mornings later, we were seated aboard the bus, on our way, once again, to the British High Commission, where I had to collect a document of identity, which I could use whilst waiting for my passport. Sadananda was in conversation with the young man seated beside him, and was telling the tale of the robbery at the well.

"This morning," replied the young man, "my wife has given birth to a son. This is a most auspicious day for my family, and I have made a vow to give away fifty rupees in gratitude for my son's birth. I am giving the entire sum to you. Please do me the honour of accepting."

"Your document is ready," said the clerk when we reached the High Commission. "The fee is sixty rupees."

My jaw dropped. But for the unexpected gift we had received that morning, there would have been scarcely ten rupees in my purse. Handing over the sixty rupees, the entire amount at my disposal, I set off to the bank with the all-important identification to collect my re-issued travellers cheques, which would be just sufficient to pay for the new passports. Truly, I was learning what it is to live as a *fakir,* in complete dependence on divine providence. And I knew that, even when I had money once again, I would still rely on God, not on pieces of paper, so easily lost or destroyed.

Next day, still in need of a dry place to sleep, we knocked on the door of a Catholic church. A tall Spanish Jesuit with a kind and graceful manner opened the door and introduced himself as Father Sopeno.

"We are all pilgrims," he said, observing our white clothing and the baggage on our backs, "but some of us more literally so than others. Come, sit down, tell me about your pilgrimage, and how I may be of help to you. I will assist you in any way I can."

Hearing that we had to remain in Bombay for some weeks more, until our new passports arrived, Father Sopeno arranged for us to stay by night in a building used as a day nursery. Following his directions, we walked up Mahakala Caves road, past the Bombay Carmelite Convent, a bakery and tea shop, a factory which thumped and clunked in the night, past the mosque and the Catholic Hospital, to the *chowkis,* slum resettlement projects. Here Father Sopeno was living, as simply as his parishioners, in a one-roomed cottage with a kerosene stove for a kitchen. And here, amid neighbours who regarded their simple dwellings as great wealth, we spent our remaining month in Bombay.

It was the Islamic month of Ramadan, and at three in the morning a crier would go from house to house, waking the Moslem families—who would not take food or water from sunup to sunset. Moslems were numerous in the *chowki,* as were Father Sopeno's parishioners, the Goan Catholics, who opened their hearts and homes to us. One evening, we made our way to the home of some Goan neighbours, who had invited us for dinner. It was a wet day, and as I walked through the narrow lanes of the *chowki* in the dusk, I stepped in some mud, arriving at our friends' house with filthy feet. The mother immediately brought me into the little bathroom area, and kneeling down, began lovingly washing my feet, and then carefully drying them. Her gesture, so natural and heartfelt, spoke more deeply to me than any Holy Thursday foot-washing ritual. Once again, I was meeting the Christ of the Indian roads.

Shortly after this incident, poised for an early morning visit to the British High Commission, we passed a rather wet night outside the Temple of Mahalakshmi in central Bombay. At break of dawn, the Goddess was wakened. We entered the temple to have her *darshan* as the *arati* bells were ringing. In the lane leading to the temple, vendors were selling freshly cut lotuses, the favoured offering for Lakshmi. We arrived at the British High Commission just as the doors opened.

"I'm glad you have come," said the clerk. "We haven't got your passport yet, but here is a telegram."

"COLLECT REMITTANCE FIFTY POUNDS THOMAS COOKS STOP LOVE DAD STOP."

I sighed. Even more than the value of the money or the kindness and care of my parents, I was touched by this gracious proof of the blessings of Mahalakshmi.

Before the robbery in Shirdi, Sadananda and I had each owned our money separately, carefully apportioning who should pay for what. Once Enrico rendered both of us temporarily penniless, we began sharing whatever came our way. Now, I did not regard the money from my parents as mine, but rather as ours. The relationship between us was definitely changing. At the outset of our pilgrimage, we had been two fellow travellers who happened to have the same destination and the same guru. After the hardships we experienced in Bombay we had grown closer together, more interdependent, more of a unit.

"I feel that our subtle bodies have united," Sadananda told me one evening as we sat in the daycare centre drinking coriander tea.

I was embarrassed. Uniting of bodies, even subtle ones, sounded rather sexual.

"My connection with you feels so deep, sometimes I wonder if I should be married to you," he went on.

"Married?" I replied timidly. "Don't you think ours is mostly a spiritual connection?"

Sadananda's American frankness was still strange to me. I had lost none of my English reticence, and was unfamiliar with discussing intimate feelings with men. Even after six months on pilgrimage together, I still had never mentioned to Sadananda my immediate recognition of him, nor the insistent inner voice that told me he was my lifelong friend and companion.

One amusing but instructive incident lightened the general intensity of our stay in Bombay. Our Sikh friend, Sant Singh, ran a small business selling parts for tube lights. Visiting his office one morning, we noticed a signboard saying, "Nature Cure and Massage Centre."

"Perhaps they can help us with our digestion," suggested

Sadananda, so we climbed the dingy flight of steps to the clinic. Evidently, they performed thorough examinations, or perhaps colonics, for the glass panel on the door was thickly curtained. When we knocked, a face peeked out, there were sounds of scurrying feet and giggles, and then a plump middle-aged woman opened the door a crack, and told us to come back later. Returning at the appointed time, we were ushered in by the matron, a Goan Catholic with a red rose behind her ear. The other staff members had all vanished into curtained cubicles.

I looked about me. There were no diplomas on the wall, no medical books, no shelves of herbs and massage oils, no filing cabinet for patient records...no equipment at all, in fact, just the plump, sexy matron. The place didn't smell right, either. It had an odour of cheap perfume, sweat, and stale, musty air, as if the windows were never opened. It was unlike anywhere I had been, but it did remind me vividly of novels I had read.

"Ours is a small place," purred the matron. "We could not do much for you on an outpatient basis..."

I struggled to suppress my giggles, noticing a lamp burning before a statue of the Virgin Mary. Our Lady of the Brothel, indeed!

Later, at Sant Singh's office, our friend asked, with an amused lift to his eyebrows, "You enjoyed your visit to the Nature Cure Centre? Will you have some tea?"

My passport, delayed for more than a month by strikes in Britain, finally arrived, and our weeks of living in Bombay without money or papers came to an end. In the cosmopolitan city of Americanized "jeanagers," God-intoxicated *sadhus,* miserable millionaires and pious prostitutes, I had learnt what it is to live in radical dependence upon Divine Providence, and had come to realize that the One who feeds the sparrows and clothes the lilies of the field will not fail to care for pilgrims also.

Our two-month stay in Bombay had been so trying that we had occasionally gone to Poona to get a break from the intensity. On one such visit, trying to find the best way to hitch-hike out of Poona back to Bombay, we had taken the municipal bus to the end of the line, and as dusk fell, found ourselves in Chinchwad, a god-forsaken industrial suburb, street upon street of dingy cement houses with flat roofs. The streets were crowded with cyclists and pedestrians, factory workers with trimmed moustaches, dressed in Western-style pants and "fashion shirts," returning home after the day's work. Roadside tea stalls and fruit sellers were doing a brisk trade. Walking out towards the edge of the town, we began rather hopelessly hitch-hiking.

"No, no, you will not be getting a ride out of here at this time!"

A distinguished-looking brahmin gentleman walking by stopped to speak to us, emanating the imperious humanitarianism of his caste. "Come with me. I am having some friends, Catholic sisters, at St. Ursula's. You may stay the night with them, and continue your journey safely in the morning."

Still weak from hepatitis, I struggled to keep up with our guide's brisk pace as he led us past the huge Baja Auto Plant. Eventually, he waved to a signboard announcing, "St. Ursula's Dispensary." As we walked down the drive, a half-grown German Shepherd rushed out, barking nervously. She was followed by a Swiss sister in a white habit, who immediately, without a single question, brought us into the dining room and set food before us.

"Stay here and rest a couple of days, then go to Bombay," said the sisters.

So began our friendship with Sister Scholastica and Sister Emilia. After our passports had arrived, and we could finally leave Bombay, we decided to make a retreat at St. Ursula's, to recover from the stress of city life. As for our pilgrimage to the Himalayas, we had reluctantly to accept that it was now September, too late in the season. We would have to wait until next May.

The sisters were delighted to see us again, though the young German Shepherd, nervous as ever, was less happy about it. We made a welcome change from the sisters' daily routine of dressing wounds, giving medicines to those too poor to buy them, distributing powdered milk to needy children—and above all serving babies. Sister Scholastica proudly showed me a little shed which she ran as a premature baby unit. Here, in cradles made from old shoe boxes, she cared for newborns who were scarcely viable. Remarkably, they lived and became bright, healthy children. Her 'special care unit' had no incubators, no oxygen, not even any nurses except herself, yet by the power of love and the sheer force of her will she cared for babies who would be lucky to survive even in the best-equipped neonatal care units in the world's leading hospitals.

On the first night of the retreat, I had a dream in which Raghudas appeared in a big, circular library, pulled out a book on Russia, and instructed me to say my *mantra* even in my sleep. Russia, home of the Prayer of the Heart, symbolized for me a deep interiority. With the lull in the outer pilgrimage, it was time for a corresponding inner journey.

Fortunately, my parents, realizing that I was likely to stay in India for some time, had sent a parcel to CPS Ashram containing some of my most treasured possessions, including my paints, brushes and canvases. Now, after hurrying to Poona to collect these, I began enthusiastically painting the images that surfaced in this inner pilgrimage, whilst experiencing a remarkably vivid series of dreams about the freeing of the nun from her cell, veil and habit.

Finding that I was so immersed in my process as to be barely relatable, Sadananda set off to make a solitary retreat at Bhaja caves, where our pilgrimage together had begun seven months previously. From the account he gave, when eventually he returned, it was a beautiful experience. Day after day, he sat in the chilly mountains, watching the purple-black monsoon clouds drifting over the opposite hill and dropping their rain into the valley, where emerald rice-grass sprang. Over the entrance of the Round Cave, a big waterfall gushed, and the whole scene was sodden yet incredibly beautiful. From time to time mists would roll in, and in the stillness he sensed the guardian spirits of the caves.

Meanwhile, Sister Scholastica was talking with me very persuasively. "Olivia, you need to go back home. You should return to England and regain your health. And your mother must be missing you very much. Why don't you go back for a while? I can get you a free flight, escorting a baby who is going over for foreign adoption—a free return ticket. That way, you will be able to come back to India whenever you wish. Think it over, think it over. Certainly, a rest in England would be best for your health."

It was a tempting prospect. I was tired of being sick and weak, and the thought of setting out on the road once more was far from inviting. And my mother had written to say that my sister Kate had just had a baby. It would be wonderful to see my new nephew. In fact, if I had only myself to consider, I would have leapt at the opportunity. After spending a few months with my parents, regaining my health, I could come back to India, go to the Himalayas, and then look for a hermitage. But how would Sadananda feel if he returned from Bhaja caves and learned that I was leaving? He had stayed in Maharashtra to nurse me through hepatitis and had been a strong support in the chaos of Bombay. Our vow to go to the source of the Ganges together was a significant consideration, for according to Indian spirituality, a resolve of this nature, once made, should be pursued even at the cost of life itself.

But the vow was not all. There was also the voice in the heart. And there was something else, something so incompatible with my chosen life as a celibate nun that I scarcely dared admit it to myself, still less to Sadananda. I was in love. The American ex-hippie *sadhu* with brown eyes had become so dear to me, so entwined in my own being, that I could not imagine living without him.

As I painted, I pondered. Since childhood I had been enraptured with a transcendent lover, with the Divine Beloved. The brief and abortive affair with the Cambridge undergraduate had only served to remind me that my love was a priceless pearl, and could not be wasted on any transitory object. Could I now see Sadananda, my guru's beloved disciple, as a manifestation of the One Love which I sought?

I was working on a painting which I called 'Immaculate Heart of Mary'. Whilst I worked with brush and palette, almost in a frenzy of creativity, thoughts and feelings about Sadananda and myself playing through my mind, the figure of the Virgin came to life, began to move and breathe, an image of radiant loveliness, an embodiment of my own highest beauty. Then, to my bitter frustration, her form merged back into the brush strokes that seemed so crude and clumsy in comparison with the vision I had glimpsed.

"If I really mean to be a nun, a hermit, a celibate," I told myself, "I'd better leave now. If I stay, who knows what will happen? Does Sadananda feel for me as I do for him?"

"You've painted what I was feeling! That's exactly what it was like." Sadananda, just back from the caves, was gazing at the finished version of 'Immaculate Heart of Mary,' a rendering of a woman who seemed to emerge through the veil of a waterfall, out of the darkness of the Cave of the Heart. "There was a great waterfall over the Round Cave, and within it, I could feel the compassion and tender love of some goddess. It was exactly like that."

As I stood beside Sadananda looking at the painting, I realized that it was actually a self-portrait. Not only did the face resemble mine; the woman emerging from the darkness was myself, pure, virginal and hidden as I had been throughout my life.

"It's you," said Sadananda, as if he read my thoughts. "You are the Maiden in the painting, you are the goddess of the waterfall."

I stared at the picture. Must I always be the veiled woman, the virginal aspect of the feminine? Were my recent dreams, the dreams of the freeing of the nun, not an invitation to cast aside the veil, to emerge from the shadows and discover the multiple faces of the Great Mother?

"I want to talk to you," said Sadananda, sitting down on his iron cot. "When I was up in the caves, meditating, I realized something. You see, I went off on retreat because I felt hurt. You were absorbed in your paintings and your process and had no energy for me. So I went to the caves. And I loved being there, in solitude. But as the days passed, I saw clearly that we are more than just companions on the way to the Himalayas. Our emotional and spiritual connection goes far beyond that. Your presence nourishes me. You keep my heart open, and I need that. I want to be with you."

I was too overwhelmed to say anything. There was a long and pregnant silence, broken only when the servant girl knocked on the door to call us to lunch.

"Tomorrow," said Sadananda, "I am going back to the caves. I just came down because I wanted to see you, and tell you what

I was feeling. It's so beautiful up there, and I got some really good luck. The head curator of the Archeological Survey of India came by on a field trip, and when he realized I was a true *sadhu*, he actually gave me permission to stay there. Till then I had been living on half an apple, half a banana and some *ghee* daily. But once the curator gave me permission to stay, the janitor started bringing me *bakeri* and curried vegetables each day. So I'm going back, and you can finish this process you're in, and think about what I told you. I'll be down again in a week or two. Then we can go on together—as more than just fellow pilgrims—or go our separate ways if you prefer."

So Sadananda left for the caves again. A few nights after his departure, I had a dream still more vivid and brilliant than those which preceded it.

I am by the side of a broad, majestic River, the Ganges, Kaveri or Godavari. At the river's edge is a grassy meadow where cows graze and go down to drink. By the water stands a ferryman's hut, where live three beautiful sisters. They are clothed in saris of brilliant silk in hues of blue and crimson, and their voices are sweet and silvery as a choir of bells. They come to the door to speak to me, passing on some message, and their communication has a fire and liveliness like the brilliant silken saris. I know that their message is really for the Pilgrim who is following behind me along the reedy path to the river. Having called him, I go to the water's edge, where I find a number of brahmins bathing. My sister Kate, she who has just given birth, plunges in for a naked bath. I too decide that the dark waters will suffice to cover my nakedness, and, casting aside my dress, immerse myself in the waters of the Sacred River.

A cycle was completed. On Easter Night, I had dreamt that I was unable to cross the Jordan because I was encumbered with money and passports. Now, after passing through the fires of hepatitis, after losing the money and passports and living in Bombay by the mercy of Providence, I was at last able to plunge naked into the river of death and rebirth, was ready to submerge my form, the body and leave only the head, the essence.

A week later, when Sadananda returned from the caves and we shared stories, we learned that on the full moon night the two of us had a remarkable telepathic experience. It was the moon of Bhadra, when Krishna dances upon the heads of the serpent Kaliya, whose venom is poisoning the Yamuna River. Sadananda, as I now learnt, had sat outside the Round Cave, watching. Behind the hills across the valley, the sun was setting. Soon the first rays of the moon would enter the stupa hall in the caves hidden in those sunset hills. So soft, so feminine, the hill across the valley, bathed in the first light of the moon, whilst behind him, the last glow of the setting sun stirred to life the echo of monks chanting. Mount Sun, Mount Moon, Yin echoed Yang across the valley. As darkness fell, a storm broke and Sadananda took refuge in the stupa hall. Lightning flashed on all sides. The moon was high in the sky when he emerged, and across the misty air arched a perfect rainbow in the subtle, silver tones of moonlight, a moonbow.

At the very time that he sat watching 'Mount Sun, Mount Moon', I was fast asleep on my iron cot in Chinchwad, dreaming.

I am in a town which lies between two mountains, Mount Sun and Mount Moon, and wish to undertake an expedition to the summit of Mount Moon. In order to do this, I first have to contact the priest of Mount Sun. The solar mountain is like a giant Glastonbury Tor, with a labyrinthine path winding up it. I climb this path to meet the priest, a tall, druid-like figure. Setting off across the town, I take a bus in the direction of Mount Moon. A few stops later, a Poor Clare nun in her veil and brown habit enters the bus. A young woman of my own age, very sweet and innocent, she begins talking to me, and then suddenly vanishes in a puff of smoke. As I disembark from the bus, the moon is high in the sky. So bright is her light that the clouds are radiant, the birds of day are soaring through the air, and all is bright as at high noon. It is Moonday, the prophetic hour of total illumination.

Both of us were awed by this experience. As Sadananda had said in Bombay, our subtle bodies were indeed united, even when we were physically in different places. He immediately began painting a shimmering moonbow in my picture of 'Mount Sun and Mount Moon.'

Sadananda decided to bring me to Bhaja caves, to see the

changes the monsoon had wrought. He also wanted me to show my paintings to two new friends, an Anglo-Indian named Tom and his Scottish wife, Fiona. The caves were beautiful indeed. There were streams everywhere, and we stood mesmerized, staring at the waterfall that gushed over the Round Cave. Months before, we had started our pilgrimage together at this very place. Then, all had been dry and austere. Now the place was totally transformed—wet, green mossy, dripping and totally alive.

Back at the village, we walked with Tom through the rice fields he cultivated, successive plantings of rice grass standing at different heights in flooded fields. Returning to Tom's bungalow, we all ate lunch at a table on the veranda. Then I showed my paintings to Fiona. Looking into her clear green eyes, I was reminded of my recent dream, the druid priest of Mount Sun. "Yes," said Fiona, as if she read my thoughts, "since coming here to India, I have felt the need to read about the Druids and the Celtic Fairy Faith. I am a Celt. And I am fey. I read Tarot. But what I really read is the person." And, so saying, she proceeded to read my paintings.

"What I see," she continued, in her soft Scottish tones, "is that, although you are painting archetypal subjects—the Virgin, the Annunciation, the Pieta, and so on—all the paintings are about you and Sadananda. You seem to be exploring the spiritual connexion between you. This one, for example." She picked up a picture of the Angel meeting the Virgin. "This one, you see, is the meeting of form and formlessness."

"That's right. The Virgin in her blue robe is form or the Christ energy; the golden angel is formlessness or the Buddha."

"But, Olivia, the Virgin is also you, the nun from the Catholic Abbey, child of tradition; the angel-bird is Sadananda, the wild and free *sadhu*, coming from years of Buddhist meditation. The meeting between the two of you has truly been a meeting of Christ and Buddha."

"It's true. He is always asking me to read the gospel to him, to find out what Jesus would do in our situation. And almost all I know about Buddhism, I learnt from him."

Fiona smiled knowingly. "In the paintings that follow," she continued, "the symbols begin to merge. The Christ energy and the Buddha energy, the moon and the sun, are merging. The tenderness of the heart and the brilliance of the Third Eye are beginning to unite. Form and formlessness are coming together."

I stared at her. Fiona really was fey! Had she seen into the dilemma I wrestled with? And if what she saw were true, did it mean that Sadananda and I would journey on together? Or, having met for a while to give and receive the gifts of wisdom and compassion, would we take our own ways, alone to the Alone?

We returned from the caves. Sadananda was still feeling restless, so he took a trip to nearby Badlapur to visit the psychic yogi who had earlier told me I would develop healing gifts. On his return, he told me the whole story.

Badlapur Baba had taken his place in his family's temple, seated on the special chair which he occupied when answering questions and giving guidance.

"Your question?" he had asked Sadananda.

"It's about Olivia and myself. I feel very confused. Raghudas gave her into my care eight months ago. Am I meant to just bring her to a suitable hermitage, and then leave for America? Will we complete our journey to the source of the Ganges and then go our separate ways? I don't know what our fate together is."

The Yogi meditated for some time, then placed a small quantity of rice in an envelope. "Take this rice, and sleep with it under your pillow. Your question will be answered."

The same question occupied my mind as I sat in meditation on the dispensary roof at sunset. The long journey Sadananda and I had made together, not just in physical miles but in spiritual transformation, the meditations we had shared . . . all the dreams that had come to me recently, the visionary paintings, the telepathic experiences . . . events both inner and outer were bringing me to a place I had not thought to reach in this lifetime, a place of willingness to accept an embodied, human, flesh and blood form of my divine consort, spouse and lover. That nun who vanished in a puff of smoke, was she not an aspect of myself? In the months of our pilgrimage together, I had been always the nun, pure, untouchable, absorbed in the ideal which I desired to emulate. I was Clare, shorn and veiled, united in heart with my Francis, yet distanced emotionally by our vows of chastity. And

Sadananda . . . he was ever the yogi, shunning woman and gold, offering me protection yet fearing the entanglement, the seduction, of the feminine. We had journeyed together as the yogi and the nun, figures from long-dead lives that we had lived before. And now, could we meet each other in the present, free from roles and past projections?

The great clouds of the late monsoon caught fire, like cow-dung at the kindling of the sacrificial flame. Suddenly, it was as if the heavens opened to illuminate my mind. Past, present and future lay before me. I saw Sadananda's *karma* as clearly as my own, his succession of lives as a yogi. In each birth, he had reached a high level of consciousness, but had been so distanced from the feminine that he was unable to attain the fullness of realization. And I, in my cloistered past life as a nun, had developed tremendous love and compassion, yet remained caught within the form. Despite great effort, neither had attained their heart's desire. We were perfect complements. Instantly I knew that we had come together to free each other from the bonds of the past—the lack of love, the lack of freedom. Raghudas had given each of us into the care of the other. Now he would withdraw from the physical plane, leaving us together, each the other's guru. Forget the free ticket to England! To leave Sadananda would be to forsake both my liberation and his.

Next day, Sadananda returned with the rice grains from Badlapur Baba.

"Look, I'm supposed to sleep with these under my pillow, and get understanding about our relationship."

I looked at the little pouch of rice dubiously.

"I don't see how it will help. We both know that things have changed, that we aren't just fellow travellers . . . or even brother and sister at this point. And I've been meditating, and I do really strongly feel that we will spend our lives together and help each other on the spiritual path."

"Our lives?" Sadananda began picking at his fingernails nervously. He was sitting on the edge of his iron cot, and I was cross-legged in the middle of mine, a seating arrangement which was very expressive of the physical distance the two of us had observed during eight months of pilgrimage together. Sadananda had been more frank and courageous than I in acknowledging and verbalizing the change in our relationship, yet the thought of a lifelong commitment—and that was what I had clearly seen in the vision on the rooftop—evidently scared him.

"Well," he said finally, looking up from his hands and meeting my eyes again, "this is a watershed for us. We need the blessings of Raghudas."

I clapped my hands like a child with a new toy. "Let's go in the morning. We can get the bus to Dehu, Sant Tukaram's shrine, and then walk to Alandi. I know the way, all along the Indrayani watermeadows. I went there before with Grandmother Shantabai."

We were sitting in Grandmother Kamalabai's tiny apartment, all three of us, Raghudas, Sadananda and myself, perched on a cot. Raghudas was reading the local paper with deep concentration, and I wondered what interested him so much. Then Grandmother emerged from the kitchen, carrying a tray with three cups of tea, which she set before us. Putting down the paper, Raghudas poured his tea into the saucer and began sipping, as Grandmother ceremoniously cut a *laddhu* sweetball into three. "Baba," said Sadananda, "Godavari Mataji gave me the name 'Sadananda'."

"Very good," Baba replied, through Indu Thai's interpretation. "Then you must be stable in bliss."

We all continued drinking tea. Suddenly, putting his saucer down with a clink, Raghudas said, "Since he is Sadananda, she must be Alakananda."

"Alak—ananda." I repeated the unfamiliar name. "What does it mean?"

"Badrinath," replied Baba, very distinctly.

"Badrinath is the shrine of God Narayan, high in the Himalayas," Indu Thai explained. "It is a holy *dhama,* situated on the River Alakananda, the chief source of the Ganges, flowing from the topknot of Shiva."

I remembered that first train ride through India, and the story of the descent of the Ganges. So I myself was Alakananda, the Ganga, whose incredible force of love and purity could be channelled to the earth only through the matted locks of Shiva. It was true. There was a Ganges of love in my heart that longed to flow out to the thirsty earth. Longed, yet held back. I needed my Shiva, the Ever Blissful, to draw me down from the heaven-realm where I habitually hid.

"So the theme of Mount Sun and Mount Moon continues," said Sadananda, as we sat in Janabai *dharmsala* that night. "Godavari named me, Raghudas named you. The moon named the sun, the sun named the moon. And the balance of Yin and Yang has been created."

In reply, I handed him a little poem.

"Do not be afraid
I will dance with you
As the dawn mist dances with the sun.
And the light of your eyes
And the rain of my tears
Shall weave a rainbow bridge
Joining form and emptiness
Heaven and Earth
In One."

When we got back to St. Ursula's on the morrow, we no longer sat each on our own iron bed, looking across the room at one another. The time for distance was past. Instead, we both lay beneath the same white mosquito net as the lights of Sun and Moon joined in one.

Exit the nun and the yogi. The divine Love Story, that most ecstatic and intense of all romances, became one with a human love story. And I, devoted with such singularity to a universal and transcendent love, found that in assuming a human face and limited form, the Eternal Beloved called forth new reserves of patience and humility. For the life of committed relationship is, in its own way, as much a spiritual discipline as the path of the monk or hermit.

This was not the ideally pure, platonic relationship which I had envisioned eighteen months ago at Shantivanam. We were now two children, squabbling heatedly, two lovers in intimate embrace, two pilgrims walking side by side, often hungry, weary and hot. Ours was not a "spiritual relationship", but a physical, emotional and spiritual union, something far more earthy and full-blooded than I had imagined. We were each other's consort, friend, sibling, parent, child, and guru.

Leaving behind us both the fear of closeness and the fear of commitment, we agreed to travel to the Himalayas next summer and then return to the West together—to America. As for marriage, it was becoming obvious to both of us that we were already married, that Raghudas had sent us on pilgrimage together, not just for a time, but for a lifetime. The seven steps by which Vedic marriage is sealed were for us but the ritualization of the seven stages of intimacy through which a couple draws closer, rediscovering commitment on each new level. From the day Sadananda had dreamed of the three of us, Baba and his two beloved disciples, enveloped in a field of blue Shakti, we had been spiritually married; all that had been needed was our discovery of this true marriage of souls. In due course, society could set its seal upon a union that had been ordained before we were born.

The retreat at St. Ursula's had now come to completion. Ironically, I had needed to return to a Catholic institution and the company of two sisters in white veils and habits to experience the freeing of my own inner nun from her cloister, veil and habit. Now we could leave Chinchwad and the Baja Auto Plant for the more congenial environment of Poona.

Within a few days, we found accommodation in a pyramid-shaped bamboo hut, abandoned by Rajneesh *sannyasins,* at Bundgarden in the Koregaon Park area of Poona. Recently, Rajneesh had suddenly departed, amid a major income tax scandal and rumours that Bhagwan himself had been murdered and an impersonator had taken his place. At his departure, many of his followers had also gone—leaving us a delightful space to live. Our hut was surrounded by a beautiful garden, with huge elephant leaves, tall bamboo plants and the brilliant flowers that burst into bloom at the end of monsoon.

There were papaya trees, banana palms, countless birds, a sun terrace, a swimming well, and nine cats. A friend we had met at CPS Ashram was staying in the same garden, whilst a couple of Rajneesh *sannyasins* lived in a tree house perched in the branches of a huge mango tree. We bathed in the cold, deep green well, diving down to find the turtles who hid in the depths. After our bath, we practiced yoga, completely naked in the secluded garden. Then we walked out into the market place as the chay shops were just opening, fragrant with incense from the first *puja* of the day.

Naturally, I was eager to revisit all my Poona friends—Dr. Lad, the sisters at CPS Ashram, and my Hindi teacher, Mrs. Laddu. Dr. Lad beamed when we walked into his dispensary on a sunny October afternoon. There was no need to explain the change in our relationship, for he was perceptive enough to see this at first glance.

"*Namaste*, my dear sister, my dear brother," he greeted us. "I am so happy that you have found each other again. This is not the first lifetime that you have been together."

I was intrigued, but he would not say more. Instead, he handed us some packets of Ayurvedic herbs.

"Eat together, pray together, and take your medicines together," he continued. "This is love."

Like all great teachers, Dr. Lad was fond of using brief and enigmatic phrases that I was to find myself pondering years later. Again I wondered whether Sadananda and I had been together as disciples of Sant Jnaneshvar. But one thing was clear. My Ayurveda guru approved our union.

We visited the Laddus on a Sunday, when the professor was home. Sitting in their simple living room, we talked as intimately as if we had known each other our whole lives. Professor Laddu, a remarkably humble and unassuming man, took a great liking to Sadananda, treating him with the same respect that he would give an Indian yogi.

When I asked the Professor the Sanskrit meaning of my new name, he, renowned scholar that he was, turned to his wife, deferring to her superior knowledge of linguistics. After some discussion, they said, "The name must come from *alaksha*, the formless, the Absolute. It may be meaning *'the bliss of the Absolute'*—or *Absolute bliss—alaksha ananda*. It could also be meaning *alaksha* plus *nanda*—daughter of the Absolute, referring to the river which issues from the supreme source, Ganga, the daughter of the Himalayas."

I was more than satisfied. So Raghudas had initiated me into absolute bliss, and given me the name of that river which flows forth from the loftiest mountains on earth, the mountains which are the terrestrial symbol of Absolute consciousness. I who had come to India as Olivia, was now named after the daughter of the Himalayas. When we left their little house, the Laddus came outside to say goodbye to us.

"I shall never forget you," I told Mrs. Laddu. "You are the embodiment of the teaching of Bhagavad Gita, the teaching of desireless action."

Mrs. Laddu, who had a hearing defect, asked me to repeat my words. Then, to be sure she understood, she asked her husband to translate them into Marathi. Finally, she nodded, with tears in her eyes. Perhaps she had an intuition that we would never meet again. I understood that my words were of great importance to her, that in some way they set a seal upon her life. Next time I returned to Poona, I was to learn from Sister Brigite of her death. So did one of the finest Hindu women I ever met pass into the arms of Lord Krishna whose teachings she had so faithfully followed.

The day after our visit to the Laddus, we went to a middle class residential area of Poona to see some friends of theirs whom they were eager for us to meet, a retired professor of archeology and his wife. This couple were both slight and thin, the Professor tremulous with age, his wife still vigorous. They were disciples of Upasani Maharaj and Godavari Mataji of Sakuri, and had found a unique way to live his teachings on the greatness and glory of woman.

"My wife is a *kanya,* a virgin, just like the consecrated maidens at Sakuri," explained the Professor. "For fifty years, she has lived on the top floor of our house, engaged in spiritual practices. We live very simply, so I have not burdened her with household duties. Though I do some *sadhana* as best I can, still, I am a worldly man, but through her influence, my mind turns more and more to God."

The elderly *kanya* smiled at me.

"Your Western feminists have done a lot to improve the condition of women," she said. "Yet, what is most important for women is that they value the women's arts. If both men and women can learn to be mothers—to feed, to nourish, to give growth to souls—this is a greater thing than for women to take to the aggression and worldly ambition of men."

This sounded to me like a new kind of radical feminism. My education had always been oriented towards making the girls and young women equal to the boys and men. We had even worn school neckties; indeed, we had learnt to become as much as possible like our male models. The thought that men might in fact need to model themselves upon women and learn from them was quite a revelation to me.

"In India," the Professor continued, "we hear a lot about *pati vrata*—a woman's vow to serve and obey her husband. Yet in the original Vedic teachings, this *pati vrata* was only half the story. Equally important was the vow the husband made to honour, support, serve and obey his wife. Now there are so many problems in society because the men lord it over their wives, just as the British lorded over us Indians. Actually, mutual service, mutual obedience, is necessary. All my married life, I have served and obeyed my wife as Upasani Maharaj instructed me. And we are very happy together."

And I was very happy to have met them. So often in the course of my pilgrimages, the male renunciants and spiritual aspirants had made it clear to me that I was, as a woman, less qualified for aesceticism. 'She is your disciple?', they would ask Francis, or with some astonishment, 'She is meditating, too?' I had needed to be reminded of the teachings of Upasani Maharaj, Godavari Mataji and Raghudas concerning the spiritual importance of women. And now that I myself was in a relationship, I was eager to learn all I could about marriage as a spiritual path.

One morning, we woke early and walked across Poona, reaching CPS Ashram in time for morning Eucharist. Sister Elisha greeted me with a long face.

"That old man who used to travel with Grandmother Shantabai came to the ashram," she said. "He was bringing the news that Shantabai has died. You will not see your friend again."

I sighed. Poor Grandmother! She had not lived to enjoy the old age for which she had so carefully provided. Now the only bank account that would serve her was the treasury of devotion she had laid up with Lord Vitthale, now the only alms she could beg was the mercy of the One who is the refuge of sinners. I prayed that she might find her place in Vaikuntha, that Heaven where all *varkaris* long to be, beholding the face of Vitthale.

Night by night the autumn moon, the moon of Vishnu's month of Kartik, grew larger. Now, in early November, it was almost full, hanging like a great lamp over our garden, ruddy, as the poets say, like fresh saffron. Inspired, we took a moonlight walk across the Mouly to the Vitthale Temple in Yeravda, erected by Poona *varkaris* who were homesick for their Lord's great shrine at Pandharpur.

The black image, arms akimbo, standing beside his consort, Rukmini, beamed at us. Devotees, old women in green or purple saris, toothless old men in yellowed *dhotis,* gathered to strum their *vinas,* clang finger cymbals, and chant *"Jai, jai Ram Krishna Hari!"*, their weather-beaten faces lighting up in ecstasy as they relished the Divine Names. The image beamed, seemed to be calling us; the devotees sang, telling the glories of Vitthale, recounting the many blessings gained by setting foot in the sacred precincts of His Temple in Pandharpur, a hundred and fifty miles to the south.

Who could be deaf to such a call? That very night found us at Poona Station, equipped with our cloth bags and bedrolls. We had with us scarcely any money. Arriving in Sholapur, the nearest large town to Pandharpur, in the small hours, we sipped tea by the light of a hurricane lantern in the late night chay shop near the station. Then, for a few hours, we slept in a little Shiva temple in the middle of a busy street, until the devotees arriving for daybreak *arati* woke us.

From Sholapur, we took the narrow gauge steam train along the branch line to Pandharpur, squashed on a wooden seat beside a family of cheerful, friendly, scabies-infested *harijan* children. We were lucky to be inside the carriage. Turbaned pilgrims clung to the doors and squatted on the roof of the little train, for we were arriving in Pandharpur for Kartik *mela,* one of the two days of the year when all the *varkaris* of Maharashtra, Goa and Karnataka descend upon the village.

Despite the crowds, we secured a room in a *dharmsala,* or pilgrim hostel, attached to a pretentious modern temple, which sported at the entrance a huge and, to me, rather grotesque image of Hanuman carrying Dronachal, the healing mountain. Unfortunately, it also had the filthiest latrines I had ever seen in my life.

From the *dharamsala,* which was on the outskirts of town, we followed the highway, past makeshift booths set up to supply the pilgrims with whatever they might need for their pilgrimage, to the cobbled, dirty streets of Pandharpur proper that twisted and wound between stone houses with finely-carved gables and doorways—streets and buildings largely untouched since the time of the Peshwas. Stately eighteenth century *ghats* led us down to the broad white sands of the Chandrabhaga, a crescent-shaped loop of the Bhima River—that same Bhima whose source at Bhima Shankar we had visited months before.

Bright-coloured saris and bleaching *dhotis* lay drying on the shore in the pleasant, sunny weather of the post-monsoon season. Marigold garlands floated in the river, and along the shoreline were little mounds adorned with sticks of incense and clay lamps. To the people of Maharashtra, this is *Bhu Vaikunta,* the earthly paradise where Vitthale, the Supreme Lord, dwells amid his devotees. Sticky and grimy from the journey, we eagerly joined the crowds of bathers, and then slapped our clothes against a laundry stone. From the burning fires of Shiva who dwelt in his *lingam* of light at the source of this great river, we had come to the white sands and cool waters of Vitthale, the embodiment of Krishna, the lovely cowherd boy. The journey of the Bhima River mirrored our own journey from stern ascetics to pilgrim lovers.

Duly bathed, we headed for the most important of the little riverside temples, the one which houses the *samadhi* of Pundalika, a Twelfth Century saint who founded the enduring cult of Vitthale. The only son of aged parents, he at first treated them in a cruel and heartless manner, forcing them to walk behind him hundreds of miles to Varanasi, while he rode on a horse. Reaching Varanasi, he visited a hermitage and there the words of a sage so touched his heart that he was converted. Carrying his parents home to Maharashtra in a wicker basket strapped to his back, he settled down by the shores of the Chandrabhaga and devoted himself to their service. Pleased with his devotion, Krishna appeared to him, but Pundalika was so concentrated on massaging his parents' feet that he scarcely noticed the Lord. "Wait a moment," he muttered. "Just now I am busy." When Pundalika returned from his duties, Krishna was obediently waiting, in the form of the Vitthale icon, and there, it is told, he has stood ever since, patiently waiting upon his devotees.

And so we came to the Vitthale Temple itself. On this festival day, simply joining the *darshan* queue was a moving experience. We passed a couple of hours waiting in line in a large hall, filled with patient devotees carrying their flower garlands and offerings of sweets, fruits and coconuts; shy girls hiding behind their shawls, women in their best gilt-bordered saris, white-clad men wearing magnificent saffron or magenta silk turbans, children, restless and eager.

I particularly noticed the Lombadi tribeswomen in mirror-patterned skirts, their arms loaded with bone bangles, heavy brass ornaments pulling down their earlobes. All these villagers, whose presence filled the air with a faith and devotion as pervasive as the scent of the jasmine flowers and marigolds they carried, had left their homes and fields, and travelled hundreds of miles—many of them going on foot—to have the vision of the sacred image whose whole message is that the Lord dwells not only in temples and images, but in all the circumstances of daily life.

He, the beloved Vitthale, drawn to earth by Pundalika's devotion to his aged parents, is the transfiguration of all these humdrum lives, of hours spent devotedly mending a husband's *dhoti* or washing children's clothes, cooking meals for aunts, uncles and parents-in-law, tending a father's field or running the business that feeds many dependents. He is the one whom faith and humility draw to those who live without choices, born to a particular village, a particular caste, a particular trade, married by arrangement, enmeshed in a complex web of duties upon which depend the survival of grandmothers and widowed aunts—He, Vitthale, transforms these lives that seem so drab, so common, with the intoxicating beauty of the Holy.

At last we were in the sixteen-pillared hall of the Temple

proper, where each pillar is so holy that the pilgrims hug them as they pass by, and every stone seems aglow with the purple light of devotion. Slowly, the queue wound around the pillars, and at last led us past the images of Jay and Vijay, the heavenly doorkeepers, into the inner sanctum. We were face to face with the image, laden with flowers, lit by flickering lamps. As Sant Jnaneshvar sang, *'When my eyes rest on your image, my beloved, I become overwhelmed with happiness.'*

The sight of Vitthale and Rukmini of Pandharpur drew tears to my eyes, and left an indelible impression on my heart.

Next day, we were invited to lunch at the house of a brahmin astrologer. Like most of the houses in Pandharpur, the astrologer's home consisted of private quarters, where the women stayed, public quarters, and cowsheds, arranged around a courtyard. As a mere woman, I was dismissed from the lofty conversation of the menfolk, but, being thus banished, had the privilege of entering the sanctum of the kitchen, to which outsiders are generally not permitted. Here I squatted on a little wooden seat and watched the cooking of *bhajis* and baking of *chapatis* in our honour. I observed closely, for occasions like this provided me with a unique opportunity to observe the techniques of Indian cuisine.

As we sat chewing cardamon pods after our meal, Sadananda asked our host, "Are there any saints or highly developed people in Pandharpur, to whom we should pay our respects?"

"Well," replied the astrologer, "Shankaracharya of Kanchi is here." Our mouths fell open in astonishment. Shankaracharya Sri Chandrasekharendra Sarasvati had been for decades the spiritual leader of millions of South Indian Shaivites, and was famed among Western seekers as the sage who had directed the English journalist known as Paul Brunton, author of *A Search in Secret India,* to the feet of Ramana Maharshi. This greatly revered *sannyasi,* now approaching the end of his days, was on his way to Varanasi to die. An old man of failing strength, he travelled only on foot. His path meandered from village to village, crowds clustering around him at each stop, begging him to stay with them longer. His progress, then, on the two thousand mile journey, was slow indeed. We had heard it rumoured that he was approaching the southern part of Maharashtra, but certainly had not expected that our paths would cross, least of all, on the auspicious ground of Pandharpur. We had arrived just in time, for Shankaracharya's public *darshan* was to start the following day.

After lunch, we wandered through the cobbled streets, passing row upon row of workshops where the traditional musical instruments for devotional song are made; finger cymbals, wooden clappers, *vinas* and *dotars,* like Sadananda's, which he had bought in Pandharpur some years ago. Suddenly a beaming figure hailed us. "*Ananda, Ananda!* Bliss!" We recognized her squashed nose and matted locks at once. She was the beggar whom we had met before at Tryambakeshvar and had affectionately named the Blissful Leper. Immediately she brought us to the portico where the lepers gathered, for the Blissful Leper and her friends had just prepared a large pot of sweet *halva,* and wanted us to share food with them.

I found the lepers of Pandharpur a fascinating group, living as they did on the margins, devoted both to God and to each other. Freed by their disease from society and its constraints, compelled by fate to live a renounced mendicant life as their physical form painlessly crumbled away, they had gravitated to the feet of Vitthale, friend of the friendless, lover of the poor. Many of them could not even be bothered to beg actively, and simply passed their time absorbed in chanting God's name, with a begging bowl beside them. I was particularly impressed by the devotion of one man whose arms and legs were mere stumps, and who lay in the dust, jerking himself from side to side with great effort as he cried, "*Shri Ram! Shri Ram!*"

Since we had no money with us, the beggars and mendicants admitted us to their fellowship, the society of the meek and lowly, that one exclusive club to which no amount of money can purchase admission. However, two cheeky beggar children, a girl of about nine and her younger brother, decided that the only white folk in Pandharpur were fair game. They pursued us, demanding, "Give us money to buy chay."

"No," we teased, "we have no money. You buy us chay!" To our astonishment, the children immediately marched us into a chay shop and bought us tea. Suddenly the two demanding little ruffians turned into dignified, friendly people, chatting with us in

Hindi. Educated foreigners from the world beyond the beggar's scarf had proved to be as poor as they, and able to receive from them, not merely to toss them a coin. From then on, whenever we met the children, they would insist on buying us tea.

Next day, lacking the money for the ferryman's fee, which rose with rising demand, we took the long walk round by the bridge to the little whitewashed monastery, or *math,* on the further shore, where Shankaracharya was in residence. Here, in a bare, simple room, a large crowd had gathered: local villagers, Sholapur factory workers, and wealthy and notable people from far and wide. Some had travelled great distances to have the *darshan* of the saint at such a privileged spot, whilst a few followed him wherever he went. The crowd jostled and pushed, the most eager scrambling in through the windows, as local police constables, almost at their wit's end, attempted to marshal the impatient devotees into an orderly queue. From an inner room, a melodious voice intoned a song resonant with the beauty of the south, *"Arunachalam, Arunachalam, Arunachalam Shiva."*

At last the waiting was over. Shankaracharya was installed in a railed-off area, and the police began ushering the crowd into, and swiftly out of, his presence. I passed. I paid obeisance. I saw a silver-haired old man in rough ochre cloth, his sole property a staff and brass waterpot, his mind immersed in meditation. I received a banana and was jostled by the crowd and hustled out by the policemen.

"Did we actually have *darshan?*" I asked Sadananda plaintively.

"Well, I guess, in a manner of speaking, he replied. "I mean, we did enter his presence." In such a noisy, aggressive crowd, the mysterious alchemy of *darshan* seemed impossible. Yet the old man had impressed both of us, and we decided to return next day.

On the morrow, everything seemed the same—the bridge, the grassy river meadows, the bare, whitewashed *math,* the crowd, still larger and more aggressive, the policemen, still more harassed, the haunting chant, *"Arunachalam Shiva."* Ladies first, men second, was the arrangement. Again, I passed, paid obeisance, saw the silver-haired old man in worn ochre robes, received a banana, and was asked to move along. Lacking the Indians' mad desire for the divine, I went outside the *math* to wait for Sadananda. Then, impressed by my politeness and status as a foreign visitor, the policemen let me back in.

The room was by now entirely filled with men, and, feeling shy, I went over to join the only women present, a group of elegantly-dressed ladies who were standing near Shankaracharya. One by one, the ladies were called forward. I had placed myself among the dignitaries who were to be personally introduced. Absorbed in gazing at the saint's face, which was a mirror of calm and holy indifference, I was startled to find myself pushed forward, Sadananda alongside, to be introduced to His Grace.

"From where do you come?" asked the interpreter. With the answer that we had given to that question ever since the day in the teashop at Nasik, we both replied, "The universe is our home."

Shankaracharya suddenly awoke from his mood of indifference and beamed a smile at us. "It is very good," he replied, "that you have taken up this way of life. Certainly, everything you need will be provided."

It was time for us to be ushered out with another banana. The saint, however, insisted on giving us two large, rosy apples which had been placed beside him, a special token of his blessings. Yes, we had certainly received *darshan;* a *darshan* we would never forget, and a blessing that would never leave us.

We remained in Pandharpur for the duration of Shankaracharya's stay, bathing each morning and evening in the pleasantly cool but silty waters of the Bhima, dotted with devotees, walking over to the whitewashed monastery twice daily to have *darshan* of the saint, and visiting the Vitthale temple each sunset, in time for arati. Then, from Pandharpur, we hitch-hiked to Akkalkot, to see the shrine of Swami Samarth, a great saint whose grace had brought Shirdi Sai Baba from the God-drowned condition to the state of *qutub,* or Perfect Master.

Arriving in the small town, with its elegant Maharaja's palace and various *maths* and temples, we found a room at the site of the banyan tree beneath which Samarth Swami used to sit. Nearby was the well which has flowed with sweet water ever since the saint, finding it dry, suddenly walked over and urinated in it.

By noon, we were very hungry. It was time to get some *bakeri,* which we usually took with water and a little salt, a menu that

SHANKARACHARYA SRI CHANDRASHEKHARENDA SARASVATI

PHOTO COURTESY OF *HINDUISM TODAY*

seemed austere even to the poorest, for we were unable to eat the fiery-hot *dal* and potato *bhaji* that was the standard village fare.

Enquiring from the manager of the banyan tree *dharamsala* where we might find some free *bakeri,* we were directed to Gajanan Math, a large stone-built monastery that lay about half a mile away through winding cobbled streets. Walking in to the main temple of the *math,* we noticed neatly typed English quotations about the holiness of fire hanging on the pillars. An immaculately clean brahmin approached and, to our great surprise, conducted us to a Western-style dining room, equipped with tables and chairs. A large party of Germans was taking lunch. Immediately, we were served a delicious Indian meal, cooked without chilies, and with the additional luxury of brown bread and butter. I relished the meal all the more, knowing that I was eating Shankaracharya's blessing. While we ate, the Germans explained to us that this *math* was the main dwelling of "Shree" Gajanan Majaraj, the "fire sacrifice Guru" of whom Lakshmi had spoken at Tryambakeshvar, the very teacher I had been longing to find.

I remembered clearly how, the moment Lakshmi told me of this teacher, my inner voice had said, "*You must meet Shree. You must learn the fire sacrifice.*" How disappointed I had been when Lakshmi had left without giving us Shree's address, or even a clue as to which town to find him in! And now, quite unexpectedly, here I was at his centre.

Next morning, well before sunrise, we returned to Gajanan Math to find the courtyard already full of devotees, chanting the great *mantra* of liberation.

"O Three-eyed Lord, by the strengthening fragrance of sacrifice, free us from evil and the bonds of death, as the ripe fruit drops from the vine!"

As the light increased, fire was kindled in a pyramidal copper pot in front of each devotee. At the precise moment of sunrise, rice and ghee were offered to the flames.

"*Suraya svahah!* I offer this to the Lord of the Sun!"

The fragrance of the sacrifice filled the courtyard, and I felt a tremendously healing and centring energy. I was thrilled to have found Shree and was eager to learn the art of *agnihotra,* the sunrise

SAMARTH SWAMI OF AKKALKOT

and sunset sacrifice—yet the full significance of our fortuitous visit to Gajanan Math was not to become clear to me until some years later. As a wandering pilgrim aescetic in India, I tended to pride myself on being in some way "above" the external rituals of ordinary devotees. *Agnihotra* was simple and essential enough not to seem to me ritualistic, but after all, what was of true importance was the sacrifice of wisdom and meditation—or so I told myself.

Later, in America, I would come to see why, despite all my meditator's hubris, I had felt such an intense eagerness to make the *agnihotra* my own. For in Denver, Colorado, no *shivalinga* nestled beneath holy *peepul* trees, no orange *sindhur* was smeared on sacred wayside boulders, nor did cries of "*Svahah!*" resound from the shores of the Platte River on auspicious days. In the absence of the thousands of ordinary devotees who had lifted me up in the arms of their daily external rituals, I would be forced to create my own sacred *mandala* of time, to anchor myself on the wheel of sacrifice. Sunrise and sunset *agnihotra* would thus become, for Sadananda as for me, the mainstay of our life, the support of our meditation.

All of this, of course, was hidden from me when, sunrise *agnihotra* at Akkalkot completed, I followed the devotees into Shree's room to receive his blessing. As I waited my turn to touch his feet, I noticed beautiful statues of Buddha, Mahavir and Christ in his room, as well as Krishna, Rama and other Great Ones. Evidently, Shree honoured all teachers, of all paths. Shree beamed at us, radiating a brilliance like the sun itself, warming us with compassion and friendliness. And like the sun whose light we take for granted in our daily lives, he had a quality of "nobodiness", a deep humility. Raising his hand in blessing, he said to us, "Take food, take food."

After we had duly eaten breakfast, an elderly Parsee gentleman gave us a tour of the *math,* talking non-stop.

"Shree is no ordinary being," he said fervently. "He is more even than a sage or guru. He is an *avatar*. In his form, the Lord himself has descended to earth to restore the ancient *agnihotra*. For the fire sacrifice had become adulterated, encumbered with unnecessary rituals and arrogated by the brahmin caste for their use alone. Now Shree has restored the original form, for the healing of the earth. It is no less a being than Parashuram, the avatar who came on earth before Lord Ram, who is Shree's guide and teacher."

"Parashuram? Who's he?" I asked.

"He was the seventh *avatar,* born in a hermit's hut, the son of the great sage Jamatagni and his Rishi-wife Renuka. He is called Parashuram on account of the Parashu, or battle-axe he wielded. With this axe he slew all the unjust kings of the world, ridding the earth of tyranny and oppression. Parashuram is a Holy Immortal. He has never left this earth. And he has paid several visits to Shree at this very *math.*"

By now we were climbing into the elderly gentleman's car. "Shree had the most fortunate of births," he continued, as he led us out of the car and into a hall which housed a larger-than-life marble statue of a sage. He was a noble figure, of stern and lofty aspect, with a great top knot crowning his head. "This," our guide continued, "is Shree's father, Shankar Maharaj, a great modern-day Rishi, a knower of *brahman,* indeed the actual incarnation of Lord Shiva. Just as Parashuram was born to the great sage Jamatagni, so our beloved guru, Shree, was likewise the son of a sage whose like has scarcely been seen in modern times."

"And his mother?" I enquired.

The Parsee gentleman showed me a painting of a beautiful girl, rapt in ecstasy before a radiant apparition of the Blessed Virgin. "This is Shree's mother, Sona Mata, a great mystic. As a young girl, she was educated in a convent boarding school, where she experienced visions of Christ and His Blessed Mother. After her husband's death, she retired to the ashram of Upasani Maharaj at Sakuri, and there she is buried."

"We have been there several times," I said, beginning to feel happier. "Godavari Mataji is our guru-mother. And our guru's sister lives with her there. Sadananda received his name from Godavari Mataji."

Our guide smiled. "Every morning," he said, "Godavari Mataji performs *arati* to the *samadhi*—the tomb—of Shree's mother. And Shree himself has spent time with Upasani Maharaj."

Here at last was something to which I could relate. As one of

Upasani Maharaj's spiritual heirs, Shree was very much a part of our family of beloved gurus. I felt that in learning and practicing the *agnihotra* which he taught, I would be sharing in the great cycle of *yagnas* offered by Godavari Ma and the *kanyas*. The fire which Sai Baba tended at Shirdi, the fire that Upasani Maharaj entrusted to the *kanyas*, had been distilled by Shree into its simplest, most essential form, the *agnihotra*, and was now being spread by his disciples to every continent.

"The great Swami Samarth himself prophesied this," explained the Parsee gentleman. "He said that he would have a successor who would be a great world teacher and who would spread the sacred fire from Akkalkot to the ends of the earth."

Next, our guide showed us a full-size marble statue of a beautiful cow. She was situated near a great firepit. "Here," said our guide proudly, "the *soma yagna*, the greatest of all *yagnas*, and the most healing for the earth, has been performed."

"And the cow?" I stared at the graceful statue.

"The cow is of paramount importance, for from her comes the ghee for the offering. It is in her presence only that the sacrifice is perfectly performed, for she is the mother, the sustainer, the nurturer. From her come five gifts—milk, yoghurt, ghee, the dung which we burn in the *yagna* fire, and cow's urine, a sacred medicine. We must never forget to honour the cow."

When we saw him again next morning, Shree requested two things of us: to help in his mission by performing *agnihotra*, and to take food at his *math* three times daily whenever we were in Akkalkot. Accustomed as we were to one meagre meal a day, eating three times daily was to us luxury indeed. When we neared the kitchen, Shree's wife, Vahini, a plump lady with soft brown eyes, would bustle out to ply us with as much food as we could possibly be persuaded to eat, well-seasoned with motherly kindness.

Meanwhile, Shree's Western disciples instructed us in *agnihotra*, taking us to Shivapuri, a comfortable centre for Western practitioners which Shree had established on the outskirts of Akkalkot, adjacent to the area with the *soma yagna* site and the marble cow. Here we learned the ancient art of Homatherapy, the Vedic method of creating a healing vibration which enables plants,

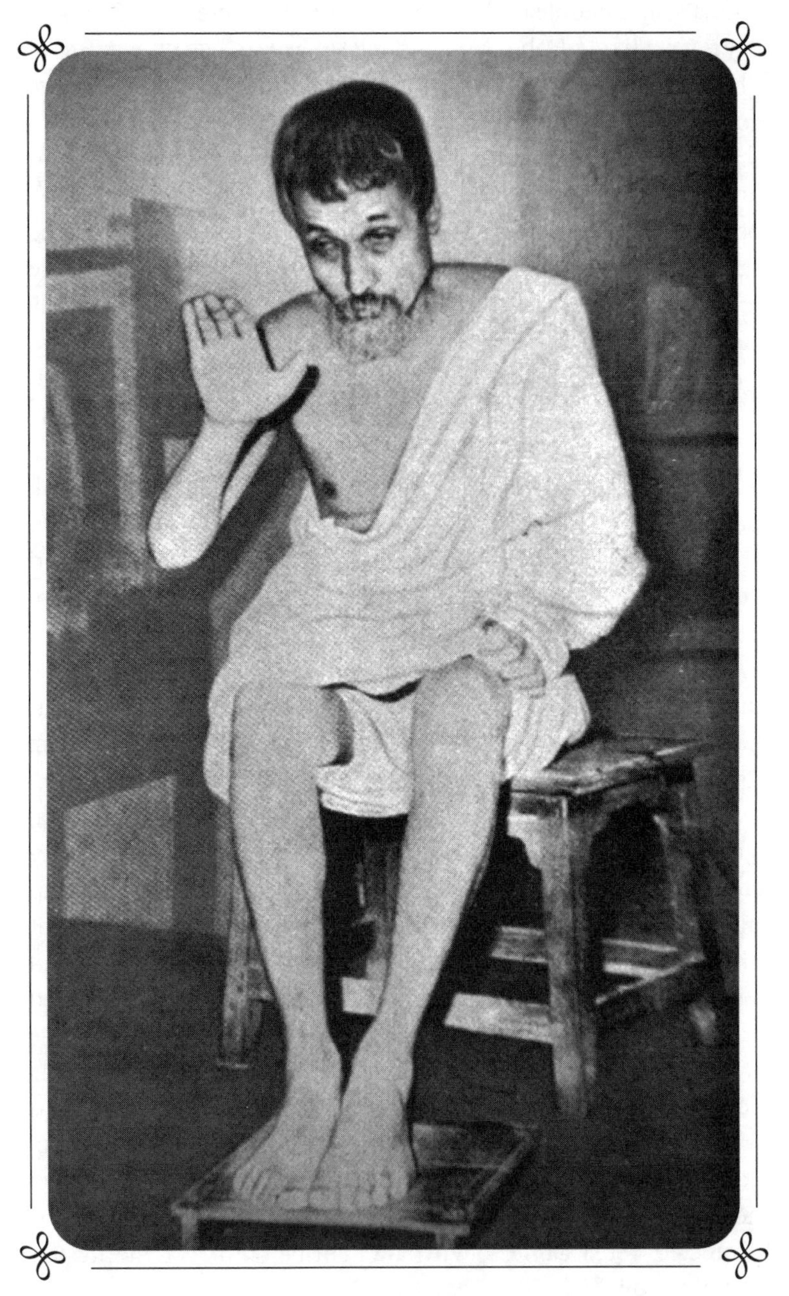

SHREE GAJANAN MAHARAJ

animals, and people to flourish to their fullest potential. Over and over we chanted the *Mahamrtanjaya mantra, great mantra* of liberation, and with the cry of *"Svahah!"* the flames leapt up, accepting the golden ghee.

When we were not at Gajanan Math or Shivapuri, we spent our time close to the banyan tree that was Swami Samarth's beloved spot. The tree, the well, the couch of the saint and the sandals he had worn, all streamed forth blessings. In the temple there was a remarkable set of paintings. The saint had personally commissioned a series of portraits, each of which depicted him, wearing nothing but his loincloth and a different ceremonial hat of one of the court functionaries at the Maharaja's palace. My favourite showed him sitting majestically, stern of face, wearing what looked to me like a green jester's hat with three large pink pom-poms.

Avadhutas like Swami Samarth, beings who have passed beyond all norms, frequently act in riddles. In the series of portraits, was Swamiji saying, "I myself am everything, from Grand Vizier to Court Jester"? Was he mocking the pride of office of the dignitaries, by showing an all-but-naked renunciant wearing their hats? Was he reminding us not to take life so seriously? Or just having childlike fun? The answer would remain an enigma.

It had been a remarkable visit to Southern Maharashtra. Vitthale the all merciful, the only masculine God whose devotees call him "Mother", had come to life for me in the form of the old man in ochre robes—Shankaracharya. From the mouth of that great devotee of Shiva, we had received a blessing more typical of Vishnu the Preserver, Vitthale the Mother, "Everything you need will be provided".

"Shankaracharya," said Sadananda, "is our desire-fulfilling cow. And you know, it's a funny thing. Some years ago, Raghudas told me to leave India because of my poor health. But I told him I couldn't leave without seeing the Ganga and the Himalayas. Then he said, 'just take Lord Vitthale into your heart, and you'll be protected.' So I came to Vitthale's shrine, and met the desire-fulfilling cow."

That cow of ancient story, whose udders pour forth whatever one wishes for, stays with those who perform the fire sacrifice.

From Shankaracharya we had come to Shree, who bestowed on us the abundance promised by Shankaracharya, and taught us the art of *agnihotra*. Now it was time to visit some real life cows. We decided to go to Goa, to visit a jungle cow ashram Sadananda knew and receive the blessings of Goa's patron deity, Shanta Durga.

The following night, as we walked down the road somewhere in southwest Maharashtra looking for a suitable spot to sleep, two great stone lions suddenly loomed out of the dark. The vehicles of Mother Durga, destroyer of Demon Death, the lions beckoned our way to her temple, where we could spend a comfortable night. The meeting with Durga's lions was an auspicious one, since we were on our way to the temple of Shanta Durga. Although we covered the distance mainly by hitch-hiking, we still spent the greater part of each day walking the open road in the hot sun, begging our food as prescribed in the scriptures, sleeping by night under a tree or at some wayside temple, and stopping to bathe whenever we came to a river or stream.

In the jungle that lay on the border between Karnataka and Goa, we came to Dwarkapuri Ashram, a forest retreat. The few buildings, a kitchen and dining area and a sleeping shelter equipped with two rows of wooden cots, were built out of mud, with cowdung floors. Rising in the chilly dawn, we would make our way to the well, where an old *sannyasi* who was visiting the ashram was already muttering *"Aum Ganga! Aum Ganga!"* as he tipped cold water over himself. After bathing, we warmed ourselves at the *dhuni* tended by "Maharaj," an old North Indian brahmin who had fasted under a tree until the government agreed to grant him this land for his ashram.

The brahmin woman who cooked and cared for the ashram served us milky tea, grumbling and complaining the while, as was her habit. *"Badmash!"* said Maharaj, nodding at her good-naturedly as he pronounced the Hindi insult, and then, in his few words of English, "Very bad woman." In fact, their relationship seemed to consist entirely of complaints on her part, and insults on his. Yet they seemed quite fond of one another.

We spent our days in the sultry jungle, meditating beneath

cashew trees, and returned to eat rice, *chapatis,* potato and buttermilk. The ashram had no electricity, and at night we would gather round the *dhuni,* wrapped in blankets, singing *bhajans* for Maharaj or struggling to follow his long, involved Hindi stories.

Apart from Maharaj, the sour-tempered housekeeper and a young cowherd, the chief residents of Dwarkapuri Ashram were a number of brown jungle cows, whose brick shelter was more convenient and better constructed than the buildings used by the humans. Each day the cows would wander off into the jungle to browse, returning at milking time. Maharaj was a devotee of Govinda, the cowherd Krishna, and his philosophy was a simple one. He served the cows, Lord Krishna's beloved companions, and the cows gave their milk, which was donated to poor local *harijans.* Thus, by serving the cow, he served both God and humanity. Each day, as I contemplated the gentle cows, I came to understand better why, in the Vedic world view, the cow is the gate to the transcendent, the bringer of the dawn of higher consciousness.

When we arrived, one pregnant cow was lost in the jungle, and everyone was worried about her. As soon as we came, she proudly returned with her newborn calf. Everyone took this as an auspicious sign. A foreign Mataji had come, and the lost cow returned safely. They all felt assured that the foreign Mother had a special connexion with Gay Ma, the great Cow Devi.

On the day when we left Dwarkapuri, there was a bus strike, and the traffic situation was chaotic. Thus, almost by accident, we began a walking pilgrimage through Goa. I loved the charming, unspoilt little state, always warm and humid, with its emerald green ricefields, shady coconut plantations, groves of mango and cashew trees, clear rushing rivers, and whitewashed churches gleaming in the sun. There is a unique combination of Latin and Indian elements, both in the landscape, adorned with Portuguese architecture, and in the temperament of the Goan people, who love singing, dancing, drinking cashew fenny, and merrymaking. *Tulasi* plants grow in the centre of the clean-swept courtyards of Hindu homes, and the *audumber,* the wild fig tree of Dattatreya, flourishes everywhere.

After a couple of days of pleasant walking, we came to Shanta Durga, the Peaceful Mother, Goa's presiding goddess. I was thrilled with the beauty of the Shanta Durga temple. In the courtyard was a free-standing lamp tower, reminiscent of a minaret. Everything was spotlessly clean and well-kept. The interior of the temple, adorned with glittering chandeliers, had an art nouveau flavour. There, in the inmost shrine, I saw the silver mask of Shanta Durga, gleaming amid silks, flower garlands and flickering lamps.

"Come," said Sadananda, leading me behind the shrine. "You have to see her bedchamber. It looks like the room of a high-class courtesan."

In the Devi's bedchamber, red velvet cushions were strewn on an ornate silver couch. Scattered around were elaborate silk saris, glittering jewellery, fans and silver-handled fly-switches. Here she was, as lush, green and fertile as the Goan countryside, as warm and seductive as the Goan people—Shanta Durga, the reconciler of sensuality and spirituality, an earthy, vibrant, colourful deity. And here was I, newly liberated from my nunnish strictness, face to face with the Goddess, as she beckoned me to the *Via Positiva*, the Affirmative Way, the way that led through the senses, not through their denial and negation. Shanta Durga was calling me to become fully woman, in every dimension of womanhood, and to follow, from now on, the Positive Way, the way of the Mother, instead of the male aescetic path that, until now, had served me so well.

Sadananda had been to Shanta Durga before, and the priests of the temple greeted him enthusiastically, as they welcomed us into their home. Over their doorway was an interesting painting, showing Shanta Durga standing, proudly and majestically. In one hand, she grasped by the tuft of hair Lord Vishnu; in the other, she held the topknot of Shiva. Both the great gods were dwarfed by the mighty Goddess.

"That's the story of Shanta Durga," explained Sadananda. "Once, Shiva and Vishnu, Destroyer and Preserver, were fighting over who was greatest. Their terrible battle was shaking all the worlds and creating chaos everywhere. So the inhabitants of the Earth prayed to the Great Mother, *Adi Parashakti*, the primordial supreme feminine power, to rescue them. Suddenly, she appeared in resplendent form as Shanta Durga. Grasping the warring gods by the hair, she cried, '*Shanti!*' And the war came to an end."

I gasped. Sadananda had brought me to the feet of the very goddess for whom I had searched so desperately in the depths of my heart for so many years. She, Shanta Durga, was the Reconciler of Opposites, the part of myself I so longed to find. She alone could end the conflict between Vishnu and Shiva, action and contemplation, love and wisdom, the heart and the third eye. For so long, I had felt myself torn apart between action and contemplation, alternating between the lives of a busy junior physician and an enclosed contemplative nun. At once, I knew that Shanta Durga was my chosen Ideal; that I must be her votary, until I became one with Her, the reconciler of opposites.

Inside the priests' house, I was introduced to the devout old grandmother, all smiles and wrinkles, the quiet, widowed mother, the young son, and a plump little girl named Smita, who seemed to hate all adults. I quickly developed an affection for all of them. After the tragic death of the head of the household, this family of *pujaris* had realized that their survival could be ensured only by deep sincerity in carrying out their priestly functions.

"The priest is the mediator between the devotee and God," one of the young men told us. "Therefore, it is necessary that he have great sympathy with the clients, and above all, that he be himself a great devotee of God."

To this end, the *pujaris* carried out their daily worship with tremendous fervour, which rendered the *arati* ceremonies at Shanta Durga quite memorable, particularly the midday worship, when, with the aid of a large mirror, the light of the noontide sun was reflected upon the face of the Goddess.

It was in the fire sacrifices, however, that the devotion of the priests reached a climax. Ranged along the walls, a row of bare-chested brahmins in red silk *dhotis* squatted on wooden stools as they chanted at the top of their voices—the senior priest, with a bald head and a great belly like Lord Ganesh, beating time with his hands, while the young men, our hosts, red-faced from the intensity of the heat, tended the fire, tipping potfuls of *ghee* down a long wooden chute into the sunken well where the fire blazed. The flames leapt up, and from the chanting priests rose a resounding "*Svahah!*"

Our hosts insisted that we stay at the temple until the Boat

Festival, which took place each month, on the fifth day following the full moon. The ceremony was illuminated by fireworks, oil lamps, spotlights and blazing torches, and orchestrated by firecrackers, drums, a loudspeaker blaring Sanskrit chant, and a seven-piece brass band. All of Shanta Durga's three images were employed simultaneously, so that the Goddess was taking an elephant ride around the temple, whilst sitting enthroned upon the edge of the temple tank, watching herself take a boat ride around the tank, escorted by her priests. The whole function was a minutely-ordered chaos.

My visit to Shanta Durga Temple was to mark a turning point in my journey. From the day when Sadananda and I had set forth together from Christa Prema Seva Ashram, Dattatreya our patron had turned towards us the face of Shiva. One by one, all my attachments had been torn from me—the attachment to regular meals and presentable clothes, attachment to the religion and culture of my birth, even the attachment to celibacy, to the way I believed a spiritual life should be lived. Each of these attachments had been offered into the sacrificial fire of the Destroyer. Now, with the *darshan* of Shanta Durga, Dattatreya revealed himself to me with a new face, the face I had seen on his statue at Kanya Kumari Sthan, the face of Godavari Mataji, the face of the Mother. And the Mother was inviting me to pass on from the first step of the spiritual journey, purification through renunciation, to the second step, mystical illumination.

Bidding farewell to the family, who begged us to return soon, we continued our walking pilgrimage. As we drew near to Old Goa, famous for the Bom Jésus Basilica which houses the incorrupt body of St. Francis Xavier, we began to notice girls in the short, Western-style dresses worn by Goan Christians, and men in suits and ties, all moving towards old Goa. They were dressed in their best and had an air of excitement.

"What's happening?" I asked Sadananda, as we reached the city. "It looks like Christmas already!"

The grandiose, crumbling ruins of the erstwhile Portuguese capital, which the colonists had abandoned when it was struck with plague, were alive with all the fun of the fair. Crowds in European dress milled around the numerous stalls, which were selling liquor, snacks, fish curry, giant sweetballs, rosaries, votive candles, statues of St. Francis Xavier, and assorted religious knickknacks. It did not take us long to realize that this was the annual fair for St. Francis Xavier's day, the greatest day on the calendar so far as the Goan Christians were concerned.

Masses were in progress continuously, and we attended three before proceeding to have *darshan* of St. Francis Xavier. Finally, we came to the gilded side-chapel dedicated to St. Francis. A magnificent Baroque statue depicted him with one hand upraised and the other stretched towards the earth, so that he looked like a whirling dervish. Nearby was a tall, marble tomb, inlaid with silver, at the top of which I could see the glass casket containing the saint's incorrupt body. St. Xavier had loved Goa more than any other place on earth, and his fervent and generous spirit filled his chosen resting place.

Next day, we set off again towards the sea, the Great Mother. In a couple of hours we reached the coast, where waves sang on the palm-fringed shore and fishing boats moved on the horizon. Turning a little inland, we came to Mapusa, a pleasant small town, in Bardez district. Here we climbed a steep hill to Sadananda's former home, the Dattatreya Temple, the place where Pilgrim Francis had first encountered the Triple-faced God. Excited to see their friend again, the temple priests hurried out with offerings of fruit.

Next morning, our yoga and meditation complete, we sat in front of Dattatreya, tuned the *dotar,* and began to chant. After a few minutes, we were joined by a devout brahmin gentleman. As we chatted with him after *kirtan,* we learnt that he was a disciple of Shree, the fire sacrifice guru. Eager for some spiritual association, he insisted on buying us bus tickets to the remote village where he was a schoolmaster. Here we found ourselves in a dark, two-roomed cottage in the green, rural heart of Goa, performing *agnihotra* with the schoolmaster and singing *kirtans* into his little tape recorder.

On the last day of our three-day stay, preparing ourselves to return to Poona, we climbed up to a spring in the jungle to wash our clothes. It was an idyllically beautiful place—a clear, cool, rushing spring, deep green foliage, leaves casting a dappled shade, the waters sparkling in the sun, birds warbling—the very essence of Goa, land of the Peaceful Mother. As we were spreading our white cloth out to dry, we heard a rustling sound in the bushes. Suddenly, to my amazement, a magnificent wild peacock appeared. I was no longer in Goa. I was in a celestial world. Sarasvati, Goddess of Song, was strumming her *vina* by the stream, whilst from behind some hidden tree in the jungle, I seemed to hear the haunting flute of Krishna. In the form of the wild peacock, the gods had blessed our Goan pilgrimage.

> *"O Goddess, abiding in all beings in the form*
> *of peace,*
> *Salutations to you, salutations to you*
> *Salutations to you again and again."*
>
> Devi Suktam

Five
The Peaceful Mother

The chilly nights and red dawns of mid-December in the Deccan ushered in a season of celebration. At Rajneesh Ashram—much changed following the departure of Bhagwan—scarlet-robed women with flowing hair danced and sang in honour of their absent Guru's birthday. Meanwhile, many of Poona's young Westerners were excitedly preparing to leave for Goa, the only place in the sub-continent where Christmas was a cultural event. And for the local people of Poona, this was the joyous season of Datta Jayanti, the birth festival of the Triple-faced God.

Amid all this enthusiasm for the nativity of the Divine Child, I woke to the sunlight of my own thirtieth birthday. Today, the fifteenth day of December, 1981 on the Western calendar, Saka Era 1903, was a date I had been anticipating for several years. The thirtieth year of my life, the inner voice had been suggesting, would bring a definite change, an unfolding of the healing work to which I felt myself called.

Sadananda ran to the bazaar to buy some sweet, sticky *barfi* in honour of the day, and the two of us sat in the courtyard of a temple near Mahatma Gandhi Road enjoying the treat. I gazed about me at the clear, bright skies, so different from those of an English December, and wondered what omen would come to me at this hour of grace.

We decided to take the bus to CPS Ashram. There we learnt of a new Christian Ashram, Aum Yeshu Niketan, which had recently opened in Goa, for the service of the "hippies," Goa's young Western visitors. Since we were already eager to return to

Shanta Durga for a special music program, we immediately set off for Goa, arriving at Aum Yeshu Niketan on Christmas Day.

"Olivia, Francis, welcome! *Namaste!*"

Santoshi, the elderly English lady, whom I had pictured as living a silent hermit life at Shantivanam, came out to greet us. She had a big apron over her sari and looked busy and careworn. "Well, Olivia," she said immediately, "there is so much to do here, caring for these young people, and many of them are sick. You are a doctor, exactly what we need. Stay here, and help us."

Eventually, we agreed to return to Aum Yeshu Niketan after the music festival at Shanta Durga. On the journey to the temple, I got a tiny blister, which immediately blew up into a major foot abscess—something you have to be very careful about in India. By the end of the first day of the classical music festival, I could not even walk. The abscess, it seemed, was a hidden blessing of Shanta Durga, for now I had to spend a full week with her.

Our *pujari* friends gave me a room with a wooden bed, and here I stayed, my foot on a pillow, meditating and writing mantras in my journal, whilst Sadananda enjoyed the music festival and meditated with Santa Durga. At lunch time, one of the boys arrived with rice, *dal, chapati* and buttermilk. The evening was the most special time of all, for it was then that I saw Grandmother. A wrinkled, bent old woman, she would tap on my door and enter softly, all smiles, her eyes lighting up as she saw me clanging my little finger-cymbals and singing, *"Shri Ram, jai Ram, jai jai Ram."* We would try to converse a little in Hindi whilst she handed me some cut fruit *prasad*—apple, banana and coconut—from the *arati* she had just attended. My all-but-wordless friendship with her was well worth the pain of the foot abscess. And during the day I had time to contemplate deeply on Shanta Durga as Reconciler of Opposites. It was a quiet, restful time. Not until we returned to Aum Yeshu Niketan did I realize what a hard taskmaster the Peaceful Mother is.

And, as soon as I could walk, return we did, and took up residence on the back porch, behind the chapel. The ashram was situated on Vagator beach near Chappora village, where the wind blew through coconut palms, the sea sang and sparkled in the sun, turnstone birds hunted at the tide line, and the local fishing fleet trawled along the horizon. Here the young Westerners sunbathed, swam, smoked dope, bought cheap heroin, ate fruit salads and danced at disco parties. And here restaurateurs, hoteliers, drivers of motorcycle "taxis", shopkeepers, police and Afghani drug pushers ministered, in a spirit of total self-interest, to the needs of the foreign visitors, who occupied a series of beaches stretching from Arambol Village at the North to Panjim, Goa's capital.

There was, as Santoshi insisted, much work to do, and she and her companions, a German priest named Anand and an Irish sister named Karuna, who was an efficient and experienced nurse, had their hands more than full. It seemed a good opportunity for us to do some service. Moreover, Anand was working closely with the local Chief of Police, and assured us that he would be able to obtain for Sadananda the visa he needed in order to travel safely to the Himalayas.

Sadananda settled into the kitchen, preparing lunch for thirty each day, whilst I soon found myself in charge of a group of young women who had been rescued from the mental hospital. My charges included two Englishwomen, two French teenagers, one of whom was an orphan, and a woman from Sweden. Cassandra, the first of the Englishwomen to arrive, actually half Greek, was slender with striking Hellenic features and a mass of wavy black hair. She was in a constant state of anxiety, wandering around the ashram moaning, "Oh dear, oh dear, everything's wrong! I'm the wrong person in the wrong place at the wrong time. Oh dear!"

Her fellow countrywoman, Ellen, a dancer from an aristocratic family, was tall, strong and athletic. It wrung my heart to see her movements slowed and stilted by haloperidol, the antipsychotic drug which the psychiatrists at Panjim Mental Hospital had prescribed. Yet if she and the other women did not take their drugs, they immediately became completely wild—"flipped out", the hippies said—and ran away. Once out of the safety of the ashram, they were in danger of being beaten by villagers and returned to the mental hospital, where they would receive massive injections of antipsychotic drugs. Thus I felt that I had no option but to continue the haloperidol, even though Ellen made it very clear to me that her "psychosis" was in her eyes a valuable process.

"Life is a cabaret!" she exclaimed gleefully, as we sat together cutting vegetables, a task I had devised as a grounding exercise. "What fun it is to be insane!" Perhaps insanity was her only route of escape from the superficiality and strictness of her upper class English upbringing, dominated by notions of good breeding and proper behaviour.

The orphaned French teenager, Cathérine, had come to India with her boyfriend, who then left her. I was uncertain whether she was suffering from the shock of finding herself abandoned in a strange land or had been administered a dose of the psychotropic herb datura, which disrupts the link between the mind and the body, sometimes permanently. In either case, she behaved like a needy and demanding six-year-old. Though I loved her, I was nearly driven crazy myself by her manipulations. Every few days she would run away. Sadananda and I then had to chase after her and would usually find her sitting at a restaurant table in Chappora with a leather-jacketed biker or some other young man who had caught her fancy, most reluctant to come home.

As for Corinne, the other French girl, she seemed more psychic than psychotic. Her trip to India and experimentation with LSD had opened up her subtle perceptions to such an extent that she was flooded with input. Since she barely spoke English, we conversed in French.

"J'ai peur," she would whisper pathetically. ("I'm afraid.") *"J'ai peur des vibrations."* There was no fear of Corinne's running away; on the contrary, she was so timid that Sadananda and I could scarcely coax her out of the ashram.

My position was a strange one. I had no privacy and was sleeping on the back porch. My health was fragile and my two saris worn from slapping on laundry stones. All this was fine for a wandering *sadhu,* a pilgrim with no concern except meditation—but very strange for a busy, important member of the helping professions. Apart from my duties at the ashram itself, which were more than strenuous enough for one person, I was supposed to be a liaison person with the Goan Chief of Police. This involved riding on the back of Anand's motor scooter to Panjim and then sitting in a black, padded chair in the Police Commissioner's office, dressed in my darned pilgrim sari, trying to look and sound like a respectable physician, someone to whom the Commissioner could entrust the psychotic Westerners who were currently in his custody.

I was caught in my own concepts. My ideas of how a doctor dressed, lived and acted were very different from my present situation. Nor did I want to be a doctor at all, still less a busy, important person. The Shiva part of me, the *sadhu,* was in all-out war with the Vishnu part, the people helper. Where, in the middle of it, was my true self?

Eventually, my physical condition improved a little. Santoshi gave me a piece of turquoise cloth to use as a *lungi,* and Sadananda and I were allocated a room, so I had a little space and privacy. And, after some intense negotiations, Anand and Karuna agreed that, as staff members, we were entitled to receive food, soap and stamps from the ashram budget.

I had been working with Cassandra, Ellen, Cathérine and Corinne for about a month when a policeman appeared at the door, to inform me that he had in his custody a Swedish woman who was completely "plipped out" [*sic*]. Would I take her, or should he have her admitted to the mental hospital? I looked at the woman, fair and beautiful, of about my own age and height, and reminded myself that she could indeed be me. If I were ever in her plight, would I not wish to have a loving friend who could care for me and keep me from the hospital? The others had all left Panjim Mental Hospital with head lice and dysentery—it just was not a safe place for foreigners. Spreading an extra mat on the stone floor of the room I shared with Sadananda, I said firmly, "She will stay here."

As I spoke these words, I had no idea that little more than a year later, my process was to take on an uncanny resemblance to the Swedish woman's. But, in my own case, there would be no Alakananda to help me.

The sleeping mat was not of any use that night, for neither Britte, as my new charge was called, nor I myself, got any sleep. She was in a manic state, violent at times, constantly moving around, endlessly ranting about her rhesus negative blood and the pregnancy she had just lost.

With the help of some antipsychotic medication and an outpatient visit to the mental hospital, Britte calmed down within three or four days, although she remained very vulnerable. She had been at Aum Yeshu Niketan for a couple of weeks when an unusually handsome young Indian man arrived, dressed in crisp, new ochre robes, his long glossy black hair neatly combed. His appearance was exceptionally tidy and his manner uncharacteristically slick for the *sadhu* he claimed to be. With shifty eyes, he scanned the ashram and its inhabitants. I took an instant dislike to him. But anyway, it was time for me to inspect a wounded ankle which Karuna was dressing for a local hippie. As soon as my back was turned, both Britte and the "*sadhu*" disappeared.

Minutes later, a young Goan man appeared, out of breath, having run all the way from the village.

"That *sadhu* boy not *sadhu*, very bad boy. He women stealing... Arabia sending. White woman, fair hair, very much liking. Much money getting."

Sadananda, an excellent runner, set off at full speed across Chappora hill, in the direction that Britte and the pimp were last seen. In great anxiety, I hurried after them. I had visited Indian families who lived in constant mourning after losing a daughter to the flourishing Middle Eastern flesh trade, and while I was in Bombay, educated Indians had regularly warned me to be extremely cautious if I did not want to find myself drugged and exported to some oil sheikh's harem. So I was not inclined to disbelieve the villagers. At Chappora fort, I caught up with Sadananda and the pimp, both trying to persuade Britte to follow them. Taking her firmly by the hand I led a very reluctant woman home, leaving Sadananda to tell the "*sadhu*" exactly what he thought of him.

In each of the women in my care I found an aspect of myself. Cassandra seemed like the embodiment of her namesake, the ancient Greek prophetess of doom. She trailed through my dreams, black hair flying, foretelling the imminent end of the world. Ellen reflected a part of my psyche that also wanted to break away from a strict English upbringing and know the fun of spontaneity. Cathérine reminded me of a sub-personality that I referred to as "Little-Girl-Lost". Corinne was a mirror of my own extreme psychic sensitivity. And Britte, like Cassandra, was a walking archetype, an embodiment of wounded motherhood, Rachel mourning for her children.

Drawing on my training at the German Hospital, an experimental therapeutic community where I had interned as a medical student, I devised a unique program for the women and a team of volunteers. These latter included a German former Jesus freak named Simon, some Rajneesh neo-*sannyasins* and a Danish couple. Each of the women received regular massage, since I hoped this would help them to get back "in touch". We spent an hour or so daily doing simple and well-supervised tasks like cutting vegetables. To restore inner harmony, each had music therapy with Sadananda, and in the evenings, we all did walking meditation, the ultimate grounding exercise.

The psychiatrists at Panjim Mental Hospital, hard-liners who believed firmly in drugs and electro-convulsive treatment, scolded me for giving my patients too little medication; the hippie volunteers told me I was cruel and heartless to give any drugs at all. Whatever I did, I found myself caught in the middle, between two extremes: tradition and revolution, the head and the heart, structure and freedom. Only when the psychiatrist in myself and the hippie in myself learnt to listen to each other would I cease to be a focus of irritation for both sides. But for now, the pragmatist part of me, the activist, the doctor, having lain dormant for two years of Indian pilgrimage, had the bit between her teeth. There was a lot of important, necessary service to be done, many people in need of help and healing, and by all means, I had to help them—never mind the cost to myself.

After a year of peaceful meditation at Shantivanam and CPS Ashram and a year as a wandering *sadhu*, with no duties except remembrance of the Holy Name and no cares except to get one simple meal in a day, I was immersed in service even more demanding than in my time as a resident house physician at Bury St. Edmund's Hospital. I never knew what might happen next. One day it was Anand waking me in the middle of the night to tell me that our Iranian cook had taken an overdose, another day Cassandra escaped and was taken back to the mental hospital, or again, it might be a call to resuscitate a junkie who had taken too much heroin.

I struggled to sustain my meditation amid my duties as doctor, psychotherapist, nurse and dietician. Physically, I was still weak from last year's bout of hepatitis and recurrent episodes of amoebic dysentery, a weakness Anand was quick to interpret as laziness. In reality, as I rather bitterly noted, few of the patients I was attending had such serious, chronic health problems as I, their hardworking physician.

Shanta Durga, the ultimate reconciler, Goa's deity, had plunged me into the heart of conflict. Here I was between the priest and the hippies; between the psychiatrists at Panjim mental hospital and my "crazy girls", who—all but Corinne—seemed to agree with Ellen's statement, 'What fun it is to be insane.' Orthodoxy and heterodoxy, sanity and madness, action and contemplation, East and West . . . Shanta Durga had me by the hair and would not let me go until I ceased to fragment myself, and came to know true inner peace.

Fortunately, I had no idea at the time just how hard-won that peace was to be. I knew—for the inner voice clearly told me so—that my task was the reconciliation of opposites, that a healing power I could not yet imagine would be the result of this reconciliation. And I had begun to see that my journey of reconciling the polarities usually involved an intensive experience of either pole. From a busy county hospital to an enclosed convent—action and contemplation. From the scientific training of a London medical school to the life of a pilgrim on the roads of India—West and East. From the Catholic Church to the feet of a Hindu guru—orthodoxy and heterodoxy. My worst fear, one that had haunted me from childhood, was that I would have to experience madness to reach the state beyond sanity and madness. When would I hear the voice of Shanta Durga in my ear, saying to me, as she said to both Shiva and Vishnu, "Peace!"?

Goddess Mariamme, too, still had her hand laid upon me, and my labours at the ashram were hampered by the foot infection which refused to heal, and left me depressed and listless. Eventually, Sadananda took me for a few days rest and recuperation in the forest. On one of our hitch-hiking journeys, we had noticed the tiny ashram of some forest yogi in the jungle between Goa and Karnataka, and now we wished to spend time there.

My spirits soon lifted, for it was the most beautiful place I had ever seen in my life. Lofty hills and steep valleys, rushing rivers and clear springs were adorned with mango trees, mighty banyans, feathery bamboos waving silver against the sky, castor oil trees, cinchonas and brilliant flame-coloured flowers. With a flash of jewel-bright wings, a kingfisher or green parakeet flew past, amid the crooning of innumerable turtle doves and the sounds of an orchestra of birds and insects. Monkeys crashed through the branches, whilst deep in the jungle hid tigers, leopards, elephants, wild boar and forest bison.

I bathed naked in a perfectly pure, deep river, with no one around except monkeys and birds, and slept outside the little grass hut of the hermit. To our astonishment, the yogi we had come so far to visit turned out to be a small, slight woman about sixty years old, who lived a solitary life in the jungle, tending the tomb of her guru, with whom she had travelled the length and breadth of India on pilgrimage. The *yogini* was delighted with her unexpected guests, and the three of us shared food, sang and prayed together, and gathered wood for her cooking fire.

In the jungle hut, I was a pilgrim, a simple *sadhu*, but back at Aum Yeshu Niketan, I was the Doctor, and Westerners were soon coming from all over Goa to see me. I treated them with a combination of antibiotics and other drugs donated by tourists, country remedies which I gathered from local trees and plants, and love. One day shortly after my return from the *yogini's* hut, Anand excitedly called me into his room. "Look!" he said proudly. Lying on his bed, neatly arranged on green surgical towels, was a formidable collection of scalpels, forceps, clamps and surgical scissors. Karuna, a former operating theatre sister, smiled happily at the sight. "Donated by the priests of my order in Germany," beamed Anand. "Now you can perform operations!" I felt as if I was turning as green as the towels. Performing minor operations for sick hippies on the kitchen table at Aum Yeshu Niketan was definitely not what I had come to India for. I began blustering about asepsis. Finally, to the great disappointment of both Anand and Karuna, I refused point blank to do surgery.

"You need to escape for at least a night," Sadananda told me. "We should go to a place I know near Mapusa. There's a beautiful jungle there with a healing spring. The local people come there to refresh themselves, bathe in the spring, and gather medicinal herbs. It's a really magical place. When I visited it, I fell in love with that jungle so much that I didn't want to leave, so I stayed there for four days, fasting and meditating, drinking pure spring water."

The journey to the jungle took us through groves of wild cashew trees, and we stopped from time to time to quench our thirst with acidic cashew fruits, red, golden and yellow. After the long walk, we eagerly approached the jungle itself. Alas! A scene of utter desolation awaited us—the jungle laid waste, the trees all felled, the Devi of the spring mourning amid the tree stumps. Thus, even in India, land of the sacred, the desires of the wealthy for quick gains and instant profit prevail over the needs of simple folk for a hallowed spot, a place of healing and restoration. Created over thousands of years by nature's cycles and seasons, the jungle was destroyed at the hands of men in but a few days. That one wealthy man might be a little wealthier, the townsfolk of Mapusa lost their greatest resource, the jungle. We left the place with heavy hearts and walked back to Assagaon, where we slept the night outside the church, as brilliant fireflies danced about the trees.

The following evening, after a busy day, we took Corinne into Chappora to visit the temple there, which housed the tomb of a naked saint beloved throughout Goa. It was difficult to think of Chappora, village of restaurants and drug pushers, as anything other than a tourist trap, yet the presence of a saint had blessed the village, and his radiance still seemed to hover over Chappora, touching both villagers and hippies in whatever way they would open themselves to his grace. Here, once or twice a week, the more devout villagers would gather to sing and praise the Name of God.

Corinne, a sensitive soul, was moved by the saint's energy, and we were all a little God-intoxicated when we left to begin our homeward walk. As I followed the other two across the road, a motorcycle with three khaki-clad men mounted on it roared over the brow of the hill, completely out of control, and knocked me flying. "Something's wrong," I told Sadananda as he helped me up. "My hand doesn't work properly." Sure enough, as the evening wore on, my wrist grew sufficiently swollen and painful for Anand and Karuna to bring me to the local hospital, where a fracture was immediately diagnosed. From now for the next six weeks, my right arm would be in plaster. Inner fragmentation had symbolised itself physically, in a dramatic way.

It was early March. The cashews had blossomed, and some were still in bloom, while a few fruits, red and gold, hung from the trees. Sadananda, who was less trapped by his role at the ashram than I, hastened to Shanta Durga Temple to celebrate Mahashivaratri, the Great Night of Shiva. Whilst he kept the vigil of Shiva, I lay on my sleeping mat in the room I shared with Britte. As I drifted into sleep, I found myself at Alandi, where Sadananda and I were in the presence of Raghudas. Baba looked much younger and very healthy, with no silver in his hair. He was sitting up in lotus position, laughing and joking, and showed great happiness at seeing us. Suddenly the scene changed, and Baba was lying on the floor in a corner of the hut near the Gopal Krishna temple, covered by a dark blue blanket. I understood that he was giving us his final message before leaving the body. "I have seen your beauty," he said. "You are so beautiful. Sadananda also, you are both so beautiful. And you two will stay together always. But you must never marry. You must be always sister and husband, sister and husband . . . ." And turning his face to the wall, he gave a gentle sigh and departed from his body.

Only years later, as I read more Vaishnava literature, did I learn the meaning of the strange phrase "sister and husband." The Vaishnava husband is counselled not to regard the woman as "my wife." Looking on her as Divine Mother, he is never to let thoughts of possession or power over her enter his heart. Thus, the union between aspirants on this path is not a "marriage" in the traditional sense, in which the wife becomes the property of the husband. Nor is the purpose of Vaishnava marriage the same as the purpose of worldly marriage, perpetuating the family tree and passing on the ancestral inheritance. Vaishnava marriage is also not the same as the more romantic marriages entered into by Westerners, whose goal is individual satisfaction and personal fulfilment. Urging us never to marry for the sake of either conventional social values or our completion as individuals, Raghudas was holding out to us as an ideal the ancient union entered into by the great Rishis and Rishi-wives of old, a relationship sustained solely by the mutual desire for God-realization. In this almost forgotten tradition, woman's primary role is neither that of physical motherhood nor of making up what is lacking in her husband, rather, she is the matrix through which the highest spiritual energies reach the physical plane. Through the agency of the woman of Truth, her husband, her family and all who know the couple are spiritually uplifted.

After this dream, I was very anxious to go to Alandi and find out whether Raghudas had actually left his body. Sadananda and I seized the first opportunity to visit Poona on ashram business, and were soon waiting in the Alandi bus queue at Shivajinagar with anxiously beating hearts. After saluting Sant Jnaneshvar's *samadhi*, we hurried to 'Baba's cave', which was ominously empty and padlocked. What had happened? "Gopal Temple, Gopal Temple," said Sheikh's plump aunt, who sat as ever behind her stall, selling brassware, *tulasi* beads and heaps of vermilion powder.

In the little Gopal Krishna Temple, where the great *peepul* tree had almost torn away the fabric of the building, we found Raghudas lying under a blanket, exactly as in my dream, whilst Surekha and her mother attended to his needs. He was too weak even to embrace his beloved disciple, Sadananda. A brahmin youth who was staying with Raghudas spoke to us in English, informing us that Baba had in fact been in the hospital at the time of my dream.

"Baba told us in advance, 'I shall become very sick and suffer much, like Shirdi Sai Baba, and then I shall leave my body,'" the youth explained. "I myself came here for a brief visit only, and was going directly to Shirdi. I am the devotee of Sai Baba. I saw Maharaj here, and immediately Shirdi Sai Baba's form appeared before my eyes. Three times this is happening to me. I am looking at Raghudas Baba, and immediately I am getting the *darshan* of Shirdi Baba. So now I am understanding that he is the same as Sai Baba. No need of going to Shirdi; Shirdi is here itself. So I made arrangements to remain here and care for Baba during his illness."

We were both very much saddened to see our guru in such a weakened condition, even though, despite his bodily pains, he still emanated both bliss and humour. Yet he was obviously well cared for by the local devotees, whilst Dr.-Mrs. Joshi, the Poona physician, whom we met the next day, had taken charge of his medical needs. After much discussion, we decided that the women in the halfway house had more need of our presence, and that the best service we could render to Raghudas would be to return to our duties in Goa. With tears in our eyes, we touched Raghudas' feet, said goodbye to Surekha and her mother, and headed for the bus station, reaching Aum Yeshu Niketan the following morning.

The Christian Holy Week was hot and humid, and an outbreak of hepatitis struck down Sadananda and some other ashram residents. Meanwhile, a lady from Panajim, wearing the short, European-style cotton frock favoured by Goan Christians, visited the ashram and was full of concern for the invalids. Surely it must be possible to get them some of the country medicine for which Goa was so renowned. True to her words, the lady returned that evening, rather out of breath and laden with bottles. The medicine she brought was a magenta liquid, of exceptionally bitter taste, four large glasses of which were to be consumed daily.

When our bottles were empty, Sadananda and I travelled to a white-washed villa in the town of Alto Porvorim, where we met the frail old woman who had received from her grandmother the family secret of preparing the remedy. "If only they would come to me," she said, in soft, sighing tones, "I could cure them. They are killing them in the hospital with that glucose and all. This medicine is working in the most severe cases. But some of them come too late." She sighed. Her words rang true to us, for Sadananda and Margaret had recovered well, and I had finally shaken off the lassitude that had plagued me since my attack of hepatitis the previous year. "The roots are scarce now. You must go far, far into the jungle to search for them. And I have a weak heart. But all my medicine is made with prayer. I pray for each one of you. I love you all." So saying, she beckoned her daughters, who brought us fresh bottles of the magenta potion and sent us on our way.

Sadananda was recovering, but needed a time of recuperation.

So, as April drew to a close, we went to visit his friends in Mapusa. The local Christians ushered in the month of May with a great festival in honour of Our Lady. In true Goan style, festival meant feasting, merrymaking, and an array of booths in the main street. Since we were completely penniless, we took the guitar Sadananda had borrowed from the Aum Yeshu Niketan, and, stationing ourselves among the booths, began to sing Gospel songs. The Goans were delighted and rewarded us liberally; yet we were most touched by the few coins solemnly offered by a group of ragged boys, who listened to the music with fascination.

The money from this venture was enough to pay our bus fare to Arambol, the hippie paradise. Disembarking from the bus at what may be India's strangest village, we stopped for a while to meditate and drink sweet well water at a little convent in the Christian section. Then we climbed up to the sacred part of Arambol, a volcanic rocky knoll overlooking the beach. To Hindus throughout the west coast, this is a special shrine to Parashuram, the immortal *avatar* who visited Shree at Akkalkot.

After he had killed all the unjust kings with his battle axe, Parashuram donated the lands he had won to the most righteous of the kings. Then to create a domain for himself, he shot his arrows into the ocean, commanding the sea to draw back and grant him a piece of land. Thus was created the entire Konkan strip, the west coast of India, from Bombay to the Indian Ocean. With his battle axe, he hacked out the passes in the Western Ghats, rendering the land accessible to the interior. And through his sincere prayer, he installed the Goddess Kanya Kumari, the Little Maidchild, at the southernmost tip, requesting her to protect the land forever from being swallowed by the sea. All these labours completed, the mighty Parashuram celebrated by performing the greatest fire sacrifice in the history of the world—right here on Arambol's rocky knoll.

We sat for awhile at the little shrine commemorating this great *yagna* and then went to the beach, where naked young Westerners were everywhere. Amid palm trees at the edge of the beach we saw many huts and visited some old acquaintances of Sadananda's. In a beautiful bamboo hut, where everything was neat and aesthetic, we met a sweet, gracious couple, artist friends of Sadananda's.

Unfortunately, they were also long-term opium addicts, so neither of us felt comfortable to stay for long.

Setting off again, we walked up the stream into the jungle. Little platforms, huts and tree houses were everywhere. Dread-locked hippies in various states of dress—some in *lungis,* some only in a loincloth, some completely naked—sat smoking chillum, playing the flute or guitar, making jewellery, or chatting. Young people strolled around, meditated beneath the trees, or were engaged in yoga. Monkeys, too, were busy with their own yogas—chattering, swinging from branch to branch, searching for food. Birds sang and insects droned. Our progress was slow, as we stopped from time to time to meet someone or listen to a song.

Finally, after several hours of slow walking, we reached a mighty banyan tree. Up in its branches we noticed a tree house and a wooden platform, on which a woman sat in meditation. She had long matted locks and wore only a loincloth. Hearing us coming along the path, she opened her eyes and beckoned us up, greeting us in a strong French accent. It was soon obvious that, despite her unusual style of dress, she was a sincere and genuine spiritual seeker, so we decided to spend the night with her.

As dusk fell, we all climbed down to the *dhuni* beneath the tree, where she prepared tea for us and cooked some rice and *dal.* After we had eaten, we sang *kirtan,* whilst she sat staring at the embers of her fire. She was truly a unique character—a young and attractive Frenchwoman who had completely adopted the lifestyle and even the mannerisms and dress of an Indian male *sadhu*. She squatted by her fire, just like an old Baba, and was as rigid as any *sadhu* about the rules and regulations of her banyan tree ashram. An introverted type, she was hospitable but not particularly intimate, keeping herself to herself. Yet she was obviously pleased when we woke early in the morning and sat for meditation beneath the banyan. After meditation, we took chay beside her *dhuni* and made our way back down the path.

As we neared the beach, a stout, tall man in a tie-dyed t-shirt approached us. He had dark hair and a reddish face. "Hi, you beautiful people! You have such wonderful vibes, brother and sister. I'm Raphael, and we have a beautiful hut over here where you can stay," he greeted us in a strong New York Jewish accent. "I'm of the Rainbow tribe," he went on, sweeping us along with him in the direction of his stone cottage. "Peace, love, and sacred ganja. I'm gonna fill the world with rainbows," and he pointed to his shirt. "I tie-dye, I make rainbows, to give joy to people. I tie-dye, give massages and feed the hungry. We have to fill the world with positive vibes, man—food, love, massage, ganja, rainbows. Wanna tie-dye those shirts you have? Here, eat some of this, brown rice and jackfruit nuts." We were inside the cottage by now. "Did you know you can eat the seeds of jackfruits? Nutty taste, real good with brown rice, and all free, man. Gotta feed the hungry." And he filled our bowls. "Did you go to the first Rainbow festival?" Sadananda had gone; I, of course, had not. "That's when I learnt the true path, man—peace, love and tie-dye."

Raphael was full of love and hospitality, so we spent a pleasant three days with him, learning to tie-dye and eating brown rice and jackfruit nuts. It was hard to tear ourselves away from such a peaceful setting and return to the stresses of life at Aum Yeshu Niketan. But of course, our service was needed. And we had, after all, a verbal promise from the Police Commissioner that he would get Sadananda a resident permit, so that we could spend tourist seasons working at the ashram and the off-season visiting the sacred shrines of India—first, of course, the Himalayas.

But once again, things did not turn out as we had expected. Long after we should have left for Badrinath and the Alakananda River, we were called to the Police Commissioner's office, where, as usual, we were greeted politely and respectfully, as Aum Yeshu Niketan staff. We sat in the black, padded chairs whilst the office boy brought us tea and glucose biscuits. From behind his desk, the Commissioner handed Sadananda a piece of paper. "Here, this is all I can do for you. Take this paper and proceed immediately to Shri Lanka. From there, you can apply for resident permit. Don't worry, don't worry, I will help you. Definitely you will be getting residency. And with this paper I am giving you, no harm will come to you."

That evening, I took my usual hour's break at the ocean. It was already June. Sitting on a rock, I watched the first white clouds roll inland, heralds of the monsoon which would break in a couple of weeks. As the sun touched the horizon, I plunged into the reddening waters of the ocean, and then sat again, reflecting on our situation. With the onset of the monsoon, the ashram would virtually close, and the work of the season would be at an end. Santoshi, who was exhausted by her diligent work, mothering and organizing us all, had already left for England to visit relatives and to rest. After waiting all winter and even through the hot season to get Sadananda's visa and go to the Himalayas, we were now being sent in the opposite direction. And we could not really 'proceed immediately'. Before undertaking such a long journey, we would need to salute all our teachers: Shree at Akkalkot, Godavari Mataji at Sakuri, and above all, Raghudas. Our visas for Shri Lanka could be obtained only at the High Commission in Madras, from where we would have to travel to Rameshvaram, at the southern tip of India, to catch the Shri Lanka-bound ferry. Instead of our usual process of taking each day as it came and moving as the Spirit led us, we now had a complex itinerary.

Our stay at Aum Yeshu Niketan had not brought the visa we had hoped for, but it had provided many lessons. Just as the inner voice predicted, I had returned to healing work immediately after my thirtieth birthday. Shanta Durga was clearly showing me that I could not choose either Shiva or Vishnu, either contemplation or action, but must learn to balance them in my life. Like Dattatreya, the Triple-faced God, on whose birth-festival I was born, like his feminine counterpart Tripura Sundari, the three-headed mother, I had three faces; as creative artist—the aspect of Brahma, as mother and healer—the aspect of Vishnu, and as contemplative renunciant—the aspect of Shiva. And in the same way that Dattatreya turns towards his devotees the face of Vishnu, I was destined, though I did not yet fully realize it, to turn towards my fellow beings the form of healing and nurturance, whilst remaining ever faithful to a more hidden life as contemplative mystic.

"*Svahah!*" Flames leapt up in fifty copper pots as the offering of rice and ghee was thrown on the fire. It was sunrise in Akkalkot, and in the courtyard of the *math,* devotees were lined up before their *agnihotra* pots to perform the sacrifice. Afterwards, whilst morning tea was served, we were introduced to Vasant

Paranjape, a leading disciple of Shree, who had commissioned him to promote the Vedic fire sacrifice in America and worldwide.

Shree was as radiant as ever. Nodding and smiling, he gave us his blessing and a handful of nuts, dried coconut and crystallized sugar. "Take food, take food."

So we made our way to the dining room for breakfast, and there met a New York Jew who introduced himself as Barry and explained that he was in Maharashtra to write a thesis on the environmental effects of Vedic fire sacrifice. Barry was enthusiastic about research data from around the world showing that *agnihotra* benefited the growth of plants and the yield of farms and gardens, reduced counts of pathogenic bacteria and moulds in the immediate vicinity and even helped to neutralize the effects of radioactive contamination of air, water and soil. Since Shri Lanka was currently afflicted with a bee disease which could have a drastic effect on crop pollination, he wanted us to do some research on *agnihotra* and bees when we reached Shri Lanka. But his own thesis concerned the effect of *agnihotra* on mental illness. Basing his research on ancient Vedic texts, Barry had accumulated a large amount of evidence showing that psychotherapy and psychiatric treatment was significantly more effective when *agnihotra* was performed in a room adjacent to the space where therapy was administered. I could not help wishing I had known all this whilst I was still at Aum Yeshu Niketan.

Shree's son came over to join us. "Here is your *agnihotra* pot. Shree has blessed it as you asked. And here is one other pot. We are giving you this one for some other person you may meet, who may be wishing to do *agnihotra*."

Carefully packing the copper pots, we made our way to Poona, and reached Alandi on the auspicious waning Eleventh. Baba's health had improved somewhat, and he was able to sit up and take a little food. As we prostrated before him in the Gopal Krishna temple, he expressed great delight in seeing us, like a grandfather greeting his favourite grandchildren.

Right after the Shivaratri dream of Raghudas, the sandalwood *mala* I had received on the day I surrendered at his feet had broken. A *neem mala* given to me at the Bombay Hare Krishna temple broke a couple of days later. The period of discipleship, of sitting at the guru's feet, was at an end. Raghudas was evidently in his last illness, and we had to leave Maharashtra.

From now onwards, the guru would no longer be 'the one who is standing before you', but the One who dwells within, to purify the depths of the heart. In token of this, I handed Baba a *tulasi mala* which I had purchased from Sheikh's aunt that day. Solemnly, Raghudas prayed a complete round on the beads, and then held with great attention the 'guru bead,' the first and last, the One that holds together the hundred and eight beads of the *mala*.

Later that evening, we were ushered into the dark little hut where Raghudas sat on a chair, his feet planted on the ground like the Buddha Maitreya.

"I have one thing to ask," said Sadananda, as we seated ourselves on a mat at his feet. "You are so stable, Baba, so steadfast, so deeply rooted in devotion. I see you as a *tulasi* tree, firmly rooted, unwavering. And I also desire to be like that. How can I become like you, like the *tulasi* tree, deep-rooted in the Divine?"

Baba smiled. 'Don't worry. Don't worry about anything. I will see to that. I will take care of you, now and always. I am with you everywhere, yes, even in New York."

We were sitting aboard a bus, headed towards Shirdi, when I distinctly heard Sai Baba say to me, "I will complete what I began in you last year."

"Oh, wonderful," I mused, "he's going to purify me."

The purification took a less than welcome form. Just as had happened the previous year, immediately I arrived within the sacred circle of Shirdi, I developed a raging fever. This time, however, it was not hepatitis, but influenza and bronchitis. It is told of Sai Baba that at times, taking a drastic method to alleviate a disciple's karmic burden, he would fly into a seeming rage and beat the poor disciple with a stick. Now, it seemed, whenever I went to Shirdi, I was to be beaten until my sins were ground to dust.

The following morning, I was standing on the upper story of the *dharmsala,* when an old black dog mysteriously appeared. He seemed to be looking for me, for he walked straight up to me, greeted me with affection, and gazed long and hard into my eyes

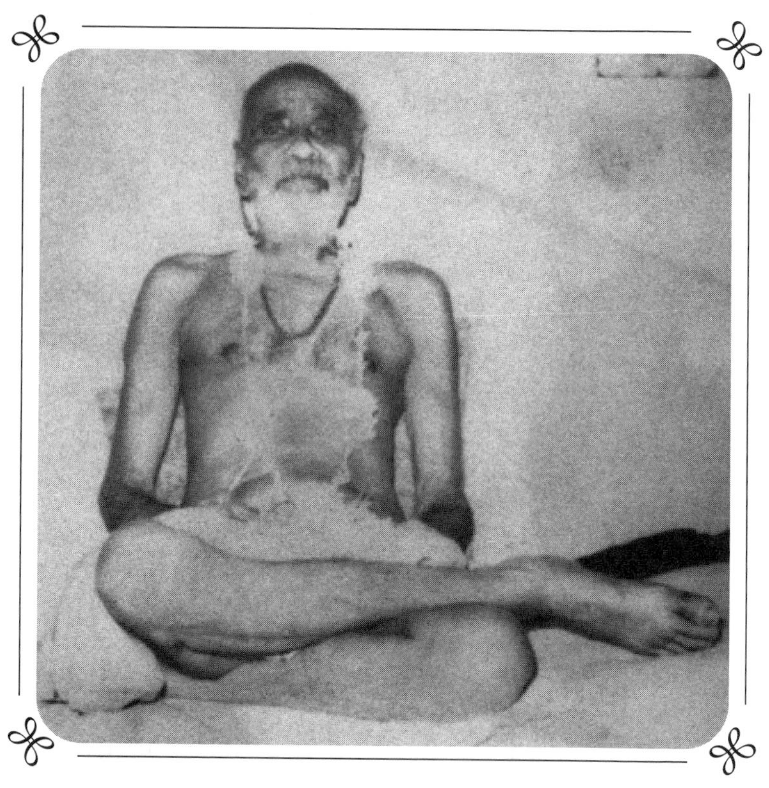

LAST PHOTOGRAPH EVER TAKEN OF RAGHUDAS MAHARAJ.

Baba attached some significance to this photograph, ordering that it not be released until one year after his *mahasamadhi*.

with great love. It was only after he had ambled off that I remembered that dogs are not supposed to be able to look people in the eyes in that way. Sai Baba, who in his lifetime would appear in canine form, had sent his dog devotee to bring me a special blessing.

After a couple of days, the fever subsided sufficiently for me to make my way to Sakuri. Godavari Mataji was standing quietly with eyes downcast and hands clasped as devotees prostrated before her. When I joined the *darshan* queue, she suddenly looked up, smiled at me, and in a remarkable departure from her usual custom, greeted me with joined palms before her face, a gesture of reverence and blessing. I might be sick and weak, but the embodiment of Divine Mother had blessed me in a way I would never forget.

From each of my three teachers I gained on this visit a special gift. Shree had given to Sadananda and myself the second *agnihotra* pot, that is, the ability to pass on the *agnihotra* to other seekers. Raghudas had blessed my new *tulasi mala,* a symbol of devotion; Godavari Mataji had bestowed the unique greeting. These were in fact their parting gifts, for I was never to see any of them in the body again. Though small gifts, or so it might seem, they were seeds that would later sprout, grow and bear fruit. *Agnihotra* fires would be kindled in the homes of my friends and associates, as foretold by the extra copper pot. The blessing given to the *mala* of one hundred and eight *tulasi* beads would gradually find its way into my heart, until I was repeating my guru *mantra* on the endless rosary of every breath, every step. At length this *sadhana*—and my life—would be fulfilled with the realization of supreme, liberating faith in the guru, a state in which everything and everyone would be recognized as the Divine Beloved. And as years passed, bringing ever greater strength and confidence, I would finally come to recognize that in greeting me with reverently joined palms, Godavari Mataji acknowledged me as a guardian of the teachings, a vessel from which seekers could drink of her grace and the grace of her lineage.

All this lay in the future, and none of it was of any consolation to me as, eager to return to Maharashtra to see my three beloved teachers again and longing to have the *darshan* of the source of the Ganges, I prepared to leave Shirdi. The bus from Shirdi to Bombay bumped and rattled its way over the Western Ghats, whilst blasting Hindi film music into the ears of the passengers. By the time we arrived in Bombay, I was in poor shape.

Godavari Mataji's blessing took a very tangible form, when the British Consulate extended my passport on the spot, without making me wait the customary three weeks. That task done, we boarded the Bombay Madras Express, equipping ourselves for the journey with some soaked mung beans, which we intended to sprout in the warmth of the compartment.

Bitterly disappointed by the frustration of all our pilgrimage plans, Sadananda and I turned our backs to the North, direction of the shining Himalayan snows, the abode of Shiva. Now we were heading due South, deep into the lap of the Mother. Forty-eight hours later, after travelling the entire thousand mile journey on two wooden luggage racks, we arrived in the capital of Tamil, Madras. Madras was in the grip of a terrible drought, for the monsoon had failed two years in a row. We searched in many places for accommodations, but nobody wanted guests who would need to bathe and do laundry.

Rather hopelessly visiting the Jesuit seminary, in the full expectation of being turned away again, we met a Jesuit father of great spiritual insight, who unhesitatingly offered us a luxurious room with fan and private bathroom in the retreat centre he ran. We were now able to make a clean and well-groomed appearance at the Shri Lankan High Commission. Within a few days, we had completed the necessary paperwork for travelling from India to Shri Lanka.

And so, like Ram of old, we came at last to Rameshvaram, on the shore of the Southern Salt Ocean. Here Ram and his army of monkeys and bears gathered, ready to cross to Lanka to rescue Sita after her abduction by Ravana, the Demon King. The remnants of the great bridge they built can be seen to this day, it is told, as Adam's Bridge. And here Ram so devoutly worshipped the shivalinga that Shiva agreed to dwell here forever, establishing Rameshvaram as the eleventh of the Twelve *jyotirlinga,* and India's southern *dhama,* or 'Abode of Light', one of the four cardinal points of the pilgrim's *mandala*. Ironically, we had come, not to Badrinath, the Northern of the four *dhamas,* but to its polar opposite. We did not know at the time indeed, we only learnt when at last we reached Badrinath—that no valid pilgrimage to the Himalayan shrine can be completed unless Rameshvaram, the feminine pole, is visited first. We felt ourselves to be going off course, yet in truth, we were right on the mark.

So important a pilgrimage place is Rameshvaram, that hundreds of pilgrims from North India crowded into the train that crossed the causeway to Rameshvaram's coral reef: ochre-robed renunciants and whole families laden with tin trunks and bed rolls, all eager to see the golden sands, gently waving palms, and crystal clear waters of the Southern Ocean. Immediately on arrival, we made our way to the temple, walking through long, cool, cloisters whose ceilings were adorned with a galaxy of *mandalas*. Having bathed in the temple tank whilst the Gods were taking their noontide slumber, we saluted the massive image of the great monkey Hanuman which stands at the entrance to the temple, covered with crimson *sindhur*. Hanuman it was, the son of the wind, who leapt to Lanka from India in a single bound to find Sita and bring her the ring of Ram. Moving on to the heart of the temple, we reverently entered the shrine of the Goddess. Unlike any of the other *jyotirlinga*, Rameshvaram also honours Amma, the Great Mother who is both India and the ocean that cradles her in her murmurous lap. Only with Her blessings did we dare to approach the *garba griha*, the womb house, to venerate the *linga* of light.

At nightfall, drums and oboe-like *shenais* struck up a meditative tune in the temple, and crowds gathered for *arati*. Local brahmins could be recognized by the huge rolls of fat hanging over the waist of an immaculate *dhoti*. The duty of Rameshvaram's pilgrims is to feed brahmins, and there appeared to be numerous brahmins whose sole ritual function was to be the recipient of food offerings. It was a task to which they clung tenaciously. As mere foreigners, *mlecchas*, it was difficult for us to obtain any *prasadam* in Rameshvaram. The numerous feeding centres were entirely oriented to feeding orthodox brahmins, who would consider themselves polluted if we so much as ate the remnants that were left after all of them were fully satisfied.

It would have been hard to find a place to stay also, had we not encountered a Maharashtran devotee of Dattatreya. From the special style of our *tulasi malas*, round, hand-turned beads obtainable only in Alandi, he immediately recognized us as fellow Maharashtrans and invited us to the small *dharmsala* he ran. The place was dark and cool, the walls hung with pictures of Dattatreya, Shirdi Sai Baba, Samarth Swami of Akkalkot and the naked saint who was Godavari Mataji's former incarnation. The environment made us feel quite at home, whilst we were able to cook ourselves some rice over our host's kerosene stove. Unfortunately, it was not only the building that was dark. The Maharashtran, a widower who had lost both wife and son, was in a permanently dark, depressed mood.

The ferry for Shri Lanka left only once a week, and we had just missed one, so we had plenty of time to experience the *darshan* of Rameshvaram. Each morning and evening we visited the temple. attending magnificent *aratis,* when the *pujaris* waved big, heavy brass lamps with numerous glowing ghee wicks. Both of us specially relished the temple music of *shenai* and drums, a specialty of the south Indian temple tradition.

We also visited the great *Math* of the Shankaracharya order, where lived the ochre-robed *dandiswamis*—brahmin *sannyasi*-philosophers, who carried the *dandi* or bamboo staff and followed the Advaita Vedanta path. It was the first Shankaracharya, the great founder of the orthodox Advaita School of Philosophy, who had identified the four *dhamas* in India's four corners. In each of them, he established a Math, where *sannyasis* who walked from *dhama* to *dhama,* carrying only their *dandi* and a brass waterpot, could spend the rainy season in scriptural study and in meditating on the great teaching "*Tat tvam asi:* You Are That".

One night, as I slept, I found myself at Raghudas' evening *satsang* in company with several other disciples. "Tomorrow," Raghudas was saying to the assembled company, "you will see me no more." Then, looking directly at Sadananda and myself, he declared firmly, "You two may come. Far in the North, you will receive my *darshan* again." I woke, convinced that Raghudas was giving me a last message before leaving the body, and certain, too, that in travelling to the Himalayas, we would meet some saint or saints through whom we could receive his *darshan*.

The day of the ferry's departure dawned, and we took a long hot walk to the boat terminus, only to learn that, in order to be admitted on the Shri Lanka-bound boat, one had to show a sizeable sum of money, in foreign exchange. What little we had was all in rupees, and the manager of the ferry turned us away. As we retraced our steps back towards the temple, Sadananda remarked, "Godavari Ma gave me her blessing to visit the Ganga and the Himalayas, and then to leave India. She never said to leave India before completing that pilgrimage. So now I cannot leave. The doors of the temple that is India are bolted, and I am inside."

Very worried about Sadananda's visa situation, we decided to take the train as far North as Madurai, the nearest large town to Rameshvaram. There Sadananda would try to extend the visa given him by the Goan Chief of Police. With an extra few days grace, perhaps we could cross India from South to North and go to Nepal instead of Shri Lanka for his new visa application.

The detective in Madurai frowned at the papers Sadananda had received in Goa. "What is this? These papers are totally invalid! Don't ask me to extend them, just be grateful that I am not arresting you. Had you tried to board the Rameshvaram ferry with these papers, you would undoubtedly have found yourself in prison. Get out! I can do nothing more for you." So much for the courtesy of the Goan Chief of Police. He had simply been trying to get rid of us, since he could not deliver what he had promised months before.

By now, Sadananda and I were both totally confused about where we should go or what we should do. Goddess Meenakshi, however, had her own plans for us. She wished to rock us in her golden lap and nourish us at her breast. Disembarking from the train somewhere between Madurai and Dindigul, we turned up a dirt road and found ourselves in a beautiful valley at the foot of the Kodai hills, accessible only to bullock cart and bicycle. In this fertile land of artesian wells, peasant farmers were growing sugar cane, millet, sweet potatoes, coconuts, mangoes, grapes, rice, vegetables of every variety, and flowers—field upon field of the fragrant white jasmine flowers which Tamilian women bind in their hair and the pink tea roses that are sold outside the Madurai temple and offered to Meenakshi.

The peasants were simple people who tilled the land with oxen and home-made tools, nominal Christians, who knew, as Father Bede would say, "No religion but love." Despite our complete ignorance of the Tamil language, they received us with great hospitality, and fed us on tender coconuts, goats milk, millet porridge, and pure artesian water.

One afternoon, we were resting in a mango grove, in the afternoon heat, gnawing on sugar cane sticks. Noticing a large white ox tethered nearby, and knowing that oxen are very fond of sugar cane, I walked quietly over to give him some. With a toss of his horns, he struck me on the brow, exactly at the symbolic site of the Third Eye centre, the point where saints bestow initiation. The force of the blow was just enough to break the skin and leave a visible mark. Shiva, Rider on the Bull, Lord of the Third Eye, had marked and claimed me as his own.

After lingering a while in golden Meenakshi's valley, we made our way up into the magnificent mountains of Shiva Sundareshvar, a place of swirling mists and shining peaks, wooded slopes fragrant with eucalyptus and pine, rushing streams edged by ferns and flowers, vistas of the sunlit valley shimmering through a veil of morning mist. Here, in the abode of indigenous tribes and their megalithic dolmens, the British had constructed a hill station complete with club house, golf course, colonial villas and Victorian Gothic churches, all built with a kind of elegant tastelessness. Kodaikanal had numerous English medium boarding schools, where the children of Western missionaries and wealthy Indians kicked balls around together in a passable imitation of the playing fields of England, and a sizeable population of hippies, attracted by good food and wild hallucinogenic mushrooms.

Having found us thin and weak, Goddess Meenakshi was eager to feed us. Kodaikanal grew an astonishing variety of produce, from tropical delights like coconuts, mangoes, papayas and avocados to such standard English favourites as leeks, rhubarb and brussel sprouts. The bees among the flowers and Jersey cattle in the lush grass made this truly a land of milk and honey.

The monsoon had not yet broken over most of Tamil Nadu, but it was cold and rainy in the hills, although water was still very scarce as a result of the drought. We found accommodation in a partitioned-off corner of a cowshed with an earthen floor and no windows, equipped with some straw mats, a broken chair, kerosene stove, and grindstone. Here we cooked, ground wheat and millet for porridge, and performed *agnihotra* according to Shree's instructions.

Each day, as I struggled to carry a jar of drinking water on my hip from the only local well that had not run dry, I admired the village women, who could gracefully carry one jar on the head and a second on the hip, or water on the head and a baby at the hip.

Slowly, I grew closer to the women of the indigenous tribes, for I shared the toil of their daily life for a full month, pounding clothing beside them in the river, and carrying cooking pots to the river to scour.

We lingered in the land of milk and honey from mid-July to mid-August. One day as we were out walking, admiring the peaks and clouds afire with the rays of the rising sun, a stocky young man with a plaintive, confused air approached us. "Amazing!" he said in a strong Swiss-German accent. "Amazing! I were just setting out to look for you, and here you have come. I saw you in the teashop the other day, and I thought, 'This couple can help me.' I have been taking mushrooms, magic mushrooms. But I need some help. May I come with you? My name is Marcel."

And from that moment, for the next month, Marcel remained with us night and day, as faithfully as Lakshman with Ram and Sita. The hallucinogenic mushrooms had left him confused and disoriented. With psychedelics, he could catch a glimpse of higher consciousness, but could not integrate that glimpse, still less become stable in *gnosis*. Now he was ready for the path of spiritual discipline, and eager to find a teacher. Since we were planning to descend the mountain to visit Mother Mary's shrine of Vailankanni, at the mouth of the Kaveri, we decided to escort him to Shantivanam, where he could be guided by Father Bede, and then to make our way from there to Vailankanni.

The Kodai hills were gently sloping on one side, on the other they fell steeply to the plain. It was agreed amongst the three of us to take the footpath down the steep side of the mountain, by way of a village which was perched on the crags, accessible only by footpath. The first day's walk down the rocky path led past fragrant mountain flowers and treacherous holes, in one of which I twisted my ankle. By nightfall, when we reached the picturesque little village with its tiled roofs and cobbled streets, my ankle was extremely swollen, and I could barely hobble. A village brahmin with shaven head and long, flowing sacred tuft was summoned to massage my foot, a task he accomplished so skilfully that after one day's rest at the village, I was able to continue the downward climb through groves of guavas and oranges, *neem* and great banyan trees. The path reached the plains at a spot where a number of natural pools had formed in a bed of volcanic lava, a sacred place where several small temples had been erected.

On the full moon, we reached the town of Bodinayakanur, at the foot of the Kerala mountains, Nearby lay the former hermitage of Sadhu Govinda, a friend of Sadananda's. An American who had now returned to his native land, Govinda had for eight years lived the life of a Hindu renunciant, loved and respected by the townspeople as much for his mastery of the Tamil language as for his austere lifestyle. Situated in a coconut grove with an abundant supply of fresh water, the little temple and *bhajan* hall which his patrons had constructed for Govinda seemed an ideal spot to make a retreat, in preparation for the pilgrimage to Mother Mary's shrine.

Govinda's friends and patrons, ever hoping that another foreign *sadhu* would come to live at the hermitage to ease their nostalgia, swiftly rallied around to offer spiritual and material support. Muttusami, the owner of the coconut plantation, a quiet, serious and very devoted man, took great pains to see that we had all we needed, and would cut tender coconuts for us each day. Govinda's friend Pandysami, who stopped by from time to time, insisted on bringing us to his very poor village to eat *pongal,* a sweet preparation of rice cooked with ghee, raisins, and cardamon, on the occasion of his daughter's betrothal. Then there was the flamboyant Ramraj, a cardamon plantation owner who was one of Govinda's chief patrons, and who supplied us with foodgrains. With Ramraj everything was dramatic, both his moods of deep melancholy and the devotional sentiments which he expressed with great feeling, but which were never followed through by any active engagement in spiritual practice.

Ramraj invited us to spend a few days at his house before settling into our retreat. Here I met his mother, a very devout old lady at whose behest any poor folk who came to the door were treated kindly and fed well, and his two beautiful almond-eyed daughters. The young women, Rani and Shanti, were never allowed out of the house and never spoke to a man other than their brother.

We passed twenty-one days in retreat at Sadhu Govinda's hermitage, waking each morning to the cry of *"Allah hu akbar!"*

from the local mosque. One evening a shower of rain drove a large scorpion out of his sandy hole and into our hermitage. Taking his presence as a blessing from Lord Shiva, we gently encouraged him to move a short distance from the temple. The next night, the dark of the moon, two men appeared in a rainstorm shortly before midnight. In the hope that they merely wished for shelter from the storm, we offered them tea, and when the rain stopped, requested them to leave. Instead, full of lust for woman and gold, they withdrew a little way into the coconut grove, to cut heavy sticks for themselves, and then returned, brandishing their sticks and flourishing long knives, to demand our money. In response, Sadananda vanished into the temple and reappeared, carrying not the money, but his dotar, which he began to play. The night was dark, the place lonely, the men well-armed, and we had no refuge except the Name of God. Seating ourselves firmly at the entrance to the temple, we closed our eyes and began to chant *"Om Namah Shivayah."*

Suddenly terrified, the men threw down their sticks, afraid that the foreign yogis would curse them or some terrible doom fall upon them for attempting to harm God's devotees. "All right, all right, enough," they mumbled, as they hastily touched our feet in apology and ran off. But by now we were wide awake and ready for action, so, since Lord Shiva had sent the men to invite us to vigil on the dark of the moon, we spent the rest of the night chanting *"Om Namah Shivayah."* Between the visit of the scorpion and our salvation from the thieves, we knew that Shiva had accepted our retreat.

Having escorted Marcel to Shantivanam, we set off for Vailankanni, carrying with us only a few rupees. We walked most of the way from Trichy to Tanjore, where we hitched a ride towards the Coromandal Coast. Next day, we reached Mother Mary's shrine on the sandy delta of the Kaveri River. Here, it is told, where the sacred river of the South merges with the ocean, a young brahmin boy on his way home from milking the cows saw a radiantly beautiful lady, holding a baby in her arms, standing by a spring. "My baby is thirsty," said the lady in sweet tones; "please give him some milk." As he hurried home, the boy was afraid he would be scolded for parting with the milk, but when he arrived, he found his vessel full to overflowing.

Near the spring was a great banyan tree, in the shade of which a lame boy used to sit and sell buttermilk. One day, the same radiant lady, again holding her child, appeared before this boy also, and healing his lame leg, asked him to go to a certain Catholic gentleman in Nagapattinam and tell him to build a chapel there in her honour. To grow to full stature, the infant Christ must be nourished with the milk of the cosmic religion, and to strike roots in India, the church must be ready to take shelter beneath the Great Banyan Tree, India's *sannatan dharma.*

The shrine was built, but the deeper meaning of the Lady's message went unheeded. Amid all the masses, rosaries and novena prayers that embodied a distinctively Roman thought form, there was little opportunity to touch the silence and simplicity in which the Lady and the children of India had met. At the little chapel by the banyan tree and well, on the sandy shore with the softly murmuring water; and in the Basilica, where the miraculous statue of Mary glowed amid pink roses, we strove to feel the touch of Arokia Maria, Mother of Good Health. She is the healer for a fractured humanity; in her new-born child, the God-Man, she unites East and West. After three days, we began to experience her presence and to sense her healing power, attested by hundreds of silver votive offerings, presented by those who had been miraculously restored to health.

The day of our departure from Vailankanni dawned. It was October the Fourth, the Feast of St. Francis of Assisi, and, appropriately enough, we had spent our last rupee the day before to buy a few potatoes to eat with our millet porridge. October, and already the snows had closed the Himalayan passes. In May, the mountain roads would open again, and surely then I would be ready to climb them.

I am the *yogini* in her forest hut, the village mother at the well, the almond-eyed maiden cloistered in her home, the mad girl running naked on the beach, the dying woman gasping her last breath. I myself am Arokia, the Virgin who heals, I am Meenakshi, bride of Shiva, the all-luminous Mother, and I am Kali the Crone, woman of wisdom, woman of tears. Rooted in the feminine, the multiple, the cyclical, I long to ascend, like the rising Kundalini, from the southern Salt Ocean to the snowcapped peaks of pure consciousness.

"Nor sun nor moon nor fire illumines It, and whither having gone people return not; That is My Abode Supreme.

Unmanifested, Imperishable is this called, and this they proclaim the Supreme State, which attained they return not, That is My Abode Supreme.

Without pride, without delusion, victorious over the blemish of attachment, ever abiding in the Self, their desires abandoned, released from the pair called pleasure and pain, they go undeluded to that Abode Immutable."

The Song Celestial by Ramana Maharshi

Six

The Maiden of the Rock

Gently here
Washed by the Kaveri
I took my birth from Mother India.
Thirty moons have waxed and waned
In the womb of night
And I return,
Hammered upon Maharashtran anvil,
Scorched by fires on burning ghat,
Drowned in a fierce Indrayani,
Carried by vultures here
Whence I began.

Here on the shores of Kaveri
Inter my mortal remnants,
I shall take birth no more within this world.
No fire can scorch me, no floods drown,
No chains can bind me—
Who can bind the wind?

Now I fear nothing,
And may none fear me.
The path lies straight to the source
I walk alone... alone
And O my friend
Your voice is calling on the breeze
Your eyes allure
Through veils of monsoon cloud.
I walk alone with you
Alone to you
O my Beloved.

With many emotions stirring in my heart, I walked once again down the sandy lane that led to Shantivanam, the ashram beside the burning *ghat,* my favourite spot in Tamil Nadu. That quiet, nunnish young woman who had come down this same lane one sunny Lenten morning two and a half years before, laden with her backpack, girt with passport and traveller's cheques, the tokens of security—where was she now? Once Shantivanam was the womb that protected me from an India I was not ready to face; now it was more like the family home to which the wanderer returns.

Due to Sadananda's visa situation, we were unable to stay in Shantivanam itself and instead, made our abode in a little mud hut in the eucalyptus grove, a short distance from the ashram. Each morning, rising in the chilly dawn, we hastened down to the river bank to bathe in the holy Kaveri. Taking water in cupped hands, we poured it out in offering to the rising sun. Then we made our way to the little painted chapel for Mass.

On the second day of our visit, we had an interview with Father Bede. As we sat on bamboo mats in his hut, he gazed at us with loving concern. He was worried about our health, which, ironically enough, had taken a sudden turn for the worse after the visit to Our Lady of Good Health at Vailankanni. Both of us were suffering fevers, exhaustion and nausea, whilst I had an enlarged and constantly painful liver.

"Stay here about three months," he advised us, "and rest and recuperate. You have been travelling too much."

The new guest master, however, was less than pleased that we were staying at the ashram, and soon seized his opportunity to make trouble for us. One noon, the Trichy CID arrived to make their annual check of foreign tourists.

"There are some people here with no passports," he told them, quite inaccurately, and called me over.

"What is your name? Your nationality?" asked the detective. Here was a dilemma. As a British citizen, I had no visa problems, and possessed all relevant papers. But what about Sadananda? These detectives could arrest him on the spot. With barely a second's hesitation, I decided to stick to the pledge I had made at Nasik, at the start of my pilgrimage with Francis, when he and I had jointly agreed not to speak of our native lands.

"My name is Alakananda," I told them firmly. "I am a pilgrim. I am God's child. I have God's passport."

Sadananda was called from the dining room to witness this scene, and had no choice but to follow my lead.

"My name is Sadananda. I am a pilgrim. I have taken a vow not to speak of the past country."

"But you must show us some papers of identification!"

"Okay. Wait here, we will bring something."

It took some time to walk to our little hut. We returned with pictures of Raghudas, Sai Baba and Godavari Mataji, and showing these to the detectives, announced firmly, "Here are our papers of identification."

The chief detective smiled. "I also pray God. You may go. I shall not harm you. But I shall have to inform the higher authorities."

In fact, whenever the higher authorities were due to arrive, the detectives sent word to the ashram, giving us the opportunity to absent ourselves.

We found at Shantivanam both old friends and new. Angelika was here again, intent upon studying Indology, and so was Kirsti, in her white sari. Kirsti was accompanied by a friend, Rosara, who was also dressed in a white sari. But there the resemblance between them ended. A tall, dark Spanish woman with piercing eyes, Rosara was as intense and wisdom-oriented as Kirsti was soft and devotional. She had spent much time in Bombay, at the feet of that same Nisagadatta Maharaj who had summarily dismissed Sadananda to Alandi. Now that Nisagadatta had cast off his body, she was eager to meet Raghudas.

"I am on my way to Maharashtra to join my sister," she told us. "I will go to Alandi, and bring you news of your guru."

I had little doubt what the news would be, for, shortly after arriving at Shantivanam, I dreamt that Raghudas had left the body, and that there was confusion concerning his tomb. Nonetheless, I questioned Rosara anxiously as soon as she returned.

"I was too late," she sighed. "It was not my fate to meet him. The night before I went to Alandi, I dreamt that I saw an old man lying on his bed. I felt his feet, and they were cold, so cold. Something told me, 'The saint you are going to visit has already cast off his body.' I was too late by more than a month. He left his body on the twenty-third of August, on the festival of Rishi Panchami, the day on the Hindu calendar dedicated to the memory of Saints and Sages."

"And his tomb?"

"There is no tomb. He was cremated by the Indrayani in the water-meadow where they say Sant Jnaneshvar used to meditate. Portions of his ashes were cast into the sacred rivers, the Indrayani, Ganges and Yamuna, to sanctify the great *tirths* like Allahabad and Varanasi. As for his bones and the remainder of his ashes, no arrangement has yet been made, and there is confusion among the devotees as to where his tomb should be."

My dream had been strictly accurate, and I felt that there was a deeper purpose in all these events. We were to find, not the tomb of Raghudas' mortal remains, but his radiant form, dwelling within our hearts.

"I dreamt of you last night," I said to Father Bede as I seated myself on the mat outside his hut, a few days after Rosara's return. "It was the most mystical dream I have ever dreamt. First I saw Arunachala, the Hill of Light. I've never set eyes on it in the waking state, just seen photographs, and yet I recognized it clearly. It seemed to be a symbol of final realization, and the opening sequence of the dream portrayed me on a journey to that sacred mountain."

"Perhaps it is time for you to go to Arunachala, to bring the symbol to life."

"Yes, I'm planning to go there soon. So in the dream I had to travel in a big wooden container lorry, a kind of Ark, that had a three-man team, like the Hindu trinity, Creator, Preserver and Destroyer. This journey was a passage to new life. Then I arrived at a big, rambling retreat house. Here there was a laboratory where a Japanese technician was performing alchemical experiments, of which I was in some sense the subject. He would not speak to me directly, or answer my questions. Then you arrived, very vivid, your ochre robes glowing and your hair and beard very silver, and began speaking with the Japanese technician about Doctor Hesyakarma, the Master Alchemist. At this point a chorus of interpreters, somewhat as in a Greek Drama, explained that Hesya came from the Russian, *hesychast,* those Russian Orthodox contemplatives who completely abstained from active life and simply prayed the Name of God, whilst Karma refers to the *karma yogi,* or Person of Action. Dr. Hesyakarma is the Supreme Alchemist, who fuses contemplation and action. The chorus quoted from Bhagavad Gita. *'He who sees the inaction that is in action and the action that is in inaction is wise indeed.'*"

"You heard that in your dream? How wonderful!" smiled Father Bede.

"That's not the most wonderful part. Then you showed me a kind of booth, or shrine on the left wall of the laboratory. Inside this shrine was no image or physical form, but the angelic form of Raghudas Maharaj, glowing with the purple of devotion and radiant with golden light. It was so incredible, I can hardly describe it in words. You know those dream colours which are so brilliant that nothing in the physical world can compare with them? Like that. He, the angelic Raghudas, is Doctor Hesyakarma, the Supreme Alchemist. Then he began speaking to me in a voice that seemed to come from the centre of my being, telling me that all these things were happening to bring me to the Fourth State."

Father Bede's face was alight with sympathetic interest. "That is the state spoken of in the Upanishads," he said. "Beyond our three normal states of consciousness, waking, dreaming and dreamless sleep, lies the Fourth State, *turiya.* It is a state of wholeness, beyond fragmentation. Thus waking, dreaming and deep sleep, fragmentary states, correspond to the letters A, U, and M, whilst the Fourth State corresponds to *Aum* as a whole, as Word, It is very auspicious to have had a dream of this kind."

"Yes, the dream left me feeling very blissful. I feel that I was brought to Shantivanam at this time to make a new contact with Raghudas, with you as intermediary. It was you who showed me the shrine at the centre left, the *sadguru* dwelling in the Heart."

That very day, the CID in Trichy sent word that they would be coming to investigate us, and that we should make ourselves scarce for a couple of weeks. Since both of us still felt nauseated and exhausted, we decided to made a journey to Goa to try some more of the bitter-tasting magenta liver herbs from the old Christian lady. Friends at Shantivanam donated enough money to cover our fare as far as Bangalore.

There is in India an unwritten rule that pilgrims and wandering monks can ride the train free, and since we had no money for the fare beyond Bangalore, we took refuge in this provision, and travelled ticketless towards Goa. But unfortunately, we had chosen to ride at the time of a major crackdown on the countless poor villagers who, compelled by a like necessity, travelled ticketless on Indian Rail. Disembarking at the junction where we had to catch the Goa train, we walked into the arms of about twenty policemen, armed with *lathis,* or big batons, who marched us to the railway police station. Unnerved, we surveyed the prospect of desperately poor villagers, unable to pay their delinquent fares, locked behind bars.

"Where are you coming from?"

I named the last major station.

"You must pay the fare from that point."

Opening my purse, I found exactly the required sum, paid the fare, and received a pink receipt.

"And what is your name, sir?"

"Sadananda."

"And you—Mrs. Sadananda?" They giggled.

"My name is Alakananda."

The giggling was abruptly silenced, and the grinning faces suddenly became respectful. Evidently, someone named for the source of the Ganges was not to be taken lightly.

"How much money do you have left?"

Emptying my purse, I revealed thirty-odd paise.

"Okay, take your receipt, board the train, and ride to Goa. No one will trouble you." As we set off down the platform, we overheard the police officers expressing their respect and admiration for these foreigners and their aescetic life.

Next day, we safely arrived in Goa, where Anand reluctantly granted us three days hospitality at Aum Yeshu Niketan. The ashram was no longer on good terms with the Police Department, and Sadananda's illegal status made him an unwelcome guest. Leaving our bags, we set off to find our herbalist friend in her Portuguese-style villa, just outside Mapusa.

"I pray for all of you. I must pray," said the old Christian lady softly, as she handed us the bottles of magenta liquid. But this time, even her miracle medicine brought only temporary relief. After celebrating the *tulasi* marriage festival at Shanta Durga, we decided to hitchhike down the Malabar coast to Kerala. Since one of the greatest shrines of the Western Quarter of India, the Mahabala *shivalinga* of Gokarn, lay on our route, we could not resist the opportunity of visiting it.

At Gokarn, it is told, is installed the *atmalinga*, taken from the heart of Shiva. Ravana, the demon king, as a result of severe penance, obtained this *linga* as a boon from Shiva. The possessor of the *linga* was unconquerable in the three worlds, and thus the power of the demon waxed. However, Ganesh, taking the form of a young brahmin boy, tricked Ravana into putting down the *linga*, which, in the shape of an unusual rock formation, became rooted on the spot—Gokarn, on the shore of the Arabian sea.

Gokarn is a beautiful and peaceful village at the mouth of the Shraptashringi River, where trees and flowering bushes fringe a sandy bay, several miles in length. Arriving late in the evening, we spent the first night on the portico of the temple, and, waking at dawn, attempted to have *darshan* of the tiny, natural *linga*. But the spirit of Ravana remained very much alive in the portly priests in spotless silk *dhotis*, their whole bearing exuding arrogance. Foreign barbarians could not be admitted to the shrine of that which lies at the centre of all beings, regardless of caste, colour, or creed.

Peeping through the doorway, we could see only the masses of white jasmine flowers that adorned the *linga*.

Angered, we left the temple, and made our way to the sea shore. No priests could debar us from bathing in the Shraptashringi River and the Western Ocean. They could not close our eyes to the sparkles of the sun on the water, nor stop our ears to the murmur of the sea, nor dull our senses to the vibrancy of the rocks of Gokarn, each of which, the *Puranas* say, is Shiva's visible manifestation. Clinging to their hereditary privileges even in an hour when the tides of history were sweeping these away as the ocean sweeps away an *Aum* traced in the sand, the priests seemed oblivious of the fact that Gokarn embodied, by its very nature, the utter obliteration of all privilege, save that of knowing the indwelling Self.

After a long walk down the bay, we came at length upon Ganesh the son of Shiva, in the form of a kindly, whitebearded yogi who lived in a cottage at the head of the bay. A man of great sincerity and humility, he utilized the small pension awarded him for service in the British Army to support a life of aesceticism, and to provide hospitality to other holy men visiting Gokarn. Two or three of these holy men were currently lodged at his hut, including one very quiet young *sadhu* who had taken a vow to wear white and eat only white food, taking little else in his diet but white rice with a tiny amount of gram. Graced by the tomb of a God-realized saint and a little temple at the mouth of a stream, the head of the bay was the true Gokarn, a privileged spot for meditation.

We returned to Shantivanam early on Christmas Eve, to find the ashram full of Westerners eager for a familiar Christmas. To me, "*Stille Nacht*" and "*Adeste Fideles*" did not ring well on the Indian air. I wanted an Indian Christmas, not a foreign transplant, but a native experience of the birth of the Christchild, something sprung from the soil of India.

On the morning of Christmas Day, Christodas sent us off for the day, telling us that the Trichy CID were coming again. Neither of us knew whether to believe him, but he was insistent that we leave, so we reluctantly set off. I felt irritated and depressed to be spending Christmas Day on the run. All in all, this seemed destined to be the worst Christmas of my Indian pilgrimage.

By evening, rather bored and very hungry, we found ourselves ten miles down the road, at a boys' school run by the Ramakrishna Mission. We were surprised to find that Christmas was being celebrated here, in memory of the exalted spiritual mood Ramakrishna's young followers felt on the first Christmas after the Master's passing. In the main hall, an elaborate *puja* was being performed before a portrait of the Sacred Heart of Jesus, whilst hundreds of Hindu schoolboys chanted fervently, *"Yeshu Nada, Christa Deva"* (Lord Jesus, Christ the Divine). Tears ran down my cheeks as the boys intoned a Sanskrit litany of the Names of Christ, "Hail to the One of Compassionate Heart, Hail the Bestower of Liberation, Hail to the splendour of the Inner Self, Hail to the Eternal Word, Hail the Virgin Born . . . " Shri Ramakrishna himself, with the help of Brother Christodas, had granted me the Indian Christmas for which I longed.

After the *puja,* we agreed, for the sake of fellowship, to share *prasadam* with the monks. Since we could not eat hot spices, we expected to take only plain rice. Divine Mother smiled on us unexpectedly, however, for the devotees had prepared a traditional Tamilian feast, consisting of five kinds of rice, using recipes that pre-dated the introduction of chilies to India. Whilst the Westerners at Shantivanam grumbled about their austere Christmas meal, we relished curd rice, tomato rice, coconut rice, lemon rice and tamarind rice, in a festive atmosphere. On our return to Shantivanam, we learnt that there had been no sign of the CID all day. Brother Christodas had been playing a typically South Indian practical joke.

In fulfilment of the dream I shared with Father Bede, we set off from Shantivanam for Arunachala, the Hill of Light, spending some time en route in Madras with Krishnamurti. It was full moon, Raghudas' birthday, when we reached the ancient temple city of Tiruvanamalai, Forest of the Holy Mountain, the *linga* of the Fire Element. Arriving by night, we walked through the sleeping town, and followed the road out towards Arunachala. Hill of Light it was indeed, standing revealed in the full splendour of the moonlight, a presence so purifying that we immediately began squabbling, as all our impurities were brought to the surface in the mysterious glow of that holy beacon. Did not even Brahma and Vishnu quarrel at this spot, their bickering as to who was the greatest giving rise to the original theophany of the Light *Linga*? For as the two gods argued, the earth split open with a great cracking sound, and an immense column of light appeared. Soar as Brahma might upon his goose, he could not reach the apex of the column; dig as Vishnu might, assuming his boar form, he could not fathom the root of the great *linga*. At last the familiar form of Shiva appeared from his primordial manifestation, to chide the two for their lack of vision of the One that encompasses and extends far beyond all that might be created or preserved.

Lacking Brahma's goose chariot, we set off on foot up the mountain to Skanda Ashram, a simple ashram built around a cave midway up Arunachala. Here Ramana Maharshi lived for some years in the company of his saintly mother, before the press of devotees eager for his darshan necessitated the construction of the larger and more commodious Ramanashram, at the foot of the hill.

And so we fell asleep, resting on what geologists have determined to be some of the most ancient rock on earth. Now a hill of no great altitude, Arunachala stood as an awe-inspiring mountain long before the Himalayas were brought forth from the womb of earth. "Himalaya is the abode of Shiva," Shri Ramana was fond of saying, "but Arunachala is Shiva himself, in the form of the Hill of Light."

Dawn woke me just as, in my dreams, a figure, neither male nor female, emerged from the darkness of the cave, robed in a softly glowing garment of flame. From our seat upon the Eastern face of the mountain, we watched the sun rise over Tiruvanamalai, drawing forth from the shadows the glittering spires of one of South India's greatest temples.

We continued to sleep at Skanda Ashram as long as there was moonlight enough to find the path, cooking our meals by a large pool behind Ramanashram. While we fanned our cooking fire one night, a young man in simple lay dress appeared and lent us a lantern. Introducing himself as Tyagiraj, he invited us to use his cooking facilities, and to sleep on the porch of his hut close by the main ashram.

Early each morning, we attended the *arati* performed at Sri Ramana's tomb, and during the day, sat for meditation in the hall where the saint used to give *darshan*. The sounds of constant repetition of the Thousand Names of Vishnu, which a group of brahmins were chanting in the *samadhi* temple, echoed through the hall, mosquitoes whined, and Ramana's couch stood as a silent witness, whilst Indians and Western seekers sat immobile, in deep meditation.

I sat also, drawn inward toward the experience of the Self of which Ramana Maharshi was so clear a mirror, but the pain in my liver had worsened since we reached Tiruvanamalai, and was now almost unbearable. I pictured Raghudas Baba, and his oft-repeated words, "As long as you are in the body, you have to bear with its pains." Everyone who had been to Ramanashram had spoken of peace and bliss in meditating there, not of the drone of Sanskrit, the whine of mosquitoes, and the aches of the body. What a lowly aspirant I was! "*Breathe, breathe, bring the attention back to the breath, be aware of the pain, see the pain as it is. Stay present, no observer.*" Sitting with the pain, sitting with the irritability of the sick body, sitting with my inability to meditate deeply, I glimpsed somehow, in the crack between breath and aching breath, that the bitter cup I was drinking was not other than the nectar of bliss, poured out for me by the one who teaches by silence.

Arunachala had many charms, the great temple, groves of bilva trees sacred to Shiva, caves where saints had found enlightenment, including the damp cave where Shantivanam's founder, Abhishiktananda lived; the monkey troop, who climbed the window bars of the dining hall to demand their share of Shri Ramana's *prasadam,* and the graceful peacocks, both blue-green and white, who ate from our hands. Above all, it boasted a living Master of the highest level, Yogi Ramsuratkumar, whose three gurus had been Shri Aurobindo, Ramana Maharshi and Papa Ramdas of Kerala.

We made our way through the narrow streets of Tiruvanamalai to the porch of Ramsuratkumar's house. After a few minutes, Ramsurakumar himself emerged, dressed in green, in a style somewhere between a *fakir's* robe and a beggar's rags, but with a distinctly kingly touch. Like the *Fakir* of Shirdi, Abdullbaba's son, he carried a peacock feather fan.

Gazing at me intently, the saint asked, "Have you seen 'this beggar' before?" 'This beggar' was the way in which he invariably referred to himself.

"No," I replied. "I have never met you before."

"Once is enough. Only see 'this beggar' once. No need to come back." And, so saying, he brought us into the house.

His door was hung with withered garlands and his pillared room was dusty, with piles of old newspapers, used bottles and assorted rubbish lying here and there. Some Indians were already present in the room, so we found places for ourselves.

"Excuse me, excuse me, madam," said Ramsuratkumar. "Would you mind moving a few inches to the right? Sir, would you move a few inches to the left?" This process was repeated several times, until Ramsuratkumar was satisfied that the three of us, himself, Sadananda and I, were positioned in a perfect equilateral triangle.

"So dirty! It's all so dirty!" he would exclaim periodically, as I glanced around the room, so different in style from the meticulous cleanliness which surrounded other saints I had met. "So dirty!" And he sighed despairingly. Gradually he proceeded to draw us out, asking about our guru and our *sadhana*.

"My guru's name is Raghudas," I told him. Ramsuratkumar laughed with delight.

"My guru Ramdas, your guru Raghudas," he crooned. 'Your guru Raghudas, my guru Ramdas." And he repeated this over and over, in singsong fashion, chuckling to himself meanwhile. I felt that he was telling me that I had found, as he had done, a *sadguru*, a Perfect Master.

"He lived in Alandi," I continued, when this refrain came to an end.

"Alandi! Ah yes, this beggar remembers Alandi well. The Indrayani River. This beggar took a bath there. He does not take bath often, but this beggar took one at Alandi. *And* he washed his clothes."

Ramsuratkumar was famed for never washing his clothes unless devotees insisted on removing and washing them.

"And you, sir," he said to Sadananda, "what is your *sadhana?*"

"I meditate," Sadananda replied, "I clean the mind."

"How interesting!" the Sage innocently replied. "You meditate and clean your mind! This beggar's mind is so dirty! So dirty!" with another sigh. "You must teach this beggar how to meditate and clean his mind."

An Indian family entered the room. It was time for us to leave. Presenting us with some crystalline sugar so charged with energy that our hands could scarcely hold it, Ramsuratkumar rose, waving his peacock feather fan and chanting softly, "I am so sorry, I must go. I am so sorry, I must go," as he danced us out of the room. For the next three days, we could do nothing but sleep and dream, for the power of the living master was working upon us.

A few days later, we walked through the town towards the bus station, for it was time to leave Tiruvanamalai. On our way, we noticed a ragged figure picking through a heap of rubbish. Yogi Ramsuratkumar, the Hill of Light in human form, looked up from the rubbish heap as we passed and raised his hand in blessing.

As India's Catholics took out their purple altar cloths at the start of the Lenten season, we arrived once more at Vailankanni, on the Kaveri delta, the shrine of Our Lady of Good Health, which we had visited after our retreat in the coconut grove. Our return to the shrine was prompted by a dream Sadananda had, in which he saw the Lady of Vailankanni as the union of the cosmic and transcendental covenants. Nonetheless, coming from the pure meditative environment of Arunachala to the Latin Catholicism of Vailankanni was something of a shock to the system. As ever, the church was bustling with Masses, rosaries and novenas. Whenever we attempted to sit in silence in front of the beautiful statue of Arokia Maria, radiant in her golden sari, a crowd of pilgrims or a group of nuns with school children would arrive and begin rattling plastic rosaries, intoning prayers, or simply chattering. One particular day, all the obstacles in Vailankanni seemed to be waiting for us. A black dog attacked me, and an Indian nun in Italian-style habit, fresh from Rome, attempted to chase me away from the communion rail, pulling derisively at my *tulasi mala.* Finally, when we went down to the ocean for an evening bath, we were harassed and pursued by a lustful drunkard.

Undeterred, we continued our efforts to enter into the presence of the Virgin of the Kaveri, sleeping by night at the little chapel near the banyan tree and holy well, and endeavouring to find, between the Masses and novenas, a quiet time for meditation. Towards the end of our week-long stay, we pierced the watchful ring of the Threshold Guardians, who were but the personification of our own impurities, our inability to reach, within ourselves, that place of immaculate purity which truly is the Virgin or Maiden state. The Khaki-uniformed watchmen, who hitherto had been industrious in shooing us out of the church, now gave us permission to remain inside the building during the siesta, showing us a small side door which was left open at this time. Thus, in the quiet hours of afternoon rest, we were able to draw close to the heart of the Maiden of Vailankanni, healer of a fragmented humanity, she who unites the Vine of Christ and the Cosmic Banyan tree.

The church might be a struggle, but the sea was always there to remind us of the true meaning of Vailankanni. Ceaselessly the fresh, sweet water of the Kaveri poured into the Bay of Bengal to renew the strength of the sea, and the music of the waves spoke to us of the fountain of youth, the enduring power of healing and regeneration which is Arokia, the Virgin of Good Health.

From the seaside shrine of the Virgin Mary, we came to Kanya Kumari, the Virgin of the Seas. Known to the British as Cape Comorin, Kanya Kumari is the tip of the peninsula, Mother India's nipple, where the Arabian Sea and the Bay of Bengal merge in the Indian Ocean. Unlike Rameshvaram, which is strictly a pilgrimage site, Kanya Kumari is also popular among Indian tourists, who come for the memorable experience of watching the sun rise and set in the same ocean. It was indeed a sight worth seeing. Day by day, I would reflect how the sun rose over Burma, stronghold of Buddhism, and wended its way Westward to the ancient home of Christendom. At Kanya Kumari, the Cosmic Covenant of immanence and the transcendent Mosaic Covenant mingle, Buddha and Christ join hands in a single ocean.

We had come to Kanya Kumari not only to have the *darshan* of the deity in the temple, but also to visit her embodied human form, the God-drowned *'Mazub'* Mai Amma, whom Kirsti had discovered in her extensive travels about South India. Following

Kirsti's directions, we came in the heat of the afternoon to a little temple of Shankaracharya at the very tip of the peninsula. There, seated on a wall, dressed in her favourite pink punjabis, was Angelika, whilst in the shade cast by the temple, Mai Amma rested, surrounded by a few devotees including Kirsti—as well as the sixteen dogs who followed Mai Amma everywhere.

A small, frail-looking old woman, Mai had the sunken nose of a leper, and was dressed like a little girl, in a simple short skirt and blouse. Reclining in the shade, she was engaged in picking pebbles out of the dogs' paws.

"Nobody knows how she came to Kanya Kumari," said Kirsti softly, as we seated ourselves beside her, "and she does not talk, but we have learnt that she comes originally from Maharashtra."

I was not surprised. Fondness for dogs and a crazy appearance are characteristic of Maharashtra's *avadhuta* saints, through whom Dattatreya turns to the world his face of Gopal Krishna, the Eternal Child.

"At first people thought she was just another leper, an ordinary beggar," Kirsti went on, "but gradually devotees became attracted by the love she radiated. Eventually the Shankaracharya himself officially recognized her as *jivanmukta,* liberated in life, a soul at the highest level of realization."

More devotees arrived, bringing great bunches of bananas, and a chicken *biryani* from a nearby restaurant. Mai took the biryani, complete with banana leaf plate and threw it to the dogs. She began peeling the bananas one by one, and throwing them also to the dogs. The dogs ate until they could eat no more, and then left the bananas lying in the dust, but Mai Amma continued peeling and throwing bananas.

"Disgusting! Disgusting!" declared an elegantly-dressed brahmin gentleman. "I am deeply scandalized! I came here to see a saint, and what is this? She is crazy! A madwoman! This food could have been taken and fed to the hungry. The money used to feed these dogs could have been given to the poor, spent usefully, to make improvements. Assuredly, I am never coming here again!"

As he stomped off, I remembered the words of the Gospel, "The poor you have always with you, but Me you have not always."

To me, it seemed fitting enough that, at Kanya Kumari, the Divine Presence appeared as a little girl.

After Mai Amma withdrew to her hut, we wandered around for a while, and then sat to rest on a low wall, gazing out at Vivekananda's Rock, with its domed meditation temple, the jewel on Mother India's nipple. Here Swami Vivekananda, the great disciple of Shri Ramakrishna, meditated for three days, receiving a vision foretelling his mission to America. Old men sat in the shade mending nets, naked children played on the beach, and out in the treacherous waters, Cape Comorin's famed fishermen stood upright on their flimsy outriggers, naked except for a loincloth. Suddenly a pure white heifer appeared, walked up to me, and laid her beautiful head in my lap. She too was a maidchild, a little embodiment of the purity of Kanya Kumari. In the form of the heifer, Divine Mother was signalling her acceptance of my pilgrimage to Kanya Kumari.

That evening, Mai Amma's devotees were gathered in a dark little room above a non-vegetarian restaurant. Mai Amma was seated on a wooden chair, whilst the women devotees, who had finished bathing and dressing her, lovingly combed her hair. The combing completed, a plate of food was brought, and, like a little child, Mai was fed by the hands of the devotees. Meanwhile, she tried to cram the food into the mouth of the devotee who was feeding her. Once Mai Amma had been fed, the remaining *prasadam* brought by devotees was distributed to all present. There were also bananas, which Mai, in random fashion, handed out to all in the room, in just the same way she had given them to her dogs. This activity completed, all sat and bathed in the stream of unconditional love that poured forth from Mai Amma, who sat diligently chewing *betel* and gazing now at one, now at another. Tuning his *dotar,* Sadananda began to sing softly, whilst Mai gazed long and hard in his direction. Finally, she daubed a smudge of vermilion powder on the foreheads of each of the visitors, as a parting blessing.

Despite the grace of Mai's presence, our stay at Kanya Kumari was by no means easy. Much of our time was spent walking in the hot sun between our sleeping place, a solitary beach three or four miles beyond the village, where we could watch the sunrise, our meditation space, the chapel of the Immaculate Heart of Mary, and the little hut constructed for Mai Amma on the rocks at the tip of the peninsula. We had nowhere to cook, and eating would have been a major problem, had Mai's most devoted disciples not taken pity on us, and offered to cook for us each day. At noon, we would arrive at Mai's hut, whilst Mai herself splashed naked in the waves, or collected a pile of rubbish, seaweed and driftwood, which she would then burn, sitting on the beach by the fire, beneath the scorching noonday sun. The woman who cooked for Mai Amma would arrive, and feed us with *idalis* or sweet rice. Indeed, our lack of accommodation turned out to be a great blessing, for we, alone of all the pilgrims in search of Mai Amma's blessings, were permitted to eat and rest in her hut, enjoying the intimate association of the simple folk who served and cared for her.

We stayed at Kanya Kumari until the day of full moon, when we stood side by side on the beach, watching the sun sink into and the moon rise from the Indian Ocean. So do all opposites meet and merge in the Primordial One who is personified as Kanya Kumari, the Little Maidchild.

Though I left Cape Comorin, I could never leave Kanya Kumari, for she was enshrined within my heart—indeed, she was my own true nature. The Little Maidchild, whom Godavari Mataji and her *kanyas* worshipped and Mai Amma so beautifully embodied, was not other than the innocence and simplicity I knew within myself. The invincible strength of the Virgin Goddess dwelt in me and had always protected me.

The diamond brilliance of Kanya Kumari was bringing a new level of clarification. Hitherto, I had seen myself as a seeker; now there was a growing awareness within me of a reality that lay beyond seeking and finding. I had played the part of searcher, yet I had been always the same. The singleness of the Virgin lay beyond dualities like ignorance and enlightenment, seeker and finder. Kanya Kumari—my own Self—invited me to live in a simplicity which left no room for either questing or attaining. Like Mai Amma, I was to be completely naked in the ocean of Mother's love. As yet, setting forth from India's southernmost tip, I had no idea that all the attainments of adulthood—mind, rationality, identity and status—were now to be stripped from me by the all-consuming love of the Virgin Mother.

> *"When this Divine Light of contemplation assails the soul which is not yet wholly enlightened, it causes spiritual darkness in it, for not only does it overcome it, but likewise it overwhelms and darkens the set of its natural intelligence. For this reason, St. Dionysius and other mystical theologians call this infused contemplation a ray of darkness."*
>
> St. John of the Cross, *Dark Night of the Soul*

Seven
The Black-Faced Physician

It was the height of hot season, and after almost three years with no southern monsoon, the drought had reached crisis proportions in Bangalore, one of India's most Westernized cities, situated in a rocky, windswept area of Eastern Karnataka. We had come here in search of some good medical care, before proceeding North to the Himalayas.

As we soon learnt, spirituality in Bangalore had its own unique flavour. It seemed to be a city of *shakti*, or spiritual power, manifesting in signs and wonders. Whitefield, our first port of call, was dominated by the ashram of the miracle-working guru Sathya Sai Baba, who has more than a million devotees worldwide. Not far from his ashram lay one of the city's numerous Pentecostal Protestant churches, whose members regarded Sathya Sai Baba as the devil incarnate. The Catholics of Bangalore were no less Pentecostal than the Protestants, for the city was a centre of the Catholic Charismatic movement. Each neighbourhood of Bangalore seemed to have its own wonder-working yogi, miraculous statue, or spirit-filled healer.

Arriving in *Shakti*-City, we went straight to the prosperous suburb of Whitefield, where we were certain that a wonderful welcome awaited us. George, an Indian Catholic friend from Shantivanam, whose family was, he said, one of the wealthiest in

Bangalore, had repeatedly invited us to stay with him, painting a glowing picture of the hospitality we would receive.

Imagine our disappointment then, when we arrived at the rather modest middle class bungalow, only to be met with unfriendly looks and embarrassed silences. As a Christian home, how could they accommodate Hindus such as we appeared to be? And the house was full anyway. But, most important, so harsh was the drought, they definitely could not spare us any water. We were an embarrassment to the family, who were determined to get us off their hands. After some frantic running around on the part of George's brothers and cousins, we were instructed to go and stay at a wayside pump house.

The pump house was by no means a comfortable place to stay. By night we were alone; by day the alcoholic watchman, his depressed wife and three quarrelsome children arrived, and we made ourselves scarce. There was nowhere to bathe except the canal. Unfortunately, after three days of bathing there, we found out from neighbours that the canal was infested with hookworms. From then on, we had to sneak showers at the Sathya Sai Baba ashram. We had a cheque from my parents, but no way to encash it. So we trailed from hospital to hospital, begging our bus fares and food money on the streets of Whitefield, and seeking out whatever free outpatient services were available. Pretty soon, the whole neighbourhood knew about the two Western yogis who lived on fruit and *kunji* (gruel—the only thing either of us could digest). Passersby would thrust fruit or rupees into our hands, or take us to the chay stall for a glass of milk.

Sathya Sai Baba was not present in Whitefield at the time, but residents soon began speaking to us of another famous saint, Shree Shree Shivabalayogi.

"You must be knowing about him," said one eager devotee. "Just now he is returning from his cave after performing so much fasting and penance for world peace. He is a great yogi, too much renounced. He was born into a poor family and had no father. Then, one day when just a boy, he had an experience of Lord Shiva, and automatically he began meditating. He meditated in *samadhi* for twelve years."

It was hot, and the *darshan* hall of Shivabalayogi ashram was crowded. Eventually the yogi himself appeared, a radiant figure, who beamed forth love for all beings, as if every cell of his body vibrated with compassion and loving kindness. But as the *satsang* wore on, I became increasingly uncomfortable. Shivabalayogi had bestowed on his devotees the initiation of *bhava samadhi,* or ecstatic consciousness, which manifested during kirtan. Suddenly I found myself surrounded by people dancing in ecstatic states, or displaying the *mudras* (hand gestures) of different gods. Women were forcibly unbinding the hair of those women who were not in *bhava,* and one particularly tall man, assuming the mood of Hanuman, rushed around with a shorter man on his shoulder. Dizzy and disconcerted, I resolved not to return. Yet the *shakti* of Shivabalayogi, Ramsuratkumar and the God-drowned Mai Amma was working within me, at a deeper level than I dreamt, and the effect of their *darshan* was to be immense.

One day, having an early morning appointment at the Baptist Hospital, we camped overnight nearby, in the village of Hebbal, on the edge of Bangalore. In the morning, we noticed a sign, '*Sumangali Seva Ashram,*' and, as the hospital doors had not yet opened, decided to drop in for a visit. As soon as we entered the ashram compound with its humble buildings, we were welcomed by a white-clad woman, Sushilamma, the head of the ashram, who invited us to bathe and take breakfast before going to the hospital. By the time breakfast was over, Sushilamma had become our firm friend, and at her insistence, we left the pump house at Whitefield, where we had been so inconveniently accommodated, and moved into the ashram.

In so doing, we entered into the deep river of Karnataka's seven-hundred-year-old devotional tradition. Sushilamma and her companions, Padmamma, Sarojamma and Karunamma, were members of the Lingayat sect, founded by the great mystic and social reformer, Sant Basava. Disdaining the traditional distinctions of caste and ritual impurity, they wore about their necks an oval-shaped *linga* in a silver case. The *linga,* symbolic of the *atmalinga* which resides in the heart, instantly burns away all impurity, and reminds the devotee that he or she is the Lord's own temple.

Fired with Basava's reforming zeal, the women were eager to

restore dignity and self-sufficiency to the poorest of the poor—low-caste orphaned children and destitute women. About fifty orphans lived at the ashram, where they received spiritual training, were educated in local schools, and learnt various crafts as a means of income. There was also a dairy, where indigent local women were allotted a cow to supplement their diet and income. Living conditions at the ashram were simple, for this was an economically depressed neighbourhood, and local residents were too poor to donate towards the ashram's maintenance. Sushilamma and her companions, educated women from good families, had completely thrown in their lot with these poor folk, sharing with them a life of little comfort or privacy, but great love, enthusiasm and devotion.

The fifty orphans included two sets of twins. Five-year-old Gauri and Ganga, the younger twins, were for me pre-eminent amongst the children. Gauri was deaf and dumb, and communicated with the rest of the world through her sister. The two children had evolved a complex sign vocabulary, which Ganga would then translate into Kannada, the local language. Ganga's patience and devotion to her sister was unfailing. Not once did I see Gauri and Ganga quarrel.

Each sunrise, whilst we sat in meditation upon the cowshed roof where we slept, the children were outside, performing Sun Salutations and other yogic postures. When their exercise was completed, we descended for *arati*. All the children joined in chanting the Sanskrit *mantras* that, for so many centuries, low caste people were forbidden even to hear. Then, after *arati*, everyone, down to the two-year-olds, sat in meditation for five minutes. As well as receiving spiritual training, the children of former Untouchables were learning to hold their backs straight and their heads high as dignified human beings. And the little girls were learning that women need not be spiritually disenfranchised; that they could dare to emulate the spiritual attainment of Akka Mahadevi, the woman poet-saint who wandered across Karnataka, clothed only in her long tresses, passionately in love with Lord Shiva.

Sushilamma and her friends were eager to introduce us to a saint whom they greatly revered, and who indeed seemed to occupy the role of guru for Sumangali Seva Ashram. Known as Yoga Swami, he was a gentle and taciturn personality who wore the customary white beard and ochre robes of the renunciant.

"His is a most interesting story," Sushilamma eagerly told us. "He was just an ordinary householder, living with his wife and children in a village some distance beyond Hebbal. Then one day, rather more than twelve years ago, he set off for his morning bath and never returned. Desperately, his family were searching for him. At last they found him in a cave not too far from their village, performing great *tapasya*. But now he was insisting upon remaining at that cave. So they returned home, relieved to know that at least he was alive, and somehow struggled along like the family of a widow. Whilst the husband purified himself through great *sadhana* and became an advanced yogi, the wife too purified herself by struggle and humble service. And at last, after spending twelve years at the cave, her former husband returned home. Now he and his wife live together as brother and sister, a holy couple, running their house as an ashram. The power of Yoga Swami's penance has benefited his entire family, and sufficient devotees come with small offerings of food or money, so the family is no longer in want."

On the new moon we, together with Sushilamma and the other women, various friends and devotees—and all fifty children—visited Yoga Swami's humble home in a cluster of dwellings grouped around a well. His imperturbable wife, now happily adjusted to running her home as an ashram, served tea to all of us, after which Swami accompanied us to the hilly area where he had found his cave. On the way, we stopped at a group of mud huts where Swami's *sadhu* disciples lived. Here a huge meal was cooked and carried with us while we hiked up to the cave. Sitting on the ground in rows, we ate our meal, and then sang *bhajans* all night, while the children slept.

Next morning we rose at dawn and climbed down from the cave to the flat area where we had taken lunch the day before. Yoga Swami's *sadhu* disciples met us here with a delicious breakfast. And so, our new moon celebration complete, we ate and made our way home.

Now scarcely two weeks remained before the full moon

festival of Sant Basava, the chief day on the Lingayat calendar. Everyone in the ashram entered a phase of feverish activity, making decorations, practicing *bhajans;* sweeping, cleaning, scouring and polishing the ashram premises and purchasing huge quantities of food.

At last, the great day came. The ashram was neatly swept and decorated, the children were dressed in their best, and all the women, myself included, were presented with new white saris to wear for the occasion, while Sadananda received a new *lungi*. Sarojamma and Padmamma decked Sant Basava's picture with garlands and performed *puja* to him, and then almost the entire village arrived for the *bhandara,* or feast. Both the dining hall and the courtyard were filled with rows of diners, as a lavish meal was served, complete with *puris,* sweets, and all the traditional accompaniments of Indian festivity. In the evening, the children, who had been practicing for weeks, gave a *bhajan* performance before an enthusiastic audience.

That full moon night, I had a vivid dream. In this dream, I was the chief participant in a ceremony which was a combination of a royal wedding and a coronation. I was clothed in a very beautiful white silk wedding dress, and was being adorned with a pale gold train, which descended from the crown of my head. The train was extremely long, and was to be carried in procession by six handmaidens. At this point an older woman with a wiry perm, who appeared to be organizing the function, informed me that the palace buildings were cramped so closely together that the train would impede the progress of the procession, and should be discarded. "No," I replied, "the train is to be worn in the ceremony for the benefit of all beings, and wear it I will. Not the train, but the palace buildings must be removed. The Royal Procession shall go forward." Thus I opened myself to the influx of a flood of grace, whose outpouring would wash away the mental structures within whose confines I had lived all my life.

Basava's festival was closely followed by Pentecost, the day of the mighty rushing wind of Spirit, and the tongues of flame upon the crown. On Pentecost Eve, we visited the Basilica of Our Lady, next to the central vegetable market. The Basilica housed a very beautiful statue of Mary, believed to have miraculous properties. We had come here for *darshan* before, but on this day Mary looked particularly beautiful, and was robed in a royal blue sari. *"My child,"* I heard Our Lady saying to me, *"I will indeed grant you the healing which you seek this Pentecost. When you leave the church, you will be given some fruit. Take it as my* prasad, *and proof of the grace you will receive on the morrow."*

Leaving the church, we walked through the noisy, echoing vegetable market, with decaying leaves on the floor, heaps of vegetables and fruits laid out on stalls, and vendors calling out their wares. Behind the market, some very poor people were selling fruit from wicker baskets. They called us over, and handed us three large lemons and eighteen finger bananas. "No money. Take." I was stunned. Not only had Mary fulfilled her promise, she had given me, as well as her own sweet fruits, three lemons, the traditional offering to the prongs of Kali's trident.

The moon was still in her days of brightness. That night, I lay on my sleeping mat on the roof, wide awake, tossing and turning. The light of the moon poured into my heart, pure white, like the white silk wedding dress of my dreams. My body was luminous white, vibrating, every cell pulsating, in the light of grace that poured into me... my body was brilliant white like Kanya Kumari, the Virgin of the Seas, like the Virgin Mary. The light that flooded my soul was inconceivably white, clear as the Immaculate Heart of Mary; it was radiantly, overwhelmingly black, black as the endless tresses of Mother Kali's hair. Deep in my heart, I knew that this was the Hour, the moment of Enlightenment. The gift for which I had longed so ardently, striven so intensely, suffered so profoundly—the gift of self-transcendence—had been bestowed upon me along with the three lemons of Kali's trident. And I saw the one I thought I was, running in horror from this great gift—my utter annihilation in the Truth.

My mind was running, jumping, flying from one thought to another, going this way and that, trying to get a handle on things, to get it together. Frantically, my thoughts chased after fragments, mind and ego becoming more and more hopelessly apart the more desperately they tried to pull 'myself' together. Personality, mind, ego—the prongs of the Black Mother's trident pierced them.

Hopelessly, as the long night wore on, I recognized that the one I had been was wrecked—beyond repair. I had sought the blessings of Mary and fallen into the terrible hands of Kali. "*Nine months must pass,*" said the inner voice. Mind grabbed at the words. "*That means, in nine months, you will be Enlightened. In nine months, you will pass from Kali to Mary.*" Mind went on and on, planning, concluding, grabbing at this and that; the voice in the heart softly repeating, "*Nine months must pass, gestation must take place. In this hour, the seed of Enlightenment has fertilized your soul. In due course the Divine Child of self-transcendence will be born. Be patient! Be patient!*" warned the voice of the heart. But mind flew on, grabbing, grasping, clutching, yet coming ever more apart.

Another night passed without sleep, my mind whirling in the intuition of the One Truth. Whirling around, seeing the correspondences, cracking the secret inner code of Sanskrit and Hebrew, dancing a crazy drunken reel among the symbols, metaphors and allusions of all religions.

All of us are on pilgrimage to that radiant city, that celestial Jerusalem, Mecca, Varanasi, Peking... Ayodhya, the home of Ram, the City-Without-Conflict; Jerusalem, City of Shalom, may Peace be upon her. All humanity without exception, a few knowingly, the rest unknowingly, converge upon that Golden City of Peace where God is worshipped in Spirit and Truth, beyond the fragmentation of mythico-cultural universes.

Given a healthy body and a calm, quiet mind, I might have assimilated, then and there, the Pentecostal wine I had so recklessly drunk. But parasites, hepatitis, and tropical sprue had weakened my body, whilst psychologically I was still tremendously overstressed from my twenty-four-hour-a-day shifts with the "crazy girls" at Aum Yeshu Niketan. So instead of arising from my sleeping mat as an Enlightened Master, I greeted the rising sun as God's Little Fool, drunk with the Divine. That which the Masters have seen, I too had seen, and the seeing thereof had cost me all the adultness that my poor ego had so painstakingly patched together. I was once more the innocent maidchild I had been at three years old.

Running down the steps from the cowshed roof, I saw Sumita, a nine-year-old orphan girl. She was dazzlingly pure, haloed in golden light, a true little *kanya.* Reverently, I prostrated at her feet, then pulled a wooden rosary from my pocket and gave it to her. As I handed her the rosary, I initiated her with a new *mantra*, the *mantra* of the New Jerusalem, of the one United Humanity of which I felt myself a prophet. Sumita carefully repeated the words, "*Shalom, Shanti, Shanti, Shanti*". With this *mantra,* I believed that the cosmic and Mosaic covenants joined hands, united forever by the little Hindu orphan girl with her wooden Catholic rosary.

Everyone was alight, everyone was glowing, but the children glowed much more than the adults. There was on the faces of the adults a tightness, a tenseness, like the wiry perm of the woman in my dream who refused to allow the procession to go forward. The children were still alive, still revelling in celebration; the adults had pulled back, substituting religion and spirituality for the boundless joy of the Royal Wedding between God and Humanity.

I stared at Sadananda. He didn't have the tightness of the Indian women, he was a great, glowing being. Three lines crossed his forehead, like the three lines of ash the Shaivites wear. In those three lines, I saw the yogi, the Buddhist, the earnest practitioner. "Just let go of those lines and fly—you are already Buddha." Grabbing a vessel of cold water, I poured it over his head, crying "Relax, let go, become a child! Be the Enlightened One you are!"

Sadananda began laughing, shaking water droplets off his beard.

"Repeat the *mantra!*" I cried, "*Amma, Aum; Amma, Aum.* Glory to the Mother of the Universe! Relax, you are a little child in Mother's lap."

Somehow, Sushilamma persuaded me to sit down with Sadananda and eat some sweet *ragi* balls she had prepared. Then I ran off to play with the children. Of course, I had no idea that the women of the ashram, talking earnestly in a corner, were deciding to take me to see Yoga Swami. All I knew was that suddenly a woman I had never seen before, dressed in a white sari, very nervous and tight-lipped, took me by the hand and led me to a bus stop. As the bus rattled along dark lanes, my mind began spinning faster and faster. Finally the bus stopped. The strange woman held me tightly by the hand as we walked down the streets of the village. Where was I? Where were we going? I knew that I had never been here before—all was unfamiliar. Suddenly, I heard a snatch of sweet, intoxicating song. *Ah! Krishna! My Krishna! He's calling me. Where is he, my beloved dusky piper? I must find him. He's calling me, drawing me, pulling at my heart, maddening me with his music.* With full force, I pulled my hand free of the woman's grip, following the strange, unearthly music, which I alone could hear. I ran full-tilt through the dark streets of the village. Without hesitation, without even looking where I was going, I ran straight to the Krishna temple—a temple of whose existence I had no previous knowledge.

It was dark, and the temple was shut. Crazed for His *darshan* as Radha herself, I persisted in hammering on the door, peering through the cracks between the double doors, chanting *"Hare Krishna"* at the top of my lungs. Until Krishna appeared to me, I would not leave. I was desperate for His vision, mad with desire to see His beautiful black form. Scarcely conscious of the outer world, all I could see was the heavy wood of those locked doors, cruelly separating me from the Beloved. Yet surely, if I cried insistently enough, knocked hard enough, the door must open.

Rough hands pulled at my body, began dragging me away. *What evil demons are these, who try to separate me from my Lord? Why, they must be my own hindrances, my own inner negativities, for what else could carry me away from Him? I must fight them, be strong... yet there are too many of them, two in uniforms and the white sari woman. They're getting the better of me, they're dragging me away! What a sinner I must be, to be thus torn from Krishna's dwelling place!*

Suddenly, I caught sight of a donkey, the beautiful beast on which Christ rode into Jerusalem. With all my might, I broke loose from my captors' hands and leapt upon the little donkey. Surely he would carry me back to the temple! But no . . . rough hands dragged at me again, pulling me off the donkey and down the street.

Soon, I was vaguely aware that my body was in a locked room at Yoga Swami's ashram. Yoga Swami...a *sannyasi. I must have been brought here to take the final step of renunciation.* Tearing off my sari, blouse and petticoat, I left them lying in a corner of the room. *I don't need these trappings any more.* I'm tugging at my blouse. Suddenly there are wooden beads rolling everywhere. *The mala Raghudas blessed for me has broken. This symbolizes a deep initiation. My very skin glows with the orange of* sannyas. *Why wear clothes? The ochre robe is within, it is the fire of Shiva.... I must be naked as Mai Amma, naked as Akka Mahadevi.*

Now I am soaring through the air. I must go up, up, for below lie the lower realms, the place of hideous demons. Rise, rise, reach the realm of the angels, of the gods. They are all here, Jesus and Buddha, dancing hand in hand, Moses and Mai Amma, Raghudas and Ramsarat Kumar, little Sumita and Shivabala Yogi. They are crowning me with the pale gold train, they are anointing me as their Queen, their servant. Yes, I am the atmalinga, *Yes, I dwell in the hearts of all....*

Sushilamma is bathing my body, pouring cold water over my limbs. I'm shivering, my teeth are chattering. Why is she being so fierce, so cruel? She is Kali, Kali Ma. I have fallen into the terrible hands of Kali, and here I shall stay.... Nine months must pass, nine months must pass, and Kali will become Mary.

Walking. Sadananda and Sushilamma are walking my body down the street, but my eyes won't open. I can't see. With eyes closed, I behold a brilliant, radiant Sun....

We're in a rickshaw, going to Hell. They're taking me to Hell, to be tortured. But I'm a spider, I'm spinning hair, my thin coppery hairs and Sushilamma's long black ones. The Three Fates spin, the sacred spider spins, and so do I. We're going through a door, into a long, dark corridor. We've entered the gateway of Hell. Now I'll be tortured, I'll be crucified by these people in the sinister white coats. My body has been handed over to ignorant people. But in my heart the work of reconciliation goes on. I'm here to heal, here to prevent nuclear war. By this suffering, by this reconciliation, by this uniting of opposites within my heart, I'm bringing war to an end. For I seem to be Alakananda, but she doesn't really exist. Shanta Durga alone is real, and She is I, I am She. Peace, peace, reconciliation. I pass through this conflict to bring peace. Peace, not this stupor that is rising. The drugs are stealing me away. I must sleep now.

So it was that after three days and three nights in the realm of the Archetypes, I woke from a drugged stupor to iron cot sides and a white hospital gown in the psychiatric ward of St. John's Hospital. The last thing I could remember from the great journey was that I had in some way realized my identity with Shanta Durga and come to understand that I was living in the world to serve Her work of peace through the reconciliation of opposites. I knew, and would never again forget, that I am Mother, dwelling in the hearts of all, and that all beings dwell in my heart.

"What do you think happened to you?" asked the young registrar, Dr. Appaya, who came hurrying over as soon as he heard that Alakananda was awake.

Despite the drugs and the hospital gown, I looked at him with great dignity and replied, "The right and left sides of my brain just came together."

Minutes later, Sadananda, who had been waiting for me to come round, was at my side. Pre-monsoon showers notwithstanding, he was sleeping rough outside the hospital. Now he was eager to make sure that I ate well, took exercise and was properly cared for.

Next day, walking up the hospital staircase, I almost bumped into a Catholic priest, running downstairs. Stopping dead in his tracks, the priest, a middle-aged European, stared at me. He seemed to be moved by some profound recognition.

Regaining his power of speech, he said, in a Dutch accent, "I sense you need some help and support. Come to my room, let's talk. My name is Father Francis." Soon both Sadananda and I were spending time with our new friend, who was indeed very supportive. "Take no notice of what the psychiatrists say," he told me. "This is not a disease or a chemical imbalance. This is a touch of God. Believe me, I envy you."

I needed his understanding, and Sadananda's, for the appearance and the reality of what was happening in my life were very different, almost contradictory. By appearance I was a sick, drugged, mentally ill foreigner on a hospital ward. Twice a day I received a substantial dose of haloperidol, the very medication which I had so hated giving to my patients in Goa. As a result of the haloperidol, I had Parkinsonism, and could not move my muscles properly. When I walked, I shuffled; when I ate, my hand shook so much that I could scarcely bring the food to my mouth. I could not turn my head or eyes to look around me, and my mind was dulled. Worse still, the drug caused a state of docile obedience, a condition of lack of will or determination which I had never experienced before. And it cut me off from my centre, from the place of causeless bliss which I had known from early childhood. Never in my life had I seemed less like an illumined being.

In appearance, my plight was pitiable. Yet in reality, I had gained a priceless pearl of which no amount of haloperidol could deprive me. With the aid of the drugs, I now had a semblance of so-called sanity, could function correctly in accordance with consensus reality. Yet I could never forget that everything I called 'myself'—my mind, ego and personality—had disintegrated before my eyes. The solid structures of the palace—my concepts and mental conditioning—had indeed been swept away by that `touch of God.' I might appear to be drugged into normalcy, yet I had not forgotten the final lesson of my journey into the other world, that Shanta Durga alone is real, and She is I; I am She. This madness, the madness of knowing that Mother and I are one, was completely incurable and brought to an end the greatest of delusions—the ego-illusion.

I could not put this experience behind me; still less could I 'integrate' it or make it my own. The intuition of complete identity with Shanta Durga and utter emptiness of what I called 'myself' was a fire in the heart which would gradually burn away all that appeared as dross. *'Nine months, nine months must pass.'* These words had come to me. Nine months is a symbolic time, a space of incubation, the period between fertilization and manifestation. An impatience remained within me, an eager desire to see the birth of what had been conceived on Pentecost Day. Yet, in truth, the 'nine months' were to last more than nine years, a space of imperceptibly growing light like the time between dawn and sunrise. Gradually, irresistibly, the mystic crowning with Pentecostal flame that had taken place here in Bangalore would illumine my entire being, making me a vessel of grace for suffering beings. What appeared to the doctors as psychosis was the black face of the Divine Physician, emerging from the churning of opposites.

I had been in the ward only a few days and was still heavily drugged when I suddenly sat up, grabbed a pen, and wrote the following lines:

Conundrum

I don't know who I am
I don't know what I want.
I feel so panicky all the time.
Expecting something terrible to happen?
No—afraid that nothing will happen
Nothing at all.
Afraid that empty hours slip past,
Past, past, past, to empty death,
A moment of ultimate horrific emptiness.
Afraid of boredom, boredom, boredom,
Bored, bored, boring, I am so boring
So afraid, afraid of nothing.
Afraid to be alone among these voices
Talking, talking, Kannada, Tamil, Telegu, Konkani,
Hindi, Sindhi, Punjabi, Marathi.
I cannot listen, cannot turn away
From empty voices, meaningless chatter
Terrified as I am of emptiness, meaninglessness,
Terrified of the unreal that masquerades
As day-to-day reality;
Terrified of the doctors who believe all this is real,
Who would have me believe this emptiness
This waking dream of sleepwalkers
—And I—
One who has fallen half-awake, a vivid dreamer,
Penalized for my dreaming, for my almost-wakening,
Given the drugs to sleep, to sleep,
And to believe the empty dream, the meaninglessness.
How can I come out?
Too terrified and jumpy to meditate,
To dream the dream of would-be wakers.
How to become free from the nightmare?

Why must I suffer in this crazy dream
Of those who know not that they sleep?
Why must I suffer here?
Why, why Guruji, why?
For I do not know who, where, what
I am, I am, I am, I am,
I, I, I, I, I.
Why, Why, Why, Why, Why
Am I, Am I, Am I?
I am, I am, I am
Soham.

My psychiatrist, Professor Subramunian, was an interesting character. As is often the case with brahmins who have received a Western education, his mind operated on two completely different tracks. He could be in one moment the psychiatrist, a firm believer in the biochemical basis of mental illness, someone obsessed with analysing brain slices taken *post mortem* from schizophrenic patients; in the next moment he was a devout Hindu, well-versed in the scriptures, aware of the mystery of consciousness and the subtlety of the kundalini shakti.

Professor Subramunian was very happy to have me as a patient, for I was an interesting case—much more appealing to him than the village woman in the next bed, who had become insane with grief when her cow died. In his eyes, I had been born to found a new world religion, one that would unite people of different cultures in one faith and cause the arrogant people of the West to acknowledge the greatness of India's *sannatan dharma.* (This, incidentally, was a destiny I had not, in my 'maddest' moments, assumed for myself.) The 'episode of acute psychosis' was in his mind just an incident, like a bout of pneumonia. The psychosis had been caused by an imbalance of the chemicals in my brain, and would be properly treated by haloperidol, which I should take for six months or a year, to prevent relapse. As for the notion that the imbalance in brain chemicals might have been caused by an uprush of the kundalini energy, he had no time for a thought of this nature. To consider any such a thing would have involved bringing the two separate tracks of his mind together, and that would disturb the tidy compartmentalization of his life.

Whilst I was in hospital, Sadananda telephoned my parents, who responded by telegraphing enough money to pay my hospital bills. I also received a beautiful letter in my father's elegant italic script.

My Dear Alakananda,

I must convey to you my firm and carefully considered opinion that you are NOT psychotic. Indeed, I almost feel that you are the opposite of psychotic, if one can imagine such a thing. What I mean is that through diligence, hardship and sacrifice, you have sought for and attained a level of mental and spiritual self-command and integrity markedly higher than is achieved or desired by the generality of people, myself included. For many of us, if not most of us, life is characterised by acquiescence in a hotch-potch of mutually contradictory or incompatible motives and emotions, including endless contrivances to evade the pain of facing squarely and clearly the fundamental questions of man and cosmos.

But in treading closer to the peaks, you are ipso facto nearer to the precipices. You have, therefore, further to fall and are the more hurt in the falling. Painful and distressing as may be what you call your "flip out", I believe it is to be regarded as an accident, by which I mean it is not of the essence, and that you will recover with or without treatment. To summarize: it is on the higher paths that the hazards are greater and the accidents more spectacular.

Enclosed is a £50 draft on Thomas Cook at Bangalore.

Much Love, Dad

After two weeks, I was discharged from the hospital on a reduced dose of haloperidol. Professor Subramunian asked me to stay in Bangalore and visit him weekly, so that he could control the dosage. So Sadananda arranged for us to stay at the novitiate house of the Little Sisters of Jesus. As long as I took the drug, I experienced the haloperidol-induced state of obedience and lack of will. And as long as I was obedient, I would continue to follow the psychiatrist's instructions to take the drug, believing his repeated claims that if I stopped it, I would relapse. I was trapped. The drug itself deprived me of the ability to choose not to take it.

On the fourteenth of June, one week after my discharge from the hospital, the Southwest monsoon finally hit land at Trivandrum. Throughout South India, all attention was focussed on the northward progress of the monsoon. We were staying at the ashram of the Little Sisters of Jesus at Kamanahalli, on the outskirts of Bangalore, when the first shower of pre-monsoon came. The Little Sisters rushed around in the downpour in their blue denim habits, placing buckets under the eves to catch the precious rainwater. Now the long months of queues and fights at public water taps, sale of drinking water at exorbitant prices, school closures and power cuts were over. At last, the rice fields could be ploughed and sown, and famine averted—as thirst and drought gave way to floods and gales. Hundreds died in cyclones, and the sacred rivers went into spate, flooding, killing, and destroying homes and cattle as they brought fertility and new life to the floodplains. The Black-faced Physician had arrived.

In addition to their main ashram at Kamanahalli, which served as an international novitiate, the Little Sisters had a small *fraternité* in a miserable slum near St. John's Hospital, to which they eagerly invited us. We had to stoop to enter the little hut, which, albeit very clean and neat, was a genuine slum dwelling, identical with those inhabited by their neighbours. When we arrived, the sisters had just completed spraying their *fraternité* to kill the bed bugs which were constantly being brought in by visitors. With great pride, they showed us their tiny prayer room with the Blessed Sacrament, a constant reminder that Christ was indeed present in the slum. Sr. Madelaine, a tall Frenchwoman whose Gallic features were alight with spiritual enthusiasm, worked in St. John's Hospital, volunteering her services to bathe and dress the wounds of the lepers. It was a task nobody else wanted, and one she performed with the greatest love.

"*Eh bien,* what if one catches leprosy?" she said. "That would be still more wonderful. Then we would really be one with them."

On my weekly visits to the psychiatrist and the gastroenterologist at St. John's Hospital, I visited Madelaine in the leprosy clinic. Not only she, but the lepers themselves, were inspiring company. The more able-bodied lepers, those who had fingers, assisted Madelaine in dressing the wounds of their brothers and sisters, for they at least had no fear of catching the dread disease. The lepers were remarkably cheerful and patient, and I felt a great solidarity with them, for as a mad woman, a 'psychotic', I understood what it was to live as they did, in the borderland. I, too, was a kind of leper.

Kamanahalli, Wed. 22nd June 1983

Broken-ness. Nervous breakthrough causes me to experience a state of brokenness. Back to square one, the frustration of all my personal efforts. I can attain—nothing. I can gain—nothing. I can reach—nothing at all. Yet I know that all these events which seem so contradictory and frustrating are the guru's teaching for my life at the present. I have to feel my inadequacy, my broken-ness, and let myself simply rest in the arms of God and guru, for it is by them alone I want to be held. The arms of ABBA-AMMA, *the great Father-Mother, the arms of the eternally full void, the arms of guru—my father, mother, brother, friend and guide—are always holding me. Divine Providence, the guru's teachings, these are simply none other than the circumstances of daily life which come to me minute by minute. I have to be able to say, in these contradictory circumstances of today, "Let it be as it is." As it is now, in this very moment of nervousness, strain and anxiety. Let what comes, come. Let it be as it is. This is the greatest teaching of both Raghudas and Blessed Mother Mary.*

I was experiencing a side effect of haloperidol—indeed, of all so-called 'tranquillizing' drugs—that nobody had ever spoken of in medical school. The Parkinsonism, of course, was expected. But not the dreadful anxiety which began midway between doses, and reached such a peak that I was almost desperate to take the next dose, knowing that the drug alone would dull the anxiety that it, itself, had created. I was hooked.

Furthermore, the haloperidol so dulled my mind, so blocked my energy, so limited my range of expression, that for the first time in my life, I was bored. I, who had been content behind the walls of an enclosed convent, blissfully happy in a mud hut beside the Kaveri, I, ever-resourceful, ever-enthusiastic, suddenly felt empty hours drag by, each day unbearably long. Enlightenment—a devastating enlightenment—the black light of truth, the "ray of darkness," had overwhelmed my soul. In such a state, joy, peace and satisfaction can come only in the depths of contemplation. And the haloperidol effectively blocked all possibility of contemplation, freezing my energy so that the mind could not sink into the heart. I was a fabulously wealthy queen, locked out of her own palace by an over-anxious gatekeeper.

Meanwhile, since the Little Sisters needed their guest room, Sadananda rented us a room nearby, a partially-built cottage. The structure itself was completed, a two-room cement house with flat roof accessible by outside staircase, but there was no plumbing nor well, and the rain blew in under the back door, completely soaking one of the two rooms. For relieving ourselves, we had to use a patch of waste ground; for cooking, a kerosene stove, and for bathing, the bathroom of our friend Alex, a former Franciscan and active social reformer, now happily married with a plump, contented baby.

Friday 24th June

A day of very ordinary things, but difficult due to lack of a timetable. Here I am, all alone—since Sadananda is taking a week's break after the stress of caring for me—in a suburb of Bangalore. I need a regime to occupy myself throughout the day. Early morning, yoga. Difficult to do when I'm so stiff with Parkinsonism, but at least try. Then go to Alex's for bath. Then go to the Little Sisters, wash my clothes, work in the garden if it's not too rainy. Do one hour walking meditation. That should make a full programme for the morning. Then leave, do shopping, prepare a meal—if I can get any kerosene, what with the shortage. Maybe go to Seva Nagar and try to buy some kerosene. Cook vegetable porridge. Take siesta. And then begins the difficult time of the day, furthest from the last dose, when the anxiety is worst. Write journal. Do walking meditation. Try to pray. Okay, so now it's time for walking meditation. Let's go and do it on the roof.

The pre-monsoon showers were heavy, but it would be a few more days before the monsoon proper brought daily deluges and unremitting rain to Karnataka. Meanwhile, as I wrestled with the most mundane details of survival, Bangalore was the site of one of the greatest Vedic fire sacrifices in history, sponsored by a millionaire industrialist. A veritable village of brahmins, naked to the waist but for the sacred thread, clad in golden silk *lungis* and besmeared with sandal paste, attended hundreds of blazing fires. The millionaire strutted about, his fat hands adorned with diamond, gold and ruby rings, exuding self-complacency. Vast vats of ghee and mounds of firewood stood in readiness, the crowd jostled to gain a better view, and the air resounded with cries of svahah! It was the last day of the yagna, and with the completion of the final offering, the ropes cordoning off the sacrificial area were removed, and the crowd swarmed in to circumambulate the firepits and smear their foreheads with ash. Afterwards, a great feast was served. In my journal, I remarked, "Yet the *yagna* with its hundreds of brahmins is nothing compared to a single person who has plunged into the fires of wisdom and become clothed in flame." Frail in health, shattered in confidence and dulled with drugs as I was, I still knew that I had no other goal than to make of my life such a sacrifice.

On the day of my next appointment, Professor Subramunian came to work in an irritable mood. Suddenly turning on me, he began saying, "Look at you! You have no independence. You depend on your parents, you depend on Sadananda, you depend on me. You're a physician, a qualified person. Why don't you go back to England and get a job? You should stop being so dependent."

When I protested, he grew still more angry, despite his suave appearance. "Aha! You are depressed. I am going to increase the dose."

I was both indignant and terrified. An increased dose of haloperidol would mean that I would scarcely be able to walk or feed myself. As soon as the appointment was over, I ran to Father Francis' room.

"Don't listen to him," said Father Francis firmly. "What does he know about you? You don't need him or his drugs. Just quit. I'm sure you won't relapse."

This was the voice of my own will, which lay bound in the chemical straightjacket of haloperidol. Suddenly, I began to feel a spark of determination and initiative within me. I didn't have to keep poisoning myself with my own hands. Grabbing a pen and paper, I slowly wrote a note to the psychiatrist, shaping the letters as clearly as the drug-induced tremor would allow.

Dear Professor Subramunian,

Thank you for your words of advice. Since you have suggested that I become more independent, I have decided to start by being independent of you and the medication. I herewith discharge myself from your care. I do not intend to relapse.

Alakananda

Placing the note on the psychiatrist's desk, I left the hospital for the last time. However, I knew better than to stop the haloperidol suddenly. Instead, I began gradually tailing off the drugs.

Both Sadananda and I needed some guidance. For years, we had worked together as a team, sharing our money and survival skills, our deepest feelings and emotions, forging together a philosophy that embraced both the cosmic and Abrahamic covenants, and above all, weaving together a unique fabric of spiritual energies. Though we could quarrel fiercely, we loved each other's company, with the challenge and energy of a fresh viewpoint. Now everything had changed. My confidence was destroyed. Between the haloperidol and the experiences I had been through, I was anxious and needy, barely able to get through a day. Sadananda had been cast in the role of caretaker, a task he had carried out with great compassion. But now he needed his own life back. What should we do?

It was agreed that both of us would travel to Shantivanam to see Father Bede. I would remain at Shantivanam for two weeks, whilst Sadananda spent time alone at Kodaikanal. Then I would return to Bangalore and wait for Sadananda, who would visit Father Bede himself and then rejoin me at the Kamanahalli apartment.

I was not completely off the haloperidol, and even at Shantivanam I was bored, since I could not meditate. Normally so self-sufficient, I eagerly sought company and friendship, ever-fearful that, drugged and dull as I was, nobody could really enjoy my company. Fortunately, I found in the Forest of Peace caring and compassionate friends who did not judge me or treat me as a leper.

"You have been travelling too much," said Father Bede, once again, after hearing my story. "You need peace and stability," he continued. "I understand that you have inwardly embraced *sannyas,* but still, a *sannyasi* need not always be wandering. One can also stay in an ashram for some time, you know, to allow for a deepening. Stay at CPS Ashram for six months or so. You need to be with women right now. And then come and stay here for some months. Above all, do not try to go to the Himalayas this summer. You don't need a peak experience just now. And . . . you and Sadananda should be apart for some extended time, until you re-find your own centre. These last weeks must have been very hard for him also, and he too will need space and solitude, after caring for you so devotedly."

It was true. Sadananda was physically and emotionally exhausted by the effort he had made in pulling me through such an intense experience. Space and solitude did indeed seem necessary for both of us. So, once we met again in Bangalore, we rather dispiritedly decided to act according to Father Bede's advice. Sadananda offered to escort me to Poona. Once I was settled in the ashram there, he would go to Gujerat, to spend some time in jungle hermitages and on the banks of the Narmada River.

Monsoon was now in full swing. We arrived in Poona during a drenching downpour. Gutters were awash, rain rebounded up from the streets, soaking us despite our umbrellas, the mud kicked up by our *chappals* spattered our white clothes, and buses and lorries speeding past drenched us with gutter water. It was, I rather bitterly noted, a most auspicious day, August the fifteenth, the Feast of the Assumption, and India's Independence Day.

A few days later, we took the bus out to Alandi, where we found Grandmother Kamalabai in her tiny apartment, together with Indu Thai and a young grand-niece who was taking care of her. They greeted the news of my 'psychotic break' nonchalantly, as if I had just got over a bad head-cold. Indu Thai reminded us that we had returned to Poona just one year after Baba's *mahasa-*

madhi, his Great Departure. On the twenty-third, a big celebration would be held, to which we were invited.

Many devotees from Poona and Bombay gathered for the occasion. A fire sacrifice was performed at the Gopal Krishna temple, and then *prasad* was served to all comers. To my surprise, I found that devotees whom I had never met before knew of me, and greeted me by name. In broken English, the family at the Gopal temple explained that Baba liked me very much and used to speak of me frequently during his last days. A mere psychotic break did not make me any less worthy an aspirant in the eyes of his devotees.

"It was an experience of *kundalini*," explained the slight, silver-haired brahmin who had officiated at the fire sacrifice, and was now seated beneath the *peepul* tree, in a position of honour. "When the *kundalini* arises to the highest *chakras*," he continued, "and any impurities are present in those *chakras*, one goes crazy for a time. It is normal, quite normal."

"He is Shri Nakhate from Poona," the devotees explained, "a retired lawyer, who gives *kundalini shaktipat* initiations. Since Baba's *mahasamadhi*, he has seen him several times in visions praying for all of us."

With a smile, Shri Nakhate handed me his card, and invited me to visit him in Poona. A few days later, I was sitting in meditation in his house in a back street near S. P. College, whilst he touched my spine in a few places.

"Now the *kundalini* is moving properly," he said with satisfaction. "As for Sadananda's forthcoming departure, please don't worry, don't worry at all. There can be no real separation between you, for you have been joined by the power of the guru. Whatever *sadhana* one of you performs, both of you receive the benefit, wherever you may be. Raghudas has made the two of you unpartable."

At CPS ashram, I was reunited with my old friends, Sara, Brigite, Arati, and Elisha. I soon made two new friends also. Rosemary, an English woman of about my own age, had a round, rosy-cheeked face and a cheerful, reassuring presence; Sister Mary was a frail-looking nun who lived in a Benedictine Abbey in Canada. She had come to India seeking a deeper contemplative experience, but, so far, had been disappointed—that is, until Sadananda and I brought her to Alandi, to the dark little room where Raghudas ended his days.

"Thank you so much," she whispered, as we emerged to the sunlight, the *peepul* tree, and the sparkling Indrayani. "My experience in that room was deeper than in any other place, even the Himalayas. Your guru must have been truly a holy man, a great saint. At last I received what I came to India to find, the experience of oneness. And I am going back to Canada in a week. Due to coming here, to Alandi, my whole Indian pilgrimage has been fulfilled."

A few days later, I accompanied Sadananda to the railway station. The train rolled out, puffing and hissing, as Sadananda waved from the window. I was alone. That night, in my dreams, Sadananda brought me to Raghudas, who very lovingly embraced me and kissed me on the cheek. I was alone but not alone, for I was in the true guru, and He in me.

Even though I was in a Christian ashram, attending Mass every day, my thoughts and meditations turned with increasing frequency to Mother Kali, the Forbidden Goddess, the black queen of the cremation ground. Only with her help could I begin to relate to those parts of myself which I had suppressed in my eagerness to be pure and holy. Kali is the emanation of the wrath of Durga. As she battled the demons, Durga Devi, the great saviouress, realized that from each drop of demon's blood that hit the ground, hundreds of fresh demons sprang forth. Then from her face, which darkened in anger, she manifested Kali the Terrible. Armed with a sword and a bowl, Kali cut off the heads of the demons and drank their blood. Now I too must learn to drink the hot blood of my inner demons.

My 'psychotic break' had cured me of the ability to pretend, to suppress, to behave, to be 'good'. With the shattering of ego, I had completely lost my false face, the 'spiritual' persona. Now I had no choice but to be spontaneous. My anger, my fear, all the demons on the battlefield were plainly there for all to see. I could no longer flee the deep, dark forces of the unconscious; I could only confront them, taste their warm blood, and transmute their energies.

I still greatly loved the Virgin Mary. But now I saw Kali, as much as Mary, as "Mother most pure, Mother most merciful." Kali's sword brought ultimate purity, Kali's wrath was ultimate mercy. The smiling Virgin and the bloodstained Black Mother were one.

Gradually I settled back into the routine of CPS ashram, cutting vegetables and cleaning rice with Sister Mary, practicing yoga, working in the garden, attending arati, taking lessons in Indian classical music with a friend of Sister Elisha.

One of my services was to help Rosemary care for sick ashram members or guests. One day in early October, Rosemary and I found ourselves unusually busy. A young man had just arrived at the ashram and promptly fallen ill.

"I don't like the look of him," I said to Rosemary. "This isn't just flu. I think he has typhoid." Sure enough, the young man was admitted to hospital next day with typhoid fever. A few days later, I was sitting in the house of a Catholic widow, recounting the tale of my pilgrimage, when I began to feel very hot. By the next day, I had such a high fever that Rosemary and Sara took me to Wardia Hospital.

The next days were a blur. I had a very high fever with rigours and night sweats and was on a noisy general ward. Hour by hour, I could feel my mind slipping towards delirium. Would the 'psychosis' come back? I had taken myself off haloperidol with great determination not to fulfill Professor Subramunian's prophecy—"You will relapse." But now, between my raging fever and the rattling, rasping breath of the patient next to me, who was dying of pneumonia, I had not slept for three nights.

I called the junior doctor, an intense young woman from Bombay.

"I'm afraid the psychosis will come back. I haven't slept for days. Can you give me something really strong to relax me and make me sleep?"

"Read. Keep your mind focussed," she said sternly, as she wrote up a tiny dose of Valium on my prescription sheet.

For the rest of the day I lay propped on pillows, desperately turning the pages of *Reader's Digest,* the only English literature I could find on the ward.

Going crazy was not my only concern. For several days I had been receiving large doses of chloramphenicol, almost the only treatment for typhoid. As I well knew from medical school, this drug had been banned in the West for causing fatal agranulocytosis, a condition where the body stops producing white blood cells. This morning the doctors muttered around my bed, then told me that I no longer needed the chloramphenicol. Crawling to the foot of my bed when nobody was looking, I grabbed my chart and read it carefully. My white blood count was alarmingly low. Would the bone marrow recover, or was I going to die here, among strangers, on this noisy hospital ward?

Nine-thirty in the evening. The nurses completed their drug round, gave me the tiny dose of Valium and switched out the lights. Now there was no more chance of reading to steady my racing, feverish mind.

I lay back on the pillows as the fever began to soar. My teeth chattered, my body shook convulsively, my head felt as if an axe had been driven through it. Could the fires of Hell be hotter than this? The woman in the next bed was worse even than last night. I lay shivering and burning, listening as she gasped desperately for the next breath. Further down the corridor, a woman moaned in pain.

The shivering stopped. Now my whole body was drenched in sweat. My throat was parched. Still the rattling, rasping breath, still the moaning.

Nurses' feet tap down the aisle; I hear the sound of curtains. They are drawing the curtains around the bed of the dying woman. Hot... so hot... my body burns. Gasp... pause... another gasp... another... another... and no more. The tortured breath has stopped, silenced for ever. No breath.

Darkness, a soul spinning in darkness, spinning in a vortex, plunging into oblivion. Nothing but darkness, raging heat, the distant moans of pain. No breath, only death, death, it is over. The sound of the breath is no more.

Finished. The body is finished. Dead. I leave the body behind. I whirl in the vortex, looking for the light. But there is no light. There is only darkness, wailing, burning. Weeping, wailing, gnashing of teeth. I am cast into outer darkness, to the place where the fires burn unquenchably. Cast into Gehenna, into Hell.

Abandon hope, all ye who enter here. Abandon hope. This darkness, this burning, this torture is for ever. It's all a dreadful mistake… no, no, not a mistake, I am guilty. Guilty and condemned. This is despair beyond despair. Forever I wander in this place of torment and darkness, all around me the souls of the damned. God Himself had cast me out in anger. This torture has no end… there is no final oblivion.

The most inhuman and horrific myth that human consciousness has ever created, eternal damnation, had seized hold of me. I descended into Hell, all hope abandoned.

Whilst my soul plunged into the darkness of the Shadow of Death, my delirious body was wandering about the ward, pulling out intravenous infusion lines. Now—much, much too late, I was given the strong dose of sedative I had demanded hours before.

Hell. I've descended into Hell and now I'm being crucified. Death, descent into Hell, crucifixion, all this has come to me. My feet, my wrists are in agony. My arms and legs are tortured, racked. My body burns, my throat is parched. I thirst. But I'm a sinner… not even vinegar for me to drink. My lips are dry, my body is nailed to the cross. My arms and legs struggle to be free, yet each movement intensifies the pain.

Daylight. A dull greyish light reflects from shiny olive green paint. The moans of the damned continue. I'm in a body of torment, a body of pain. My hands and feet are tightly bound to the bed. There's a demoness who looks exactly like Rosemary, solicitously spooning curds and rice into my mouth.

"Why are you being so kind to me?" I demanded. "I'm supposed to be in Hell aren't I?"

I was back in my body, a miserable, painful body, weakened by fever and fasting, dulled once again with haloperidol. This was not Hell, but a hospital ward, and the people who had tied me to the bed were not demons, but nurses.

I wriggled my fingers, begged to be untied. As soon as I was free, I felt my pulse. Yes, my heart was still beating. I was alive. I had returned from Hell.

I was alive, and the whole thing had simply been a delirium. Or, as the doctors insisted, another 'psychotic episode'. Yet I had passed through crucifixion, death, and descent into Hell, a passage as real and vivid to me as any other episode of my life. My physical body had not actually died, yet in my own experience, I had returned from the dead, broken the chains of Hell. In fact, there had never been any Hell; it was the creation of my own fear. Hell was a product of mind; Hell was my own thought form. My mind could create heavens and hells, gods and demons, but beyond all this lay the clear light of awareness. Mind alone had created everything I feared.

My white blood count was still dangerously low. I had not eaten for days and had slept only when drugged. Physically I was too weak to brush my own hair or to walk down the ward unaided. I had survived, but barely so. If my bone marrow recovered, I would live. If not, I would die of some infection. My body waited between life and death, uncertain which way to go.

Night. As I slept, I saw the infinite Light of *brahman*. For so many years, I had devoted myself to the realization of this Light. Now, the splendour of formlessness beckoned me. Would I choose to pass from embodied life, to enter this Light?

The radiance of *brahman* called me, invited me—and I was not ready to go. I knew, clearly enough, that to merge into the Light at this moment would be to leave the physical plane. And this I refused to do. Pitched between life and death, I chose life—embodied human life in all its frailty. I would not enter the radiance that was the face of death. With total determination, I rooted myself in form.

When I woke from the dream—if dream indeed it was—I felt surprised. Why should I choose to stay here, in the place of impermanence? Why had I lacked the courage to plunge into the splendour of *brahman*? Yet to remain in bodily form had been my deepest instinct.

Dimly, I began to sense that I was crossing some kind of watershed. The grace of Pentecost, a grace that still blazed in my heart, had fulfilled my deepest longings to be utterly consumed by the Divine. My life, my old life, was over. Three times, I had died—in the fever flames of hepatitis, in the mighty rushing winds of Pentecost, in the fathomless abyss of descent into Hell. In these triple deaths, Mariamme, Mary and Kali had devoured my conditioning, mind and ego. Now I was a helpless baby on the threshold of a completely new life—a life in which I would learn to dwell in the infinite splendour of *brahman,* here and now, in this body, on this earth.

For as long as I could remember, I had experienced a dichotomy between form and formlessness, between action and contemplation, between Shiva and Vishnu. The doctor and the contemplative nun, fragmentary beings, had both tugged at me. It was a conflict that had resurfaced with a vengeance during my time at Aum Yeshu Niketan, in the land of the Peaceful Mother. Now, in the dream-vision experience, this struggled reached its zenith. The choice that faced me was to merge into the Light and lose embodied form, or to retain form—and pull back from the Light.

Next day, I lay propped on pillows, playing with some crayons and paper Rosemary had brought for me. Suddenly, I stopped scribbling and began drawing in earnest, sketching the union of the Vine of Christ and the Cosmic Banyan Tree. The mighty arms of Shanta Durga, the Peaceful Mother, could bring together these two, the Cosmic and the Transcendent covenants. Moses and Krishna could join hands. I could find the unity of the crucified Christ and the smiling Buddha. From the very heart of conflict and dichotomy, I could reach inner peace in the union of opposites. I could know, as the mystical dream at Shantivanam had prophesied, the action that is in inaction and the inaction that is in action—Dr. Hesyakarma, the Supreme Alchemist.

The crayon fell from my hands as I gazed at the picture, a representation of my heart, the heart of Shanta Durga. The battle had been ferocious, but I knew that I had won a spiritual victory. Henceforward, I would not see dichotomy. Work had become my prayer and prayer my work. Though I had almost died in the attempt to scale the peak of unity and integration, I now stood on that peak.

But my days in India were numbered. Whilst I tottered around the ward on wasted limbs, gradually gaining the strength to bathe and dress myself, telephone calls and telegrams were flashing between the hospital, the British High Commission in Bombay, the Foreign Office in London, and my parents in Ipswich. The pilgrim whose home was the universe, had suddenly become a British National in distress, and as such, obviously needed to be sent home to England.

Apparently, at some time during my delirium, I had said that I wanted to see my mother. This was taken as meaning that I wanted to go to England. Even before I was fully conscious, my parents, eager to be of help, had bought a ticket for me, having been informed that this was my wish.

I did not want to hurt and disappoint my parents, who were in any case the only people willing to have me at this time. Sister Sara made it clear that I could not return to CPS Ashram. It was tourist season, and Father Bede's ashram, Shantivanam would be fully booked for months ahead. I did not know where Sadananda was, and moreover, he needed space from me. I was sick, weak and exhausted. All these considerations played a part in my sense of the inevitability of the journey to England. Yet most significant of all was my drugged state of docile obedience and lack of will. 'They' were telling me that now I must leave India and visit my parents. Once again, I was caught in the haloperidol trap.

It all seemed like a bad dream, the trip to Bombay, the plane flight, with images of violence and abusive sex unrolling on the movie screen, the ambulance in which my father met me at London airport . . . . Almost before I knew what was happening, my father was helping me out on to the gravel driveway, and my mother and aged grandmother were waving excitedly from the steps of the tall red brick house with blue paintwork. And there I was, in my white sari, with my few worldly goods in a worn cloth bag, standing in the front garden, on a damp autumn day, at the place I had called home before the Universe became my home.

I was in Ipswich. Almost four years ago, on a grey leap year day, I had set forth from here, with butterflies in my stomach and a bulging pack on my back, called, by some mysterious inner urge, to India. Now I had returned, the pilgrimage to the Source still incomplete, to a leafless, drizzling November. The disruption was total.

India, the heat, the light, the animated voices, ashrams, *sannyas,* the pilgrim way; everything of the life I had chosen was suddenly rolled into the wings, and in its place was the whole scenario of middle-class English life; bacon and eggs sizzling at breakfast time, *Idomeneo* and *Hamlet* on the video player, afternoon tea for Grandmother at four o'clock sharp, trays of coffee and finger foods for the Ladies' Club meetings, Saturday visits to the hypermarket.

My parents were loving and sympathetic, my grandmother solicitous, the ginger cat sporadically affectionate, the new Sheltie puppy adoring, and my siblings, who visited occasionally, unconditionally supportive. And yet I was alone. Where I had journeyed, inwardly as outwardly, they had never been.

For almost four years I had sojourned not just in the Republic of India, but in ancient Bharat, the land of *brahman,* the place of mythic consciousness and cyclical time. Now I had returned to history, linear time and the problems and complexities of the modern world. As if to symbolize this return, my father bought me a wristwatch.

Days after my arrival in Ipswich, the first Cruise missiles landed in Britain. Our island was now equipped with the weapons of mass destruction. My parents and their fellow parishioners were up in arms. Rosalind, my sister, joined a peace camp outside a nearby U.S. Air Force base, living in the freezing damp cold in a dugout shelter. Both she and Kate joined thousands of other women in encircling Greenham Common, the home of the Cruise missiles. The women decorated the barbed wire fence with baby clothes, a symbol of life. I was cheered by the courage and resolve of my sisters. To me, Kate, Rosalind and the Greenham Common women were embodiments of Divine Mother, bringing grace, sweetness and hope to a psychotic world.

"Olivia, Olivia, there's a letter for you! From India!" my mother called excitedly. The postman had arrived earlier than usual. I leapt down the stairs two at a time, skidded along the hall, and grabbed the letter. The address was in Sadananda's handwriting, and I rushed off to read it in solitude.

Beloved Alakananda,

Here in Lonavala after three days in Alandi, where I had the good fortune to stay in Raghudas' room, sleeping and meditating there for three days. You were very much with me in my prayers. The family at the Gopal Krishna Temple were very kind in offering food without chilies, and tea, and good overall energy. I really hope and pray you're finding peace and happiness. I'm sending you a mala *of* tulasi *beads, which has been put on Baba's bones and ashes and shoes; also some ash from the Fire Sacrifice we attended, on his death anniversary. I was really able to feel his presence this time. I'm on my way to Gujerat. There is a Spanish priest there, Shubhananda, whom I met at the Christian Ashrams Conference in Bangalore. He invited me to come and stay with him for a month.*

I paid a brief visit to Shri Nakhate but I missed CPS as I didn't want to go through explanations, etc. Some prasad *from Shri Nakhate is enclosed. I keep praying for you with each breath.*

Be Happy. Peace.

Love, Sadananda

From then on, I lived for letters from India. The postman's visit, which could take place any time between eight and noon, was the most important event of the day. I received letters not only from Sadananda, but also from CPS ashram, and from Kirsti, who wrote her epistles on the back of pictures of Murugan or Hanuman, and enclosed peacock feathers from Arunachala.

Each Sunday, as the churchbells rang out across the park, I walked past the beautiful Gothic Anglican churches—St. Margaret's with its magnificent tower, St. Mary-le-Tower with its graceful spire and full peal of twelve bells—to the squat Victorian building, placed under the unlikely patronage of St. Pancras, that served the local Catholics, my old fellow-parishioners. Climbing into the choir loft, I sang my way through the Mass. I found the service stiflingly European, patriarchal and lifeless, but at least it was essentially concerned with the Spirit.

The ladies of the choir, simple, devout, warm-hearted people, welcomed me enthusiastically, and so did my old friend Mr. Smith, the sacristan. It was he who reminded me that Ipswich, ancient Gippeswyk, was itself a place of pilgrimage, a holy place. In medieval times, it had been the shrine of Our Lady of Grace, a town to which pilgrims streamed from far and wide to obtain the blessings of Mary's miraculous statue. With the Reformation and Dissolution of the Monasteries, the statue disappeared, and the chapel was demolished. Earnestly, I prayed that the Lady of Grace, despite the absence of her statue, would still be present in Gippeswyk, to turn her merciful gaze upon me, for surely I was mourning, in the vale of tears, an exile from the homeland of the Heart.

I was still caught in the haloperidol trap, mainly out of respect for my parents, who did not have the facilities to deal with me having a relapse. At their request, I agreed to see a psychiatrist and follow his advice. With a slowness typical of the National Health Service, I received an appointment at the end of November, almost four weeks after my arrival.

Sitting in the psychiatrist's office, I felt uncomfortable. So did he. The more I said about my experience, the more disturbed he became. I was very, very threatening to him.

"Look," he interrupted me, "you're seeing all this in a psychodynamic way…almost as a positive experience. But, look, I mean, come on, what is the illness where there are recurrent episodes of mania, and apparent normalcy between episodes?"

He was addressing me now not as a patient but as a negligent junior physician, someone who should know better. A chill crept over me as I heard myself coldly reply, "Manic depressive psychosis." I had been tricked into labelling myself with my own lips.

"Exactly, exactly," he said rapidly. "You're young, and it's a severe case. The episodes will get worse and worse, more and more frequent. You must take lithium for the rest of your life."

It sounded like a curse. Depressed, I left the hospital. I had been given one week to decide whether to start on lithium.

My mother, a leading community physician, brought home learned papers on manic depressive illness. The more I read, the more gloomy I became, and the more I felt trapped into seeing myself in terms of the medical model. An eminent psychotherapist who was a friend of my parents suggested that two or three years of twice weekly analysis might take care of the problem. There was no psychotherapist in Ipswich, nor had I the funds for such a process. At length, intimidated by the possibility of having another 'psychotic episode', I agreed, with deep misgivings, to start the lithium. The diagnosis seemed to place an enormous distance between Sadananda and myself. As the victim of a crippling, lifelong disease requiring constant medical supervision, how could I ever rejoin my fellow pilgrim in his wild, free life of abandonment to the spirit that blows where it wills?

The days grew colder. My artist father, who stood on street corners making sketches for his urban landscapes, complained that his new ski suit was not warm enough. Accustomed to the heat of India, I was always chilled, as the damp, biting wind blew from the Northeast, crossing no land mass between the Arctic Circle and East Anglia. I felt more and more stifled within Western post-industrial society, a world of concrete and plastic, artificially heated, artificially lighted, electronically monitored, where experiences come cellophane-wrapped and everything from food to entertainment is instant. Fondly I remembered the simple life of harmony and communion with nature that had been mine in India, sleeping on the earth, bathing and washing clothes at the river, cooking over a fire, eating only the few fruits and vegetables that were local and seasonal, telling the time by the cosmic clock of sun, moon and stars. After the visit to the psychiatrist, it seemed as if a killing frost had shrivelled whatever hope remained for me. It was the darkest time of the year and of my life.

Tapovanam, Gujerat

Beloved Alakananda,

I got your letter on returning to Shubhananda's ashram. It's my intuition that what doctors label as Manic Depressive, psychotic, etc., are precisely that, labels. Some in India would call it kundalini. *Few really know what is happening with the mind; we've just scratched the surface. Alakananda, beloved jewel in a world of rust, I have a very strong feeling that you will make a rather fast and good recovery. Pearl diver, extractor of precious metals, let this be another expedition. Just gather the nectar in the bowl of poisonous substances. You'll grow to be of much help to others after this passes and the gold has been extracted.*

Alakananda, child of the garden, child of the cave, child of the water, child of the depths, the evening is coming. The night and day will soon mingle and night will swallow the day. The moon is waxing towards the full. Today I spent in a long walk through the ravines in the lap of nature, among the springs and the leaves, sheep and shepherds. Bathed naked in the sun, not a soul around. Drank deep from the lips, pure water, poured through sand and mud, reeds and rocks, to empty in my thirsty thought. Walked up on a hump to gaze out across the land below, plains and a lake, a Holy Jain mountain full of hundreds of temples. Down back to the path to the Banyan tree to eat and see a ten foot black cobra in the garden. Hens, peacocks, squirrels, pigeons, buffaloes and cows, serpents and holes of rodents all mingle and pass the day together under the winter sun of this day. Tomorrow I'll post this letter to England. I may have to take a bus to Palitana unless I can get stamps in the village. I'm on my way to Varanasi via Bombay. Write care of Charandas in Varanasi.

Be happy, Be peaceful, Be liberated.

Love, Sadananda

Sadananda's letter was reassuring. Meanwhile, at the beginning of Advent, a letter had arrived from Father Bede himself.

Dear Alakananda,

Thank you for your letter. I was glad to hear from you. I met Sadananda in Bangalore at an ashram conference and had a long talk with him. He is rather at a loss as you are as to what he should do.

But of course, the first need is that you should get well again. You are having a very difficult time, but I think that you should try to see this as a creative and transforming experience. Often on the mystical path one has to undergo a breakdown of one's personality, involving both physical and mental illness. But if you hold on in faith, you will emerge into a new level of consciousness and experience of God.

So don't be discouraged. God is working through all this 'dismemberment', as they often call it, and will build you up into a new person in Christ. Gradually your inner life will be restored, and you will be able to continue your meditation. But it will be at a new and deeper level.

We are all keeping you in our prayers, and I am confident that God will see you through this. It isn't that you have done anything wrong, but that you have a psyche which is extremely vulnerable, and you have to go through much suffering to reach inner peace.

With my love and prayers.

Yours ever in Christ, Bede

In my heart of hearts, I knew the truth of his words. The gusts of madness had blown through my mind to shatter the fundamental illusion, that I am the mind and personality. Henceforth, I would never feel security in anything except the dimly glimpsed perception of the Dweller in the Heart. Perhaps years more of 'dismemberment' lay ahead of me, for even if I rejoined Sadananda, I would have to suffer the shocks of America and the struggles of poverty in the land of the self-made millionaires. Yet henceforth, I stood securely on Nothingness. I would never again place my trust anywhere but in the Absolute Reality.

Receiving Father Bede's letter was a major turning point. His understanding restored my confidence in myself. Immediately, I stopped the lithium, completely dropped the diagnosis of manic depressive illness, and applied myself to studying the *Upanishads.* In the pages of these ancient scriptures, my own insight was validated. I had experienced what the *Upanishads* teach: that I am not this, not this; not mind, ego, nor personality. I am That, the Dweller in the heart.

A few nights after I received Father Bede's letter, I dreamt that I entered a room in which Raghudas was lying in state. Certain horrific ordeals had to be undergone in order to bring him to life. I was unable to fulfill these demands, but I went up to him, and spontaneously he awakened to life. Like the leafless trees, like the fallen acorns and chestnuts, buried in the earth, forgotten by the squirrel, I waited, through the brief days and long nights of the Northern winter, for the rebirth of the sun, for the distant promise of spring.

Then, two days before my birthday, I had another dream.

Ipswich, 13th December 1983

In my dream, I am wandering round a large supermarket, looking at racks and racks of Western clothes. Then I return to the entrance, where, in Indian fashion, I left my sandals, my beloved chappals *from the Indian roads. Some naughty children have taken away my old, worn* chappals, *and in their place is a single, enormous, brand new sandal, particularly large about the heel.*

My old wandering life has been taken from me, and in its place is a single, amazing new opportunity. I have received the seven-league boots, the magic shoe. I don't have to walk any more, now I fly. And my shakti, *my heel, my energy, is tremendously strong. The old pilgrim life was the life of a seeker. Now my journey has taken a new direction, though I don't yet know what it is.*

My birthday came, soon followed by a typically English Christmas Eve; holly on the mantelpiece, tinsel on the Christmas tree, chestnuts roasting on the hearth in front of a blazing log fire, carols from King's College, Cambridge on the radio. My brother, Nick, an undergraduate, arrived from Cambridge, together with his ginger kitten and his classical guitar. Neighbours dropped in for mince pies and sherry, groups of carol singers went from house to house at dusk, and my mother iced the Christmas cake. In a packed church, bells pealed out, and the Babe was solemnly laid in the crib. After midnight Mass, I sat in bed sipping hot cocoa. On the morrow, there would be Christmas pudding with rum butter, and my grandmother would insist upon watching the Queen's speech on television. I thought of the previous Christmas, the schoolboys of Ramakrishna mission chanting in Sanskrit, "Hail to the Virgin's Son."

On New Year's eve, I sat by the embers of the fire in vigil until the moment when ships' sirens rang forth all along the Orwell River, announcing the arrival of nineteen hundred and eighty four, another year, another page of time and history. I shivered and stretched my hands to the glowing coals. On the fortunes of this particular year, my whole future rested. Would Sadananda and I be reunited and continue our life together?

My parents and I celebrated New Year's day by driving fifteen miles down the Orwell estuary to the open sea. Well wrapped up, we crunched across the shingle beach, feeling the salt spray on our cheeks and gazing out at grey seas, grey skies, grey sea mists.

Seagulls wheeled and cried, ships moved along the horizon. The arctic wind that before had felt so chilling now seemed to stir strength and vitality within my soul.

With the rebirth of the sun at the solstice, my life took a more positive turn. Instead of repining, I began to see the beauty of being right here, right now, in Ipswich. Throughout my pilgrimage in India, I had been cradled in the lap of wise and loving teachers: Father Bede, Sister Arati, Raghudas, Grandmother Kamalabai, Godavari Mataji, Shree of Akkalkot. Sadananda's protective presence had always been with me, as had the association of loving friends like Kirsti, Angelika and Rosemary.

Now the doors of the temple that was India were locked again, as they had been at Rameshvaram—but this time I was outside. The warm womb of Mother India, her gurus, her peasants, her dedicated seekers, no longer sheltered me. I was on my own, sent back to gain a strength and confidence that I could find only outside the womb. In the very place where once I grew from childhood to adulthood, I was now passing from spiritual childhood to spiritual maturity. As I sat at my old oak desk—the very spot where I used to do homework—poring over the *Upanishads,* I was learning the Buddha's final message, "Be a light unto yourself."

I read and I wrote, reflecting on the shattering experience at Bangalore and on the new turn my life was taking.

Yes, I was free in a way I had never been before. I had discovered the forbidden Gods, Kali the Black Mother, Queen of the nightmare kingdom, and Krishna the Dark Lord. In Jesus and the Virgin Mary, I had experienced the Divine as Love. In Mariamme and Kali, I had met Her as Ruthless Compassion. In the ecstatic ring dance of Lord Krishna amongst the Gopis, I realized God as Bliss. It was a totally new, totally overwhelming experience, so overwhelming, at last, that my mind and personality had been shattered. That Pentecost Day in Bangalore, Krishna had blown through my spirit like a cyclone and deluged me in a flood of grace. Now here He was in the centre of my Patchwork Mandala. Not exactly what might be expected of a middle class English Catholic! Not even one with a Jewish father.

Krishna had freed me not by making me a Krishna *bhakta,* not by converting me from one religion to another, but by liberating me from all religions. Since the day when I, the naked mad-woman, had hammered in frenzy on the locked doors of the Krishna temple outside Bangalore, I had been freed from every religion, for I had glimpsed the source from which all religions flow. I loved Jesus, Mary, Krishna and Kali, yet I was no longer the prisoner of any culturally conditioned view. In my heart, the Vine of Christ and the Cosmic Banyan Tree grew entwined.

Now there lay before me a new life, symbolized by the single, enormous shoe. For as long as I could remember, I had been seeking the answer to the question, "Who am I?" Pentecost Day at Bangalore had clearly revealed to me that I am not the mind. I am not the body, the senses, the personality, the personal history. I am That. Yet as long as I was unable to realize self-transcendence here and now, in this world, in this body, the question "Who am I?" could lead only to disintegration in the formless light of *brahman.*

Now that I had returned from death and Hell, surviving despite a shockingly low white blood cell count, I had a new question. "Why am I?" Why am I this person, with this history, in this body, at this time? It was a question that led back into the world from which I had fled in search of Enlightenment.

"You were born to heal," said my grandmother Emily in one of her sudden flashes of prophetic insight. "You just have to find the right way to go about it."

"Who am I?" is the question of the seeker, the aescetic; it leads away from the world to renunciation, contemplation and the bliss of Self-Realization. "Why am I?" is the question of the *bodhisattva.* It leads back into the world in love, compassion and service. My old shoes, the shoes of the seeker, were worn out. The time had come for me to cease the search and begin the journey of Return, flying on my single enormous shoe. With the illumination of my soul by the "ray of darkness", I had attained everything I desired. I had reached the goal of which I had read in the mystical texts; I had tasted *brahman,* the Real, the Transcendent. My new shoe was to carry me into territories uncharted by the authors of books of mysticism. At journey's end, I realized that this was only a beginning.

I had recovered, even from the crushing blow of the diagnosis of manic-depressive illness. I had turned from external valuations of who I was to my own intuitive self-knowing. And in that recovery, I was finding within myself an inexhaustible strength, a light that nothing could dim.

From the churning of opposites within me, the Divine Physician had emerged, His face as black as a storm cloud. Though the monsoon flood of His grace had all but drowned me in Bangalore, I now realized that He had not come empty-handed. Just as Dr. Lad told me, Dhanvantari carried the jar of healing nectar. First had come my own healing, my own experience of the reconciliation of opposites. But this was not all. The precious gift of the Divine Physician went far beyond either my medical training or my inborn propensity for healing. Having passed through disembodiment, madness, death and Hell, I myself had become Dhanvantari, the bearer of nectar. Wherever I went, a healing grace went with me.

It was late January. The nine months foretold at Pentecost had passed, and I was sitting once again in the office of my counsellor, that same wise friend who, four years ago, had sent me to Shantivanam.

"I had such an incredible dream last week," I told her. "I was at Tiruvanamalai with Sadananda. It's a very holy place in south India, with a most ancient sacred mountain. Suddenly my Third Eye opened, and I saw the top of the mountain, Arunachala, sparkling and glittering. In the mists at the foot of the mountain, myriad sparkles of energy were playing. I saw figures moving on the mountain, with glowing golden auras. Really, it was like being present at the Transfiguration."

"That's what you have done in your life. Climbed the mountain of the Transfiguration. And what did Peter and the others do then?"

"Come down the mountain to teach and heal. It's happening in small ways."

"And what I see, Olivia, is that the cloud, the symbol of the numinous, is not on the mountaintop, it's on the plain below. The experience of the Divine is dwelling on the plains of earthly life."

"Exactly! All my life it has been a conflict—action or contemplation. Those so-called psychotic episodes—they were the resolution of the conflict. I'm not torn apart any more. When I serve, it's prayer, when I pray, it's service. Deep in my heart I know this as I never knew it before. It's the lesson of the pilgrim way, where your walking, your cooking, your eating, your bathing, all is sacred ritual. I have been studying the lesson for years, but I couldn't truly learn it without a breakdown of the old structures."

"Wonderful! So through the Shadow and dismemberment you have found healing."

It was February. In his next letter, I learnt that Sadananda had arrived in Varanasi, ancient Kashi, the Luminous One, the centre of India's *mandala* and chief of all her *tirthas*. I knew that in India it was the season of Vasanta Panchami, the beginning of spring. Although the nights of the Northern plain would still be chill, the watermeadows would be ablaze with golden mustard flowers.

Sadananda's presence at the very heart of India's spiritual life fanned the flames of my desire to return to Holy Bharat and complete my pilgrimage. Now that I was gaining confidence, and was free of all medications and physically fairly fit, there seemed to be no reason not to fulfill my vow to visit the source of the Ganges with Sadananda. The visit to England had done its work in bringing me to a new level of spiritual maturity, a level where I felt able to share the light with others. It was time for me to return to India and complete the pilgrimage to my Name, the Alakananda River.

Writing to Sadananda, I asked him to wait for me in Varanasi. From there, we could visit Bodh Gaya in time for the Buddha's Enlightenment Festival and proceed to Badrinath after the snows melted. By midsummer our pilgrimage in India would be complete. Then Sadananda could visit my parents, and we could relax together in Cathy's country cottage in Scotland before heading to America. I had a strong sense of confidence and had grown accustomed once more to the orderly punctuality of the West. Had I forgotten that in India things never go according to plan?

My ticket was booked for the Tuesday in Easter Week. On Easter Saturday, churches all over the land prepared their Easter gardens. After a damp winter of leafless trees, the bleakness unrelieved by snow, after the short days and lingering twilights, in the Armageddon shadow of the Cruise missiles, at last the paschal moon arose, and Easter came with a blaze of daffodils. There were lambs in the fields and primroses in bloom, and the heat of Easter Saturday broke open bud and blossoms; the magnolia unfurled, flower by flower, pink blossoms glowed in the light of the setting sun, tender leaves appeared on the horse chestnut tree. At dawn on Easter Sunday, a friend and I drove to church at Shelley village, and standing beside a brook, heard the first cuckoo of spring, as children skipped along the lanes, past blossoming hedgerows.

Easter Monday, my last day in England, was a perfect, cloudless spring day. Driving with my parents to Shotley peninsula, I went to pay my respects to the River Orwell, by whose sunset-dappled waters, nearly twenty years before, I had heard the call to be a healer. No scene could have been more English than that Bank Holiday afternoon. White-sailed dinghies raced down the brilliant blue river, a brisk breeze carried a salty tang to the nostrils, the gorse was in bloom, the silver birches just at bud-break. Sunlight glittered on green winter wheat, celandines nestled around the boles of trees. Spring had broken forth with a rush of life energy, the hillocks were aglow, and the air filled with myriad silver sparkles. As I took a token ablution at the Orwell, I thought of Sadananda in far-away Varanasi, where temples graced the banks of Ganga Ma. It was hard to believe that I would soon be back again in the beautiful and bewildering subcontinent, from Orwell to Ganges, from motherland to Mother India.

"Of all immoveable mountains I am the most holy Himalaya. Of all streams I am the Ganges, brought down from heaven by Bhagiratha . . . the only river of the three worlds."

Bhagavad Gita

Eight
To the Source

At four in the morning, the hour sacred above all others, the plane touched down at New Delhi International Airport. Once again, my feet stepped upon the holy soil of India, bramha bhumi, the land of the immanent Divine. From the airport lounge, I watched the Eastertide dawn and the thin wedge of the waning moon, praying that under these auspices I might die to the old self and rise to newness of life. I savoured every moment of that first day; the simple pleasure of sitting in a chay shop once again, a siesta on the cool, quiet portico of the cathedral, the mynah birds, even the intense heat of the height of the hot season.

I had been unable to get a reservation for Varanasi and so was condemned to pass seventeen hours confined to the corner of a wooden seat in the third class compartment. The train was so crowded that it was impossible to get to the latrine or go to the platform for drinking water. A desperately poor woman was sitting on the floor, leaning against my legs, her head pillowed in my lap, whilst her two daughters, dressed in dirty, ill-fitting clothes, sat propped on either side of her. The elder girl was seriously ill, short of breath and pitifully malnourished. Hours passed, as the night breeze gave way to the sticky heat of morning. My head nodded, the children cried intermittently, the wooden seat grew harder. Crowded stations passed with cries of "Chay! Chay!" and loading and unloading of sacks and tin trunks through the compartment windows.

Escaping into my thoughts, I called to mind all that I knew of my destination, Varanasi. Titled Kashi, the luminous one, the city is said to have been brought forth at the dawn of creation. I thought of the great column of light that split the earth and blazed forth into the sky at the moment of the original hierophany of Shiva, the column whose depths Vishnu as boar could not plumb, whose heights Brahma, riding his goose, could not attain. There are many places where this *lingam* of light has shone forth in the vision of pilgrims, great Shiva shrines such as Arunachala, Hill of Light, and the twelve acknowledged *jyotirlinga,* or *linga* of light, including Tryambakeshvar, Bhima Shankar and Rameshvaram. Yet of all these shrines, the greatest is Kashi, where the light *lingam* has manifested as Shiva's City, "the auspicious essence of brilliance extending to five *kroshas,*" and is worshipped as Vishvanath, the Lord of All.

Kashi is the centre, to be reached only by the Perilous Way. "The other holy centres are easily accessible," says the *Shiva Purana,* "but the city of Kashi is difficult of access." I squirmed on my wooden seat. Kashi was difficult of access not only by virtue of the long, crowded train ride. This was the fourth summer that I had planned the journey to Kashi, without which the long-promised pilgrimage to Badrinath could not be completed. Before journeying to the Himalayas, one must come to Kashi, centre of India's *mandala,* vow one's intention, and depart from there. Difficult of access indeed was Kashi. The first year, hepatitis had put me in hospital, and our passports had been stolen. Delayed in Maharashtra, I had visited Pandharpur, learnt the fire sacrifice at Akkalkot, and met Shanta Durga. The next year, visa problems had sent us, not North but South, our road to Kashi and Badrinath going by way of Rameshvaram, Arunachala, Vailankanni and Kanya Kumari. And so the Perilous Way had led to Bangalore, Poona, the Valley of the Shadow of Death, and Gippeswyk of Our Lady of Grace, a journey back to my roots. Sadananda had already come to the Ganga at Kashi, via the Narmada, River of Penance. And now, I too was arriving, as the train at last pulled in to Varanasi.

From the station, I took an auto rickshaw to Lanka Bazaar, at the southern end of the city, near the Durga Temple and Benares Hindu University. At Lanka Bazaar, I transferred to a bicycle rickshaw, which took me through narrow, winding streets to Nagwa village, situated on the banks of the Ganges, just south of the Asi River, the traditional limit of Varanasi, which is said to lie between the Varuna and the Asi. The address Sadananda had given me was "Krist Panthi Ashram," Nagwa, the place where Father Francis ministered to poor rickshaw *wallas*. After much enquiry, I found the ashram, and from there was directed down the street to the little storefront building where Sadananda was staying. No one was home, and after more enquiry, I found the house where Govindanand, a Canadian *sannyasi,* and Charandas, Sadananda's old friend, were staying. "He is not here," Charandas told me. "He's probably sitting by the river, waiting for you. For the past two weeks, he has been sitting by the river, waiting for you to come." Sure enough, as I made my way down to the water meadows, I met Sadananda, returning from the river. Our meeting was joyous, yet tinged with the pain of all that had passed. Returning together to Charandas' house, all of us chopped vegetables and shared an evening meal.

It was the dead of night, and the dark of the moon when finally I came down to the Ganges. Walking carefully down the slippery clay bank, a *lungi* tied loosely about me, I descended into the night-black starlit water. It felt as if I were plunging into the breast of Kali, the Midnight Mother. the waters of Ganga Ma closed over me. She, daughter of Himalaya's Lord, eternally pure fount of nectar, moon-crested, the eternal peacemaker, destroyer of sorrow, poverty and sin, purifier of the three worlds—Ganga, the Soul of India, took me in her embrace. As I began to swim, the water snatched away my *lungi,* and I was indeed taking that naked bath in the Sacred River which had haunted by dreams for years.

I had journeyed through the realm of the Great Archetypes and found my identity as a beat of Shanta Durga's heart; I had descended to Hell and had seen that Satan is but my own thought-form—then returned to England as a pilgrim whose home is the nowhere and everywhere—and now I had come at last to the Centre. I was in Varanasi, City of Shiva, the hub and heart of India's sacred universe.

Retrieving my *lungi*, I stepped out of the river. Then, from my seat on the bank, I gazed at Sadananda who was swimming fearlessly in the dark waters . Sometimes I could see his form, sometimes he seemed to evaporate before my eyes, completely one with the river, the starlight, the night. During the six months of separation, our relationship had passed from form to essence, as, across thousands of miles, we sought and found each other in the heart. At last, we were reunited in physical form. Emerging from the river, Sadananda sat down beside me and took my hand.

Now, at India's heart, in the city where, according to the scriptures, any pilgrimage to the Himalayan shrines must begin, we renewed our vow to visit the source of the Ganges together. Our commitment was not just to a physical pilgrimage. On a deeper level than ever before, we pledged ourselves to journey together to the source of Being—and from there, to take the way of Mystic Return.

Late though it was, Sadananda wanted me to see his beloved Varanasi right away. As soon as we were both dressed, he led me across the River Asi, which marks the southern boundary of the sacred zone of Varanasi. We began to walk downstream along the *ghats,* past sleeping temples and the narrow black shapes of boats, heading North, for at Varanasi the Ganges makes a great loop to the North. Soon we came in sight of the smoldering fires of Harishchandra burning *ghat.*

"These fires have been burning for thousands of years," murmured Sadananda, "the greatest of fire sacrifices. The brahmins here say that Kashi is ten thousand years old."

Yet ancient Kashi is also a vibrant modern city. Turning in to the bazaar, we found an all-night tea stall and sat down to drink chay. An old, blind man, his turban tied in the Maratha style, came to join us. Evidently a Maharashtran who had come to Kashi to end his days, he praised God for the miraculous gift of a cup of tea at two in the morning, and chanted over and over, in soft, nasal tones, the *mantra* of the Varkaris, *"Jai jai Ram Krishna Hari."* With the sound of his chanting still ringing in our ears, we returned to the *ghats,* and fell asleep for a few hours under a great tree, the rustling of leaves and the lapping of Ganga Ma our lullaby.

"Shri Ram, jai Ram, jai jai Ram!" At dawn, white-robed Vaishnav

sadhus sang the praises of Ram as they took their morning bath, while the thump, thump of laundry upon stone slabs broke the silence of night.

"*Ghar ap log ke pas nahi hai?* [You people have no house?]" asked a lady devotee in a white sari, smiling at us as she came to pour water over the *shivalingam* beneath the tree. It was time to rise and take the bath that washes away all sins, for my bath at Nagwa last night, just south of the City, had not, strictly speaking, constituted a bath in Kashi itself. I made my way to the water's edge, where women were bathing, wet saris clinging to their bodies, and stepped into the River of Heaven. Three times, I plunged beneath the waters of the Ganges, and emerged gasping for air, as the rising sun appeared before my water-blinded eyes.

"Behold, I make all things new," renewing the sun from the shadows of night, the moon from her darkened form, purifying the jaded and clouded vision of the city dwellers. After the baptism of fire on the scorching plains of Maharashtra, the flames of *yagna* and the fever heat of hepatitis, after the rushing winds of Pentecost had torn through my mind in Bangalore, after dying all these deaths, I am reborn of water and spirit, the spirit of Ganga Ma, the feminine Divine. And as I plunged in baptism in the waters of the Ganges, knowing her in her inner nature, as the River of birth and death, of time and Eternity, not only did I receive from her my Name, I also became the Namer of Ganges, one by whom she is known as she truly is.

After bathing, my hair still wet, I walked on, startled by the *digambara,* a completely naked Jain renunciant who passed briskly and with intense concentration through the crowd. At Dasashvamedha Ghat, I received a dot of coloured sandalwood paste from one of the semi-priests who sat on wooden platforms beneath tattered straw umbrellas, surrounded by ritual paraphernalia. My eyes fell on the sick and aged folk who lay dying on the broad stone steps of Godaulia, gaze fixed on the river. Their condition touched me with pity, yet I knew that for them this was the supreme achievement, for death in Kashi brought the promise of certain liberation.

Bells clanged in the flat-roofed temple of Shitala, the fever goddess, children played in the water, and boatloads of staring foreign tourists passed by. At the great burning ground Manikarnika, funeral pyres blazed, bystanders looked on. I saw the boatloads of wood, the Dom workers (an untouchable caste who are the undertakers of Varanasi) stoking the fires; a procession carrying a corpse on its decorated litter; flames consuming the body of a woman, her purple sari still recognizable; half-burnt corpses; heaps of smoking ashes. A sweet, heavy smell, reminiscent of roast meat but much more intoxicating, filled the air. In the city of Shiva, the great, final fire sacrifice is always burning.

I knew that I would never forget the scene, that the fires of Manikarnika, the broad sweep of the river, the eyes of the dying, the great span of Malviya bridge, were engraved upon my heart. In the secular cities of the West, I would remember Kashi, its crowded bazaars and spacious *ghats,* its flies and scorching heat, the black waters of Ganga washing the shadowy further shore, the columns of smoke rising from funeral pyres. Wherever my body might be at the hour of death, my spirit would return here, where Kali dances in the cremation ground and Shiva bestows the gift of final liberation.

In Kashi, *shivalinga* are everywhere, but it is Ram and Kali who are the most prominent faces of Shiva for the city. Their images are painted on whitewashed walls, calendars and icons depicting them hang in the shops, and the city resounds with the name of Ram. They are the twin roots through which Shiva's celestial city strikes the rock of earth. As the City of Death, the City of the great burning *ghats,* Kashi has the face of Kali, Shiva's spouse, popular amongst the numerous Bengalis who have journeyed upriver from the Ganges delta to make their home here. As a city of learning, culture and commerce, it has the face of Ram, the ideal King, who has given his name to its centre of government, Ramanagar.

In its manufacture of silk saris and handmade sweets, its universities and magnificent temples echoing with Sanskrit chant and classical music, Kashi pursues *kama* or Pleasure through the arts, *artha* or wealth, through trade, and *dharma* through Vedic learning and temple worship, striving toward the realisation of Ram's Ayodhya, the ideal city of the ideal realm. In its flies, its dirt, its malarial mosquitoes, its monsoon floods and scorching heat, in the columns of smoke rising from the funeral pyre, the spacious calm of the ghats, the black waters of the Ganga washing the shadowy further shore, it is the city of Kali, where the bitter taste of ignorance is recognised, and the gift of *moksha,* final liberation, is bestowed.

One morning, Sadananda and I were walking briskly down Bengali Tola, a crowded street. Pictures of Kali were everywhere, and shops sold the bracelets of red coral and conch shell traditionally worn by the women of Bengal. Walking on, we crossed Godaulia, a broad thoroughfare lined with fruit stalls and peddlars' carts, and began threading our way down the narrow, congested Vishvanath Lane, past shops displaying brassware, silk saris, tiny *shivalinga* of soapstone or marble, heaps of vermilion *kumkum,* bangles, rosaries, trinkets, jasmine garlands and milk sweets for pilgrims to offer to Lord Vishvanath. We were on our way to the Kashi Vishvanath temple, home of Shiva, Lord of the Universe, the temple that is first of the twelve *jyotirlinga,* and centre of the Hindu *mandala.*

Evening worship was in progress at the temple. The great bell was tolling, and Sanskrit chants boomed from the inner sanctuary. We had little chance to enjoy the chanting, however, for our way was immediately barred by temple guards and brahmins. A guard ushered us into the Temple office, where the priest explained, with unctuous scorn, "We have in Hinduism a caste for everyone. There are castes even of thieves, robbers and cheaters." But there was no caste for us, and as non-Hindu foreigners, we were not allowed in the temple. After extensive persuasion, we were permitted to stand just outside the sanctuary, to have, as best we might, the *darshan* of the polished black *linga* in its silver pit, almost hidden beneath sandal paste, bilva leaves, garlands of marigold and jasmine—and a coiled, five-hooded silver cobra. Amid a deafening clamour of drums, bells and Sanskrit mantras, priests waved the *arati* flame before the *jyotirlinga,* symbol of the primordial Light.

Adjacent to the Vishvanath Temple was the shrine of Shiva's consort Annapurna, the goddess of abundant food, who brandishes a cooking pot and spoon. After circumambulating her shrine, we walked down narrow lanes towards Manikarnika burning *ghat.* In the streets just above the cremation ground are sold the finest handmade sweets in India.

"It's no wonder that we know how to do this," smiled a woman and her son, as, seated on the porch of their shop, they expertly rolled sweetballs. "This shop has stood here for more than one hundred years. For so long, our family has been making sweets."

The taste of sweets was on my tongue, the smell of burning flesh in my nostrils; Annapurna and Shiva, the twin rulers of Kashi.

Returning to Assighat by bicycle rickshaw, we heard the sound of solemn chanting, *"Ram nam satya hai! Ram nam satya hai!* God's name is truth!" A funeral procession was passing on its way to the *ghats,* carrying the bier shoulder-high through the streets. The monotone of the chant merged into the music of a brass band, and from the other direction appeared a joyful, brightly clad crowd with elaborate head-dresses—a wedding procession, escorting the bridegroom, who was seated upon a prancing white horse. I watched in amazement, as the two processions passed in the narrow street. Here, in the Centre, in the Place beyond destruction and re-creation, the twin processions of Life and Death meet, merge, and again flow out to generate the world-illusion.

Back at Nagwa, we cooked some rice, and called our dog friend to share the remnants. I had begun to grow quite fond of the black and white mongrel, until one morning, on our way across the water meadows, he trotted past us with the happy expression on his face of a dog who has just found a bone—and in his mouth, a human femur.

As we walked through the village to buy milk, the women and girls who were squatting on the ground making cowdung patties for their cooking fires greeted us in a respectful and friendly manner. Before I arrived, the villagers had regarded Sadananda as a *sadhu.* With my appearance, the people became disillusioned. We were just "hippies", after all. However, their view of us rapidly changed when they observed our regular daily practice of floating down the river after performing *pranayama.* According to their beliefs, only a highly accomplished yogi could execute such a feat.

Thenceforward, they addressed not only Sadananda, but even me, as "Maharaj", a term of ultimate respect.

As the moon reached the seventh day of her waxing course, Varanasi celebrated one of its great festivals, Ganga *saptami*, the day of the descent of the Ganges from heaven to earth. All along the *ghats*, decorated booths were erected, adorned with rows of coloured electric lights. Within each booth, the image of Ganga was enshrined, in the form of a beautiful woman, draped with green or red silk brocade and hung with flower garlands. As we wandered along the *ghats* at dusk, the air rang with a haunting refrain, *"Shri Ganga Maharani, Shri Ganga Maharani."*

As the moon grew brighter, we realized that it would soon be Buddha Purnima, the festival of Buddha's Enlightenment. It was time to travel to Bodh Gaya, Shrine of Gautama Buddha.

Scrambling out of a crowded minibus, we gazed around us at the *ashoka* and *kadambara* trees with their scarlet and orange flowers, the hibiscus blooms and the silvery leaves of *peepuls*. It was Buddha Purnima, and we had arrived at Bodh Gaya, the place where Prince Siddhartha became the Buddha—the Awakened One. The area had an extraordinary feeling of peace, and the trees were sparkling as nowhere else. "This," said Sadananda, "is the place where the peace bomb exploded."

At moon rise, we made our way to the Bodhi Tree Temple. Large numbers of Indian Buddhists, mostly low-caste villagers, had gathered for the occasion, and were assembled in the temple, chanting refuge vows and praises of the Buddha, the *dharma* and the *sangha*. After the ceremony, we all went outside, behind the temple, where the Bodhi Tree itself stood, festive candles and oil lamps around it. All of us—shaven-headed monks and layfolk, Tibetans in their purple robes, saffron-clad *bikkus* from Burma and Thailand, Zen monks dressed in grey, and western meditation students—circumambulated the Bodhi Tree. On this great day, when the minds and hearts of the entire Buddhist world reached out to Bodh Gaya, picturing the Buddha seated beneath his chosen tree, the Bodhi Tree shone forth with a body of golden light. Here the Blessed One attained the vision of all his past lives, insight into the vastness and intricacy of the entire universe, and complete understanding of the nature of suffering. And here, as the sun rose in the East, lighting the hills and setting the leaves of the Bodhi Tree asparkle, Siddhartha attained Buddhahood.

During the long dark months in the land of leafless winters, while I sat in meditation on the little bed in which I slept as a child, or studied the *Upanishads* at the oak desk where my former self had struggled with equations and Latin grammar, I had been reflecting on the Buddha and his final teaching, "Be a light unto yourself." In the town that was once my home, now emptied of all my schoolmates, I had found new friends, longtime Buddhist practitioners. Now the hours of meditating in front of a plump, laughing Buddha in Cathy's art studio, surrounded by easels and canvases, had brought me to a tree beneath which nobody sat. Buddha, like Christ, was the One Who is Not Here, not here, but beyond; not here—outside—but within.

Bodh Gaya was an interesting combination of a Buddhist pilgrimage centre, a Hindu town, and a central market for local hill tribes, the *adivasis* or "original ones", who were neither Hindi nor Buddhist, but animist. On the Buddhist side, it was a larger version of Sarnath, with temples sponsored by every Buddhist country, to provide accommodation for monks, retreatants and pilgrims. The Hindu population gained much of their income from pilgrims and tourists, and the streets were lined with chay shops, restaurants and stalls selling Tibetan rosaries of jade and crystal, silver prayer wheels, soapstone Buddhas, *rudracksha* seeds and so forth. In addition to the Hindu temples frequented by the local population, there was a large Shankaracharya Math, a reminder of the ancient struggle between the heterodox creed of the Buddha and Vedantic orthodoxy. As for the tribals, they arrived for weekly market day, when they squatted beside their wares—squashes, bitter gourds, greens, fresh turmeric root, and local fruits.

On the day after we arrived, we wandered into the monastery that served the main temple and were greeted by the monk in charge of the Bodhi Tree Temple, a brahmin who had converted to Buddhism.

"Ah, so you are Alakananda," he said, after I had introduced myself. "That is the pure, pure source of the Ganges, as it flows from the Himalayan snows. Well, Alakanandaji, we have prepared a feast in honour of the occasion of Buddha's Enlightenment. Please, take *prasad*. You will have the opportunity to meet the most distinguished members of our local community."

From then on, we regularly visited the brahmin monk, who would invariably offer us a chair on his veranda, where he sat beside an electric fan, with cold drinks and snacks close at hand, whilst our discussion traversed the whole range of Indian spirituality, both Hindu and Buddhist.

Bodh Gaya is known for its scorching heat, and this was the longest, hottest summer of the century. Local people draped a cloth over mouth and nose as they bicycled around, for the hot wind burnt the eyes and nostrils and made the throat sore. Birds lay in the streets, felled by heat stroke; wooly Tibetan dogs, hundreds of miles from their homeland, quivered and panted miserably, and the tar on the roads melted and stuck to our shoes. After spending a day prostrated with heat stroke, I learnt to water my wooden bed to cool it off before I slept and would get up in the middle of the night to shower and cool down.

Images of Bodh Gaya mingle and merge in the heat haze. A Tibetan child monk in his purple robe plays with a blue toy car, lamas chant in the dark temple where butter lamps burn before a huge golden Buddha, a French Kagü monk speaks of former days when he toured Britain with a rock band smoking marijuana and trying to "bring in the New Age." At the Madras Restaurant, Tibetans relish *masala dosas* and other South Indian delicacies. An English-born, Catholic-bred Chinese youth practices his hundred thousand prostrations in front of the Bodhi Tree, whilst a *bikku* gathers Bodhi leaves.

Birds sing and the leaves of the Bodhi tree rustle in the breeze. Buddha, serpent-hooded, rises from the centre of a lotus pool as Theravadan monks walk mindfully around the pool, and in a shady corner, an Indian woman wearing a saffron sari—formerly a Catholic nun—is meditating. Down the road struts a *sadhu* who wears nothing but a loincloth decorated with tassels and metal pendants.

The local madwoman wanders down the main street and is offered a meal by Shivanath, a pious restaurateur who feeds her daily. "This is a place of peace," he tells us. "I have noticed that if any mad person comes here, after living here for some time, they become quite all right again." Shivanath's restaurant is filled with Westerners waiting for money to arrive from overseas, for only he will give them credit.

As Shivanath began his morning routine, offering incense before the icon of Shiva and throwing the first handful of food he cooked into the fire in oblation, we chatted over tea with Peter, a Bangalore-born Englishman about fifty years of age who "dropped out" in the early sixties and wandered India, first as a black-robed *aghori,* practising an extreme form of tantra, then as a Tibetan monk. Now wearing western dress, he described himself as a "free form tantric pilgrim." Peter's manner was mild, English, but penetrating blue eyes flashed above his silver-flecked beard.

The expensive new Japanese Temple had an elegant, air-conditioned visitors' lounge, and we went there from time to time, just to feel cool for half an hour. Politely, the young Zen Master offered us tea, which we sipped from bone china bowls. He had been studying Zen from the age of seven and had a great sense of humour and lightness. Soon, he was laughing about the earnest heaviness of American Zen students. Tensing his body and breathing deeply, he imitated an effort-filled Western student. "Ah, Americans. Very good meditators. *Samsara*—cut!" He screwed up his face in a parody of intense concentration, paused, and then started giggling. "Satori—Enlightenment—also cut. Unfortunate." And he collapsed with laughter.

Day after day, we walked round the Bodhi Tree, mindfully, mindfully, for hours on end. Candles offered by the faithful flickered in the shrine before the Buddha. One morning, we found a tiny Vietnamese nun about fifty years old, who was also meditating on the Bodhi Tree; her name was Dhamma Deepa. She took a great liking to us, and invited us to her dark, cluttered little room in a back alley. We soon fell into a pattern of spending each noon with Dhamma Deepa, who chattered excitedly whilst she cooked delicious Vietnamese food.

"Since a child, I run to forest, meditate. My family very rich, not like me meditate in forest, but I must do. I want be Buddhist nun. My mother not like, but I make nun. Meditate and go to Pure Land."

"Dhamma Deepa, you're following Mahayana Buddhism?" I asked.

"Yes, yes. Get robe from Japanese nuns. Mahayana."

"So, will you follow the way of the Bodhisattva, the Mahayana way?" I was questioning eagerly, for to me this was the most wonderful aspect of Buddhism. "To refuse to enter Nirvana until all sentient beings are freed from suffering? To be reborn until the end of time to help suffering beings?"

"No, no! Go to Pure Land of Buddha! Never come back this *samsara* again. Never come back!"

Dhamma Deepa had no desire to live through more Vietnam Wars.

Our friend was, like most Vietnamese, very musical, and fell in love with Sadananda's gourd-and-bamboo *dotar*. She was so eager to have one of her own that we decided to return to Varanasi and get one made by a *sitar* maker. We had time on our hands, for we were waiting for a travel agent in Patna, near Bodh Gaya, to return from his vacation. For a hefty fee, he would rectify Sadananda's visa situation, so that we could travel safely to the Himalayas.

"You have come back to Varanasi just in time," said our old friend Charandas, the American *vairagi* sadhu who was now living in Nagwa village outside Varanasi. Charandas was the same as ever, beaming smile, white robes, matted locks majestically coiled atop his head.

"These are the most auspicious days of the year for bathing at Dasashvamedha Ghat," he went on. "It's Ganga Dasahara. Each bath you take during this festival will destroy ten lifetimes of sins. And you're even more lucky, because Deoria Baba has come. He's living just across the river from us, a very eminent *vairagi* Saint. The villagers claim that he's three hundred years old. Anyway, he must be over a hundred." Charandas had a sceptical nature.

By the further shore, just opposite Nagwa village, a bamboo hut on stilts had been set up in the waters of the Ganga. Deoria Baba, who spent half the year at the Yamuna and half at the Ganga, was living here, whilst his entourage of white-robed

Vaishnav *sadhus*—with clay tilak on their foreheads and matted hair—had built their huts on the beach. Next morning after our bath, we climbed into a ferry, together with a full boatload of Indian villagers. The boatmen rowed across the river and anchored a short distance from Deoria Baba's hut. And here we all sat, the sun beating down upon us mercilessly, as we chanted *"Sitaram, jai Sitaram."* At last Deoria Baba appeared from the recesses of his hut, a lean, brown figure clothed only in a loincloth and his long matted locks. Sitting in the doorway of his hut, one leg crossed over the other so that a foot pointed at us, he said a few words in Hindi, and then began throwing fruit into the boat.

I sat in the ferry, sari over my head, lulled into a deeper state by the chanting, the boat's gentle motion and the presence of the Sage. The guru was Deoria Baba, sitting in front of his hut, the guru was the villagers, droning *'Sitaram!'*, the guru was the stately Ganges and the sunlight on the water, the guru was Sadananda, the guru was myself. The physical form of Raghudas Baba had gone, leaving me to discover the inner guru. And last Pentecost the inner guru had scattered like the beads of my broken *mala*. In every face, in every moment, I found another of those beads, and each one was the Whole. Baba was everywhere, and in all things.

Dasashvamedha Ghat had undergone a complete transformation. A large tent had been erected for the distribution of *prasad,* whilst Vedic fire sacrifices were continuously in progress. Accompanied by cries of *"Svahah!"*, we took our bath, and then lined up to receive *prasad*. This year, the ten days of the great bathing festival coincided exactly with the Pentecost Novena, so I prepared myself for Pentecost by bathing at Dasashvamedha, sitting in the boat waiting to catch sight of Deoria Baba.

Meanwhile, I was about to have an unusual experience, one that clearly showed me that the feelings I experienced were not merely my own—that my heart was one with the heart of humanity, of the earth, and of Ganga Ma, the River of Heaven.

The nights were unbearably hot, and we were sleeping beneath a large *peepul* tree on the banks of the Ganges. Usually, I slept well there. A night came, however, when I was unable to sleep at all. I felt racked with psychic pain, deeply suffering. It seemed as if the *peepul* tree was shedding tears and Ganga herself groaning in agony. When we rose at dawn I told Sadananda, "Something terrible must be happening. Some great calamity is in the air, I know it!"

We were walking along the main street towards Charandas' house when I saw the newspaper headlines. *"Golden Temple stormed by Indian Army." "Hundreds killed in Amritsar."* As I had lain awake beside the Ganges, in the grip of an unknown sorrow, telegraph wires were flashing the news of "Operation Bluestar" and the destruction of the Akhal Takhat of the Golden Temple, Sikhdom's most sacred shrine, several hundred miles to the Northwest. That day of shock and grief was for me a profoundly spiritual experience. As I sat beside the river, pondering the events which had come to pass, I realized that since Pentecost Day in Bangalore, my pilgrimage had entered a new dimension. I was no longer the raw, ignorant young traveller in search of her guru, her *mantra* and her name.

Something new had begun from the moment I returned to my old home, Ipswich, reaching Britain synchronously with the coming of the Cruise missiles. Now I was in India during her hour of strife and sorrow, and soon, I was to be in the United States, a few miles from Rocky Flats nuclear weapons plant. With the force of a deep inner conviction, I realized that I was no longer wandering in search of myself; rather, I was being led on a pilgrimage of peace, for the benefit of the Whole. Where prayer and healing was most needed, I would be present, either physically or in spirit. Beneath the *peepul* tree at Kashi, a messenger had come to me. Ganga Ma herself, after whose source I was named, called me to pour myself out freely, as she did, for the healing and cleansing of all beings.

Pentecost Day came. The Eucharist was over, it was a hot noon, and we were far from our favoured bathing spot just above the city. Eying the water, which was adorned with marigold garlands, refuse and scum, Sadananda decided that it was not clean enough here for swimming. We should take a boat to the further shore and bathe there.

"Are you sure the other shore is auspicious?" I asked dubiously. But Sadananda was insistent, so we hired a boat and set off across the Ganges. In midstream, Sadananda grew impatient, leapt out of the boat, and had his swim. He scrambled back inside, and we neared the further shore. Human bones were littered everywhere, indeed, the very sand seemed made of powdered bones. Hearing the sound of our boat, two lean grey dogs appeared, staring at us with ears cocked and a strange expression in their eyes. Clearly, they were scavengers, eager for the corpse they hoped we were about to drop in the river.

"You're right," said Sadananda. "This shore is not at all auspicious for bathing. Let's go back."

Still I had not had my bath, and was hot and miserable. After much persuasion, I agreed, poor swimmer though I was, to jump off the boat in the middle of the Ganges. As I descended into the waters, I heard a splash a short distance away. Thrown into the river from a nearby boat, a corpse plunged into the water with me. The corpse vanished beneath the waters, and I emerged into the sunlight alone. The burden of *karma,* of the one I took myself to be, sank like the lead- weighted corpse and was seen no more. Pentecost had come indeed, and I was reborn in the waters of the Ganges.

The side of the boat was slippery with algae, and despite several attempts, I could not climb back in. Clinging to the bulwark with all my might, I was towed half the width of the Ganges, swimming to shore in those very scum-covered waters which had been deemed too dirty for bathing. Tired, cross and utterly blissful all at once, I recalled what the elders of India often said—that the sight of a corpse is auspicious, a symbol of the death of ego. And I remembered also that "for one who dies in Kashi, liberation is certain." The corpse which dropped into the Ganga brought me the promise of final liberation.

At sunset, we were wandering through narrow lanes, when we heard the sound of women's voices chanting—in Latin! Here was a tiny convent of Indian contemplative nuns, set in the very heart of India's holy city. Tapping on the window, we were admitted to vespers with the sisters. It was an extraordinary experience, for the premises in which the nuns live adjoin a popular Kali temple. On one side is the Black Mother, whose great, lolling red tongue was once stained with human blood. On the other side of the wall, the sisters have enshrined a charming statue of the Immaculate Virgin, with a pastel blue robe and a sweet smile.

"She is so horrible, so hideous, that Kali," said the sister who was showing us around, "and those poor people are worshipping her with great devotion. But if they come here, they will see how beautiful is our Mary."

Leaving the convent, we went to pay our respects to Her of the lolling tongue. For me, neither Kali nor Mary was lesser or greater. If the Virgin Mother is the crown of womanhood, the Black Mother is undeniably the root. In the course of my pilgrimage, each symbol had gained vitality and significance from the other. Their counterpoint here in Kashi reminded me of the moment, one Pentecost ago, when I had received, as Mary's *prasad,* the three lemons of Kali's trident. Kali and Mary had become, in my patchwork mandala, the twin faces of Her, most pure, most merciful, awesomely terrible and full of Grace, the Mother of the Universe.

We returned to Bodh Gaya with Dhamma Deepa's *dotar* just as the pre-monsoon arrived, in all its glories and inconveniences; rainbows and mud, dancing fireflies and whining swarms of malarial mosquitoes, lotuses, magnificent clouds, gales and rainstorms. In the soft rustle of leaves, the Bodhi Tree whispered, "Find me within your own heart."

It is said that the Buddha attained Enlightenment on the banks of the lovely stream Niranjana. Today, the Niranjana is dry most of the year, flowing only in monsoon. We were walking beside the river bed when with a great rushing sound, the waters appeared, turbulent and red with mud. Suddenly the village was alive with excitement. Hitching up our garments, we joined the villagers in a breathless race to ford the river. Further upstream, we reached the Shankaracharya Math just at the moment when the sacred elephant was led out for his first river bath of the year. The elephant's joy at the coming of the waters seemed even greater than that of the villagers, and he happily frolicked and showered himself, whilst the trainer scrubbed him down. It was a day of auspicious omens. Our presence at the coming of the waters, the first fording and the elephant's bath augured success in obtaining the visa for which we were negotiating in nearby Patna and good fortune on our way to the Himalayas. On a deeper level, these events spoke of the coming into our hearts the stainless purity which is Niranjan and the proverbial wisdom of the Elephant.

Just before leaving Bodh Gaya, we set off for an outlying cave where the Buddha is said to have performed penance. After getting thoroughly lost and spending a night in the hut of some tribal people, we reached our destination, a small Tibetan monastery with a temple of Mahakal, Great Death, in the cave itself. I had little experience of Tibetan Buddhism, and was shocked by the monstrous, grinning faces of wrathful deities, the murals depicting flayed human skins and a wheel of life showing the tortures of hell. For a moment I wondered if the Tibetans were indeed, as earlier European writers had asserted, engaged in demon worship.

When we left the monastery and began walking back over the bare, rocky hillside, we became embroiled in a furious argument about whose fault it had been that we got lost on our way to the temple. As anger eventually receded and some lucidity returned, I realized that the tortures depicted on the wheel of life at the Mahakal temple were nothing to those we inflicted upon ourselves and each other. We were arguing about who was to blame, essentially about what to do with our negativity, the very question which the Mahakal Temple sought to answer. The Tibetans were not worshipping demons, but acknowledging and transmuting the anger and negativity that each of us must encounter on our journey into the Cave of the Heart.

After several tedious trips to Patna and some intricate negotiations with the corrupt travel agent, Sadananda received legalization of his status, with instructions to leave India within two weeks. We had barely time to visit Badrinath, our long-sought goal, and then hasten across the Nepal border to make arrangements for our flight back to the West. Immediately, we thanked the brahmin monk for his hospitality, said a tearful goodbye to Dhamma Deepa, saluted the Bodhi Tree, and caught the minibus. Within a couple of hours we were aboard a train, heading northwest.

Next dawn, hanging out of the door of the little passenger train, I gazed at an unforgettable sight. Peak upon snowcapped peak, stretching, it seemed, to infinity, was set aflame in shades of crimson, rose and red-gold, as the sun of a new day appeared over misty mountain tops. The long-time object of my dreams, hopes and aspirations—the Himalayas—at last granted me their *darshan.*

"It has been worth everything," I murmured as the colours faded. "All the waiting, all the hardships, all the sickness, the thousands of miles—it is all worthwhile, just for this moment."

Sadananda nodded. "This is the magic of pilgrimage. For the rest of your life, wherever you are, these great holy places will never leave you. The sound of the Southern Salt Ocean on the corals of Rameshvaram, the rustling leaves of the Bodhi Tree, the full moon over Arunachala, the midnight waters of Ganga, and now the sunrise on Himalayan snows—nothing can take these gifts from you. Even in a prison or concentration camp, these sacred spots will always be with you, because they are not only outside, but inside, too, and when you see the symbol, you begin to wake to the reality."

Disembarking at Haridwar, the gateway to the Himalayas, we found a fellow passenger, a lean, energetic *sadhu,* who was also bound for Rishikesh. Doing our best to keep up with his fast walking pace, we followed him to the bus station. And so, after about an hour on a crowded bus, we came to Rishikesh, the 'Place of Seers', at the base of the Himalayan foothills. Here the Ganga flows, swift and glacier-cold, past a city of riverside ashrams, silent meditators and *sadhus,* both beggarly and sincere. Choosing a suitable spot with a grassy bank and an iron chain to grip in the strong current, we took our sacred bath. Further upriver, we paid our respects to the tomb of Swami Shivananda, a great master of the yogic path, whose ashram is one of the largest and most famous in Rishikesh.

Since the ashram could not provide lunch *prasad* to non-residents—except genuine *sadhus,* who were by definition all Indian—we dined on *idalis* and coconut chutney at a little shack that called itself "Madras Vegiterian [*sic*] Hotel". That night, as I lay in a secluded grassy spot, listening to the music of the river, I was too excited to sleep much. Tomorrow, at long last, we were headed for the source of the Ganges.

"*Challo bhai, challo bhai!* (Let's go!)" Sikh soldiers called to their companions, as the Badrinath-bound bus throbbed and roared in the chill dawn. For the next two days, we, together with the soldiers and some poor Indian pilgrims, rattled at terrifying speed up the muddy, precipitous road in a decrepit local bus. As the driver hurtled around hairpin bends, I gazed at the sheer drop below me, and, with a sinking feeling in the pit of my stomach, recalled the previous week's tragedy: on roads made treacherous by monsoon rains, a tour bus en route to Badrinath had plummeted over the edge.

Spurred on by an enthusiastic Indian family, who like us were making the pilgrimage of a lifetime, but one that had cost them many years of meagre savings, we plunged into the bone-chilling Ganges at every stop along the way. Each pilgrim station on the Badrinath trail marks a sacred confluence where a fresh tributary joins the Ganga, and the literature of pilgrimage extols the merits of a bath at each stop, merits which our friends haltingly but nonetheless persuasively explained to us in a few words of English and a wide vocabulary of signs.

We reached our night halt just as sunset coloured the monsoon clouds. Nervously, all eight of us, the family, Sadananda and myself, stood at the water's edge while a brisk mountain breeze raised goosebumps on our arms. It would be the fourth icy bath of the day.

"Well," I declared bravely, "if we catch cold, it will last only four days or so, but the merits of this bath will endure for lifetimes and reach out to generations of our ancestors." And in we all jumped. With teeth chattering and hair still dripping, Sadananda and I followed the shivering Indian family to a *dharmsala,* and sat around a kerosene stove whilst the women prepared food for all.

This first day, the road had led through rice terraces and remnants of the Himalayan rainforest, with its great broad-leaved trees and huge flowering cacti. On the second day, we saw shrubs and occasional trees, hemp plants which were taller than I was and countless beautiful wildflowers and rock plants; a wild strawberry with blood red flowers, gracious mountain asters, and most beautiful of all, bush after bush of fragrant wild roses in full bloom. Streams, torrents, springs, cascades and cataracts poured down the mountainside, each one revered as the very source of

Ganga Ma, the river of heaven. Glaciers glinted in the sun. For all its discomfort, the journey to Badrinath was such a profound experience that the sufferings of four years in quest of the Himalayan snows paled into insignificance.

I thought of the Poona shopkeepers and bank clerks lovingly pouring pure spring water over the *linga* at Pateleshwar cave temple, of the cold Indrayani water dripping, dripping on to Shiva's stone at Alandi, of the *atmalinga* of Gokarn, buried beneath a heap of white jasmine flowers. I recalled the priests pouring milk and curds over the *jyotirlingas* at Bhima Shankar, Tryambakeshwar, Ellora and Rameshvaram, and I revisited in spirit the fire *linga* of Arunachala and the great light *linga* of Kashi Vishvanath. Gazing out of the bus window, I suddenly understood the meaning of all the *shivalinga* worship I had seen. The curds are glaciers, the milk the Himalayan snows, the water poured out upon the *linga* embodies the streams and torrents that course down the mountainside. The *yoni,* the well into which the water flows, is the Ganges floodplain. And the black columnar *linga* stone itself is the Himalaya. And as the symbol sprang to life on Badrinath trail, the *linga* before which I had knelt, from Rameshvaram to Varanasi, rooted themselves more deeply in my soul, and I knew that the snowcapped Himalaya, the mere sight of which wipes out the sins of countless lifetimes, is not other than That which dwells in mystery in the Cave of the Heart.

But of all the sights and sounds and smells of the journey to Badrinath, nothing could raise me to so great an ecstasy as the sight of my namesake, the Alakananda River, a rushing, foaming, frothing mountain torrent cutting her way through a deep ravine in the great, glacier-carved valley which led from Devaprayag to Badrinath. She it is who flows forth from the foot of Vishnu, and is caught in Shiva's matted locks, the high Himalayas. The music of her waters, echoing and re-echoing across the steep canyon, stirred my soul, and mingled with the repetition of the *mantra* which Raghudas had empowered for me.

Around noon on the second day, the bus ground to a halt. Rubble from a big landslide blocked the way, and in front of us several luxury buses and an "All India Tour Coach" were stranded.

It was not the first heap of landslide rocks and mud we had encountered that day, but it was by far the worst. My heart in my mouth, I scrambled out of the bus. We were but a few hours journey from the goal that had eluded us for so long, the shrine which we had vowed to visit—the place so holy that the scriptures say no pilgrimage of India can truly be deemed complete unless the pilgrim visits Badrinath. And now, would we be forced to turn back before we had seen the renowned temple of Badri Narayan?

Like the other passengers, we squatted on the ground and munched apples, whilst the drivers, helped by the soldiers, set to work with pick and shovel to clear the road. Hours passed, the river roared, and we chatted with four Sikh children bound for the shrine of Hemkund Sahib. One by one, the luxury buses were freed. The children and their family departed amid shouts and waves of jubilation. But the "All India Tour Coach" which blocked the road in front of our bus was too low slung for the rough road. Try though the volunteer roadworkers might, and hard though all the men in the party pushed, the coach could not be freed. Its wheels spun hopelessly. I began to despair. Just then, our driver leapt aboard his rickety bus, took off at top speed, and, mounting the sloping mud of the landslide, somehow maneuvered past the coach. A cry of victory arose as we boarded the bus and raced up the trail at breakneck speed. The driver, who knew every bend in the road, drove like a fiend, intent upon reaching Joshimath, the last way station, before it grew too dark to see.

At dawn the next day, we boarded the bus once more for the final run up to Badrinath. The precipices became more dizzying, the hairpin bends more violent, the road narrower, and small heaps of landslide rubble more frequent as we ascended to ten thousand feet, negotiating the portion of the road that is snow-bound from October to May. We were travelling up a steep valley between the Nar and Narayan peaks which flank Badrinath on either side. As we came to the head of the valley, a great cry arose. "*Shri Badri Narayan ki jai!*" The pilgrim occupants of the bus raised joined palms in awe and reverence. We had reached Dev Darshan, the point from where pilgrims toiling up the Badrinath trail caught their first glimpse of the temple. There before us rose the glittering spire of the shrine of Badri Narayan. Motor vehicles were allowed no further into the sacred zone. Disembarking from the bus, we proceeded on foot a quarter of a mile to the pilgrimage town of Badrinath proper.

For the Indian pilgrims, who had learned of the glories of Badrinath at their mother's knee and had planned and saved for years to make the pilgrimage, reaching here was a moment of supreme fulfilment. Rameshvaram in the South, Krishna's city of Dwarka on the West coast, Puri on the Eastern seaboard, and, above all, Badrinath, the hermitage amongst the snowcapped peaks of the North were for them the four *dhamas,* the abodes of Light which uphold the four corners of India's *mandala*. Yet even their joy could scarcely exceed that which filled my heart as I stooped to touch the rock of Badrinath. Year after year, obstacles had been placed in my way. Now at last I was completing the journey to my Name. "Badrinath," Raghudas had said when he named me Alakananda—"the river that flows through Badrinath."

Walking around Badrinath, we gazed at the snowcapped peaks, the great glaciers which brooded over the valley and the wildflowers splashing alpine meadows with colour. The Rishi Ganga poured down from a glacier to join the foaming Alakananda, whose icy waters breathed forth steam at the spot where a sacred hot spring mingled with her current. As I sat on a flat rock to watch the rushing, steaming river, I realized that the obstacles I encountered had never been outside myself. Through the death experience of hepatitis and the loss of the money and papers which guaranteed my security, through the demanding service Om Yeshu Niketan had called forth and the nurturance I had received at Divine Mother's breast on the shores of the Southern Salt Ocean, through the agony of madness, the descent into the Valley of Shadow and the struggle to regain my dignity whilst winter gales lashed the island of my birth—through this whole odyssey, layer upon layer of pretenses, defences and disguises had been stripped off, and now my soul lay bare as the naked rock on which I sat.

"You know," I told Sadananda, "it is really a great mercy that I didn't get here any sooner. The energy is so high, so powerful, and I am so sensitive to this place, that I really believe it would have killed me if I had come before I was ready. I would have caught some drastic disease and died. But instead, the person who set off in quest of the Source has died—is no more."

As the only foreigners present in Badrinath during the first onslaught of the monsoon, we attracted considerable attention, indeed, too much attention. Our presence was immediately noticed by wary local officials who politely but firmly informed us that, as foreigners, we were obliged to stay in the Government Rest House, a concrete building that was soul-less, uncomfortable, and, for our budget, expensive. Fortunately we had passed only a couple of days in this incongruous situation when we met a charming and warm-hearted *sannyasi* who introduced himself as "Gujerati Swami."

"You must come and stay with me at Guru Kripa," he insisted. "I have a room where you will be most conveniently accommodated. My ashram is right opposite the confluence of the Alakananda and Rishi Ganga, downstream of the temple. It is a more auspicious area, where most of Badrinath's aescetics have made their hermitage, and will be quieter and more convenient for meditation than your present quarters. Please come with me."

Ambiguously informing the warden of the Rest House that we were departing this place and going down river, we joyfully followed our new mentor, who for the duration of our stay in Badrinath would be our host, friend, guide and untiring teacher.

"Here at Badrinath," he informed us, "Lord Vishnu himself performed penance (he pronounced it *pee-nance*) beneath the *badari* tree. From the heat of his aesceticism was formed Tapt Kund, the hot spring. As for his wife, Lakshmi, finding that she was left alone, she too performed penance on the other side of the Alakananda. In the golden age, Lord Shiva's shrine of Kedarnath was also at this very spot. So Vishnu performed his penance here under the guidance of Lord Shiva. Though the Kedarnath *linga* is no longer here, Shiva remains as the guru of this place, in the form of Mount Neelkanth," and here he pointed out to us the great peak which towered above the glacier. "Even Sir Edmund Hilary has not climbed that unconquered peak. It is called Neelkanth, Bluethroat, because when poison came forth at the churning of the Ocean of Milk, Shiva drank the poison, and his throat turned blue."

"So as guru of Badarik Ashram, he teaches us to transmute the negativities which arise during the meditative churning," I mused.

"Quite so, quite so. At the time of *Mahabharat*, Krishna and Arjuna performed penance here in the forms of Nar and Narayan, and their presence remains here still in the twin peaks which guard this valley."

Even in the hazardous monsoon season, Badarik Ashram was a microcosm of India. Sadhus puffed clay chillums of ganja and beggars congregated on the bridge. At the free kitchen run by the Badri Narayan temple, broad-shouldered Sikhs plied us with *puris*, fried potato, and sweet halvah. A very old Gujerati man, too poor to afford even the local bus, arrived on foot, greeting us proudly as he panted and leant on his staff. City brahmins in silk lungis and elegant saris crowded the flat rock that jutted out into the river as they offered riceballs for the liberation of their ancestors. Rajasthani women milled about in bright mirror-studded shawls, and the local mountain people, more Chinese than Indian in appearance, sported colourful folk costumes.

"Our life is *seva*," said the manager of the Telegu pilgrim hostel. "The pilgrims come here to serve God, and we come here to serve pilgrims, to cook for them and care for their needs. There are at least eight such establishments here, serving free meals. In this cold place everyone, beggars, *sadhus*, poor villagers, priests, must eat their fill two or three times a day."

Spotting the ochre pennant of the *varkaris*, we walked over to find a poor Maharashtran couple who spent their entire life on pilgrimage. As he introduced their nine year old daughter, the varkari father told us in broken Hindi, "She has been to all Twelve *jyotirlinga*, all four *dhamas*. She has never gone to school, but she has travelled to the greatest holy places in the land. What better education could there be?"

Just then, a South Indian family appeared, with three slender-waisted daughters in full skirts and half sari. Greeting us reverently, their father said, "I just wanted to tell you that immediately I am seeing you, I am thinking of our great sages Gautama Rishi and Ahilya his wife. You are living exactly as they did. Today, there are so many swamis, so many *sadhus*, but in ancient days, sage and his wife retired to the forest together. Just like that, you are performing penance side by side."

We listened to his words seriously. On our pilgrimage together, as we gradually lost our identification with the "holy" images of the nun and the yogi, we had come to realize that our calling was indeed to the ancient life of *vanprastha,* or forest dwellers, the third *ashrama,* designed for those couples whose inclination was towards contemplation rather than active involvement in business, agriculture, government and so forth. Our new acquaintance had been inspired to confirm to us the path that we felt called to follow together.

The biting cold of monsoon season at ten thousand feet largely determined the pattern of our days. Having shivered all night, afraid to huddle together for warmth lest there be any suggestion of impropriety in Swami's ashram, we awoke at dawn to do vigorous yoga and energetic *pranayama,* before cooking breakfast. Around midmorning, when the sun finally appeared over the peaks that rose more than ten thousand feet above the narrow valley, we went to bathe in the hot, sulphurous waters of Tapt Kund, revered as both holy and healing. Then, still dripping and blister red, we raced to the edge of the Alakananda and dowsed ourselves with icy water. Thus invigorated, we sat to meditate beside the river.

Every sunset, we joined the pilgrims flocking up the steps of the carved and brightly painted temple where Vishnu sat in meditation, with Nar and Narayan on either side. Songs of praise filled the crowded *mandir,* ghee lamps waved before the deities, and the priest invariably presented us with a garland woven from the magnificent wild *tulsi* plants that bloomed in the alpine meadow.

The sanctity of Badrinath arose from the alchemical fusion of the majesty of nature, the faith of countless pilgrims and the presence of sages, both living and dead, who emanated the peace that passes understanding. In this, Badari Dham was the quintessence of India, land of the immanent divine.

"There are a number of saintly and respect-worthy persons," Swami told us, "whose *darshan* you should have whilst in Badarik Ashram. Above all, there is one Paramananda Avadhut, who is a very advanced personality, a *mahatma*. Even in this chilly weather, he is wearing only a loincloth."

Sadananda and I glanced at each other. Our thin cotton clothes were so unsuitable for Badrinath that we wore goat hair sleeping blankets all day. Evidently the yogi in question had mastered the internal heat, an esoteric yoga said to be essential for prolonged *sadhana* in the Himalayas.

After some searching, we found the big boulder that marked the sage's hermitage. Inside the bare, dark room, Paramananda sat on a wooden bed, naked except for his loin cloth and long silver matted locks. Apart from his beard and hair, the resemblance to Raghudas was striking. Paramananda Avadhut emanated the same quality of love, purity, simplicity and spiritual power as that in which we had basked when in the presence of our guru. After we had sat for some time, he began speaking slowly and clearly in Hindi.

"What *sadhana* do you practice?"

"Just sitting meditation and some devotional singing," I replied. "A little hatha yoga for health."

"Silent meditation, that is good. By *dhyan,* meditation practice, one comes to gyan, intuitive wisdom. Meditate much. But only through bhakti, through devotion to Ram, can we attain prema, attain pure love of God. And without love, wisdom is vain, without *prema,* nothing can be accomplished. Love is the most essential quality for spiritual life. So sing, praise Ram, and chant his holy names." He waved an eloquent hand towards Sadananda. "Since you have been given the gift of music, sing, chant, until your heart overflows with love."

In ungrammatical but comprehensible Hindi, I told him of the dream I had received at Rameshvaram.

"My guru informed me then that he was leaving his body, but that after many travels and much confusion, I would have his *darshan* once more, far to the North. And so we have come for your *darshan.*"

The saint nodded. "You have my blessing. Come here again."

As I left the little hut, I felt a renewed sense of gratitude for the chain of circumstances that had led us to Rameshvaram exactly two years ago. Like an axis of light, like Kundalini in the spine, a column of energy flowed from Rameshvaram at India's root to Badrinath at her crown. The promise given in Rameshvaram was fulfilled at Badrinath.

"Indeed," Gujerati Swami told us, "had you not first visited Rameshvaram, your vow to come to Badrinath would not have been paid in full. Rameshvaram must be visited first. That is clearly stated in the scriptures. It is like the grounding in an electrical system. The energy of Badrinath cannot be assimilated without the *darshan* of Rameshvaram."

Meanwhile, fervour was mounting amongst Badrinath's pilgrims and aescetics as the orb of the moon increased. Tonight, the full moon would signal the festival of *guru purnima.* The mysterious dynamic of pilgrimage which had brought us to Shirdi on Ram *naumi* and to Sakuri on Upasani Baba's birthday, to St. Francis Xavier's tomb on his feast day—conveying us time and again to the most auspicious place on the most auspicious day—had now led us to Badrinath for the holiest festival of the Himalayan pilgrimage season.

We found Paramananda leaning against his beloved boulder, luxuriating in the sunlight like a resting lion, whilst a *sadhu* disciple massaged his legs. There was no need to talk, and we just sat quietly in his presence. Then, after going through our hot-soak and ice-bath routine, we sat on the bank to contemplate the Alakananda.

I gazed at the waters, "the pure, pure source of the Ganges", as they rushed and foamed. The power of the river's purity awed me. Dammed, she could light cities; free, she lit countless hearts. Wild, untainted, cutting her way through rocks, she, the pure feminine power, flowed down to the plain as limitless compassion. Had Raghudas really seen in me this boundless freedom, this eternal power of purity? If so, then no wonder the floodgates of my heart had opened at Pentecost last year. My Alakananda had indeed been dammed behind a wall of inhibitions, fears and conditioning. And the tide of her release had, temporarily, drowned sanity and reason. The river sang in the channel she had carved, at play between her banks, knowing her power, knowing her limits and her destined course.

As I sat on the rock, my face wet with spray, I realized that this day, this full moon at Badrinath, marked both an ending and a beginning. From the moment when I lay prostrate on the stone flags of the Abbey choir in the white robe and veil of a novice, my life had been a relentless journey of purification. In all sincerity, I had requested the grace of monastic conversion, had expressed my willingness to die to self in order to live in Truth. On the shores of the Kaveri, I had reaffirmed the commitment to live and move and have my being in *brahman.* And plunging fearlessly into the fires of Shiva, I had vowed, together with Pilgrim Francis, to journey to the Source. A cloud passed, and I shivered on the cold rock. Could I have made the journey, had I known what lay ahead, known how terrible is the compassion of the Divine? At the hands of the Dark Mother, Mariamme the fever Goddess, Kali, drinker of the blood of Ego, my soul had been stripped, dismembered, unmade and wrought anew. I had set forth, still very much the innocent youth, in search of Enlightenment, seeking to find within myself the immaculate purity of the Maiden. Now I had reached a state of spiritual maturity, spiritual motherhood. I was ready to face the challenges of mid-life.

"In my end is my beginning." The time of purification was done, the journey to the source complete. The wandering course of that journey from the South to Maharashtra, back again to the South, winding from East coast to West, and even across continents, had mirrored the spiral course of the *kundalini,* had vividly shown that the inner journey is not linear, but circuitous, complex and multilayered. There would be other purifications, but these would take place within the context of a new dynamic. I had reached the Source. Now I, like the Alakananda, must travel forth from that pristine, elemental world of glaciers, snow and ice caverns; must descend the valley to the plain with all its colours and forms. The journey was over; the Return had begun.

Knowing the unlimited, I must learn to live with the limited. I had entered into silence; speech was now required of me. From her Himalayan home, the river would journey down to the cities of the plain, to the bustle of the market place, embracing those who bathed, washed their clothes, and watered their cattle, giving of her purity to each according to their need, accepting in return the burden of sin and pollution, flotsam and jetsam; watering ricefields, nourishing the fish, and at last entering the ocean. Her journey was mine. I too must return to the marketplace as a channel of the healing and purifying power of the Source; I too must shoulder my neighbour's burdens of sorrow and care, on my way to the shoreless Ocean. Demanding as the journey had been, I sensed that the returning would be harder still. Much growth lay ahead before I could flow broad and serene as the Ganga at Kashi. The season of purification had passed. That of empowerment was just beginning.

"Today you are most fortunate," beamed Gujerati Swami as he entered our room the next morning. "The Nepali Mothers have specially invited you to their *guru purnima bhandara* ceremony. We are due there at nine-thirty. Hurry, get ready." Hastily, I donned my best sari, the one with no rips or stains. I knew that Swamiji highly esteemed these two mothers. The senior of them was the oldest aescetic in Badrinath, whilst her young companion and disciple was about seventy. Because the old lady could no longer make the journey to Joshi Math, they spent their winters alone, in snowbound Badrinath.

Inside the Mothers' dark room with its thick walls and big fireplace, the aged aescetic sat in an armchair, swathed in shawls. Her wrinkled, leathery face smiled at us benevolently, her fingers ceaselessly moving over prayer beads—whilst her disciple, also a very serene and saintly personality, bustled about, serving us a sumptuous feast of Nepali cuisine. I felt that the two wise women, sprung from indigenous mountain stock, had completely merged with the spirit of the Himalayas during their long years of penance here. In a unique way, they were at Home in Badrinath. And I, too, had come home. I, named for the Alakananda River, had reached my goal. I had returned to the source of my being; now I was ready to return to the world.

The crone of Badrinath was myself, and I was she. The Nepali mothers would remain here, immersed in contemplation; I would journey to the West—yet the three of us were one. Young though I was, I had become a wisewoman, a knower of the mysteries of life, death and healing. Within my own heart was the purity of Mai Amma, the Maiden, the love of Godavari Mataji, the Mother, and the wisdom of the Himalayan Crone. I was that wisewoman I came to Badrinath to find, and my hands would cook her delicious dishes for the hungry hearts of the West.

Bibliography

General

Hindu Places of Pilgrimage in India: A Study in Cultural Geography. Berkeley: University of California Press, 1973.

Narayan, R. K. *The Ramayana: A Shortened Modern Prose Version of the Indian Epic.* New York: Viking Press, 1972.

Panikkar, Raimundo, ed. & tr. *The Vedic Experience: Mantramañjari.* Berkeley: University of California Press, 1977.

Radhakrishnan, S. *Indian Philosophy.* London: G. Allen & Unwin; New York: Humanities Press, 1941.

Sargeant, Winthrop, tr. *The Bhagavad Gita.* New York: State University of New York Press, 1984.

Swami, Shree Purohit and W. B. Yeats, tr. *The Ten Principal Upanishads.* London and Boston: Faber and Faber, 1970.

Chapter 1

Abhishiktananda. *The Further Shore.* Delhi: I.S.P.C.K., 1975.

________. *Hindu-Christian Meeting Point.* Delhi: I.S.P.C.K., 1969, 1976.

Griffiths, Bede. *Christ in India: Essays Towards a Hindu-Christian Dialogue.* New York: Scribner, 1966.

________. *A New Vision of Reality: Western Science, Eastern Mysticism and Christian Faith.* Felicity Edwards, ed. Springfield, IL: Templegate, 1990.

________. *Return to the Centre.* Springfield, IL: Templegate, 1977.

________. *River of Compassion: A Christian Commentary on the Bhagavad Gita.* Narwick, NY: Amity House, 1987.

Chapter 2

Abbott, Justin E., tr. *Stotramala: A Garland of Hindu Prayers, A Translation of Prayers of Marathai Poet-Saints from Dnyaneshvar to Mahipati.* Poona: Scottish Mission Industries, 1929.

________, N. P. Godbole, & J. F. Edwards, trs. *Mahipati Bhakti Lilamrita: Nectar from Indian Saints,* chapters 1-12; 41-51. *Poet Saints of Maharashtra II.* Poona: J. F. Edwards, 1935.

________. *Life of Tukaram.* Poona: Motilal Banarsidas, 1930; Delhi, 1980.

Deleury, G. A. *The Cult of Vithoba.* Poona: Deccan College, 1960.

Deshpande, P. Y. *Jnanadeva.* New Delhi: Sahitya Akademi and Sterling Press, 1973.

Fraser, J. Nelson & K. B. Marathe, trs. *The Poems of Tukarama.* Delhi: Motilal Banarsidas, 1909, 1981.

________ & J. F. Edwards. *The Life and Teaching of Tukaram.* Madras: Christian Literature Society for India, 1922.

Jnaneshvar, Shri. *Jnaneshvari.* Translated from the Marathi by V. G. Pradhan, edited and with an Introduction by H. M. Lambert. Albany: State University of New York, 1987.

Lad, Dr. Vasant. *Ayurveda: The Science of Self-Healing.* Santa Fe: Lotus Press, 1984.

Lipski, Alexander. *Life and Teachings of Sri Anandamayi Ma.* 1977. Available from Matri Satsang, P.O. Box 876, Encenitas, CA 92026.

Lutyens, Mary. *Krishnamurti: The Years of Awakening.* London: J. Murray, 1975.

Shepherd, Kevin. *A Sufi Matriarch: Hazrat Babajan.* Cambridge (UK): Anthropographia Publications, 1985.

________. *Gurus Rediscovered: Biographies of Sai Baba of Shirdi and Upasani Maharaj of Sakuri.* Cambridge (Cambridgeshire): Anthropographia, 1986.

Chapter 3

Bahadur, Sri Jaya Chamarajendra Wadiyar. *Dattatreya: The Way and the Goal.* London: George Allen & Unwin, 1957.

Briggs, George Weston. *Gorakhnath and the Kanphata Yogis.* Delhi: Motilal Banarsidas, 1973.

Chatrabhanu, Tjunider Shree. *Twelve Facets of Reality: The Jain Path to Freedom.* ed. Clare Rosenfield. NY: Dodd, Mead, 1980.

Ghurge, G. S. with L. W. Chapekar. *Indian Sadhus.* Bombay: Popular Prakashan, 1964.

Gross, Robert Lewis. *The Sadhus of India; A Study of Hindu Aesceticism.* Jaipur Ravat Publications, 1992.

Jaini, Padmanabh S. *The Jain Path of Purification.* Berkeley: University of California Press, 1979.
Rogopoulos, Antonio. *The Life and Teachings of Sai Baba of Shirdi.* Albany: State University of New York Press, 1993.
Tobias, Michael. *Life Force: The World of Jainism.* Berkeley: Asian Humanities Press, 1991.

CHAPTER 4

Deleury, G. N. *The Cult of Vithoba.* Poona: Deccan College, 1960.
Metzger, Werner. *Shree, His Life and Works.* 1982. Available from The Copper Works, R D 1, Box 121 AB, Madison, VA 22727.
Paranjape, Vasant V. *Homa Therapy, Our Last Chance.* Fivefold Path, Inc., 1989. Available from The Copper Works, R D 1, Box 121AB, Madison, VA 22727.

CHAPTER 5

Mookerjee, Ajit. *Kali, The Feminine Force.* New York: Destiny Books, 1988.
Pattner, F. A. (with photographs by B. Moosbrugger). *Christian India.* London/NY: Thames and Hudson, 1957.
Pearson, M. N. *The Portuguese in India.* Cambridge (Cambridgeshire): Cambridge University Press, 1988.
Rao, R. P. *Portuguese Rule in Goa 1510-1961.* London: Asia Publishing House, 1963.
Rémy. *Goa: Rome of the Orient.* Lancelot E. Sheppard, tr. London: A. Baker, 1957.
Schurhammer, Georg. *Francis Xavier, His Life, His Times.* M. Joseph Costelbe, tr. Rome: Jesuit Historical Institute.

CHAPTER 6

Abhishiktananda. *The Secret of Arunachala.* I.S.P.C.K.
Osbourne, Arthur. *The Sage of Arunachala.*
The Spiritual Teaching of Ramana Maharshi. Boston & Shaftesbury: Shambhala, 1988.

CHAPTER 7

Ramanujan, A. K., tr. *Speaking of Siva.* London: Penguin Books, 1973. (Includes poems and brief biographies of Sant Basava [Basavanna] and Akka Mahadevi [Mahadeviyakka].)

CHAPTER 8

Kashi: Myth and Reality of the Classic Cultural Tradition. Simla Institute of Advanced Study, 1975.

Varanasi: The Heart of Hinduism. Varanasi: Orient Publishers, 1969.

The Sacred Complex of Kashi. Delhi: Concept Publishing Company, 1949.

Varanasi Down the Ages. Varanasi: Bhagava Bhushan Press, 1974.

The Chequered History of the Golden Temple of Kashi Vishwanath. Kashi.

Davids, Caroline Rhys, tr. & ed. *Stories of the Buddha: Being Selections from the Jataka.* New York: Dove Publications, Inc., 1982.

Eck, Diana L. *Banaras: City of Light.* Princeton: Princeton University Press, 1982.

Joshi, Lal Mani. *Studies in the Buddhist Culture of India.* Delhi: Motilal Banarsidass, 1987.

Naran, A.K. and Lallanji Gopal, eds. *Introducing Varanasi.* Varanasi: Banaras Hindu University, 1969.

Pannikar, K. M. *The Himalayas in Indian Life.* Bombay: Bharatiya Vidya Bhavan, 1963.

Rommel and Sadhana Vaima. *Ascent to the Divine: The Himalaya Kailasa Manasarovar in Scripture, Art and Thought.* Switzerland: Lotus Books, 1985.

Schumann, H. W. *The Historical Buddha.* M. O'C. Walshe, tr. London: Arkana, 1989.

Singh, O.P., ed. *The Himalayas, Nature, Man and Culture with Specific Studies on the U. P. Himalaya.* New Delhi: Rajesh Publications, 1983.

Warder, A. K. *Indian Buddhism.* Delhi: Motilal Banarsidass, 1980.

Resource Guide

Agnihotra

In the U.S.A.:

The Copper Works, Rt. 1, Box 121 AB, Madison, VA 22727 (403) 948-5463.

In Europe:

Deutsche Gesellschaft für Homa Therapu, e V Schützonstraße 49, Radolfzell, Germany 07732/54803.

In India:

Abhay V Paranjape, Srinivas 40, Ashok Nagar Dhule 424001 Maharastra 2562-24093.

Ashrams

Alandi Ashram, 1705 14th St., #392, Boulder, CO 80302. (303) 786-7437. The "smallest ashram in America"—Kirtans, classes, resources in connection with Raghudas Maharaj and Godavari Mataji, networking.

Christa Prema Seva Ashram, Varkari Wadi, Shivajinagar, Poona, Maharashtra, India.

Shantivanam, Thannirpalli, PO Kulithalai, Dr. Trichy, Tamil Nadu, India.

Shivabalayogi Ashram, 11A, 3rd Phase, J. P. Naga. Bangalore 560 078. Tel. 648-243. Very good ashram.

Shri Upasani Kanya-Kumari Sthan, Sakuri, Post-Rahata. Dr. Ahmednagar Pin 423 107, Maharashtra, India. Tel. Rahata 42227.

Sri Ramanashramam, PO Ramanashramam, Tiruvanamalai, Tamil Nadu, India.

Ayurveda

Dr. Vasant Lad, *The Ayurvedic Institute,* PO Box 23445, Albuquerque, New Mexico 87192-1445. (505) 291-9698.

Dr. Alakananda Devi, 1705 14th St., #392, Boulder, CO 80302. (303) 786-7437.

Temples

Shanta Durga Mandir
Shri Shantadurga Sansthan
PO Kavlom, Ponda Goa 403 401

Share the Blessings of the Pilgrimage

Alakananda has created the *Rocky Mountain Wildflower Essences* to share with westerners what she experienced on her pilgrimage.

CHAKRA KIT: $39 per kit

Seven 1 dram bottles of the concentrates of our chakra flower essences. Take singly or sequentially to clear and strengthen the chakras.

MEDITATION ENHANCERS: $8.50 each or all eleven for $85.00

King's Crown ~ Self Initiation
Ninebark ~ Inner Silence
Osha ~ Paradise Here
Purple Fringe ~ Spiritual Emergence
Purple Groundcherry ~ Soul Retrieval
Serviceberry ~ Meditation
Shrubby Evening Primrose ~ No Mind
Tulasi ~ Sacred Space
White Rose ~ Purity of Heart
White Stemless Evening Primrose ~ Inner Guru
Valerian ~ Peace

DIVINE MOTHER FORMULAS: $10.00 each or all three for $25.00

Maiden Formula:
The purity of the virgin, eternally sixteen, renews our hearts and opens us to Divine Love.

Mother Formula:
The Mother, Empress of the Universe, bestows abundance and peace. Releasing our false ego-identifications, we realize that what we were seeking is always right here, right now. In the midst of daily life, we experience the richness of inner silence.

Grandmother Formula:
Only the spiritual warrior can worship the grandmother, who overthrows all that is known. She heals our wounds and softens our hardened hearts by teaching us that sorrow, frustration, loss and failure are opportunities for spiritual growth. She destroys negative influences and grants us safe haven and protection.

Alakananda Devi is a revealer of Divine Mother, and a spiritual guide. Sent by her spiritual grandmothers to bring the teachings to America, she and her partner, Sadananda, run an urban contemplative centre, Alandi Ashram, in Boulder Colorado.